CH00747035

Analytical Psychology in Exile

A list of Jung's works appears at the back of the volume.

Analytical Psychology in Exile

The Correspondence of
C. G. Jung and Erich Neumann

C. G. JUNG AND ERICH NEUMANN

EDITED BY MARTIN LIEBSCHER
TRANSLATED BY HEATHER MCCARTNEY

Ⓟ PHILEMON SERIES

PUBLISHED WITH SUPPORT OF THE PHILEMON FOUNDATION
THIS BOOK IS PART OF THE PHILEMON SERIES OF THE
PHILEMON FOUNDATION

PRINCETON UNIVERSITY PRESS
Princeton and Oxford

Copyright © 2015 by Princeton University Press
Published by Princeton University Press,
41 William Street, Princeton, New Jersey 08540
In the United Kingdom:
Princeton University Press,
6 Oxford Street, Woodstock,
Oxfordshire OX20 1TW

press.princeton.edu

Jacket Art: William Blake, *Job's Evil Dreams*, illustration for The Book of Job. 2001.73.
Courtesy of the Morgan Library & Museum.

Library of Congress Cataloging-in-Publication Data

Jung, C. G. (Carl Gustav), 1875–1961.
  [Correspondence. Selections. English]
  Analytical psychology in exile : the correspondence of C.G. Jung and Erich Neumann
/ C.G. Jung and Erich Neumann ; edited by Martin Liebscher ; translated by Heather
McCartney.
     pages cm. — (Philemon series)
  Includes bibliographical references and index.
  ISBN 978-0-691-16617-9 (hardcover : alk. paper) 1. Jung, C. G. (Carl Gustav), 1875–1961—
Correspondence. 2. Neumann, Erich—Correspondence. 3. Psychoanalysts—Switzerland—
Correspondence. 4. Psychologists—Israel—Correspondence. 5. Psychoanalysis. 6. Jungian
psychology. I. Liebscher, Martin. II. Neumann, Erich. Correspondence. Selections. English.
III. Title.
  BF173.J85A4 2015
  150.19'54092—dc23   2014033960

British Library Cataloging-in-Publication Data is available
This book is published with the support of the Philemon Foundation and is part
of the Philemon Series of the Philemon Foundation. philemonfoundation.org.
This book has been composed in Sabon Next LT Pro
Printed on acid-free paper. ∞
Printed in the United States of America
10 9 8 7 6 5 4 3 2 1

Contents

Acknowledgments

OVER THE LAST FEW YEARS MY RESEARCH FOR THE EDITION OF THIS CORRESPONDENCE FOUND ME MOST OF THE TIME ALONE AT MY DESK OR IN OBSCURE ARCHIVES AND LIBRARIES AROUND THE WORLD. Despite this lonesome task I was always aware that at the end of the day this work has always been a team effort and would not have been possible without the support and help of many who need to be mentioned here as an integral part of this project.

Up and foremost, it was the Philemon Foundation that made this publication possible. In particular, I would like to express my deep gratitude to its president, Judith Harris, for her invaluable contribution, and to the board of the foundation, Michael Marsman, Craig Stephenson, Caterina Vezzoli, and Beverley Zabriskie. The Philemon Foundation would like to acknowledge that this edition was made possible by Nancy Furlotti through a donation from the Furlotti Family Foundation.

It is to the credits of the heirs of both C. G. Jung and Erich Neumann that this important piece of intellectual history can now be presented to the public for the first time. The Community of Heirs of C. G. Jung and the Foundation of the Works of C. G. Jung was always supportive of this publication. Ulrich Hoerni and his successor as head of the foundation, Dr. Thomas Fischer, not only granted me access to the relevant material in the Jung archive at the ETH Zurich and the library in Küsnacht, but also helped me through their knowledge and expertise in matters Jung. The same is true for Andreas Jung, whose warm welcome to Küsnacht was very much appreciated.

My special thanks also go to the heirs of Erich Neumann, his daughter Rali Loewenthal-Neumann and his son Professor Micha

Neumann. They supported me with information and help throughout the duration of my work. Rali welcomed me with open arms to her home in Jerusalem while I was looking through the papers of her father. Thanks to her these days will always be a precious and unforgettable memory to me.

Of course this correspondence would never have seen the light of the day without the constant struggle of Professor Sonu Shamdasani, my friend, colleague, and main editor for the Philemon Foundation. As always I profited enormously from his advice and expertise as the eminent scholar on Jung history.

I would also like to thank translator Heather McCartney for providing us with an excellent translation of this correspondence. Working together was a great experience for me.

It was during my research stay in Israel that I met Dr. Erel Shalit in person for the first time. Erel was instrumental to the publication of this correspondence. As spokesman for the family Neumann, expert in the psychology of Erich Neumann, and through his careful reading of the manuscript Erel has become indispensable to this project.

My thanks also go to Dr. Heide Kunzelmann (University of Kent) and Christopher Barenberg, PhD (University of London) for their willingness to take on the laborious and difficult task of transcribing the letters.

The following persons and institutions helped me with my research: the Jung archive at the library of the ETH Zurich, especially Dr. Yvonne Voegeli, whose help and expertise facilitated my archival research a great deal; the Curatorium of the C. G. Jung Institute Zurich, especially Daniel Baumann, dipl. Arch., Robert Hinshaw, PhD, and the librarian Vicente de Moura; the Psychology Club Zurich, its president Dr. Andreas Schweizer, its curator Emanuel Kennedy and the club's librarian Frau Gudrun Seel; Frau Bettina Kaufmann at the Foundation of the Works of C. G. Jung; the archive of the Zentralbibliothek Zurich; the Eranos Foundation, especially Frau Gisela Binder, for her warm welcome at the Casa Gabriella, and Dr. Sandro Rusconi; the Frankfurt Exil Archiv and its archivist Dr. Sylvia Asmus; the Literaturarchiv Marbach; the librarians of the Kunsthaus Zurich, especially Thomas Rosemann and Tina Fritzsche; Safron Rossi, PhD, curator of the OPUS Archives & Research Center at the Pacifica Graduate

Institute; Aletha van der Velde of the Philosophy Department at the Internationale School voor Wijsbegeerte; Lance Owen, MD; Dr. Giovanni Sorge; Dr. Ernst Falzeder; Professor Graham Richards; Eve Devoldere (Dutch translation); and Angus Nicholls, PhD.

For assistance with the publication of this work I would like to thank the team at Princeton University Press, especially Fred Appel, Juliana Fidler, Leslie Grundfest, and Dawn Hall, who copyedited the volume.

The photographs for this volume have been provided by Mrs. Rali Loewenthal-Neumann and Dr. Paul Kugler, for which I would like to express my gratitude. We are indebted to the Fondazione Eranos, Ascona, for granting the permission to consult its archives and print the photographs figures 1, 3, 5, 6, 7, and 9. The cover picture by William Blake belongs to the Morgan Library, New York, who granted permission to use it; the William Blake archive provided us with a copy.

Finally I would like to thank my wife Luz Nelly for her ongoing love and support.

Dr. Martin Liebscher

The Neumann Heirs would like to express their gratefulness to Dr. Martin Liebscher for his excellent editorial work. Likewise, they recognize and express their deep gratitude to Dr. Nancy Swift Furlotti, who has financed this project. As co-president, and together with Dr. Stephen Martin, the co-founder of the Philemon Foundation, she pursued the project unyieldingly for many years. The cooperation with the Foundation of the Works of C.G. Jung has been very fruitful, and thanks to Fred Appel and Princeton University Press this important volume can now reach the public.

Introduction

I. The First Encounter

The first known document of the correspondence between Erich Neumann and C. G. Jung—a correspondence that lasted from 1933 to 1959—is a short note from Jung to Neumann dated 11 September 1933: "Dear Doctor, I have reserved an hour's appointment for you on Tuesday, 3rd October at 4 pm. Yours respectfully, C. G. Jung." Unfortunately we do not have the initial letter by Neumann, which instigated the correspondence with Jung in the first place. But the two men had met earlier that summer, when Jung was in Berlin to hold a much-acclaimed seminar from 26 June to 1 July 1933.[1] The handwritten attendance register lists around 145 names, including those of Erich Neumann and his friend Gerhard Adler.

Jung's note to Neumann was sent to the following address: Weimarischestrasse [sic], 17, Berlin-Wilmersdorf. Berlin was the place where Erich Neumann was born in 1905 and where he grew up. His father, Eduard, was a merchant, married to Zelma. Erich was their third child. Adler has given us an account of young Erich Neumann during the Berlin years:

Erich Neumann and I were connected by a close friendship of almost 40 years, a relationship that went back to our student days. Even as a student and young man his creative personality was clear and impressive. We belonged to the same circle of friends, a circle, which was interested in and engaged with all those life-problems

[1] Jung (1933b).

of the immediate post-war period—problems that were a focal point for Germany at that time: philosophy, psychology, poetry, and art, and last but not least the Jewish question—were only a few topics that touched us deeply in our hearts. How many nights did we not spend conversing intensively and never endingly about all sorts of potential life-questions! And in all of those instances the depth and breadth of his view, the intensity of his passionate nature, contributed original and creative answers.[2]

This creative side of Neumann's character found its early expression in literary ways: poetry exists from as early as 1921 and continues until 1929,[3] when his creativity was focused on the novel *Der Anfang* (1932).[4] Alongside his literary ambitions he studied at the University of Berlin, where he sat in courses of psychology, philosophy, pedagogy, history of arts, literature and Semitic studies (1923–26). In 1926 he went to Nuremburg to finish his studies of philosophy and psychology at the University of Erlangen with a dissertation on the mystical language philosophy of Johann Arnold Kanne (1773–1824).[5] He also wrote a commentary on Kafka's novel *Das Schloss* and fifteen of his short stories, which he sent to Martin Buber.[6] His ever-increasing interest in psychoanalysis and psychotherapy[7] led him to embark on the study of medicine at the Friedrich-Wilhelms-University in Berlin (Charité). He completed his studies there but could not undertake an internship because of the race laws the Nazis had implemented.[8]

---

[2] Adler (1980), p. 181.

[3] The published collection *Sonnensucher* (1926) is likely to be written by an author of the same name. This is strongly suggested by the lament for the poet's father, "Tod des Vaters" ("Death of the Father"), whereas the father of the psychologist-to-be Erich Neumann was still alive at that time.

[4] Second chapter was published in an anthology of young Jewish authors titled *Zwischen den Zelten* (Neumann, 1932).

[5] Neumann (1928).

[6] A part of Neumann's commentary on "The Trial" was published in Neumann (1958). Its English translation together with comments on the chapter "In the Cathedral" can be found in Neumann (1979), pp. 3–112. For a detailed list of Neumann's unpublished typescripts on Kafka, see Sotheby's catalog (2006), pp. 146–47. On Neumann and Buber, see n. 215.

[7] There is a psychological and philosophical text by a young Erich W. A. Neumann in the Zionist journal *Proteus* titled "Die Schmerzlüsternheit: Fragmente einer Psychologie des Pessimismus" (Neumann, Erich W. A., 1924). However, there is no evidence that this text was written by the future psychologist.

[8] Micha Neumann quoted in *Haaretz* (Lori, 2005); see also Rali Loewenthal-Neumann (2006), p. 149. Erich Neumann would receive his medical doctor degree from the University of

The year 1933 was a turning point in his life in many ways. In contrast to his father, Erich was a dedicated Zionist[9] and was readily prepared to leave Germany with his wife, Julie (née Blumenfeld) when Hitler seized power in January 1933. Together with their one-year-old son Micha the family left Germany for good. The first station on their way to Palestine was Zurich, to meet up with C. G. Jung. This is where Neumann's (missing) letter to Jung comes into play. Jung's reply from September 1933 was the invitation that followed. So Erich Neumann and his family left Germany for Zurich at the end of September 1933.

When Neumann met Jung he was already acquainted with the works of Jung and Freud, which he had read during his student years.[10] According to Jung's letter, they met on 3 October 1933 for the first time in Zurich and we know that they continued their therapeutic sessions until spring 1934.[11] On 14 December 1933, Jung writes an official letter stating that "Dr. Erich Neumann is engaged in psychological studies with me" (2 J) and that his work would resume on 15 January.

The next letter from Jung to Neumann is dated 29 January 1934 and was published in Aniela Jaffé's edition of Jung's *Briefe*. In this letter Jung already refers a patient to Neumann. One should not be surprised about the brief period of analysis that saw Neumann as being fit to take on his first patient—at least in Jung's eyes. This was common practice and was already an improvement on the couple of instructive weeks that were seen to suffice as training at the beginning

---

Hamburg in 1959, when *The Origins and History of Consciousness* was accepted as his doctoral thesis.

[9] In his seminar on the *Seelenproblem des modernen Juden: Eine Reihenanalyse von Träumen, Bildern und Phantasien* (*Soul Problems of the Modern Jew: An Analysis of a Series of Dreams, Images, and Phantasies*) (Tel Aviv, 10 November 1938–29 June 1939) Neumann recalls the following dream: "I remember a dream, a mixture of a dream, a childhood memory and fantasy, there was a moment when the parents appeared as a very negative authority, in a devouring form, an image reminds me of grandfather. The main thing was the long beard, association: this is why I became a Zionist—Herzl-beard and the memory that the picture of grandfather that hung in my childhood home was connected with the Misrach" (1 June 1939, p. 360). On his father's Zionism, see also Micha Neumann (2005), p. 18.

[10] Micha Neumann (2005), p. 19.

[11] Micha Neumann indicates summer 1934. As a handwritten biographical cursory by Erich Neumann shows, Neumann did leave earlier, namely, in May 1934 (RA). This fits with Jung writing in a letter to James Kirsch dated 26 May 1934 that Neumann was now living in Palestine (Jung-Kirsch letters, p. 46).

of the psychoanalytic movement. We do not know if Neumann took on this patient. We also do not know if Neumann had already experienced therapy during his Berlin years—as, for instance, James Kirsch had done before he met Jung in Zurich for the first time.

II. C. G. JUNG IN THE 1930S

When Neumann met Jung in Zurich in the autumn of 1933, the Swiss was fifty-eight years old and thirty years his superior. Jung had established himself as one of the leading psychologists of his time and as the founder of his own brand of psychotherapy under the name of "Analytical Psychology" or "Complex Psychology." His reputation was internationally acknowledged through invitations to lecture in England, the United States, and India, where honorary doctorates from Harvard (1936), Oxford (1938), and the Indian universities of Hyderabad, Calcutta, Benares, and Allahabad (1937/38) were bestowed upon him. His travels and lectures abroad are also reflected in the correspondence with Neumann, for instance in his letter of 4 April 1938 where he apologizes for his lack of writing due to his lecture series at Yale in October 1937 ("Terry Lectures"), which was followed by a dream seminar at the Analytical Psychology Club in New York,[12] and his journey to Calcutta. Jung also visited Palestine once, albeit as a tourist when he traveled with Hans Eduard Fierz through the Aegean in 1933, a year before the Neumanns settled in Tel Aviv. Jung refers to this visit in a letter to Neumann on 19 December 1938: "I am right in the thick of it and am following the Palestinian question on a daily basis in the newspapers, and think often of my acquaintances there who have to live in this chaos. When I was in Palestine in 1933, I was unfortunately able to see what was coming all too clearly. I also foresaw great misfortune for Germany, even quite terrible things, but when it then shows up, it still seems unbelievable."[13]

Closer to home he got involved in the business and politics of the General Medical Society for Psychotherapy (Allgemeine ärztliche Gesellschaft für Psychotherapie, AÄGP), the later International General

---

[12] Jung (1937; 1937a).
[13] Jung to Neumann, 28 J. On Jung in Palestine see n. 216.

Medical Society for Psychotherapy (IAÄGP), when he became second chairman in 1930, after Ernst Kretschmer's resignation as acting president in 1933, and finally president in 1934. His chairmanship of a society that was dominated by its national-socialist German section was heavily criticized at home and abroad. In reaction Erich Neumann, who was undertaking training with Jung in Zurich at that time, wrote a letter to Jung expressing his concern and urging Jung to justify his decision (4 N). (See chapter on "Discussing Anti-Semitism.") Less controversial was the foundation of the Schweizerische Gesellschaft für Psychotherapie in 1935.

Another institution that originated from those years and that is inextricably linked with the names of Jung and Neumann is the Eranos conference. Founded in 1933 by Olga Fröbe-Kapteyn, the annual gathering in Ascona was an exchange of thoughts between scholars of different fields. Neumann expressed his fascination with the event in an almost hymnic way, calling it a link in the *aurea catena* of the great wise man leading through the ages: "Eranos, landscape on the lake, garden and house. Unpretentious, out of the way, and yet . . . a navel of the world, a small link in the golden chain."[14] Whereas Jung took part and gave lectures at most of the Eranos conferences from 1933 until 1951, Neumann presented an annual paper from 1948 until 1960. Aniela Jaffé, referring to the famous "terrace-wall" sessions when Jung used the conference intervals to discuss the psychological relevance of the presentations outside on the terrace, gave this account of Neumann's impact on Eranos: "These wall sessions were the unforgettable highlights of the summer. They acquired a different character when Erich Neumann of Tel Aviv was there for then a dialogue developed between the two and we listened."[15]

The Eranos meeting always took place for eight days in August. In those summer days Jung was free from many obligations that were bestowed upon him during the rest of the year. Besides seeing his patients, writing books and articles, leading his correspondences with colleagues and scholars, and looking after his vast family, teaching increasingly added to his workload. Since 1925 Jung had been holding seminars at the Psychological Club on a regular basis. The

---

[14] Erich Neumann in Fröbe-Kapteyn (1957), p. 20 (translation by Robert Hinshaw, 2004).
[15] Jaffé (1968), p. 119.

Figure 1. Jung's "terrace wall" session at the Casa Eranos veranda in 1951 (Eranos Archive; courtesy of Paul Kugler).

seminars in the 1930s—which are occasionally mentioned in the correspondence—included the vision seminar (1930–34) based on the visions of Christiana Morgan,[16] the seminar on Kundalini yoga (1932),[17] and the seminar on Nietzsche's *Thus Spoke Zarathustra* (1934–39).[18] Jung sent a copy of the manuscript of the latter to Neumann in 1935 (14 N, n. 269). As the letters show, Jung tried to keep Neumann informed about the theoretical developments in analytical psychology by sending him his latest publications and copies of seminar notes. Jung also gave lectures at the ETH (Swiss Federal Institute of Technology) from 1933 to 1942 on a vast range of topics from the historical roots of complex psychology to Patanjali's *Yoga Sutras*, sometimes accompanied by seminars such as a seminar on children's dreams from 1936 to 1940.[19]

In 1935 Jung was awarded a professorship at the ETH (12 N, 9 February 1935). Jung sent Neumann a copy of his inauguration lecture from 5 May 1934 titled "A review of the complex theory" ("Allgemeines zur Komplextheorie") to which Neumann referred in his letter 14 N.[20] That was only one of the many decorations that came with his sixtieth birthday in 1935. To honor the birthday occasion a festschrift was organized and published under the title *Die kulturelle Bedeutung der komplexen Psychologie*, which included articles by many of Jung's most ardent followers and collaborators (17 N, 29 October 1935; 18 J, 22 December 1935).[21]

The 1930s also saw a change in Jung's theoretical interest. His work on the *Liber Novus* and his attempts to explore and depict his experiences of self-observation, which had occupied him since 1913, ceased and were gradually replaced by an ever-growing fascination with alchemy and its importance for the individuation process.[22]

---

[16] Jung (1930–34).
[17] Jung (1932).
[18] Jung (1934–39).
[19] Jung (1936–40).
[20] Jung (1934b).
[21] Psychologischer Club Zurich (ed.) (1935).
[22] See Shamdasani (2009).

III. Correspondence between Palestine and Zurich, 1934–40

Whereas Julie and Micha had already left for Palestine in February 1934, Erich remained in Zurich until May when they met again in Tel Aviv. Their first address was 37 Sirkin Street, where the family stayed until they moved to 1 Gordon Street in 1936. Dvora Kutzinski, who Julie analyzed and who subsequently became an analyst and lifelong friend of the Neumanns, described the apartment (on Gordon Street) as follows:

> It was an apartment they bought with "key money." Old. Modest. Two children. When patients came, they had to disappear. One waited in the children's room, and the front room was for his mother. Erich's patients waited on one side of the curtain. Julia's patients waited in the children's room. He had patients on the hour; she on the half hour.[23]

Soon after his arrival in Tel Aviv, Neumann writes a long letter (seven pages) to Jung. And already in this first letter from Palestine we can find many topics that will occupy their correspondence until 1940, when the war interrupted their exchange.

Zionism, the Jewish People, and Palestine

Neumann's first impressions from Palestine showed signs of disappointment. His high expectations of the Jewish people and their ability to create an idealistic Jewish state were shattered during these first weeks in Tel Aviv. As his son Micha Neumann put it: "Father thought he would come here and find all his good buddies from Berlin but instead he found a great many Poles, very simple people, artisans, builders, merchants, speculators, people of the Fourth Aliyah (1924–1931)—not idealists like those from the Second Aliyah (1904–1914)."[24]

---

[23] Abramovitch (2006), p. 166.
[24] Micha Neumann, quoted in Lori (2005).

Figure 2. Neumann at his desk (RLN).

Erich Neumann felt alienated by those immigrants, and equally he had nothing in common with the Jewish orthodoxy around him. Though he had nothing but praise for those who worked behind the scenes for the coming generation that would be the first to form the basis of a nation: "We are Germans, Russians, Poles, Americans etc. What an opportunity it will be when all the cultural wealth which we bring with us is really assimilated into Judaism" (5 N, June/July 1934).

Accordingly he rejected Jung's assumption that the Jewish migration to Palestine could not lead to a form of Alexandrianism.[25] For Neumann, the ability to assimilate would create something new, but it would also unleash the Shadow, the effects of which had been repressed by external forces during the diaspora.

[25] See n. 171.

The Earth Archetype

Whereas Neumann seemed partially disillusioned with the Jewish people in Palestine, he discovered to his astonishment an archetypal connection with the land. He describes how his anima started to connect to the earth, suddenly "appearing in dreams all nice and brown, strikingly African, even more impenetrable in me, domineering" (5 N, June/July 1934). It is most fascinating to observe how the thoughts that occupied Neumann during those first weeks in Palestine returned almost twenty years later in his 1953 Eranos lecture on "The Meaning of the Earth Archetype for Modern Times" ("Die Bedeutung des Erdarchetyps für die Neuzeit").[26] There, his personal encounter with the anima and her expression as an earth archetype is amalgamated with his psychological findings on the development of consciousness, his new ethics of shadow integration, and his research on the archetype of the Great Mother, which he was undertaking during these years. In his lecture he shows how, in its weaker states, the patriarchal view of consciousness had to repress the earth archetype, which threatened to swamp consciousness completely. Hence consciousness had to reject its unconscious and matriarchal origins, a rejection that can be seen in the Platonic-Christian hostility toward the body and sexuality. As modern man has been unchained from the heavens, the sky and the spiritual realm, he falls prey to the cruel manifestations of the Great Mother. Only the conscious acceptance of this dark side of the earth archetype, meaning the integration of the instinctual unconscious forces—here Neumann's ethics come into play—will make it possible for the archetype to express itself creatively rather than through cruelty. Together with the Great Mother appears the serpent (see Neumann's dream): The evil serpent of the Old Testament changes into the serpent of redemption as depicted in the Gnosis or the Sabbatean myths. What we can see in this example is the significance of Neumann's experience of *Eretz Yisrael* not only for his own individuation but also for the development of his psychological theories.

[26] Neumann (1954a).

Discussing Anti-Semitism

Another topic Neumann raises in the first Tel Aviv letter to Jung concerns an article by James Kirsch in the *Jüdische Rundschau*.[27] This article, from 29 May 1934, is a reaction to Jung's article "The State of Psychotherapy Today" ("Zur gegenwärtigen Lage der Psychotherapie") published in the *Zentralblatt für Psychotherapie und ihre Grenzgebiete*,[28] which was the journal of the General Medical Society for Psychotherapy (Allgemeine ärztliche Gesellschaft für Psychotherapie). In his article, Jung emphasized the importance of the "personal equation" in psychotherapy. He deploys the idea that the analyst must be conscious of his own shadow and uses this argument in order to attack Freud and Adler, who allegedly ignored or repressed their Jewish resentments toward non-Jews. This, according to Jung, led to a fatal situation in which Jewish categories were wrongly applied to the unconscious of Christian Germans or Slavs.[29] Especially the argument that "the Jew is a relative nomad" and would never be able to create his own form of culture because of his need for a civilized "host people" (*Wirtsvolk*), was received with a certain bewilderment among his Jewish followers in Palestine.[30]

Given the nature of Jung's arguments, Kirsch's article exercised a kind of constraint. He accuses Jung of exercising a one-sided view of Jewishness: Jung, according to Kirsch, sees Freud only as a Galuth Jew[31] and projects this image of Freud onto the entire Jewish people. In so doing, Jung ignores the latest developments of a specifically Jewish culture, of which the most significant sign could be seen in the return to the old land. But one could also learn from the great psychologist Jung about how to engage with these elementary primal forces that have been unleashed, through the return to the Jewish land, onto the individual soul.

[27] Kirsch (1934).
[28] Jung (1934a).
[29] Jung (1934a), § 354.
[30] Jung (1934a), § 353
[31] Galut(h), Hebrew for exile, has become a synonym for Jewish diaspora.

The article by Kirsch came in the aftermath of a debate that had been triggered by Gustav Bally's article "Therapy of German Descent" ("Deutschstämmige Therapie") in the *Neue Zürcher Zeitung* dated 27 February 1934.[32] Bally had been less apologetic than Kirsch in his article. Not only did Bally accuse Jung of open anti-Semitism but also of taking over the presidency of the General Medical Society for Psychotherapy (succeeding Kretschmer) at a time when the German section was "gleichgeschaltet" and Jewish membership prohibited. In his opening address as the new president (published in December 1933 in the *Zentralblatt*) Jung demanded that in the interests of scientific clarity, the confusion between Jewish and Germanic psychology should cease.[33] The pledge for allegiance (*Treuegelöbnis*), as Jung later called it, to the Führer by the German section of the society, which was originally meant to be for the German edition only, was distributed along with the international edition—according to Aniela Jaffé without Jung being informed—and caused fury among many supporters. Bally replied to this as follows:

> He who introduces himself as editor of a "gleichgeschaltete" journal by raising the race question has to know that his demand rises against a background of organised tumult, which will interpret it in the manner implicitly contained in these words.[34]

Jung reacted to Bally's attack with an article in the NZZ titled "Rejoinder to Dr. Bally" ("Zeitgenössisches").[35] There he defended his presidency as an act of self-sacrifice for the sake of the survival of German psychotherapy. Regarding the accusations of anti-Semitism, Jung repeats his arguments and talks about the imponderabilities of the soul differences between Jews and Christians—everyone, he argues, would know about those differences.[36] And he opposes the argument that he only dared to engage with that topic now that the

---

[32] Bally (1934).
[33] Jung (1933).
[34] Bally (1934).
[35] Jung (1934).
[36] Jung (1934), § 1031.

Nazis were in power in Germany, by stating that he had already es-poused race-psychological ideas in articles in 1918 and 1927.[37]

In a letter dated 26 May 1934, written a week before Kirsch's arti-cle in the *Jüdische Rundschau*, Jung tries to appease Kirsch, who had told him about the hostile reactions in Palestine toward his state-ments. Referring to the internationalization of the AÄGP, now IAAGP, he reports on the new statutes from the congress in Bad Nauheim that would make it possible for German Jewish physicians to join the international organization as individual members.[38] He also re-fines his argument about the impossibility of forming a unique Jew-ish culture:

This view is based on (1) historical facts, and (2) the additional fact that the specific cultural contribution of the Jews evolves most clearly within a host-culture, where the Jew frequently becomes the very carrier of this culture, or its promoter. This task is so unique and demanding that it is hardly to be conceived how, in addition, any individual Jewish culture could arise alongside it. Now, since Palestine presents very unique conditions, I have cau-tiously inserted "presumably" in my sentence. I would not deny the possibility that something unique is being created there, but I don't know that as yet. I positively cannot discover anything anti-Semitic in this opinion.[39]

And Jung continues: "Regarding your suggestion that I write a spe-cial piece about this question, this too has already been anticipated, in that I suggested an exchange of letters with Dr. Neumann, who has worked with me and now lives in Palestine, which would deal with all the contentious questions. Up to now, though, I've heard nothing from him."[40] He returns to this at the end of the letter by saying: "When you see Dr. Neumann, please greet him from me and remind him that I am waiting to hear from him."[41]

---

[37] Jung (1934), § 1034.
[38] Jung and Kirsch (2011), p. 45.
[39] Jung and Kirsch (2011), p. 44.
[40] Jung and Kirsch (2011), p. 46.
[41] Jung and Kirsch (2011), p. 47.

Kirsch seems almost insulted about the fact that Jung wished this exchange to have been with Neumann and not with him:

> In closing, I would like to inform you that Dr. Neumann, who for some time apparently has been living in Tel Aviv, just around the corner from my place, has not yet found an occasion to get in touch with me. To be ignored in this manner does not really surprise me since—as I mentioned to Miss Wolff in Berlin—he was already describing himself in June 1933 as the only Jungian analyst in Palestine.[42]

Of course Neumann had only recently come to Tel Aviv and therefore could not have described himself as the only Jungian analyst in Palestine in 1933. During the Bally affair Neumann had been in Zurich undertaking his training with Jung. There is one letter from him to Jung from that time (4 N). Although the letter is neither dated nor given a location, the content suggests that it was written between March and May 1934, which means that it was written from Zurich. That Neumann felt it necessary to use the written form instead of talking to Jung personally shows the shocking impact that Jung's race-psychological remarks must have had on him. In the opening lines of the letter Neumann makes it clear that he does not write from idle personal reason, but because he feels obliged to take issue with Jung "on a matter which goes far beyond any merely personal concerns" (4 N, March–May 1934).

This fascinating document, an expression of Neumann's disgust, is an outspoken critique of Jung's positions regarding Jewishness and National Socialism. Neumann questions Jung's positive understanding of the Germanic unconscious, which had seized the German people, accusing him of turning a blind eye to the collective shadow. He asks if this easy affirmation, this throwing himself into the frenzy of Germanic exuberance, could really be Jung's true position or if he misunderstood him, and he wishes to change Jung's picture of Jews, which he criticizes as being one-sided and full of misunderstandings. He contends that Jung knew more about the India of two thousand

---

[42] Kirsch to Jung, 8 June 1934 (Jung and Kirsch, 2011, p. 53).

years ago than about the development of Hasidism 150 years ago. But, and here Neumann argues in a similar way to Kirsch, that Hasidism and Zionism proved the ability of the Jewish people to form their own culture and that Jung was mistaking Freud for the entire Jewish people. As Jung had once declared Freud as a European phenomenon, he, Neumann, could not understand why Jung would repeat the National Socialist notion that Freudian categories are Jewish categories.

Apparently Jung and Neumann talked about this letter in Zurich and agreed that they would discuss the issue in their subsequent correspondence. This is what Jung indicated in his letter to Kirsch. Neumann also refers to this in his first letter from Tel Aviv: "I've set myself the big challenge of getting you to write something fundamental about Judaism. I believe I can only do this by simply speaking to you about what is very important to me" (5 N, June/July 1934). He attaches the uncut version of his rejoinder to Kirsch published (as an abridged version) in the *Jüdische Rundschau*.[43] The printed version, at least, defends Jung against the allegations Kirsch brought and stands in sharp contrast to Neumann's Zurich letter. He sides, in part, with Jung by arguing that the Jews have a special ability to focus upon, recognize, and also to endure the shadow. To see this as a negative quality of the Galuth Jew, as Kirsch did, would mean taking away the fundamental principle of the moral instinct of the Jewish people. What Neumann did not add to his argument (in the abridged version) was a point he had made in the letter to Jung—namely, that Jung did turn a blind eye to the shadow side of the Germanic people.

Whereas in his Zurich letter (4 N) he doubts Jung's ability to talk about Jews, since he sees Jung's Jewish patients as a small and sad remainder of assimilated Jews and therefore not as true representatives of the Jewish people, his reply to Kirsch sounds rather differently:

Even the objection against Jung that he "has not progressed from dealing with the phenotype of the Jew who lives in exile from the Shekhinah to the genotype of the real Jew" is wrong. Jung as a psychologist sticks to his experiences of his work with Jewish people, and we all belong to "the phenotype of the Jew who lives in

[43] Neumann (1934).

exile from the Shekhinah," meaning the Jew as he is—and we don't need to escape to an image of a non-existent "real," "authentic" Jew.[44]

And he finishes his contribution by putting his faith in the idea that Jung and his psychology will help the Jewish people to reunite with their primal roots, for which the integration of the shadow is a necessary prerequisite.

The debate in the *Jüdische Rundschau* also includes letters to the newspaper by Otto Juliusburger (in the same issue as Neumann),[45] by J. Steinfeld,[46] and is concluded by a statement by Gerhard Adler on behalf of Jung, who had asked Adler in a letter of 19 June 1934 to write to the *Jüdische Rundschau* and the *Israelitische Wochenblatt für die Schweiz* in order to clarify Jung's position in this debate:

I am always being assailed by letters which accuse me of the craziest anti-Semitism and I can hardly find the time to reply to these letters. You will no doubt have heard of Kirsch's article in the "Jüdischen Rundschau." I had already written a letter of clarification to Kirsch before I knew of the existence of this article. He seems to be stuffed full of all sorts of rumours of lies. I would be very grateful to you if you would perhaps highlight my position regarding the Jewish question—in my name and under my orders—for this publication.[47]

He also mentions Neumann's contribution, which he had not read at this stage.

In the issue of 3 August 1934 of the *Jüdische Rundschau* the editor summarizes the arguments of Kirsch and Jung and declares an end to the debate with the publication of Adler's text. In his contribution titled "Is Jung an Anti-Semite?" ("Ist Jung Antisemit?"), Adler underlines the importance of Jungian psychology in integrating Jews into a bigger picture and reuniting them with their culture and primal

---

[44] Neumann (1934).
[45] Juliusburger (1934).
[46] Steinfeld (1934).
[47] Jung to Gerhard Adler, 19 June 1934 (JA).

ground.[48] He differentiates between the "form of culture" ("Kultur-form") and "culture" ("Kultur") itself, stating that Jung had never de-nied the existence of the latter. Finally he points out the successful therapeutic processes that Jewish patients have experienced with Jung.[49]

Kirsch-Neumann Controversy

Due to Jung's preference for Neumann as his spokesman in matters Jewish there was a kind of tension between Neumann and Kirsch right from the outset. Neumann's open reply in the *Jüdische Rund-schau* certainly did not help to calm things down. In his first letter from Tel Aviv, Neumann reports to Jung that he had met Kirsch after the publication of his rejoinder. Kirsch had conveyed Jung's com-plaint that he (Neumann) had not written earlier and had told Neu-mann that Jung agreed with Kirsch's theory that the Jews had been subject to neurosis for two thousand years. And then Mrs. Kirsch got involved in the discussion, accusing Neumann of breaching an un-written rule among Jungian analysts by responding in a public letter. She also asserted Kirsch's authority in psychological matters, en-dowed, as it was, with the complete trust of Jung. Neumann reports this meeting to Jung asking if he has misbehaved in any way. Given these animosities that arose almost immediately after Neumann's ar-rival in Palestine, Thomas Kirsch's judgment of Erich Neumann as a "member of the German Jewish group in Berlin whom my father had befriended" does not give an accurate account of their relationship.[50]

Jung's reply of 12 August 1934 (7 J) assured Neumann that no se-cret committee of Jungian adherents was in existence. But as the re-marks and reaction of the Zurich Jungians regarding the publication of his book on *Depth Psychology and a New Ethic* in 1949 demon-strated, Neumann was indeed on the periphery of these circles—his remote and isolated position in Tel Aviv made it difficult for him to

---

[48] Adler (1934).

[49] Kirsch wrote a follow-up of his initial text for the *Jüdische Rundschau*, which was not pub-lished. He sent it to Jung attached to his letter of 8 June 1934. The text is printed in Jung and Kirsch (2011), pp. 54–56.

[50] Thomas B. Kirsch (2011), p. xiii.

lobby for his cause during those years. In his letter, Jung continued to thank Neumann for the intelligent and proper elucidation of Kirsch's article and assured him he had acted in the right way. (This small victory for Neumann was probably diminished by Jung's apology that he had to send his letter via Kirsch, as he did not know Neumann's exact address.)

At the beginning of 1935 Kirsch took center stage once more in the correspondence between Jung and Neumann. This was the year in which Kirsch divorced his wife Eva and moved with his second-wife-to-be, Hilde, to London. According to their son Thomas, "they had experienced the early Zionists as more fanatical than they were comfortable with. Living conditions in what was then called Palestine were also considered too primitive for those who were used to the modern conveniences of European life."[51] As Neumann wrote to Jung on 9 February 1935 (12 N) Kirsch's decision to leave Palestine did not go down well with his Jewish colleagues and patients, who still recalled his emphatic praise of the formation of a unique Jewish culture in the promised land.

In his reply from 19 February 1935 Jung distanced himself from Kirsch and confirmed Neumann's suspicion. He had been unable to open Kirsch's letter—"a very pathetic story." And he ended with the remark: "I can only tell you how glad I am, firstly that I have not started a religion, and secondly that I have not founded a church. People may cast out devils in my name all they like or even send themselves into the Gergesene swine!" (13 J).

The Rosenthal Review

In 1934 Jung published a collection of articles titled *Wirklichkeit der Seele* (*Reality of the Soul*).[52] One of the contributors was the German Jewish pedagogue and Zionist Hugo Rosenthal, who in the aftermath of the controversy with Bally was included "in order to annoy the National Socialists and those Jews who have decried me as an

---

[51] Thomas B. Kirsch (2011), p. xiv.
[52] Jung (1934c).

anti-Semite."[53] His article, "Der Typengegensatz in der Jüdischen Religionsgeschichte" ("The Type-Difference in the Jewish History of Religion"),[54] was reviewed by Neumann in the *Jüdischen Rundschau* on 27 July 1934.[55] Although Neumann gave credit to Rosenthal for being the first one to apply Jung's typology to the history of the Jewish religion and culture, he also criticized his contribution for only scratching the surface of the problem. By sticking to an internal Jewish perspective Rosenthal would fail to follow up the wider consequences of his discovery of the Jewish people's introversion and its sharp contrast to the extraverted non-Jewish environment of the diaspora. Nevertheless, the polarity between introversion and extraversion within the Jewish tradition itself would still reveal remarkable results, especially where Rosenthal used biblical material—most importantly the story of Jacob and Esau—to show the typological polarity.

Based on this review Neumann began to elaborate on the questions Rosenthal raised (5 N). In his first letter to Jung from Tel Aviv he told Jung about this attempt to engage with the question of Jewish psychology and announced a typewritten text that would follow the letter (5 N). This letter of content, which Neumann and Jung referred to as "Annotations" ("Anmerkungen"), was—together with two other letter attachments—believed to be missing until recently, when the editor identified it in the Neumanns' heirs' collection of unpublished material in the home of Mrs. Rali Loewenthal-Neumann, Erich Neumann's daughter, in Jerusalem in 2012. "Annotations" has been published as attachment to the letter 5 N as 5 N (A). Although one has to

---

[53] Jung and Kirsch (2011), p. 47. Next to Rosenthal's article the volume also contained two contributions by the National Socialist psychiatrist and psychotherapist Wolfgang Müller Kranefeldt (Kranefeldt, 1934; see also n. 531). Jung himself contributed nine articles to the volume. In "The Development of Personality" ("Vom Werden der Persönlichkeit") Jung wrote about the problem of the peoples' desire for the great individuals: "The huzzahs of the Italian nation go forth to the personality of the Duce, and the dirges of other nations lament the absence of strong leaders" (Jung, 1934e, pp. 167–68; German: p. 180). This text was a reprint of a lecture originally delivered in November 1932 at the Kulturbund in Vienna. In the 1934 publication Jung added the footnote: "Seitdem dieser Satz geschrieben wurde, hat auch Deutschland seinen Führer gefunden" ("Since this sentence was written, Germany too has found its Führer"). Cocks interpreted the phrase "has found" as a positive endorsement of the role of the strong leader by Jung (Cocks, 1991, pp. 160–61; also 1997, p. 147). For Sherry the footnote "makes it clear that Jung saw Hitler's coming-to-power as the outcome of a natural, almost inevitable process" (Sherry, 2012, p. 100).

[54] Rosenthal (1934). On Hugo Rosenthal (a.k.a. Josef Jashuvi) see n. 176.

[55] Neumann (1934a).

see it as a thought experiment and brainstorming on Neumann's part, it undoubtedly formed the backbone of the initial discussion between Neumann and Jung on Jewish psychology. The "annotations" are mainly concerned with the typological opposition in the biblical story of Jacob and Esau elaborating on Rosenthal's article. On Jung's recommendation Neumann used the material of the letter to write an (unpublished) article on the topic of Jacob and Esau.

Before Jung was able to reply, another letter with attachment followed on 19 July 1934 (6 N and 6 N [A]). This second attachment, subsequently referred to as "Applications and Questions" ("Anwendungen und Fragen"), was even more elaborate and dealt with the question of Jewish psychology, typology, and individuation. It was around this time that Neumann started to work on his (unpublished) text *Ursprungsgeschichte des Jüdischen Bewusstseins* (*On the Origins and History of Jewish Consciousness*).[56] For the next six years Neumann would work on two volumes, which are concerned with the depth psychology of the Jewish psyche and the problem of revelation on the one hand, and the psychological relevance of Hasidism for Jewry on the other hand. But it is not incorrect to say that the beginnings of this project can be found in "Applications and Questions."

Although Jung's reply to these extensive letters took a while, the letter of 12 August 1934 (7 J) is probably his most substantial contribution to the question of Jewish psychology in his correspondence with Neumann. Here, Jung engages with the contents of Neumann's letters, amplifying on the material presented to him. But still not enough for Neumann, who expressed his disappointment that Jung did not sufficiently elaborate on the content of "Applications and Questions" and subsequently sent a final attachment together with the letter 8 N, referred to as "Letter III" (8 N [A]).

Last Time in Zurich

At the beginning of 1936 Neumann expressed symptoms of exhaustion. He explained his need to withdraw from his considerations of Palestine and the Jewish question in order to dedicate his time to his

---

[56] Neumann (1934–40).

individuation process and expressed his desire to come to Zurich (19 N, 30 January 1936). Indeed, in May and June 1936 Erich and Julie Neumann visited Zurich. It would be the last time before the war, as they would not return to Switzerland until 1947. In Zurich Erich worked psychotherapeutically with Jung and Toni Wolff, who also became Julie's therapist. During their stay the Neumanns took part in the Jungian life of Zurich, as Erich's participation of Jung's seminar on Nietzsche's *Thus Spoke Zarathustra* showed.[57]

Nietzsche's philosophical text also played an important role in Jung's *Wotan*, which was published in the same year.[58] According to Jung the return of the Germanic God Wotan to Nazi Germany, the archetypal seizure of the German people by the pagan God, had been anticipated in certain sections of Nietzsche's *Zarathustra*, a book Jung praised for its visionary qualities.[59] In an interesting exchange in 1939, shortly after the beginning of the war, Neumann reported a dream in which he identified himself with a pilgrim wearing a wide-brimmed hat, easy to recognize as Wotan (29 N). In his reply Jung shifts his previous argument about the pure Germanic character of this archetype, indicating the psychological regression in Nazi Germany, to a wider understanding of Wotan as a wind god, who, archetypally, also bears universal significance.

Closer to home, the Neumanns moved to a different apartment in 1936. The new address of 1 Gordon Street would become a household name among therapists and patients. Not only would Erich and Julie have their practice in the modest apartment, it also became a place for Erich Neumann's weekly seminar series. In the 1930s topics ranged from the theory and teachings of Jung to Hasidism, from the psychological characteristics and problems of the modern Jew to the archetypal contents of fairy tales.[60]

In the same year Erich's parents came from Berlin for a visit—a brief moment of calm joy in those troubled days. But it was the last time that Erich Neumann would see his father. In the following year Eduard

---

[57] See Neumann's question on 24 June 1936 (Jung, 1934–39, pp. 1021–22). See n. 269.

[58] Jung (1936).

[59] On Jung's *Wotan* article in connection with his reception of Nietzsche's *Zarathustra*, see Liebscher (2001) and Dohe (2011).

[60] See Neumann (1937–38, 1938, 1938–39, 1939–40).

Neumann died of the injuries sustained in a beating by Nazi thugs.[61] But this personal tragedy would not come on its own. On the night of 9 November 1938 a pogrom of unprecedented scale against Jews had taken place in Germany, the so-called Kristallnacht (Crystal Night).[62] In a moving letter to Jung dated 5 December 1938 Neumann expressed his shock about recent events in Germany (27 N). Neumann's letter is an expression of perplexity and ambivalence. He praises Jung for an assurance that there is still a place left for the Jews in Europe, but remarks at the same time that Jung's ivory tower position would make it more difficult to communicate the horrors bestowed upon the Jewish people. In regard to Germany he writes about the personal debt of gratitude toward the German people that would not allow him to simply identify it with the symptoms of its schizophrenic episode. And in a twist that for us today, in hindsight, is difficult to grasp, he links the atrocities committed against Jews in Nazi Germany with the hope for a rejuvenation of the Jewish people, thereby going back to his previous thoughts about Jewish extraversion:

> Added to this is the fact that I believe that these entire events will be, in brief, the salvation of Judaism, while at the same time I'm clear that I do not know if I will be among the survivors of this upheaval or not. The enormous extraversion of Judaism which has led it to the brink of its grave will be cut off with the inexorable consistency of our destiny, and the terrible state of emergency which has gripped the entire people and will continue to do so will inevitably compel the inner source energies either into action or to their peril. (27 N)

IV. THE LONG INTERVAL, 1940–45

The correspondence between Jung and Neumann broke off in 1940 and was only resumed in 1945. During those years Palestine, still

---

[61] The exact circumstances of his death are not entirely clear. According to one account he was beaten up by the Gestapo during an interrogation. (Information by Rali Loewenthal-Neumann, personal conversation in Jerusalem, December 2012.)

[62] See n. 335.

under British mandate, was threatened by the swift advances of German troops in North Africa. Jewish support of the British war efforts ranged from the involvement of Haganah units, the Palmach, against Vichy French forces in Syria in 1941 to the formation of a Jewish Brigade Group as a front-line unit in 1944. Palestinian Jews were parachuted over Nazi territory to gather intelligence and get in contact with surviving Jewish communities. In total more than thirty thousand Palestinian Jews served in the British Army and fought in Greece, Crete, North Africa, Italy, and Northern Europe.[63] Since 1941 news of the systematic mass murder of European Jews had reached Palestine and made the abolition of the immigration quota ever more urgent. In spite of the efforts of well-meaning supporters such as Winston Churchill, the British policy did not change until 1943, when, at last, any refugee coming via the Balkans and Istanbul would get entry permission regardless of the existing quotas.

The war years saw Neumann at his most productive. Although the only text to be published as it was conceived during the war was *Depth Psychology and a New Ethic*, the foundations of many of his later writings go back to that time. The unpublished texts written in this period were "Zur religiösen Bedeutung des tiefenpsychologischen Weges" ("On the Religious Significance of the Path of Depth Psychology") (Neumann 1942) and "Die Bedeutung des Bewusstseins für die tiefenpsychologische Erfahrung" ("The Role of Consciousness in Depth-Psychological Experience") (Neumann 1943). The latter consisted of four parts: "Symbole und Stadien der Bewusstseinsentwicklung" ("Symbols and Stages in the Development of Consciousness"), "Bewusstseinsentwicklung und Psychologie der Lebensalter" ("The Development of Consciousness and the Psychology of the Life Stages"), "Der tiefenpsychologische Weg und das Bewusstsein" ("The Path of Depth Psychology and Consciousness"), and "Stadien religiöser Erfahrung auf dem tiefenpsychologischen Weg" ("Stages of Religious Experience on the Depth-Psychological Path"). As the chapter titles reveal, Neumann's mind was already occupied with the question of the development of human consciousness, which would become the major topic of his magnum opus *On the Origins and History of Consciousness*.

[63] Gilbert (2008), p. 119.

On an everyday level he continued to see his patients and ran the usual seminars for colleagues and those interested in analytical psychology in his flat.[64] He also had to look after the household that had grown by one member, when his daughter Rali was born in 1938. There was also concern for the fate of the German relatives. Most of them had been able to flee Germany and immigrate to England.[65] Erich's mother Zelma, who was supposed to come to Tel Aviv and was taken by surprise by the beginning of the war while in London, had to spend the war years with her other son, Franz, and his family in England and would only be able to continue her journey in 1947.

V. CORRESPONDENCE BETWEEN ISRAEL AND ZURICH, 1945–60

In Touch with Europe Again

After the end of the war, Palestine was still under the mandate that had been given to Britain by the League of Nations in 1922. The attacks against British military targets by Jewish paramilitary agencies such as the Irgun, its offshoot the Stern gang, and the Haganah, which had ceased while under the threat from Nazi Germany and its allies, were resumed. The excessively rigid anti-immigration policy of the British authorities meant that Jews, among them many Holocaust survivors who wanted to come to Palestine, were detained in camps in Europe. Jewish agencies organized "illegal" immigration to Mandatory Palestine. The unresolved immigration situation increased the tension in the region and led to ever more violence. After a number of Zionist leaders were arrested in 1946, the Irgun blew up a wing of the King David Hotel and killed ninety-one people. In 1947 Britain asked the United Nations for help in solving the crisis. The UN General Assembly voted on 29 November 1947 for the creation of two separate states. The decision was welcomed by the Jews

---

[64] From 12 November 1941 to 24 June 1942 his seminar was dedicated to the alchemical symbols in dreams (Neumann, 1941–42).
[65] See n. 355.

in Palestine but was rejected by the Palestinian Arabs, who used this dangerous moment of lawlessness to start—with large support of the Arab world and some involvement of volunteers from neighboring Arab countries—hostilities against the Jewish community. This resulted in the killings of Jews not only in Palestine but also in its Arab neighbor states. The situation led straight to the war of independence of 1948.

In October 1945—after an interval of five years—the correspondence between Neumann and Jung resumed. The first sign Jung received from Palestine was a small parcel containing a typescript titled *Tiefenpsychologie und Neue Ethik* (*Depth Psychology and a New Ethic*). To reestablish contact by sending this text was a significant gesture by Neumann, as the book can be read as his personal reaction to the atrocities of the Holocaust. And he sent his text to a man whose race-psychological considerations had prompted an international outcry in 1933–34 (and continued to do so after the war) and had led to Neumann's discussions with Jung about the specifics of Jewish psychology in the first place. In the years to come this little book would shake the foundations of Jungian theory in regard to ethics and led to hefty attacks against Neumann from within Jungian circles in Zurich.

The first letter arrived separately from the parcel on 1 October 1945. Therein, Neumann stressed the importance of his contact with Jung and Toni Wolff as representatives of German culture, which never ceased to be of vital importance to him. He reported a change in his scholarly interests, stating—and this puzzled him—that precisely at the time when the question of the Jewish psychological condition was of paramount global necessity, his personal interest in the subject had faded away. Once he had completed his book on Hasidism, which formed the second and final part of his unpublished *Ursprungsgeschichte des jüdischen Bewusstseins* (*On the Origins and History of Jewish Consciousness*) (Neumann 1934–40), he turned his focus toward more general psychological problems.

The letter reached Jung at a critical point in his life. In February 1944 he had suffered a heart attack with almost fatal consequences, which was followed by another one in November 1946. Neumann did not realize how fragile Jung's health was at that time. Although he had heard from Gerhard Adler of Jung's illness, he probably did not understand its severity and assumed that Jung was well again.

In the twilight zone between life and death in which Jung found himself in the days after the first heart attack, he experienced a series of visions that had a profound effect on him. And it is fascinating to notice that one of the visions was of a kabbalistic nature:

> I myself was, so it seemed, in the Pardes Rimmonim, the garden of pomegranates, and the wedding of Tifereth with Malchuth was taking place. Or else I was Rabbi Simon ben Jochai, whose wedding in the afterlife was being celebrated. It was the mystic marriage as it appears in the Cabbalistic tradition. I cannot tell you how wonderful it was. I could only think continually, "Now this is the garden of pomegranates! Now this is the marriage of Malchuth with Tifereth!" I do not know exactly what part I played in it. At bottom it was I myself: I was the marriage. And my beatitude was that of a blissful wedding.[66]

It is as if the intellectual development of the two men had crossed paths during the long years without contact. Neumann, who had accused Jung in 1934 of knowing more about ancient Indian philosophy than about contemporary Jewish culture and religion, had refocused his research interest from Jewish psychology to questions of ethical behavior and developmental psychology. For Jung, in contrast, Jewish mysticism had become increasingly important, and the symbolism of the separation and reunion of the male and female aspects of God, of Tifereth and Malchuth, does not only feature in his vision of 1944 but also informed his understanding of the *Mysterium Coniunctionis*.[67]

Neumann's main contact with Switzerland and Europe in these immediate days after the war was Gerhard Adler. And it was Adler who worked on a plan to connect Neumann once again with the wider Jungian world. In a letter to Jung on 12 December 1945 he wrote:

---

[66] Jung (1961), p. 294.
[67] See also Jung's letter to Neumann, 5 January 1952 (89 J).

It concerns my friend Dr. Erich Neumann in Tel Aviv. He sent me a whole series of manuscripts, which I find in part excellent. I know that he writes entirely without echo and without much prospect to publish. Do you think it would be possible to invite him to Ascona for a presentation? I am certain that he would deliver something valuable and original, and it would be equally as interesting to others as it would be of help to him to find an echo—and eventually even a publisher! I would not bother you with this question, if I were not to be absolutely certain that he could do more for the understanding and the dissemination of "Analytical Psychology"—especially in Jewry—than most of the others I know.[68]

In his first letter to Neumann after the war, in August 1946, Jung mentions his efforts to bring Neumann back to Europe and the difficulties that attended them. And it would take another year for Neumann to achieve this return.

Coming Back to Switzerland

In summer 1947 Erich and Julie Neumann met Gerhard Adler and his wife in Switzerland. Together they attended the Eranos conference in Ascona in August 1947 (see Jung's letters of reference 45 J and 48 J). Although Jung was not present that year, Neumann had a chance to discuss his ideas with other prominent scholars, such as Karl Kerényi, Gilles Quispel, and Victor White to mention a few, and also to link with those Jungians who had come from Zurich. Of special importance was his meeting with Olga Fröbe-Kapteyn, the organizer of the conference, who was particularly impressed by Neumann's personality and intellect, so much so, that she—of course after consulting with Jung—not only invited Neumann to speak at the next Eranos conference about the mystical man (his first of thirteen annual consecutive presentations until 1960), but also to write an introduction to the first Bollingen publication of material from the Eranos picture archive.[69] The volume was to be comprised of the

[68] Adler to Jung, 12 December 1945 (JA).
[69] Olga Fröbe-Kapteyn to Erich Neumann, 30 October 1947 (EA). See n. 423.

images from the exhibition held on the occasion of the 1938 conference on "Gestalt und Kult der Grossen Mutter" ("The Nature and Cult of the Great Mother"). In the years to come, Neumann's "introduction" grew to such an extent that when it finally came out in 1956, it had become a substantial book in its own right with an appendix of images from the Eranos archive.

Neumann and Jung also met again in person that summer—after eleven years. During their meeting they discussed another of Neumann's texts, a volume that would later be published under the title *The Origins and History of Consciousness* (*Ursprungsgeschichte des Bewusstseins*), which was to become Neumann's main work. The text is split into two complementary parts. While the first half is concerned with the mythological stages in the evolution of consciousness, the second corresponds to these stages on an ontogenetic level following the psychological stages in the development of the personality. Neumann calls the first developmental state the uroboric one, here referring to the symbol of the serpent biting its own tail. In this state of complete unconsciousness there is no separation between the ego and the world. The participation mystique (Lévy-Bruhl) of this animistic belief equates to the embryonic state of the womb. Only slowly does the ego work its way toward consciousness. It passes through the stages of the "Great Mother"—(Neumann elaborates on the cult and the characteristics of this archetype in his second major work of 1956)—and the separation from the world-parents, until it enters the stage depicted by the hero's quest. It is here that the ego begins to differentiate itself through the "slaying" of the parental couple, a prerequisite for reaching the final stage, that of the highest consciousness, which is the point of departure for the assimilation of the unconscious as part of the psychological process of individuation.

Jung was deeply impressed by Neumann's study, his only reservation was Neumann's use and understanding of the concept of the "castration complex," which he wanted to see replaced by the term "Opferarchetyp" (archetype of sacrifice). When Neumann insisted on the importance of the concept, Jung replied with a phrase that would ironically anticipate the events to come: "You still have to gain experience for yourself as far as being misunderstood goes. The possibilities

Figure 3. Neumann, Jung, Mircea Eliade, and others at the Eranos Round Table (Eranos Archive; courtesy of Paul Kugler).

exceed all terminology" (54 J). Not least due to Jung's intervention, both volumes—*Die Ursprungsgeschichte* and *Tiefenpsychologie und neue Ethik*—were accepted for publication by Rascher in Zurich.

Neumann returned to Ascona in 1948 to address the audience at the Eranos conference for the first time. His lecture on "The Mystical Man" was not received with unanimous appreciation.[70] Carl Alfred Meier apparently stormed out of the room in the midst of the lecture, an action Neumann referred to in a letter to Meier as "complex driven."[71] Jung defended Neumann against the accusations of Meier and Jolande Jacobi that he was advocating a new dogmatism, stating that "Dr. Meier, for instance, would fare better to elaborate on the connection between his Asclepius and psychotherapy than to run away from the lecture. He would discover some tricky problems, where groundwork, such as Neumann's, might be more than

[70] Neumann (1949).
[71] See n. 472.

welcome."[72] But that was not the end of the affair, which would shed an unfortunate light on some of the most important members of the Zurich followers of Jung, if not on Jung himself.

In the spring of 1948 the Jungian community in Zurich celebrated the foundation of the C. G. Jung Institute for the teaching of analytical psychology. Although Jung was the president, it was the vice president, C. A. Meier, who was the quasi–acting director, the same Meier who would leave Neumann's lecture in protest in the summer to come. Another member of the institute's board, through the personal insistence of Jung, was Jolande Jacobi. Here is her description and opinion of Neumann's 1948 Eranos lecture expressed in a letter to Jung:

> I could not follow your advice to engage with Neumann's thoughts, as I did not like his presentation at all. He did precisely what you always rejected, namely, to create a "system" from your teaching. Though he warned of "dogmatization" in his introduction, he did not follow his own warning. [...] By the way, it was quite interesting how easily the women—almost every one of them—were fascinated by him, whereas the men rejected him strongly. It was equally informative how, during his lecture of two hours, he was completely withdrawn and did not notice his audience at all; he was very odd. Of course he is ingeniously talented at formulation, has an abundance of words, and an eloquent and beautiful style, which can be used to express everything magnificently. It seems almost too easy for him. Does this pose a danger for him? I did not only have to disagree with his schematizing manner, but also with the content of his deliberations. I did not think that those "exceeded yours," as you were allegedly quoted as saying, but remained way *below* yours. Everything that you have revealed about Christian symbolism and the understanding of Christianity over the years, is wiped away, if Neumann's account were to be the *authentic Jungian teaching*. The most important of your principles, namely,

---

[72] Jung to Jolan[de] Jacobi, 24 September 1948 (JA). Meier's comparison of the ancient divinatory understanding of dream with modern psychotherapy was finally published as *Ancient Incubation and Modern Psychotherapy* (Meier, 1949).

that "the damaged," "the crippled" is also the chosen one, would collapse.[73]

Thus Neumann's Eranos lecture had already antagonized two of the key players of the Zurich Jungian circle: Meier and Jacobi. But at least at this stage, Jung did not give in to their critiques; on the contrary, in his reply to Jacobi he told them off:

> I think that Neumann's work is excellent. It is not a dogmatic system, but a structured account, thought through in minute detail. Admittedly he does not take the feelings of his audience into consideration. That is the reason why he does not mention the positive aspect of the damaged. But it is certainly not unknown to him. [...] His style of presentation must have had a particularly unfortunate effect. But his intellectual achievement is outstanding. You are all a bit spoiled by my anima, which is capable of switching between light and dark—nothing is entirely dark and—thank God—completely light! That is why I am accused of contradictions! With Neumann it is more complex. One needs to think with him, otherwise one is lost. I even recommend a careful reading of his lecture. Neumann comes from his eremitic existence in Tel Aviv, which is unknown to us. The house opposite to his was bombed to the ground and "Israel" is suffering in labor. N. is strongly infected collectively due to his anxious rejection of the outer world. This attitude is responsible for his lack of emotions and thus has to be taken into consideration. [...] According to my opinion Neumann is a scholar of the first order, and it is up to my students to prove that he does not teach a dogma, but attempts to create a structure.[74]

As Jung mentioned, Neumann's participation at Eranos in 1948 was overshadowed by the war in Israel. In response to the UN plan of a two state solution, the country had plunged into a war between the Jewish and the Arab communities of Palestine. The British, who were still holding the mandate until 14 May 1948, hardly intervened, which

---

[73] Jacobi to Jung, 9 September 1948 (JA).
[74] Jung to Jacobi, 24 September 1948 (JA).

Neumann described in a letter to Jung as the "betrayal of the English" (62 N, 24 January 1948). When the state of Israel was declared with effect from 15 May 1948, troops from neighboring Arab countries attacked Israel and the internal conflict became a war between states. The Arab-Israeli war, or War of Independence, lasted until 10 March 1949 and ended with an Israeli victory. As a result, the state of Israel kept almost the entire territory allocated by the UN plan and occupied in addition large parts of the land proposed for a Palestinian state.

Given the dangerous situation in Israel, it is not difficult to imagine that Neumann would have seemed quite tense when he came to Switzerland in August 1948. Earlier that year a bomb had destroyed the neighboring house at 3 Gordon Street and brought the realities of war very close to home. In a letter to Olga Fröbe-Kapteyn from 12 July 1948 he described that incident: "As long as we are meaninglessly bombed—only yesterday, directly next to us, one child dead, eighteen wounded; while I am writing this there is another warning—I cannot, as you will understand, make a final decision to come." And he continued to express the feelings that he probably shared with the entire Jewish population of Israel during those days, and that also explains his difficulty in reestablishing contact with Europe:

> Nevertheless, I very much believe that I belong here, even when I am standing here totally on the edge of Europe. You will have difficulties in understanding that, but there is the gassing of 6 million Jews hanging over Europe, and this weighs more heavily than wild Arabs, who are primitive barbarians, but you would not expect otherwise from them. More when we meet.[75]

Enemies in Zurich: The New Ethic

Depth Psychology and a New Ethic can be read on a personal level as Neumann's attempt to understand how a civilized nation such as Germany, in whose society and culture Neumann was deeply rooted,

---

[75] Neumann to Fröbe-Kapteyn, 12 July [1948] (EA).

was able to commit atrocities on a scale never seen before. His psychological answer goes back to the heart of the Judeo-Christian ethical system. This old ethics, according to Neumann, was based on the opposition between good and evil—and their mutual exclusion. At its core, one would find the psychological principles of repression (*Verdrängung*) and suppression (*Unterdrückung*). This kind of ethics demanded the complete identification with its positive values, which made a recognition and integration of the other side or the shadow impossible. The consequence of such an exclusive identification of the good with the conscious side and the consequent repression of evil created an unconscious feeling of guilt, the pressure of which was relieved through the projection of the shadow on to the other. The rage against the foreigner or the supposed ethical inferior, or even the sacrifice of the best of society for the greater good, is an expression of this primitive scapegoat psychology. Neumann demanded a new ethics that would replace the old dichotomy of good versus evil with the integration of the individual shadow in the sense of Jungian psychology.

How little sensitivity Neumann could expect in regard to his ethical demand is revealed by an exchange with Rascher, who asked Neumann "to change the first section [of the foreword], as we do not want 'the Nazism of Germany' to be mentioned."[76] Neumann replied that his book dealt with contemporary historical facts and German Nazism would undoubtedly belong in this category.[77]

But *The New Ethic* was not the only book by Neumann that would be published by Rascher that year. Originally intended as a volume to be published on its own, *The Origins and History of Consciousness* had previously been chosen to become the first volume in the institute's series Studien des C. G. Jung Instituts (Studies from the C. G. Jung Institute).[78] This meant that it would now be published under the auspices of the institute. One has to call it at least unfortunate, that the institute's vice president, C. A. Meier, was just about to finish his major study *Antike Inkubation und moderne Psychotherapie* (*Ancient Incubation and Modern Psychotherapy*), which was only second in the

[76] Rascher to Neumann, 19 April 1948 (RA).
[77] Neumann to Rascher, 2 May 1948 (RA).
[78] Rascher to Neumann, 6 July 1948 (RA). See n. 444.

pipeline of the series of books. And when Jung, as seen in the letter to Jacobi, presented Neumann as a role model for Meier, tempers must have flared. In her letter to Jung in the aftermath of Neumann's Eranos lecture of 1948, Jacobi also started to stir up emotions against the inclusion of Neumann's book in the series:

> I have great concerns as to how such an account will look in a volume of more than 800 pages and if such a book at the beginning of our series won't dominate all the others to come? There is also the danger that it will be understood as the "official," approved Jungian teaching and *not* the Neumannian understanding, which in fact it will be. And as Dr. Neumann seemed rather unhappy that his book has not appeared yet, he might, perhaps, be delighted anyway, if his book were to be published outside of the series—it would stand up independently, which would be justified by its size anyway. I have only spoken to him briefly. His interest towards me was only limited to business (i.e., the printing of his book) and that has not prompted me to attempt further conversations. The entire Eranos was—even when Mrs. Froebe saw it as the best conference so far—a "failure."[79]

On this occasion Jacobi's worries did not fall on fertile ground. Jung emphasized the value of Neumann's study and honored the book with an extraordinarily generous preface, stating that Neumann had continued laboring at the place where Jung had had to stop in his pioneering work—effectively declaring Neumann to be his successor.[80]

But Neumann's opponents found another opportunity to oppose the publication of *The Origins and History of Consciousness* in the institute's series, when his *Depth Psychology and a New Ethic* was finally published at the end of 1948. On 10 December (72 J) Jung wrote to Neumann telling him that *The New Ethic* had sparked harsh reactions and discussions and that there was a debate going on as to whether the institute should publish the *Origins and History of Consciousness* in its series. Of course Jacobi had already set the tone for this discussion after the Eranos lecture. But in his letter, Jung enthu-

---

[79] Jacobi to Jung, 9 September 1948 (JA).
[80] Jung (1949).

siastically assured Neumann of his support and emphasized the importance of the cathartic effect of such a controversial text.[81] Yet Jung's remark that a "small institute, which still stands on weak legs, must not risk too many opponents. (Side glances to university and church!)," should have been a warning sign to Neumann. In his reply he attacked the idea of an institute that would compromise its academic credibility in order to avoid confrontations (73 N, 1 January 1949) and added that he would gladly withdraw his book from the series if he were asked to do so. The use of this more rhetorical addendum turned out to be fatal for the book's inclusion in the series, when, a month later, he received a letter from C. A. Meier in his capacity as vice president of the institute:

> Dear colleague, as you have already heard from Jung, in the aftermath of the public and private controversy that was sparked by your *New Ethic*, the institute has discussed the question as to whether it was right to publish the *Origins and History of Consciousness* in the publication series of the institute. After an extensive discussion in the board we came to the conclusion that the young institute should not expose itself too much to hefty public controversies. Hence we prefer, for the time being, to publish texts of a monographic character on detailed questions of complex psychology, which still need a better material and scientific underpinning. It therefore seems also personally right, if your big summarising work is published as a separate publication, and I can understand the decision of the board. I hope that you do not have any difficulties with this decision and assure you that we all await the publication of your book with anticipation. Best wishes, always yours, C. A. Meier.[82]

Neumann responded to Jung, the president of the institute, in a fuming letter, reiterating his accusations of opportunism and hypocrisy

---

[81] A letter from Neumann to Olga Fröbe-Kapteyn from 25 December [1948] showed Neumann's delight about Jung's reaction, which seemed to indicate that Jung would take side with Neumann: "In the meantime, 'Ethic' has come out; I hope that Rascher has sent you a copy, and, as Jung wrote in his very nice letter, it has already caused a stir. To my greatest surprise, even in the Institute itself" (EA).

[82] C. A. Meier to Neumann, 3 February 1949 (NP).

(74 N, 10 February 1949). Jung, in return, referred to Neumann's previous letter according to which Neumann did not seem all too eager to publish in the institute's series (75 J, 29 March 1949).

At the same time that the shock of Neumann's *New Ethic* was causing outrage among Jung's supporters in Zurich, Kegan Paul informed Neumann that they would publish an English translation of the book. Neumann asked Jung if he would be willing to write a preface for the English edition. Jung agreed to it, but suggested some changes to the text, as one could not expect any knowledge of psychological or philosophical concepts from an English audience. He sent Neumann his detailed amendments and suggested revisions of the text.[83] What kind of ambivalent role Jung played in this affair is revealed by a letter to Cary Baynes from May 1949:

> He [Neumann] wanted me to write a preface to the English edition of it. I have written it but not sent it to him yet. Instead I have sent him a whole list of propositions that he might consider if he wants to have my foreword. His reply was not altogether favourable. He says that he could not write in the way I would, that to him the whole problem is as hot as hell and of immediate urgency.[84]

Cary Baynes was also stirring up the mood against Neumann, as a letter from Marie-Jeanne Schmid, Jung's secretary, to her shows:

> What I would like to write to you about—and how I would wish I could *talk* it over with you!—is the "new star" Dr. Neumann, i.e., his books. What you wrote about his "New Ethic" made me long for your presence here. Discussion about it is running rather high over here, both in the "outer world" and in the "inner circle." We are even going to have a discussion evening about it among the members of the club.[85] Personally I absolutely agree with you, namely, that one wonders whether he knows what he is talking

[83] See appendix II.
[84] Jung to Cary Baynes, 9 May 1949 (CFB).
[85] On 26 March 1949 a discussion on Neumann's *Depth Psychology and a New Ethic* took place in the Psychological Club Zurich.

about and—although his big book on the "Origins and History" is better—I also wonder with you whether it "really does all that" namely, what C. G. says in his foreword. I wish C. G. had never written it.[86]

Another opinion came from R.F.C. Hull, the translator of Jung's works into English, who would also translate Neumann's *Origins and History* in the years to come. He expressed his initial reaction to *Depth Psychology and a New Ethic* in a letter to Michael Fordham from 6 August 1949:

> I hope I am not putting my foot in it when I say that this Neumann book seems to me singularly ill conceived and possibly a dangerous interpretation of Jung's ideas? If Jung's strictures on Freud and Jewish psychology have led, in America, to the wild accusations that he was a Nazi, anything may happen if Neumann's account of the Jungian "new ethic" is taken at its face value—there may be a hurling of epithets like "Communist," "immoralist," "Antichrist" and who knows what![87]

Neumann was deeply disappointed about this affair, though in his letters to Jung himself, he seems to hold back his anger. To justify his relationship with Jung, he begins to differentiate between Jung, the president of the institute, and Jung, the admired scholar, who challenges the status quo and defended Neumann's book. In a letter to Olga Fröbe-Kapteyn, Neumann summarizes his relationship with Jung after these events as follows: "Personally, Jung is still nice to me, sometimes even movingly so, but it remains that he is not reliable—an old man."[88] He reiterates this argument in 1954 vis-à-vis Aniela Jaffé, calling Jung an uncertain friend in particular matters. In her reply Jaffé assures Neumann of Jung's deep affection, which had never been disturbed by the circumstances that surrounded the publication of Neumann's book. Here, she continued, one can see the

---

[86] Marie-Jeanne Schmid to Cary Baynes, 15 March 1949 (CFB).
[87] R.F.C. Hull to Michael Fordham, 6 August 1949 (MFP).
[88] Neumann to Fröbe-Kapteyn, May [1949?] (EA).

development of the son surpassing the father: in which what had not been possible between Jung and Freud came to an end. [89]

In the case of Toni Wolff, Neumann was less willing to excuse her behavior. At the beginning of April 1949 she wrote to Neumann that his ethical concept would not belong in the theoretical framework of depth psychology (see 76 N, 6 April 1949). Neumann interpreted her letter as the manifestation of hostile sentiments toward him in Zurich. He replied to her expressing his disappointment in a harsh and unambiguous manner.[90] In an unusually defensive way Toni Wolff justified her critique of Neumann's book:

> I do not know if it is of much use to talk once again about the "Ethic." I did write to you everything that I needed to say. Apparently, you have indeed mixed me up with everything else. I was not in Ascona last year, I have absolutely nothing to do with the publication of your book, I am a completely ordinary lecturer at the institute, and besides other women make the decisions. I also have told every one I know personally that your book should be accepted as a publication of the institute. You, hopefully, remember that I was one of those who advised you to publish the Ethic. But I have to confess once again that I am unable to read a manuscript equally critically as a printed book. And it was important to me, with regard to the English translation, to revise certain critical passages. I know England pretty well, and it was only in your interest. Why should I then make all this effort to go into such detail? It was quite some work. It is a shame that the Ethic came out first. Thus it became, in a certain way, almost too important.[91]

Finally, Neumann and Wolff found a way to reconcile, and when Toni Wolff died in 1953 Neumann wrote a moving letter of condolence to Jung, which gives an insight into the important role that she had played in the lives of both Erich and Julie Neumann.

The most intimate account of the affair around the publication of Neumann's books can be found in his correspondence with Olga

[89] Aniela Jaffé to Neumann, 11 January 1954 (NP).
[90] See n. 465.
[91] Toni Wolff to Neumann, 20 July 1949 (NP).

Fröbe-Kapteyn. The outsider's position that both had held in the Jungian world of Zurich was what brought them closer together. To Neumann, the annual conference in Ascona was of much greater significance than the visits to Zurich. In the letters to Olga Fröbe-Kapteyn he did not hold back his anger. In March 1949 he wrote of severe tensions between Jung and himself, calling Jung's dissociation from the institute's decision ironic. The entire affair was a shameful disgrace, and he had written to Jung, whose role in all of this he called outrageous.[92]

There is another aspect that comes into play when Neumann reflects upon those incidents, and that is anti-Semitism. One has to imagine that the Jung Club still had its notorious regulation in place, according to which only 10 percent of members were allowed to be Jewish. This clause was only abandoned when Neumann's Jewish friend Siegmund Hurwitz refused to become a member under such circumstances. And Neumann believed that the rejection of his new ethic and the refusal to include his book in the series was part of the same anti-Semitic agenda, driven, according to Neumann, by catholic circles around Jolande Jacobi—though Jacobi was herself of Jewish descent. In the aforementioned letter he continued to write about his sadness: "This is how it was in Nazi Germany, cowardly and opportunistic, but while it was truly dangerous there, it is only business in Z.—and one that is wrongly understood to boot, but this is no consolation."[93] In a letter from May he is even more explicit about his understanding of the affair:

Jung's behavior toward me is extremely moving and he cares in a way that truly affects me. Of course this has to be of higher importance to me than his weakness in individual cases, where, in my opinion, he is also factually wrong at times. Nevertheless, the whole affair is important to me in a tragic way, as it demonstrates to me the emergence of a reactionary Europe, which takes possession of Jung. Catholicism, individualism—well, those are words, but they are also powers, and everything rhymes in such a sad and fitting way with fascism and national socialism. Because of Jung's

[92] Neumann to Fröbe-Kapteyn 14 March [1949] (EA).
[93] Ibid.

carelessness it has already been tremendously difficult so far to separate Jung and his work from the embarrassing, even catastrophic, closeness to it. I am afraid the Zurich circles, including the readmitted Kranefeldt with his "archetypus sinaiticus" from 33, won't improve the global situation.[94]

On a number of occasions he mentioned the psychological and physical impact that affair had upon him.[95] Although he recovered, and his relationship with Zurich improved steadily over the years to come, the most important aftermath of these days was that his relationship with Jung changed. As the letters reveal, Neumann seemed to realize at that point that Jung was an old man who would not be able to defend Neumann against the Zurich circles. He continued to honor and respect Jung and his work, but this also meant that Neumann would be able to free himself from Jung's influence and could start developing his own theories beyond those of Jung.

Partial Reconciliation with Zurich

Over the coming year, things calmed down, at least on the surface. Jung retreated slowly into the quiet background of his Küsnacht mansion, leaving space for others to take over a leading role. In the case of Eranos Jung's successor was Neumann. In 1951 he wrote to Olga Fröbe-Kapteyn:

> Even if you very much overestimate my role at Eranos. It has indeed turned out that Eranos has become a friendly island for me to which I belong. Zurich however [. . .] anything but—after the Ethic experience. But I have had so many positive experiences with individuals there, that it is some comfort.[96]

Even in Zurich Neumann earned the respect of some parts of the Jungian circle, especially through his *Origins and History of Consciousness*. Richard Hull, for instance, working on its translation, reversed

[94] Neumann to Olga Fröbe-Kapteyn, 22 May [1949] (EA). For Kranefeldt see n. 531.
[95] See Neumann to Fröbe-Kapteyn, 13 December [1949] and 11 [or 14] May [1949] (EA).
[96] Neumann to Fröbe-Kapteyn, 20 January 1951 (EA).

his previous judgment: Though the book was indeed a "modern myth," he wrote in a letter to Herbert Read in 1951, it was an absolutely fantastic one. Still one cannot help reading a hint of animosity in verdicts such as that, for Neumann, analytical psychology comes very near to being a substitute religion.[97] Or when he calls Neumann's system "a little too perfect," blaming Neumann's Jewish origins for its rigidity.[98]

For sure, Neumann would count among the positive and comforting experiences a letter by Helene Hoerni-Jung, the youngest of Jung's daughters, who wrote to him in September 1950 of how much she and her sister enjoyed his lectures, especially the exciting and new perspectives of someone outside the Zurich circle. "What we enjoy less are the theorising and pseudo-intellectual critiques which are getting quite clamorous."[99]

Neumann lectured not only in Ascona but also in Zurich and Basel on a regular basis. In Zurich he was invited to lecture at the Jung Club on a number of occasions,[100] and he even taught at the institute. It is one of the ironic aspects of the affair around the publication of *The Origins and History of Consciousness* that the board, consisting of the very same people who decided to ditch the book from the institute's series, wrote to Neumann five months later to invite him

---

[97] Hull to Read, 25 May 1951: "I have reverted to my original opinion of the Neumann book. . . . The thing may be, as the opponents of Jung claim, a sort of modern myth, but what a fascinating myth it is! In that sense analytical psychology comes very near to being a substitute religion" (RKP).

[98] Hull to Read, 16 October 1951: "My one misgiving is that it tends to turn analytical psychology into a 'closed circuit' on the pattern of the uroboros itself; the system is a little too perfect. To parody one of Neumann's own observations: he, as a Jew seems to have broken out of the 'womb of the Torah' only to land himself in a system that is just as absolute. . . . It would be a pity if this brilliant systematisation of Jung should lead to the kind of fanatical dogmatism one often finds among psychoanalysts" (RKP).

[99] Helene Hoerni-Jung to Erich Neumann, 25 September 1950 (NP).

[100] The club program register lists the following lectures by Erich Neumann: "Towards a Psychology of the Feminine in the Patriarchy" ("Zur Psychologie des Weiblichen im Patriarchat") (7 October 1950); "On the Dominance of the Feminine Archetype in the Creative Man" ("Über das Dominantbleiben des weiblichen Urbildes beim schöpferischen Manne") (13 October 1951); "A Structural Analysis of the Archetype of the Great Mother" ("Zur Strukturanalyse des Archetypus der Grossen Mutter) (27 September 1952); "Primal Relationship and the Self: Remarks on 'Symbolic Wish fulfilment'" ("Urbeziehung und Selbst: Bemerkungen zu 'Symbolische Wunscherfüllung' von M.-A. Sechehaye") (1 October 1955); "On the Problem of Reality" ("Zum Problem der Wirklichkeit") (29 September 1956); "The Fear of the Masculine" ("Die Angst vor dem Männlichen") (10 October 1959).

to teach their students at the institute. The invitation letter was writ-ten in Ascona on 25 August 1949, and was signed by Binswanger, Frey, Jacobi, and Meier.[101] Neumann accepted and became a regular teacher at the institute.[102] An attempt at a personal reconciliation with the institute came probably in 1954, when he accepted the pa-tronage of the institute.[103]

Although Neumann and Jacobi would never become friends, her annual letters to Jung from the Eranos conferences started to ex-press a slightly more positive attitude toward Neumann: The con-ference in 1955 did not offer a lot, nothing stimulating, "Neumann spoke in a dogmatic and seductive way,"[104] and in 1956 she writes that it even gained quality through Neumann's presentation: "He was absolutely excellent."[105] In contrast, although Neumann seemed to respect her strength and courage in comparison with the other Jungians in Zurich, he would not reconcile with her that easily. Even in 1959, while teaching a course at the institute in Zurich on child psychology, Neumann and Jacobi would clash with each other. Mario Jacoby, at that time a student at the institute, gave us an ac-count of that confrontation:

> Neumann had the characteristic of radiating great powers of per-suasion in support of his ideas—which were new at that time—by using well-polished linguistic expression. Only the ever undaunted Jolande Jacobi, who was also present, dared to contradict him. She was not happy about Neumann's notion of equating the infant's experience of the mother with that of the Self in the Jungian sense. [...] She was—as she said—convinced of the fact that the Self is a metaphysical reality which extends into human experience. "This is exactly what the Self is not" interrupted Neumann. With his

---

[101] Curatorium des C. G. Jung Instituts Zürich to Neumann, 25 August 1949 (NP).

[102] Neumann's seminars at the institute were not without controversies. In autumn 1950 he was attacked by Meier and other members of the Curatorium for his interpretation of *Amor and Psyche* (see n. 518).

[103] Curatorium des C. G. Jung Instituts Zürich to Neumann, October 1954 (NP).

[104] Jacobi to Jung, 5 September 1955 (JA).

[105] Jacobi to Jung, 22 August 1956 (JA).

humour, his clarity of thought and his persuasive clout he could hold his own, even in the face of some training analysts who were present who were all direct students of Jung.[106]

A damning letter to Aniela Jaffé in 1959, written in the aftermath of this incident and apparently in a state of depression, shows that Neumann's general reconciliation with the Zurich Jungians was not successful after all. Here, Neumann explained his wish not to lecture in Zurich any more. The letter is a reply to Jaffé's attempt to emphasize Neumann's importance for Zurich, especially for the institute and the club. She wrote about her impression that the general appreciation that Neumann received by the members would not be reciprocated by him:

Perhaps it is due to past experiences that even today you find yourself in a sort of defensive position in Zurich, and one sometimes gets the impression that you operate according to the principle: "Attack is the best form of defence." That has a remarkably divisive effect on your audience. Two camps immediately form: pro Neumann and contra Neumann—a fact which is then, of course, for the most part ignored and not discussed.[107]

Calling Jaffé naive, Neumann set out to strike a balance in his relationship with Zurich over the last decade. There would be no community waiting for him in Zurich. Since Jung had left Eranos, the Zurich Jungians would shun Ascona. This ignorance, which he also had to face in Zurich, would have tragic consequences, as he would put his fingers on wounds and problems that needed discussion in order for analytical psychology to survive.[108] He would be prepared to forget the past insults by Jung, Jacobi, Meier, and Frey for the sake

---

[106] Mario Jacoby (2005), p. 38.

[107] Jaffé to Neumann, 24 October 1959 (NP).

[108] Neumann to Jaffé, undated letter, written around late October/November 1959 (NP): "Even more, behind the Eranos work, there is much more inner inspirational experience; the system is, in part, difficult work which seems necessary for me, and whether analytical psychology will survive depends in part, I sometimes fear, on this."

of the cause, but his opinion would be sidelined.[109] And his final verdict sounds devastating:

> You know, I put up with some things from C. G. that I am still amazed at today, but at least I know who he is in spite of this and in relation to me. I do not have the feeling that the same is required of me in relation to the Zurichers.[110]

Late Recognition

During his lifetime Neumann saw the translation of his works into several languages. Along with Hull's English translation, *The Origins and History of Consciousness* was rendered into Italian and Dutch, and a Spanish translation appeared in 1956. Translations of *Depth Psychology and a New Ethic*, the three volumes of *Die Umkreisung der Mitte*, *Eros and Psyche*, and the *Great Mother* followed suit.[111]

At the forefront of interest in things to do with Neumann were the Dutch. This special relationship becomes apparent not only through the number of translations but also through Neumann's regular lectures in the Netherlands. In 1952 he was invited to the Internationale School voor Wijsbegeerte in Amersfoort for the first time, which was followed by several other visits in the years to come. Presentations in Amsterdam, Arnhem, Leiden, and The Hague followed.[112]

Neumann's international recognition reached a new height in 1958 when he participated in the First Conference of the IAAP (AGAP) in Zurich and in the Fourth International Congress of Psychotherapy in Barcelona, both marking milestones in the history of modern psychology. A year later he took part in a conference in Germany, something he had rejected until then.[113] In 1960 he returned to Germany

---

[109] Ibid: "A lunch with Frau Dr. Frey and Brunner belongs, as kind as they are, in the same category. I have tried hard—for the sake of the cause—to forget the old insults of C. G., Jacobi, Meier, and Frey—which does not come easily to someone like me."

[110] Ibid.

[111] For the contracts with Neumann regarding translations, see RA.

[112] See nn. 545 and 551.

[113] Neumann participated in the Evangelische Akademie in Tutzing at the Starnberger Lake, which took place from 18 July to 4 August 1959.

one more time to lecture in Munich on the topic of "Consciousness, the Ritual, and Depth Psychology."[114]

At home he began to institutionalize the small group of analytical psychologists and to secure its future by founding the Israel Association of Analytical Psychology (1959). His reputation was steadily growing. He was even asked to become the head of the Psychological Institute of the University of Tel Aviv, an offer he gratefully declined.

Among all these signs of international and national recognition, signs Neumann had waited for desperately over all those years, fell the sudden and unexpected medical diagnosis of his fatal cancer. The last Eranos conference in the summer of 1960 was followed by a visit to London to see his brother and to seek specialist medical advice. But his condition deteriorated rapidly, and after the return to Tel Aviv Erich Neumann died on 5 November.

VI. THE LEGACY OF ERICH NEUMANN

Two monographs by Erich Neumann were published posthumously: *Crisis and Renewal* (1961) and *The Child* (1963).[115] The latter was regarded as one of the first major studies on child psychology by an eminent Jungian scholar. Neumann's interest in the subject went back to the 1930s as an (unpublished) essay from April 1939 titled "Remarks on the Psychology of the Child and on Pedagogy" ("Bemerkungen zur Psychologie des Kindes und der Paedagogik") proves.[116] In the 1950s he held seminars for child psychologists at his home in Tel Aviv on a regular basis.[117] As mentioned before, Neumann also held a course on the subject at the institute in Zurich in 1959, which provoked a conflict with Jolande Jacobi.[118] In the aftermath he expressed his disappointment about the lack of support from the Zurich school, warning of the skeptical attitude toward the possible

[114] Presentation at the conference "Der Kult in den Kulturen der Welt" ("The Cult in the Cultures of the World"), 31 July–5 September 1960 (Neumann 1961c).

[115] Neumann (1961b); (1963).

[116] Neumann (1939).

[117] Fragmentary notes of the 1954 and 1955 seminars can be found in NP (Neumann 1954; 1955).

[118] See introduction, pp. lii–liii.

practical application of analytical psychology by the "regressive English school of Fordham," which would endanger the entire project.[119] In his 1954 seminar he noticed a rapprochement between the Kleinian and Jungian school in England:

> What is being reported from England is that the therapy of Klein and the Jungians is almost one and the same. Because Melanie Klein keeps on mythologising. I wonder whether the child understands her interpretations—which are strongly mythologically based—from what she refers to as myth; that this is the basis of the child's understanding and interpretation of symbols. The question is whether the intellectual interpretation which she attributes to this is an essential component or not.[120]

Fordham's use of the Oedipal complex in *The Life of Childhood* is also criticized by Neumann in his letter to Jung of 1 October 1945 (33 N).[121] There Neumann also emphasized the importance of child psychology, which Jung had neglected because of his interest in the individuation process of the second half of life.

The antagonism between Neumann and Fordham came to the surface when Neumann wanted to publish an article in Fordham's *Journal of Analytical Psychology*.[122] Fordham rejected the article in the first instance on grounds of theoretical differences, to which Neumann responded: "I did not know you have a critical attitude towards my work and should be thankful to get known with your criticism. Never did it occur to me that you might reject essays from me for such reasons. This would mean that you do not feel as editor of a Journal for Analytical Psychology, but as a censor who has to judge about what Analytical Psychology has to be."[123] Subsequently, Fordham sent Neumann his latest book and the two men agreed to have a further discussion. Due to Neumann's premature death there was

---

[119] Neumann to Jaffé, undated letter, late October/November 1959 (NP). On Fordham, see n. 366.

[120] Neumann (1954), p. 12. Fordham's interest in Kleinian thought would even lead him to undertake a Kleinian analysis in his later years.

[121] Fordham (1944).

[122] "The Significance of the Genetic Aspect for Analytical Psychology" was finally published in the *Journal of Analytical Psychology* in 1959 (Neumann, 1961a).

[123] Neumann to Fordham, 30 January 1958 (NP).

no further debate to bridge those differences. However, in 1981, Fordham published an article on "Neumann and Childhood" in which he heavily criticized Neumann's theory of childhood psychology: "I can enjoy the experience of his 'poetry', especially when he interprets myth and legend; that, however, no longer justifies using vague, contradictory metaphor with which to capture states of consciousness in infancy and childhood. It was a device which used to pass muster, but today research has made that approach inappropriate. Both Jungians and psychoanalysts have constructed theories of childhood."[124] Fordham's article was a hatchet job in every sense of the word: besides accusing Neumann of being dogmatic and non-Jungian, his main critique was targeted at Neumann's lack of empirical data and use of out-of-date scientific theories such as the relation between phylogenesis and ontogenesis or Adolf Portmann's extrauterine first year.[125] Fordham's conclusion, that after detailed scrutiny almost nothing of originality remained from Neumann's child psychology, was a dire verdict.[126] In defense of Neumann, it has to be said that his theory of childhood was informed by years of weekly exchanges with child psychologists and that the project of the Neve Ze'elim Children's

[124] Fordham (1981), p. 100.

[125] Adolf Portmann (1897–1982): Swiss zoologist. From 1946 on he was a regular participant of the Eranos conference in Ascona, where he used to give the last and concluding presentation. After the death of Olga Fröbe-Kapteyn in 1962, he—together with Rudolf Ritsema—took over the presidency of the foundation. His last presentation at the Eranos conference took place in 1977. The Portmann theory of the extrauterine first year states that the newborn human—in contrast to other primates—endures a premature birth in a physiological sense. Due to its vulnerability the infant is completely dependent on the mother or other adults for a year. After this time in the "social womb" the infant experiences a "second birth" as a cultural and social human being. His works include *Animal Forms and Patterns* (1948) and *The Animal as Social Being* (1953). On Portmann see Ritsema (1982).

[126] In his attempt to discredit Neumann's work, Fordham went even further and questioned Jung's appreciation of it. In a private conversation with Sonu Shamdasani, Fordham gave the following account of a verbal exchange with Jung: When he asked Jung why he wrote of Neumann's work in such laudatory terms, when he often criticized it in conversation, Jung stated that it was to prevent Neumann from having a psychosis (personal communication, Michael Fordham to Sonu Shamdasani). Fordham's antagonism aside, Mircea Eliade reports of an equally critical remark by Jung: "He [Jung] finds Neumann too rationalist (Jung gives this interpretation of a dream of Neumann that has a little girl in it: Neumann hasn't integrated the 'the feminine creativity' of which he has spoken so much in his writings" (Eliade, Journal II, p. 41 [6 June 1959]). But for every reported negative remark one can find a statement of Jung's deep appreciation for Neumann such as this: "I have a huge correspondence, see innumerable people but have only two real friends with whom I can speak about my own difficulties; the one is Erich Neumann and he lives in Israel and the other is Father Victor White in England" (reported by F. Elkisch, 29 October 1976; quoted in Cunningham, 2007, p. 334).

Home, a long-term treatment center in Israel, was based on the find-ings of his child psychology.[127]

In his article Fordham refers, as unlikely as it may sound, to none other than Wolfgang Giegerich, who wrote a fundamental critique of Erich Neumann's analytical psychology in 1975.[128] Both agree that Neumann was not Jungian at all, because he confused—in spite of Jung's warning—the archetypal with the empirical child.[129] Whereas for Fordham *The Child* is weak because of the lack of empirical data, Giegerich, in contrast, criticizes Neumann's research for the attempt to base his findings on empirical facts, thereby fudging amateurishly in the realm of biology. Psychological truth should not be concerned with the empirical but with the imaginal.

As far as *The Origins and History of Consciousness* is concerned, Gieg-erich finds the opposite aspect worthy of critique. Quoting a passage from the introduction to Neumann's book, he concludes that "such utterances, although limited to the castration complex and other such 'symbols' may by implication suggest that in the last analysis, Neu-mann wants everything he says to be understood as 'symbolic facts' which then could not be located in empirical ('personalistic') his-tory."[130] This is important, as Giegerich can only build his verdict about the book as a myth in itself, an archetypal fantasy, on this lack of empirical concreteness. What Giegerich did not know is that this passage in Neumann about the symbolic character of the castration complex was only included because of Jung's intervention, who had concerns about Neumann's usage of the term.[131] This shows—and the correspondence between Neumann and Jung confirms this— that Neumann's writing and thinking was often much more in tune and accordance with Jung than critics like Fordham or Giegerich would have liked it to be, insofar as their critique of Neumann would implicitly become one of Jung also.

There have been a number of attempts to revive the legacy of Erich Neumann. The volume *Zur Utopie einer Neuen Ethik* (2005), based on

[127] See Abramovitch and Badrian (2006), pp. 182–99.
[128] Giegerich (1975).
[129] Giegerich (1975) refers to Jung (1941), § 273, n. 20. Fordham (1981), p. 101 follows Gieg-erich on this point.
[130] Giegerich (1975), p. 115.
[131] See the letters 52 J (1 July 1947) and 53 N (8 July 1947), n. 412.

a conference organized by the German language organization of analytical psychology,[132] and a special issue of *Harvest* (2006) marked the anniversary of Erich Neumann's one-hundredth birthday.[133] In 2007, a memorial plaque was revealed at Julie Neumann's house in Berlin (Pariser Straße 4). The proceedings of the accompanying conference, organized by the Arbeitskreis für die Geschichte der Analytischen Psychologie, were published in the journal *Analytische Psychologie* (2008).[134] In Germany his Eranos lectures have been republished, and there are regular conferences and seminar series on Neumann's thinking. The high esteem in which Erich Neumann, the founder of the Israel Association of Analytical Psychology, is held among analytical psychologists in Israel cannot be doubted. There is hope that the publication of the correspondence between C. G. Jung and Erich Neumann will create an international revival of the interest in the thinking of Erich Neumann, which will make it possible to revaluate his position within the history of analytical psychology.

Editorial Remarks

The first attempt to publish the correspondence between C. G. Jung and Erich Neumann dates back to the early 1980s. Aniela Jaffé was supposed to be the editor, assisted by Julie Neumann and Robert Hinshaw.[135] Due to the unexpected death of Julie Neumann in 1985, the project was delayed and finally abandoned. In 2010 the Philemon Foundation obtained the permission to publish the correspondence.

Jung's letters were in the private collection of the Neumann family in Jerusalem until 2006. During Jung's lifetime no copies of handwritten letters were taken, whereas the secretaries would take and file copies of typewritten letters. These copies are kept in the Jung archive of the ETH Zurich. When Aniela Jaffé edited the selection of Jung's

---

[132] Österreichische Gesellschaft für Analytische Psychologie (2005).
[133] Harvest (2006).
[134] *Analytische Psychologie* (2008).
[135] Personal information from Robert Hinshaw.

letters, she received copies of Jung letters from all over the world.[136] It is probably due to this that the Jung archive possesses a set of Jung's letters to Neumann. This was completed for the use of this edition by a set of copies from the Neumann heirs in Israel. In 2006, thirty-four letters by Jung to Neumann were auctioned and sold at Sotheby's in London.[137] In two cases, Jung's letters from 22 September (100 J) and 9 July 1954 (103 J), lines are missing due to the bad state of the copies. As the whereabouts of the actual letters are currently unknown it was not possible to fill these gaps. The letters of Erich Neumann were sent back to Tel Aviv by request of Julie Neumann after Erich's death. Fifty-five letters by Neumann to Jung were sold at the 2006 auction.[138]

In total this correspondence consists of 124 documents. Of these there are thirty-nine letters by Jung to Neumann, seven attests or references written by Jung for Neumann, and one letter from Jung to Julie Neumann. The Neumann documents consist of fifty-eight letters from Neumann to Jung, three letters to Marie-Jeanne Schmid, and the three attachments 5N (A), 6 N (A), and 8 N (A).[139] As the contents of these three attachments is an integral—if not even the essential—part of the letter exchange between Jung and Neumann in the 1930s, the editor has decided to publish them—regardless of their length—in the sequence of the correspondence.

In addition there are ten letters by Marie-Jeanne Schmid and three letters by Aniela Jaffé, which they wrote to Neumann in their capacity as Jung's secretaries. Appendix I is a copy of Neumann's contributions in the *Jüdische Rundschau*[140]—his rejoinder to Kirsch and his review of Rosenthal's article. Appendix II is the list of amendments and revision Jung wanted Neumann to implement for the English edition of *Depth Psychology and a New Ethic*.

The letters are placed in chronological order. Neumann's letters are sometimes not dated and the dates had to be reconstructed from

---

[136] See Jaffé's preface in Jung (1973).

[137] Sotheby's (2006), pp. 132–37.

[138] Information on the holdings of the Jung archive collection was given by Ulrich Hoerni (e-mail correspondence, 22 October 2012) and Yvonne Voegeli (e-mail correspondence, 20 September 2012).

[139] On those attachments see introduction, p. xxix–xxx.

[140] Neumann (1934).

the content. In such cases the reasons have been given in the footnotes. Neumann's handwriting caused problems—not only to Jung—hence he decided to use a typewriter in the later years. Where Neumann wrote by hand—this concerns mainly the early letters—the transcripts needed to be checked a number of times. Despite this painstaking work there have been a few occasions where it was not possible to decipher a word—in those cases the problem has been indicated in the footnotes.

There exist a few letters of Jung in a handwritten and a typescript version, for instance letter 15 J of 27 April 1935. In those cases Jung wrote by hand and the secretary produced a typewritten version, which Jung corrected by hand before it was finally typed and sent to Neumann. Substantial differences between the different versions have been highlighted in the footnotes.

Translator's Note

In keeping with the values of the Philemon Foundation, I have sought in this translation to remain as true as possible to the style and meaning of the German original, opting, where necessary, for accuracy and faithfulness to the sometimes obscure German, rather than English idiom. It must be remembered that the original texts were letters between friendly colleagues, and as such punctuation, especially, at times reflects this personal medium in that it can deviate from the norms expected for scholarly publication. Where possible I have retained this punctuation, except where meaning would otherwise have been obscured. I have adopted the use of capitalized "Self" for the translation of Jung's "Selbst" for the sake of clarity.

I acknowledge with gratitude the patient proofreading and editing collaboration of Martin Liebscher.

Heather McCartney

Analytical Psychology in Exile

List of Letters

1 J

[Küsnacht, Zurich,] 11 September 1933

Dr. Erich Neumann,
Weimarischestrasse 17,
Berlin-Wilmersdorf[141]

Dear Doctor,

I have reserved an hour's appointment for you on Tuesday, 3rd October at 4 pm.

Yours respectfully,
C. G. Jung

---

[141] From 1928 to 1932 Erich and Julie Neumann lived in Hindenburgstraße 86 (Berlin Wilmersdorf; today's name: Am Volkspark). In 1932 they moved to Weimarische Straße 17 where they stayed until they left Germany in autumn 1933. (Information from Micha Neumann and Rali Loewenthal-Neumann.)

2 J

CERTIFICATE [142]

I hereby confirm that Dr. Erich Neumann is engaged in psychological studies with me, and that my work will begin again on 15th January 1934.

Küsnacht, Zurich, 14th December
[C. G. Jung]

---

[142] Presumably written for the Swiss Federal Department of Justice and Police in order for Neumann to obtain a temporary permit of residency.

3 J

29. I. 1934

To: Dr. Erich Neumann,
Zurich

Dear Colleague,

It is possible that a Dr. Ernst Harms[143] will make contact with you. He is desperate for therapy, and needs it too—as he basically consists of an intellectual halo wandering lonely and footless through the world. He would not be uninteresting, but there would be no money in it.

With best wishes,
Yours truly,
[C. G. Jung]

---

[143] Ernest [Ernst] Harms (1895–1974): Jewish child psychotherapist. Studied with Freud and later with Jung; defended Jung against accusations of anti-Semitism (Harms, 1946). In 1934 he had already published articles on topics such as psychology of religion (Harms, 1931), pedagogy of psychology (Harms, 1931a), and German idealism (Harms, 1933a). Later works include *Psychologie und Psychiatrie der Conversion* (*Psychology and Psychiatry of Conversion*) (1939) and *Origins of Modern Psychiatry* (1967).

4 N

[no date][144]

Dear Dr. Jung,

When I spoke—in some dismay—with Miss Wolff[145] today about
the partial validity of Dr. Bally's[146] article and she gave me your paper

[144] The letter was written in Zurich between the publication of Gustav Bally's article on 27
February 1934 and Neumann's departure in May 1934.

[145] Toni Anna Wolff (1888–1953): Born into a wealthy and distinguished Zurich family, Toni
Wolff was sent to Jung for treatment in 1910 after the death of her father the previous year. She
became the soul mate, mistress, and companion of Jung and was of particular importance for
him during the time of his crises and subsequent exploration of the unconscious in the years
after 1913. She played a pivotal role in the foundation of the Zurich Psychological Club in
1916 and presided over it from 1928 to 1945. Patients coming to see Jung for therapy would
often see her as well. When Erich Neumann came to Zurich in 1933 he underwent therapy
with both. Toni Wolff also became the therapist of Julie Neumann when Erich and Julie visited
Zurich in May and June 1936 (see Neumann's letters to Jung from 30 January 1936 [19 N], and
15 April 1953 [95 N]). Neumann and Toni Wolff wrote to each other on a regular basis from
1934 until her death of a heart attack on 21 March 1953. Neumann wrote a letter of condolence to Jung (see letter from 15 April 1953 [95 N]). Toni Wolff is the author of *Structural Forms
of the Feminine Psyche* (*Strukturformen der weiblichen Psyche*) (1951) and the collection of essays
Studies on the Psychology of C. G. Jung (*Studien zur Psychologie C. G. Jungs*) (1959). On Toni Wolff
see Molton and Sikes (2011).

[146] Gustav Bally (1893–1966): German-born psychiatrist and psychotherapist. Studied medicine in Zurich and Heidelberg from 1913 to 1920 and had psychiatric training at the university
clinic of Zurich with Eugen Bleuler and the Münsingen Sanatorium in Bern from 1921 to 1926.
From 1924 on, he trained at the Berlin Psychoanalytic Institute among others with Hanns Sachs
and Karen Horney. Professor at the commercial college of St. Gall from 1947 to 1956, thereafter
he held the chair for psychotherapy at the University of Zurich. In 1948, he founded—together
with Manfred Bleuler and Medard Boss—the Zurich Institute for Medical Psychotherapy. His
published works include *On the Scope of Freedom* (*Vom Ursprung und den Grenzen der Freiheit*)
(1945) and *Introduction to the Psychoanalysis of Sigmund Freud* (*Einführung in die Psychoanalyse
Sigmund Freuds*) (1961). When Jung was elected president of the General Medical Society for
Psychotherapy (Allgemeine ärztliche Gesellschaft für Psychotherapie) and demanded in his editorial to the society's journal *Zentralblatt für Psychotherapie und ihre Grenzgebiete* (Jung, 1933)
that the differences between the Germanic and Jewish psychology should no longer be blurred,
Bally wrote a harsh critique of Jung's race-psychological arguments and his presidency of the
AÄGP in the *Neue Zürcher Zeitung* of 27 February 1934 (Bally, 1934). Jung responded with a
"Rejoinder to Dr. Bally" ("Zeitgenössisches") on 13/14 March 1934 (Jung, 1934). Despite their
controversy in 1934, Bally and Jung remained in collegial contact and worked together on a

"The State of Psychotherapy Today,"[147] I could not have imagined what a controversy of such fateful personal significance was about to unfold! I know I don't have to tell you what you mean to me, and how hard it is for me to disagree with you, but I feel I simply must take issue with you on a matter that goes far beyond any merely personal concerns. I will refrain from commenting on whether the reverberations that your words are bound to have were indeed what you intended, and I will be silent about whether it is truly a Goethe-inspired perspective[148] to view the emergence of National Socialism in all its human-lashing, bloodthirsty barbarianism as a "mighty presence"[149] in the Germanic unconscious. I will also ignore the fact that I am perplexed that—though you cited in your lecture "the more obscure reference" to the ecstatic "Allah il Allah"[150] wail and that you spoke out against the idea of the "Führer as idol,"—here you are asserting that "a movement that takes hold of an entire nation, already has each and every individual in its grip."[151] As a Jew, I do not feel I have any licence to intervene in a controversy that no German can avoid today when they encounter this Germanic unconscious,

---

regular basis as members of the Commission on Psychotherapy of the Swiss Society of Psychiatry. See introduction, pp. xxii–xxiii.

[147] Jung, "The State of Psychotherapy Today" (1934a). In his text Jung reiterates and elaborates on his race psychological considerations raised in his editorial to the *Zentralblatt* (Jung, 1933), calling it a big psychological mistake of medical psychology to apply Jewish categories to the Christian Germans or Slavs (Jung, 1934a, § 354). See introduction, pp. xxii.

[148] In Johann Wolfgang Goethe's (1749–1832) tragedy *Stella* (1806), Fernando exclaims at the end: "Great God!—you who sends angels to us in our extremities, grant us strength to support their *mighty presence*" (editor's translation) ("Gott im Himmel, der du uns Engel sendest in der Not, schenk uns die Kraft, diese *gewaltigen Erscheinungen* zu ertragen!" [Goethe, 1806, p. 346–47]); The phrase "Goethesche Blick" might also refer to Goethe's holistic view of natural phenomena, which he opposed to the analytical method. In his discussions with Friedrich Schiller (1759–1805) Goethe expressed his high esteem for the *Gestalt* (morphé), which can only be perceived by immediate sensual perception (Goethe and Schiller, 1794–1805).

[149] Jung (1934a), § 354.

[150] The first *Kalima* (testification) of Islam, "La ilaha ill Allah," means "There is no God only Allah." Jung uses the term in his lecture at the ETH on 23 February 1934: "The fanatic 'il Allah' clamour is an ecstatic cry that pulls out the human being from its instinctive animal side" (Sidler, 1933–41); "as the collective consciousness may move to the Right or the Left. With the rise of certain religious movements, when general consciousness soars, the curve will reach Right V. To give an historical example I will mention the wave of ecstasy which swept over the ancient world with the rise of Islam. In our present time there is a appreciable movement of the consciousness towards the Left side, the interest shown in psychology, for instance, illustrates this" (Hannah, 1934–41, vol. 1, p. 73).

[151] Jung (1934a), § 354.

but as it is certainly correct that we Jews are accustomed to recognizing the shadow-side,[152] then I cannot comprehend why a person like you cannot see what is all too cruelly obvious to everyone these days—that it is also in the Germanic psyche (and in the Slavic one) that a mind-numbing cloud[153] of filth, blood and rottenness is brewing.

It may well be that the immemorial history of my people with its long recurrence of prophets, judges, Zaddikim[154] and elders fills me with implausible and completely ungermanic ideas (ungermanic for sure), but, where I come from, great men have always been called upon to exercise discernment and to stand against the crowd—and it is precisely my conviction about the uniqueness of your own nature that causes me now—(not only in my own interest)—to ask you if this easy affirmation, this throwing yourself into the frenzy of Germanic exuberance—is this your true position or do I misunderstand you on this point?

More importantly though, I would wish to disabuse you of the conviction that Jews are as you imagine them to be. I do not know the Jews you have treated, but I know you consider even my friend Gerhard Adler[155] to be exceptionally Jewish. I believe myself to be

---

[152] Jung (1934a), § 353.

[153] Neumann's handwriting could not be deciphered here. The transcription "Qualmsee" is not definite.

[154] Zaddikim, plural of Zaddik (also spelled Tsaddiq or Tsaddik), in the bible (Genesis 6:9) the term is used to describe a man of a particularly just and righteous character; in the tradition of the eighteenth-century Eastern European Chasidism the Zaddik occupies a central role as the mediator between the believer and God. In his 1939/40 seminar on Hasidism, Neumann writes about the Zaddik: "And when you look at the Zaddik, he actually stands beyond the law and all limitations. Everywhere in everything that we will come to hear of the teachings of the Zaddik it can be said that this is the prototype of the doctrine of the individual. He is the only one who is able to be an authentic human being. This is the precursor of that which appears in the process of individuation as finding one's own way to the law" (Neumann 1939–40, p. 79).

[155] Gerhard Adler (1904–1988): Psychotherapist, born in Berlin to German-Jewish parents; in analysis with James Kirsch in Berlin in 1929 and with Jung in Zurich from 1931 to 1934. Adler left Germany with his wife-to-be Hella in 1935 for London (see Jung's letter to Neumann from 22 December 1935 [18 J]). He collaborated with Aniela Jaffé on her German edition of Jung's published letters, edited the English edition, and was a member of the editorial board of Jung's *Collected Works* in English. He was president of the IAAP from 1971 to 1977 and, after the split of the Society of Analytical Psychology (SAP), founder of the Association of Jungian Analysts (AJA). His best-known works are *Studies in Analytical Psychology* (1948) and *The Living Symbol* (1961). Adler was a lifelong friend of Erich Neumann going back to their youth in the 1920s (see Adler, 1980). When Erich and Julie Neumann visited Switzerland for the first time after the war in 1947, Adler introduced Neumann to Olga Fröbe-Kapteyn, who invited Neumann to speak at the Eranos conference. On Neumann and Eranos see introduction, pp. xv–xvi, xxxvii–xli.

completely certain of his agreement when I say to you that, even among our own people, things are not so unfortunate as for either of us to be considered typical representatives.

The rather sad Jewish remnants that have wound their way to you are those that remain, the most diasporic, assimilated and national-ized Jews, individuals and stragglers, but from where, dear Dr. Jung, do you know the Jewish race, the Jewish people? May your error of judgment perhaps be conditioned (in part) by the general ignorance of things Jewish and the secret and medieval abhorrence of them that thus leads to knowing everything about the India of 2000 years ago and nothing about the Hasidism[156] of 150 years ago? Further-more, is there not the remnant of a misunderstanding in a sentence such as: "The Aryan unconscious has a higher potential than the Jew-ish (one)"[157] which allows a primitive race to claim that 'they are the ones who are."[158] The Hasidism movement as well as that of Zion-ism[159] demonstrate the inexhaustible liveliness of the Jewish people, as only a deficient interest can overlook the outrageousness of a phe-nomenon such as, for example, the renaissance of the Hebrew[160] language that was dead for 2,000 years and the settlement in Pales-

---

[156] Chasidism, also Hasidism (from Hebrew *Hasid* "the pious one"), originally a twelfth- and thirteenth-century Jewish religious movement in Germany that combined austerity with over-tones of mysticism. But Neumann refers to the Hasidic pietistic tradition that arose in Eastern Europe in the eighteenth century following the kabbalistic teachings of charismatic leaders such as Rabbi Israel Ba'al Schem Tow (1700–1760), known under the acronym Bescht, and Dow Baer of Mezhirich (1704–1772), also known as the Great Maggid. Hasidism teaches a panentheistic world, according to which God is in everything. Its emphases on the role of the *zaddik*, the spiritual leader of a Jewish congregation, as the god-sent envoy who mediates be-tween God and man, splits the orthodox Jewry into Hasidim and Mitnaggedim ("opponents"). In 1927, Martin Buber (1878–1965) published a collection of Hasidic stories under the title *Die chassidischen Bücher*. This collection formed the textual basis for a seminar on Hasidism, which Neumann held in Tel Aviv from 9 November 1939 to 30 May 1940 titled *Analytische Psychologie und Judentum: Der Chassidismus* (Neumann 1939–40). Between 1934 and 1940 Neumann wrote a two-volume manuscript on the *Ursprungsgeschichte des jüdischen Bewusstseins* (*On the Origins and History of Jewish Consciousness*) (Neumann 1934–40; see n. 273) that has not been pub-lished. On Hasidism see Scholem (1941) and Dan (1999).

[157] Jung (1934a), § 354.

[158] Allusion to Exodus 3:14: "And God said unto Moses, I AM THAT I AM: and he said, Thus shalt thou say unto the children of Israel, I AM hath sent me unto you" (KJB).

[159] Jewish nationalist movement that aimed at the creation and subsequent support of a Jewish national state in Palestine, the ancient homeland of the Jews (Hebrew: *Eretz Yisra'el*, "the Land of Israel"). The political goals of Zionism have been formulated by the Austro-Hungarian journalist Theodor Herzl (1860–1904) in his influential book *The Jewish State* (1896).

[160] Neumann replaces "living" ("lebend") with "Hebrew" ("hebräische") language.

tine that you, albeit tentatively and skeptically, consider to be roman-
tic, while, as a Germanic person, you seem to wish to have a monop-
oly on all romanticism and illusion and value them highly. Of course
I have to laugh at this exaggerated formulation, but there is much
truth in what I am saying. This Jewish renaissance seems to me to be
more embryonic, youthful and full of energy than the Nazi-rigid,
brutally organized and stolid, extreme submissiveness of the Aryan
revivals.[161] Believe me, as a Jew, I quite love the Germanic potential as
far as I am able to see it and get a sense of it, but to equate National
Socialism with the Aryan-Germanic is perhaps ominously incorrect
and I cannot understand how you reach this conclusion and whether
you must reach it. Is Bolshevism also a feature of the Aryan unconscious? Or what does it imply that there, as you told me, all bad instincts have been called upon—which is apparently completely different in Germany.

I believe, even, that in both there are seeds of things to come, but I
believe and know I have learned from you, and had it confirmed by
you, that the most precious secret of every human being—not only
of the Germanic race—is, in essence, the purely creative prescient
depths of one's soul. Far beyond the fact that your Jewish diagnosis
is not right, I simply cannot see that it is possible that the collective
unconscious, in its deeper layers, can have greater or fewer tensions
within it among the different races. It seems to me that, as is the case
for the individual, it is contingent on the consciousness of the race
that changes through history and that, expressly in the case of the
Jewish people, has changed repeatedly and will change again, and
this engenders new developments over and over again. I fear you are
confusing Freud—whom you have classified sociologically as European[162] by the way—with the Jew, and therefore the use of Nazi
terminology—simply to identify Freud's categories as "Jewish categories"[163]—is doubly puzzling coming from your pen, especially

[161] Jung (1934a), § 353.
[162] Jung (1934a), § 352.
[163] Jung (1934a), § 354.

when previously—before the rise of Hitler—Freud's extraverted theory was contrasted with Adler's introverted theory.[164]

I do not wish to change anything in this letter. It will remain as it is written. Hopefully you will appreciate how it is intended. It seems to me that it is precisely my gratitude toward you that obliges me to be candid. I hope there is not too much "Mars"[165] in this, but that there is some "Mars" here, I know, and I stand by it.

Yours,
Erich Neumann

---

[164] In *Psychological Types* (1921), Jung writes: "Freud would like to ensure the undisturbed flow of instinct toward its object; Adler would like to break the baleful spell of the object in order to save the ego from suffocating in its own defensive armor. Freud's view is essentially extraverted, Adler's introverted" (Jung, 1921, § 91).

[165] Roman god of war.

5 N

[no date][166]

Dear Doctor Jung,

I had actually intended not to write to you from here[167] until I had really settled in and had begun to form at least the start of my own perspective. In the meantime I have realized that this is impossible, for my need to write to you grows rapidly while settling in takes longer. In the first part of my time here, although there were a lot of practicalities to sort out, I was more in Zurich than I was in Palestine. That was not such a bad thing, as only in that way could I get to grips with the not insubstantial surprises. I did not, by any means, come here with any illusions, but what I have found extraordinary was that I haven't found a "people" here with whom I fundamentally feel I belong. I might have known that before, of course, but it was not the case, and the fact that the Jews here as a people, as a not-yet-people, seemed so extremely needy was a shock at first. On the other hand, though, the landscape gripped me in such a compelling way that I couldn't ever have thought possible. Precisely from the place I hadn't expected it, a vantage point emerged. I haven't fully made sense of this. Anyhow, as you prophesied, the anima has gone to ground. She made an appearance all nice and brown, strikingly African, even more impenetrable in me, domineering—with a sisterly relationship to many animals—a boa constrictor, a panther, an elephant, a wild horse and a rhinoceros—thus speaks an image.[168] That this gives me strength, however, I feel strongly. Even dreams are confirming it.

---

[166] Tel Aviv, written between 15 June 1934—the publication date of Neumann's rejoinder to Kirsch—and 19 July 1934.

[167] Neumann immigrated to Palestine in May 1934. His first address in Tel Aviv was Sirkin-street 37.

[168] On 11 October 1933, around the time of Neumann's arrival in Zurich, a panther escaped the local zoo and was on the run for ten weeks (see *Neue Zürcher Zeitung*, 17 January 1934). Perhaps the image of the panther in the dream was informed by this incident that caused

The situation here is exceedingly serious, as I see it. The original spiritual, idealistic forces who established the country, the core of the working class and of the land settlements are being repressed by a growing wave of undifferentiated, egotistic, short-sighted, entrepreneurial Jews, flooding here because of the economic opportunities.[169] Thanks to this, everything is escalating more and more, and a growing politicization of the best is obstructing all horizons. But this politicization is inevitable as the situation of the country is devoid of all state authority and gives power to the negative individual like nowhere else does. So everything points to fascism regardless of where it might originate. As a people, the Jews are infinitely more stupid than I expected, while only a concerted effort could overcome the difficult situation of being sandwiched between the Arabs and the English.[170] Please don't misunderstand me—I am not reproaching the Jew. How could it be any different? We come, as individuals, from who knows where and are then supposed to be one people. That all takes time, but I must state it as it is. So, I believe, the situation is rather muddled—but I'm not qualified politically and I haven't been here long—and herein lies my hope. I can well imagine that Palestine will get dangerously close to the abyss and I assume that the Jews, in a paradoxical situation, will then come to their senses—as ever. Everywhere the economy is booming, it's all hard work and speculation. There is little interest in intellectual things except among the workers and almost none in things Jewish. A newly prospering petit bourgeois middle class is evident everywhere, not only in Tel Aviv. All of this is quite natural. We find ourselves in a strongly extraverted phase—how else could Palestine be developed? The Jews are coming to a—terrible—civilization. It cannot be changed. The

---

widespread concern in Zurich at the time. Exotic animals feature also prominently in a number of unpublished poems Neumann had written in the years 1926–30, as well as in some of his drawings (NP).

[169] For Neumann's first impression of Palestine, see introduction, pp. xviii–xx.

[170] The British Empire occupied Palestine—then part of the Ottoman Empire—in 1917, the same year the British foreign secretary Arthur James Balfour (1848–1930) declared in a letter to Baron Walter Rothschild (1868–1937) that "His Majesty's government view with favour the establishment in Palestine of a national home for the Jewish people, and will use their best endeavours to facilitate the achievement of this object" (2 November 1917). On the Balfour declaration, see Schneer (2010). In 1922, the League of Nations granted Britain a mandate for Palestine, which it held until 14 May 1948, the day the state of Israel was proclaimed.

traditionlessness of this struggle that has no core gives everything a rather ghostly demeanor. It is a people of infinite opposites. What orthodoxy does exist here is so immeasurably foreign to me that I'm shaken by it. Alongside this are the unprincipled speculators and then the hordes of people who, by the investment of their substance, have constructed the prettiest villages and landscapes out of deserts and swamps. Overall, there are many individuals who are not yet visible, but who are there and whose time will eventually come, individuals for whom it will be worth it.

It is strange to recognize that my generation will only be an interim generation here—our children will be the first ones to form the basis of a nation. We are Germans, Russians, Poles, Americans etc. What an opportunity it will be when all the cultural wealth that we bring with us is really assimilated into Judaism. I don't share your opinion at all that there will be no Alexandrianism[171] here, but rather, either nothing at all or something completely new, if, as I believe, despite everything, the Jews have retained their incredible ability to assimilate.

The way forward, as I see it, is certainly as hard as it is dangerous. I actually fear that all our repressed instincts, all our desires for power and revenge, all our mindlessness and hidden brutality will be realized here. Indeed, the ongoing development of the Jews failed precisely because, on the one hand, they were united in a collective-religious bond and, on the other, they were under pressure from other nations as individuals. After the emancipation they caught up unnaturally quickly and powerfully with the Western trend toward the individual (secularization, rationalization, extraversion, the break with the continuity of the past), and thereby the shadow was finally "liberated," and here in Palestine it can reveal itself for the first time as, here, there is no external pressure. That will not be pleasant—perhaps we will all be killed, but it's no use—it simply must be out in the open at last and worked through. (I wonder often if I am

[171] German historian Johann Gustav Droysen (1808–1884) used the term *Hellenization* in order to describe the spreading of Greek culture and language in the former Persian Empire during the conquest and reign of Alexander III of Macedon (356–323 BCE), known as Alexander the Great (Droysen, 1833). Jung's usage of the term *Alexandrianism* might refer to this model of cultural insemination where the incoming culture is integrated and assimilated by the hitherto prevailing culture.

projecting all of this, but it does seem to me to be more than mere projection.) In the face of this apparently historic necessity, the chaos here becomes not only bearable to me but I also feel myself to be infinitely closely bound up with it; I emerge out of this to my own "people." I must, though, confess that I am quite often afraid at the same time. I feel myself here to be quite accountable and I still know that my place is here, quite independently from whether the Jews will grant me this place one day or not.

Of course, I have very little to do, although there is still something, but I am not worried as I had reckoned with an extended lead-in time. I am preparing a great deal, am absolutely not unproductive, and now—and this is new—and for this, along with infinitely more, I thank the work with you—it is no longer work "for me"; on the contrary it wants to exist in reality.

This includes a response to an article by Dr. Kirsch[172] in the *Jüdische Rundschau*[173] of which you will be aware. As it appeared in a very abridged version, the strongly critical Zionist aspect was deleted, so I'm sending you a copy. I have now made contact with Dr. Kirsch whom I only knew fleetingly. He gave me your reminder[174] about

[172] James Isaac Kirsch (1901–1989): Psychotherapist of Jewish origin. Studied medicine at the University of Heidelberg; analysis with Toni Sussmann in Berlin from 1922 to 1926 and, from 1929 on, with Jung and Toni Wolff in Zurich; in later years he had also professional training with Liliane Frey-Rohn and C. A. Meier. In 1933 Kirsch immigrated with his wife Eva to Palestine where they settled down in Tel Aviv; in 1935, he, now together with his former patient and second wife-to-be Hilde (née Silber), left Palestine for London, where he continued to practice until 1940, the year they moved to California. Kirsch helped to found the Medical Society of Analytical Psychology in London in 1936 and was pivotal in building up the Jungian community in Los Angeles. Jung and Kirsch were in correspondence until Jung's death in 1961 (Jung and Kirsch, 2011). Kirsch wrote two books: *Shakespeare's Royal Self* (1966) and *The Reluctant Prophet* (1973). On Kirsch see Thomas B. Kirsch (2003; 2011) and Lammers (2011).

[173] James Kirsch, "Die Judenfrage in der Psychotherapie: Einige Bemerkungen zu einem Aufsatz von C. G. Jung" ("The Jewish Question in Psychotherapy: Some Remarks on an Article by C. G. Jung") was published in the *Jüdische Rundschau* on 29 May 1934. Neumann's rejoinder came out on 15 June 1934 (Neumann, 1934). In his letter to Gerhard Adler from 19 June 1934 Jung asks Adler to write to the *Jüdische Rundschau* on his behalf in order to clarify his position in regard to Jewish psychotherapy. Adler's clarification, titled "Ist Jung Antisemit?" ("Is Jung an Anti-Semite?") was published on 3 August 1934 (Adler, 1934). In his letter Jung also states that he had heard about Dr. Neumann's rejoinder but had not been able to read it yet (Jung to Adler, 19 June 1934 [JA]). See introduction pp. xxi–xxvii and appendix I.

[174] Jung to Kirsch, 26 May 1934: "Regarding your suggestion that I write a special piece about this question, this too has already been anticipated, in that I suggested an exchange of letters with Dr. Neumann, who has worked with me and now lives in Palestine, which would deal with all the contentious questions. Up to now, though, I've heard nothing from him"; "When

writing to you—I hope though, dear Dr. Jung, that you will understand that I needed a short break to settle in here. Now I'm ready. Dr. Kirsch is of the opinion that you shared his perception of the 2000-year-old collective neurosis of Judaism.[175] I explore this as well as the essay by Rosenthal[176]—which is equally as interesting and important—in a longer elaboration that I do not wish to send you in my barely legible handwriting.[177] In the course of next week I will send you a typed version. Many questions are raised in it and only the typed piece will be the letter of "substance." I'd like to add something else too. I've set myself the big challenge of getting you to write something fundamental about Judaism. I believe I can only do this by simply speaking to you about what is very important to me.

After all, my efforts around the Rosenthal essay have taken me much further as I can show you here—but these are just notes for you, perhaps they'll develop into more.

---

you see Dr. Neumann, please greet him from me and remind him that I am waiting to hear from him" (Jung and Kirsch, 2011, pp. 45–46, 47). See introduction pp. xxiii–xxiv.

[175] Jung to Kirsch, 26 May 1934: "The Jewish Christ-complex is a very remarkable business. As you know, I completely agree with you in this respect. The existence of this complex predisposes to a somewhat hystericized general mental attitude, which has become especially clear to me in the course of the present anti-Christian agitation against me" (Jung and Kirsch, 2011, p. 46).

[176] Hugo Rosenthal (1887–1980): German-born pedagogue and Zionist, immigrated with his family to Palestine in 1924, but had to return to Germany after five years due to ill health. In autumn 1933 he became director of the Jewish School of Herrlingen, where he followed a liberal pedagogical concept that enabled students to create a positive Jewish identity. He published numerous articles during those years. When the school was closed in 1939, Rosenthal went to Palestine, changing his name to Josef Jashuvi. He founded and established the Ahawah home for children. On his biography, see Rosenthal (2000). Rosenthal contributed also an article to Jung's *Wirklichkeit der Seele* (*Reality of the Soul*) titled "Der Typengegensatz in der jüdischen Religionsgeschichte" ("The Typological Contrast in Jewish History of Religion") (Rosenthal, 1934). As Jung wrote in a letter to Kirsch, the article by a Jewish author on Old Testament psychology was intended to upset the National Socialists and his Jewish critics in the aftermath of the Bally affair (Jung and Kirsch, 2011, p. 47). Neumann wrote a review of this article, which was published in the *Jüdische Rundschau* on 27 July 1934 as "Zur jüdischen Religionsgeschichte" ("On Jewish History of Religion"). Neumann writes: "The application of analytical psychology to theology of which the Rosenthal piece is just a beginning, communicates not only new answers and questions, but it can make a decisive contribution to the re-rooting of the Jew into Judaism by making possible to modern man a personal entry point into the religious and general foundations of Jewish literature" (Neumann, 1934a).

[177] See attachment to the letter 5 N (A).

By the way—something else. Mrs. Kirsch[178] informed me at the end of a detailed conversation about my response, which confirmed my impressions of Dr. Kirsch's essay, that I had gone against the comment of the Jungian analysts by responding in public. I replied that I considered my response to be objectively necessary and important, and that I am not willing to retract factual material out of affiliations unknown to me. It had been unpleasantly gossiped about, apparently, and I hope it is now over with, but I'd like to ask you to tell me if I have behaved incorrectly. I do believe I can communicate with Dr. Kirsch within certain limits, but for me he is anything but authoritative, although, as Mrs. Kirsch informed me, in your opinion, he articulated the best thinking on the Jewish problem years ago, and has been authorized to educate Jungian analysts, and his opinion coincides with yours, for example, on the Yahweh complex, the Christ complex, and on collective neurosis. I very much strive for objectivity; I see much in these issues very differently from Dr. Kirsch, and would like to find out for myself whether your opinion deviates so much from mine. Until now I had formed a very different impression about this. It would not have occurred to me to write to you about this were it not for Mrs. Kirsch's intervention. I have considered myself (and still do) to be very attached to you and your work—does this oblige me to a public conformity with your students? I would be very concerned if that were the case, but I am convinced that it is not so. To the best of my knowledge my response to Kirsch is free of personal issues.

I hope you will be able to make sense of my handwriting; if not, let me know and I will write my letters on a typewriter.

Dear Dr. Jung, it still seems too crass simply to thank you for what I have received from you; I am ambitious enough to say that I hope to be able to give something to you in return too. I don't think it is

[178] Eva Kirsch (1901–1999): Physical trainer and psychotherapist; underwent a Freudian analysis first, followed by a Jungian training—also with Jung himself. She married James Kirsch in 1926. Together with their two children they left Berlin for Tel Aviv (Palestine) in 1933. They were accompanied by James's patient Hilde Silber, who would become his second wife in 1935, and her children. After her separation from James, Eva went back to Berlin and opened a private practice. In 1938, she fled to Wales and settled down as a physical therapist and psychotherapist. See Thomas B. Kirsch (2011, p. xiii) and Jung and Kirsch (2011, pp. 5–6, n. 8).

that I cannot say thank you—that is just not enough. This is connected to the fact that I did not know what to do when you gave me the gift of *The Sermons*.[179]

Forever yours,
E. Neumann

---

[179] *Septem Sermones ad Mortuos* (*Seven Sermons to the Dead*) (Jung, 1916), a text written by Jung but attributed to the semilegendary Gnostic teacher Basilides of Alexandria. The *Septem Sermones* originated from the visions that Jung had in the years from 1913 to 1917 and which would form the contents of *The Red Book*. Jung had the text privately printed in a limited edition in 1916. He gave copies to a selected few of his students and friends. Toward the end of his life Jung agreed that the text should be published as an addendum to *Memories, Dreams, Reflections*. Neumann's copy holds an inscription by Jung: "zur freundlichen Erinnerung. C. G. Jung" ("in fond memory. C. G. Jung") (NP).

5 N (A)[180]

The Rosenthal essay is, without question, exceptionally interesting and important, my remarks, observations and objections seek only to take further the problems under consideration in it. Firstly I wish to go into the Jacob-Esau problem, the Samuel-Saul story, which has occupied me for a long time, I see actually quite differently in a crucial way. It seems to me an addendum is much more necessary than for the Jacob-Esau section. Dear esteemed Doctor, I gladly take this opportunity to write you some of my thoughts on the Jewish problem at the same time as "Applications." Please regard these things as questions, wherever they certainly occur, for this is what they are. Perhaps then something definitive will emerge through your response.

Principally, it seems to me to come down to an application of the whole of your psychology to religious-historical problems, the confinement to typology is not without risk despite its fruitfulness. The Rosenthal essay does not go far enough in some things, this is apparently due to some sort of perhaps moral restriction. Only in this way is it comprehensible why R. does not push forward to obvious consequences. A systematic basic objection concerns the fact that it seems impossible to me to treat the mythical-historical Jacob-story in exactly the same way as the historically individual books of Samuel.

Jacob cannot be analyzed as an individual human being without a psychological understanding of the basic religious concepts that shape the foundation of the events. One misses the point if one does not first understand what "blessing," and what "first-born" mean. One might only speak of "hoodwinking the firstborn" if this were a report about a modern person, which R. almost seems to assume. Here

---

[180] This is the separate content letter Neumann refers to in 5 N. It was probably attached to 5 N and titled "Letter I." Subsequently, Jung and Neumann refer to this manuscript as "Anmerkungen." See introduction, pp. xxix–xxx.

lurks another unanalytical prejudice that knows nothing of early psychology.

I do not mean a defense of Jacob, but one must pursue the inequality of the brothers much further into the deeper layers of the collective unconscious. R. does this only insofar as, in his opinion, the private individual Jacob is in touch with the collective unconscious. Thus, he himself emphasizes the myth as a dream of the people; but if a people dreams and particularly if it dreams such things as these, then this is always a matter of fundamental conflicts with the collective unconscious. For sure, the people—individual correlation is present, and for us, the starting point is the individual, because a "people" barely still exists. On the other hand, one must proceed in reverse in the analysis of texts such as the Bible. The events are a given fact in the collective unconscious and we can press forward from there, perhaps, to the "individual," as far as that existed then. But the average biblical person is still fully unconscious, only a pure exponent of the collective unconscious, and it is precisely the patriarchs, prophets etc. who enter into dialogue with the collective unconscious and in this way they are "heroes" and individuals.

One has to proceed from the basic introversion of Judaism, which, according to the biblical account, was shaped by the patriarchs and prophets who were essentially introverted intuitives with thinking, so belonged to the "moral variety." The decisive turn inward is common to them all, to a world whose center manifested itself to them as Y.H.W.H. in visions and prophecies. This radical bias toward internal demands explains substantial parts of Judaism. The emphasizing of the subject and fear of the object lead first to segregation, chosenness, holiness, to the tendency of not intermingling with the world, of privileging the inner voice and of changing the world according to this. The exponents of this inner tradition from the patriarchs until the Zaddikim must express what Y.H.W.H. has to say on every situation and make sure that He reigns, i.e., by creating institutions so that Y.H.W.H. becomes the center of the inner world as well as the Lord of the reluctant object world, that this latter submits itself and becomes holy.

Now the essential thing is that the inferior function of the introverted intuitive is "an extraverted sensation type of a lower, more primitive variety."[181] Hence, the correlate to the extreme introverted intuition of Judaism is the almost compulsive neurotic seeming exterior of Judaism, the "Law." The negative side of the Jew, an object-addicted, voracious sexuality, an obsession with power, money and acquisitiveness, and a murderous intent constitute the Jewish shadow, which intuitive nations such as, for example, the Germans alone[182] see. This explains, I believe, a part of anti-Semitism with its belief in the Elders of Zion, the ritual murder tale and the devilish image of the Jew. In an ingenious way—after all a symptom always has a teleological propensity—the Law tames the propensity of the inferior function to realize itself and thereby guarantees at the same time the introversion of the libido toward Y.H.W.H. Judaism's hostility toward nature is only a projection of the fear of its own inferior extraversion.

So the Jacob-Esau conflict is, for sure, the mythological struggle of the patriarch as a representative of introversion with the natural inferior inherent extraversion. But this conflict is fundamental for Judaism; I would like to pursue it further as it seems to be one of its essential components.

(From: M. J. bin Gorion, "Jewish Legends and Myths," Volume II, "The Patriarchs," pp. 353ff. to be found in the appendix "Sources.")[183]

II.

"At the very creation of the world, the Lord determined that the sun would be the Kingdom of Esau, and the moon, the Kingdom of Jacob."[184]

---

[181] Jung, 1921, § 663.
[182] Handwritten addendum.
[183] Bin-Gorion, 1919 (subsequent translations from Bin-Gorion by Heather McCartney).
[184] Bin-Gorion, 1919, p. 354.

I.

"It is said that when Jacob and Esau were still in their mother's womb, Jacob spoke to Esau: 'My brother Esau, here are the two of us and two worlds lie before us, a world on this side and a world on the other side. The one world is the world where one eats and drinks, the world of trade and change; but the other side has nothing of all those. If it is your will, you take this side and I will keep the other side for myself.' In this moment, Esau took his portion in this world, but Jacob chose the next."[185]

III.

"Know that Isaac had two faces, one holy and one wicked; the face that was turned inward was holy, but the one turned outward was unholy. From the inner one, Jacob earned his support; but Esau cleaved to the external one; to him in turn do the rulers of the left-hand side of the world cling."[186]

(Note on Esau as ruler of the left-hand side of the world. The right is always—in kabbalah too—the masculine side of grace, blessing, Michael is its angel, the guardian Lord of the Jews. On the left, Gabriel often stands, the highest Lord above all courts of the world, also on the left in kabbalah is the feminine side, the court.

It seems to me that this can be deduced from the introverted intuitive structure of Judaism—at least of the Midrash[187] and the kabbalah. In general, the left is the unconscious, but that is initially the shadow that is experienced as a projection onto the world. It is extraverted: "courts of the world," because at the same time the "court" considers this extraversion as a sin. That this is the feminine side is unquestionably associated with the anima, which is known to play

[185] Bin-Gorion, 1919, p. 353.
[186] Bin-Gorion, 1919, pp. 354–55.
[187] *Midrash*, pl. *Midrashim*, Hebrew for interpretation or exposition, is a homiletic methodology of biblical exegesis; it also refers to a compilation consisting of the Jewish interpretations of the Old Testament. In contrast to the Bible the Midrashim belong to the oral tradition.

a very negative role as Lilith. I think too that the visibility of the shadow that you stress is connected to this. It is exactly the intuitive who sees the world under the projection of his shadow. Likewise Judaism. C./f., hostility to nature and later the moral problem.)

That the Jews have a very particular relationship to the moon does not only originate in the places cited, but even more from the meaning of the new moon festival which in no way corresponds to the last vestiges of sun worship. It transcends by far the fact of the moon calendar, which is certainly symptomatic. The historical relationship of Abraham with the Babylonian moon-worshipping cities of Ur and Haran may also play a part here. Equally, I would like to mention that the first law given to Moses at the exodus from Egypt is the institution of the moon calendar and the instigation of the new moon festival. The Israel-Moon identity seems to find its beginnings here already. Later it is expressed clearly: "As the new moons are renewed and sanctified in this world, so will Israel maintain its regeneration and sanctification in the future."[188] The moon, not the sun is, for the Jews, renewal and rebirth; the ebb and flow of the moon's phases correspond, according to old tradition, to the image of the historical life of the Jews.

I would like to go into the moon problem more comprehensively because only in this way can the Jacob-Esau conflict become visible to its full extent.

The consecration of the new moon plays a decisive role in biblical Judaism; at the new moon and on the Sabbath one went to the prophets (IIK4:23),[189] in Isaiah it says of the messianic time: "From new moon to new moon and from Sabbath to Sabbath all flesh will come to bow down before me" (66:23) and again, from the second century, a saying has been handed down: "Had Israel inherited no other privilege than to greet the presence of their Heavenly Father once a month, it would be sufficient."[190] Characteristically, in the XVII century, through the influence of kabbalah, the day of the new

---

[188] According to the *Pirke de-Rabbi Eliezer* (chapter 51, p. 410) this saying is attributed to Rabbi Gamaliel: "Just as the New Moons are renewed and sanctified in this world, so will Israel be sanctified and renewed in the future world just like the New Moons."

[189] 2 Kings 4:23: "And he said, Wherefore wilt thou go to him to day? it is neither new moon, nor sabbath. And she said, It shall be well" (KJB).

[190] *Babylonian Talmud: Tractate Sanhedrin* (Folio 42a): "In the school of Rabbi Ishmael it was taught: Had Israel inherited no other privilege than to greet the presence of their Heavenly Father once a month, it were sufficient."

moon gained a new significance as a minor "Day of Atonement" and with this we are getting close to its real content.

You will be familiar with the central place of the day of atonement in Jewish life. At its heart is the following ritual: the High Priest had sacrificed one of two rams, on the other one, which had been chosen by lots, he laid the confession of sins of the entire people, where, on one single occasion in the year, while people and priests fall to the floor, the name of Y.H.W.H. is proclaimed aloud and he cries "you shall be clean." Then the goat, the scapegoat, is sent into the desert to Azazel. According to Goldberg, El ha-es means Goat-god.[191] At the new moon consecration also, the sacrifice for sin is a goat. The sanctification declares: You have given your people new moons, a time of atonement for all descendants, as they offered sacrifices to please you and scapegoats to create atonement for themselves, they should be a reminder for all and *a redemption of their soul from the hand of the enemy.*[192]

Here a small digression on the "goat" should be interpolated. The goat is, in contrast to the "'smooth moon," (Jacob see also [unreadable]) also the hairy, radial sun. Among the Germans he is clearly a sun symbol. Esau-goat-hairy-ruddy sun stands in contrast to Jacob-flat-white-moon. This goat-sun means negative extraversion, c./f. the lasciviousness of the goat is its own impurity and—projected—the impurity of the world. This is why the goat later becomes the devil. (I don't know whether all this was familiar to you; it was new to me.)

The further development of the problem can now follow the rite of the new moon celebration. Pleas for the restoration of Zion, of the ministries, etc., are connected to the cited sanctification, and it is stated in the worship for the consecration of the moon: "and he spoke to the moon, that it would be renewed, as a crown of radiance for those blessed from their mother's womb, which shall be renewed in

---

[191] Goldberg, 1925, p. 281.

[192] The musaf recited on Rosh Chodesh (New Moon): "New Moons have You given to Your people, a time of atonement for all their generations; that they should sacrifice before You sacrifices for favor and goats of sin-offering for their atonement. It shall be a remembrance for all, their souls' deliverance from the hand of the enemy."

the same way."[193] (Those blessed from their mothers' wombs refers to Isaiah 46:3 where it is written that Y.H.W.H. carries the Jews from their mother's womb onward.) Then follows, as a new important motif, a request to abolish forever the darkening of the moon and its diminution. "And the light of the moon shall be like the light of the sun."[194]

At the creation, moon and sun were in fact equally large. Some texts on this problem: (Gorion, ibid., Vol. 1, pp. 15–16).

"Sun and moon were both equally large, as it is written: God made two great lights. And they remained equal in greatness until the moon came and complained. It spoke before the Lord: Lord of the world, why did you create your world with Bet, the second letter? (Start of the Torah: Bereshit).[195] Thus spoke the Lord: So that it will be manifest to all my creatures that I placed the letter two at the beginning (Hebrew Beth = 2),[196] in the beginning I placed the letter two because I also created two worlds, and so shall the word of only two witnesses be heard. The moon spoke: but which of the worlds is greater than the other? Is it this one here or the world beyond? The Lord spoke: The other world is greater than this one. The moon said: Behold, you created two worlds, a world beyond and this world. The world beyond is great, this world is small; you created a heaven and an earth; the heaven is greater than the earth; you created the fire and water; water extinguishes fire. Now you created the sun and the moon; must not the one be greater than the other? Thus spoke the Lord: It is evident and clear to me that you think I will make you great and the sun small. But because you wished evil to the sun, you shall become the smaller and your light will be sixty times less than that of the sun. The moon said to the Lord: O Lord of the world! It was just one word that I said and because of this I must be so harshly punished? The Lord said: One day you will be as great as the sun once again and the light of the moon will be like that of the sun."[197]

---

[193] *Babylonian Talmud: Tractate Sanhedrin* (Folio 42a): "The moon He ordered that she should renew herself as a crown of beauty for those whom He sustains from the womb, and who will, like it, be renewed in the future, and magnify their Maker in the name of the glory of His kingdom."

[194] Isaiah 30:26: "Moreover the light of the moon shall be as the light of the sun" (KJB).

[195] Insertion by Neumann.

[196] Insertion by Neumann.

[197] Bin-Gorion, 1913, pp. 15–16.

Unquestionably the moon here is the representative of introversion, the inner world, it knows itself to be a symbol of the other side. Characteristically enough, its claim to power demands that it should become the greater. Thus it is made smaller. The inadequacy of the inner moon world is achieved along with the awesome, greater, more powerful object-sun world. This motif of making the moon smaller contains, however, very much deeper things. A problem arises here which is the problem of the introvert, of the Jew: Is Y.H.W.H. not the center of the inner world? Why does he allow the powerlessness of his—the inner—world? The psychic problem that is concealed in this symbolism leads directly to an indictment against God. (We shall soon see that yet another basic problem is lurking behind this subjectively determined indictment.) In any case the indictment against God is clearly expressed in the following story: (Gorion, Vol. 1, pp. 6–7).

"God seeks two great lights, the sun and the moon. The moon spoke before the Lord: O Lord of the world: Is it proper that two kings have only one crown? The Lord replied: Go forth and become the smaller light. Then spoke the moon before the Lord: Because I have spoken a true word, am I now to become smaller? And the Lord replied: For this, you shall rule by day and by night. But the Lord saw that moon did not become quieter and he regretted doing this thing and he commanded Israel after this and said: You shall bring a sin offering for me because I have made the moon smaller. And this is the new moon goat that was sacrificed when the temple of God still stood there."[198]

Here God's guilt is very clear, it is in order to absolve him that the sacrifice is brought. Before we attempt the interpretation of this problem, we must draw on a third text that seems to stand in contrast to both of the others and in which making the moon smaller is attributed to evil powers, as is common amongst many peoples. (Gorion, ibid., Vol. II, pp. 356–57.)

"In the writings of the Gaonim we read: Seven days before the rising of the moon, the multitude of the meek prepare themselves for battle with Semael and his legions because of the diminution of the moon; but the hairy one got into an argument with the smooth one

---

[198] Bin-Gorion, 1913, pp. 6–7.

out of envy of the beauty of the moon, and Michael and Gabriel made war with the accusers. But at the end of the seventh day, Gabriel weakens her strength and the High Priest Michael takes the Semasael that stands by the side of the hairy one and that looks like a ram and brings it as a type of sacrifice onto the altar that is built at the start of every month for atonement. Then the will of the Most High is appeased, the moon becomes great and full and the power of the ram is consumed by the fire of the Almighty. At the time of the waning of the moon, the ram rejuvenates itself and grows all over again, and this is how it has been until doomsday shall come of which it is said: the light of the moon will be like that of the sun."[199]

Therefore we must take two facts into consideration. The moon is made small by God and by the evil one. But beside this, the smallness of the moon is closely connected with its opacity (both have been simultaneously reversed messianically). What does this mean, which facts of the matter are intended?

Obviously it is a matter here of a double division of the world. On the one hand, of a division into a sun and a moon world, into an inner and outer, for which, from the introverted perspective, the inner world is smaller and weaker. But at the same time, this weakening is due to the repetition of this split world in the interior. The moon is also split, subject to changing opacity, the "evil one" lies in the interior; the inferior function, which is coupled with the external world, lies behind the double nature of the collective unconscious. On the one hand, the opacity of the moon, the fact of the inferior function, is the source of the moral problem. But on the other hand, ultimately the moral problem and its source, i.e., evil itself, seem to be inherent in God's division into an inner and an outer world. This means, in the end, the demand of the moon that does not desire this twoness but rather unity, the supremacy of the inner world, if one disregards its undoubted will to power. As far as there is a will to power, it is the inferior function, opacity, which leads to diminishment, as far as the objection refers to the split, God has done the moon an injustice. (Text 2) In this context belongs something that has already been brought to our attention—that, on the second day

---

[199] Bin-Gorion, 1919, pp. 356–57.

of creation, at the separation of the water above and below the firmament, the exclamation "And he saw that it was good" is absent.

First, we wish to further pursue only the moral side of this problem. The inadequacy of the internal world for the external one is due to the fact that there is an inferior part within it. Only when this disappears does the opacity disappear, the light of the moon becomes like that of the sun, and Self and the world become appropriate sizes. This opacity is removed in Judaism and in Christianity, which succeeds it, by the *sacrifice of the inferior function*, i.e., the sacrifice of the inferior object relationship, which atones, i.e., the outwardly projected libido is reinstated to the inner side, to Y.H.W.H. Thus, by the sacrifice of the goat, the moon becomes "large and full." This moral process is, however, unavoidably eternal, only in the messianic time is the opacity and smallness of the moon redeemed.

The Jacob-Esau problem is situated with this background of the polarity of the collective unconscious with its moon-sun symbolism. The cited points prove that the problem is such that it almost came to the conscious formulation of the world's polarity, the following location proves this: (Gorion, see Vol. II, p. 354).

"On the fifth day God created the great whales, which are Jacob and Esau, and all creatures that live and weave—these are the levels that lie between the two."[200]

After this comprehensive excursion, I think I can still bring another contribution that, it seems to me, illuminates the whole profundity of Jacob's wrestling with an angel.

I am fully aware that I am, in part, saying the same as R. and where my perception differs from that of R. will hopefully have become clear. A basic error seems to me to be that R. apparently considers Jacob to be an extraverted sensation type in whom intuitive introversion thus resides as an inferior function in his unconscious, and that he assumes a fundamental character transformation in Jacob in order to square things. There is absolutely no such transformation of character in the sense of a conversion. If you look more closely, R. is prevented by a remnant from rationalism from seeing things correctly. One must start with the text, otherwise there is nothing to be done

[200] Bin-Gorion, 1919, p. 354.

with such an analysis that must proceed like a dream analysis. According to this text, however, Jacob's consciousness is completely occupied by the internal reality of Y.H.W.H., only in this way does he achieve his role as father of his tribe and his visions.

From his earliest youth, Jacob has full consciousness of being the carrier of God's blessing. This begins with the fact his mother Rebecca—whose superior significance both he and his father Isaac defer to—attributes this function to his attaining the firstborn privilege from Esau, the achievement of the blessing from Isaac. The great vision at his exodus makes that absolutely and undoubtedly unequivocally clear. His inferior extraversion, which lies in his unconscious, finds expression precisely in the place he lives unconsciously, i.e., this means for these early people as far as he lives every day. For sure, through the fight with the angel, something new happens in Jacob, a transformation, but, to my mind, not at all in the way R. means. (In this way, one can also avoid the contradictions that are present for R., as on the one hand the appearance of Esau requires the enlivening of what is living in Esau's unconscious, on the other hand, according to R., Jacob's consciousness is negative, and the positive of the promise of the fathers lives in his unconscious. I think my interpretation simplifies not only the fact, but allows the text's meaning to emerge.)

For clarity's sake, I would like to assemble the text which has been rather abbreviated by R.

1) Before Jacob approaches the Esau problem, angels of God meet him, and Jacob mysteriously names the place: Double encampment, with the justification: This is an encampment of God ([Gen.] 32:2–30), then he sends messengers (= angels) to his brother Esau.

2) The renaming of Jacob as Israel is interpreted: "Fighter of God, for you have struggled with God and man and overcome."[201]

3) Jacob names the place of the struggle Peniel, the face of God, for "I have seen God face to face and my soul was spared." ([Gen.] 32:31 c./f. Hallowing of Moon)

4) Jacob says at the meeting with Esau: For I have now seen your face as one sees the face of God and you have shown me kindness. ([Gen.] 32:10)

[201] Genesis 32:28.

Before and during the struggle, Jacob does not know whom he is fighting with, this can be seen clearly enough from the question about the name of the "he." In contrast comes the naming of the place "Peniel" and the later remark to Esau that shows that the opponent was "God" in Esau's form. What does this paradox mean? Here, too, R. is centrally correct in his holding to the idea that Esau becomes the divine principle, the evil one moreover, but also with this formulation R. does not penetrate to the root of the event.

The apparition, being the inferior part within Jacob and, at the same time, the representative of the "negative" world, is engaged in the battle with Jacob. The same formulation that Jacob speaks at the end of the battle—"and my soul was spared"—occurred, as we saw, in the hallowing of the moon: "brought the scapegoat to atone for . . . to save your soul from the hand of the enemy",—and yet it is a matter here of a fundamental opposition. The collective solves the problem of evil in a moral way, through the sacrifice of the inferior function. In Jacob, something takes place that is evidently diametrically oppositional. The inferior function is compelled to bless Jacob and with this, its structure is changed. In or after the fight, Jacob recognizes that evil, the negative world, is likewise God. Esau, as the face of God, that is the terrible expansion of the issue, the assimilation of the inferior part of one's own structure and thereby also of the structure of the world is thus achieved. Only this realization makes Jacob capable of coming out of the "half world" of introversion, by experiencing the "other side" of the world as divine. With this experience, he has "fought with man and God and overcome." This struggle is a process of individuation, being an assimilation of the shadow and of the adversarial figure from the collective unconscious that is identical to him. In him, humanity—his own inferior function, and "Godhood"—the negative world-side of God, is overcome, which was already implied in the Midrash in the problem of splitting. But Jacob fights as a fighter of God, it is a matter of a face-to-face fight, the God-side of Jacob fights with the God-side of Esau. Both are God. But, while Jacob's realization is the exterior, even the evil one. [. . .]²⁰²

---

²⁰² The end of the letter is missing.

6 N

Dear Doctor Jung,

As I'm sending you the anticipated "Applications and Questions,"[203] I am myself equally surprised at how many typewritten pages it has turned into, and I fear that you will be surprised by this "flood." I know well that this is a certain imposition, but I don't know what else to do. I've been agonizing about what position you will take in response to my remarks, but gradually I've been coming to the conclusion that it would be more sensible for me not to worry on your behalf. I am fully aware that you may not be in a position to respond as comprehensively as my letters seem to "demand," but you will understand that these things matter to me a great deal, and it seems better in this case to "demand" too much rather than too little, as the planned letter exchange has come to nothing anyway and I am only "demanding" for myself. It is up to you, dear Doctor Jung, to respond with as much or as little as your time and work allow, but I have firmly resolved not to let up, so I must warn you against me once again in good time. I have the firm intention not to give you any peace about the Jewish problem and, if necessary, I will earn again the lost tenacity and stubbornness of my race in order to be taken into the depths of these problems by you so that I no longer see them from a blinkered standpoint. I think I must also make a confession, although it is not pleasant to do so. Before I came to you, I was rather sad that I was not able to go to a Jewish authority because I wanted to go to a "teacher" and I found it typified precisely the decline of Judaism that it had no such authoritative personality in its ranks. With you, I became aware of what was prototypical in my situation. According to Jewish tradition, there are Zaddikim of the nations,

---

[203] Attachment 6 N (A).

and that is why the Jews have to go to the Zaddikim of the nations—perhaps that is why they do not have any of their own left. This Jewish situation, the beginning of an exchange, of an understanding *sub specie dei*[204]—this is what makes this "letter exchange" so important to me. Please do not misunderstand me. This is not supposed to be a presumption on my part, I am really no "legitimate" representative of Judaism, although you are absolutely a legitimate representative of the Occidental world; I know therefore how unevenly the weights are distributed. But I am only writing to you about my perceptions and, if I can see the symbolic character behind it, then this should simply point you to my situation and explain to you why I am not afraid to start with Adam when it would be easier to speak only of "now."

Yours,
Erich Neumann
19. VII.

---

[204]"under the sight of God"

6 N (A)[205]

[HANDWRITTEN ADDENDUM:] II TO C. G.

Applications and Questions.

Some problems arise in connection with the Rosenthal essay to which the solution is still not at all clear to me. What does it actually mean when one speaks of a nation's "type" as R. does when he observes absolutely correctly that the Jew—or better, Judaism itself—is introverted?

Actually, in the case of Judaism, we are dealing with an intellectual cultural structure that is "introverted." I am referring here to my note in the "Annotations" about *Y.H.W.H. as an immutable center of devotion* and the law as a means to this end. If one starts with the individuals who informed this structure it is clear that they were introverts and intuitives. Even so, there must have been a certain *national disposition* in this direction, otherwise it would have been impossible for *the whole history of a people* to be seen in terms of turning toward and away from Y.H.W.H., and this, even though deviations from and extraverted violations against the required fundamental attitude not only frequently occurred, but dominated the entire historical picture.

How was it possible that the introverted intuitive created a national consciousness, formed a tradition, shaped a history and so transformed a people, that it repeatedly came back to introversion and thereby to a religiously based ongoing existence? As long as a people lives as a tribe in *participation mystique*[206] one can speak of

---

[205] See introduction, p. xxix–xxx.

[206] Concept developed by the French anthropologist Lucien Lévy-Bruhl (1857–1939) in *Les fonctions mentales dans les societiés inférieures* (1910) in order to describe the subject's relationship to an object where it cannot distinguish itself from the thing. Jung used the term from 1912 onward and defined it as follows: "It denotes a peculiar kind of psychological connection with objects, and consists in the fact that the subject cannot clearly distinguish himself from the object but is bound to it by a direct relationship which amounts to partial identity" (Jung, 1921, § 781).

human types probably as little as one can of "individuals," because it is only the progressive development of the ego that first leads to differentiation and thus to the emergence of types.

All the same, a very remarkable and distinctive kind of human being, the *medicine man*, exists in these primitive communities, who can be traced back to the earliest times and whose most developed stage is represented by the prophet. The chance emergence of the introverted intuitive's ability of seeing into the future elevated the bearer of such a characteristic always and everywhere to an important member of the tribe and for this reason he was probably compelled to differentiate his intuitive function very early on. So it can be assumed that the introverted intuitive was a type that developed relatively early, perhaps even one of the first human type formations ever. This supposition is reinforced by the fact that traditions that support the differentiation of the intuitive aptitude are demonstrable everywhere. But for other reasons, too, a stronger development of the ego is to be expected, especially in the case of this type. The medicine man did not only have a position of relative power but also found himself in a marked isolation within his tribe who surrounded him in fear and awe so that, for good or ill, he was compelled to a certain emergence out of *participation mystique* and toward an extended development in ego-consciousness.

The working out of the crucial differences between the *medicine man and the prophet* requires a greater examination that is not yet possible for me, but all the same I would like to note a few points.

What does the emphatic "imagelessness" in Judaism mean—which is seemingly not inconsistent with the abundance of apparitions, visions and dreams, whose narratives extend from the patriarchs to the prophets? I have come across two facts (?) which perhaps give us some purchase on this. It seems to me that out of your distinguishing between aesthetically and morally introverted intuitives it follows that the former has feeling as an auxiliary function, and the second has thinking. In contrast to the aesth. Int. who, as the artist shows, is directly giving his attention to the symbols of the collective unconscious, it seems to me that the moral Int. is orientated around the actual *energy of the collective unconscious*. To think is always to abstract, and thus for the moral Int., it is not the individual symbol that is the crucial thing, indeed he sees this as an individual aspect only with great effort because he is primarily orientated toward the energetic connection that *goes beyond the individual symbol*. (Your principle of the assimilation of the unconscious makes this very clear; in the foreground stands the energetic component, the capacity for transformation into consciousness; a symbol is never autonomous nor the final authority.)

Now, the "energetic stance" is crucially linked with the *imagelessness of Y.H.W.H.*, by Y.H.W.H., as an elementary energetic principle of the world that is, that breaks through, expresses itself, speaks, appears, comes into operation, but never in an ultimate form, never in a definite form, but only ever for the situation in question, for a consciousness that captures it in turn. Every form, even the one in which Y.H.W.H. appears, is only a husk (shell). Hence, Y.H.W.H.'s fundamental imagelessness. The "unveiling" is always a transformation into the energetic, be it an event, be it an extending of consciousness. This is why the energetic aspect of the moral Int. invariably aims at being "superior in every case." Y.H.W.H. is always fundamentally superior to all concreteness, to all realization, to every state of being. He is always the impossible possibility, therefore he also always requires the paradox, the absolutely improbable, i.e., he requires the knowledge of him as the one who is superior in turn. That a people should emerge out of the One, that an old woman should conceive children, that the son of the future should be slaughtered and despite this, a people should emerge out of him, that an enslaved people is chosen, that salvation comes from the meek, all this is Y.H.W.H. It is the insight of the intuitive that *possibility stands behind all reality*, that all reality is mere possibility made real, that precisely the impossible is always the most real thing, that out of the small, the greatest grows—but all this only if one looks on Y.H.W.H. who breaks through into the world and changes its apparently fixed structure.

Alongside this structural-psychological insight into the imagelessness of Y.H.W.H., who is equally superior to every image, stands a quite conscious fixation on imagelessness because here again the *danger of enantiodromia* threatens. The inferior function in fact threatens the introv. Int. with a strong negative object-imprisonedness, but this leads moreover to the concretization of the symbol and to its being confused with the thing—i.e., to idolatry. This explains the tendency of the Jews to repeatedly succumb to images, "strange Gods" and equally the embittered battle against them. (It is equally evident that this principle of imagelessness as a demarcation of the aesth. Intro. Int. leads to the demise of Jewish art, and that this people has an eminent musical giftedness precisely because music is energetic.)

The *Jewish prophets* and patriarchs, as moral intuitives, distinguish themselves from the medicine man by the quite particular role that *consciousness* plays among them, as is then proved by Jewish development in its entirety. They are in fact not only "the mouth of God," but also, in a certain sense, his "head." I want to leave this here to pursue how crucial a role the stance of consciousness and the work of consciousness have always played in the Bible and in Judaism—this goes as far as the meticulous and painstaking work of Talmudic discussion. The decisive difference between true and false prophecy is the attitude of consciousness, the sharp delineation of the prophet from the magician and sorcerer requires a critical stance toward the influx of the contents of the unconscious, an ability to discern that has its basis in contents that are in control of consciousness, hence the "moral" intuitive, i.e., evaluation, critique, in contrast to the mediumistic self-abandonment of the medicine man. The exceptional role that man plays in being the image of Y.H.W.H. is closely connected to this. Man, whose prototype is the prophet, has great power in relation to Y.H.W.H., Y.H.W.H. is in a certain sense dependent on him. The significance of a prophet as that of a man can be deduced moreover from the degree of his own initiative in relation to Y.H.W.H. This personal initiative is indeed in no way exclusively tied to consciousness, but, in any case, the ego and consciousness with its contents participate centrally in it. The crucial role that consciousness plays in Judaism corresponds moreover with man's initiative in the image of God, who has to draw Y.H.W.H. into the world, but at the same time he influences and regulates this reaching out into the world—at least on the highest prophetic level.

The stance of consciousness is on the one hand energetic, i.e., it goes beyond the symbol, progressing to the superior in turn; on the other hand it is critical, in that it confronts the contents of the unconscious with the contents of consciousness. But one can also call this stance reductive in a very central sense. In a creative form, in the case of the prophet, the concrete world as well as the symbols of the collective unconscious are reduced in relation to Y.H.W.H. This last reduction is admissible there although it leads to a metaphysical "rootlessness" that distinguishes authentic Judaism—but even you will call the individuated man "rootless," for one arguably cannot take root in the immensity of the Self. I will mention later what dangers arise from the quasi-reduced structure of the Jew as soon as his creative relationship with Y.H.W.H. ceases.

Two remarkable phenomena that belong in this context give me cause to reflect. *Judaism*—as it still existed around 150 years ago—excluded the individual and *individuation* from its fundamental attitude with remarkable consistency. I will ignore the fact that the Jews lived partly in a *participation mystique*, this is a matter of a more central fact. Thus, as the prophet principle consists in capturing Y.H.W.H.'s impetus and leading it into the world, the people of Israel is "intended" as a prophet among the nations. But this means that the goal of its development is never a self-sufficiency, a limited development of culture, but constant attendance on Y.H.W.H. From this point of view, existence as a whole becomes "incidental" and "nothing but." The fullness of the world seems normatively lost under the force of the law that is expected to create the constant attendance, the purity and holiness of the people, and a never-failing consciousness of being Y.H.W.H.'s people and of doing "service unto him." Doubtless, such an existential stance must lead to a forcible impoverishment of life, as well as the fact that its central content gets lost and only its rational framework remains in existence. Characteristically the "internalization" of Judaism always starts from the sequence of intellectual history that Rosenthal has correctly located on the introverted side: Prophetism, Essenes,[207] Early Christianity, Midrash, Kabbalah, Hasidism.

The actual and original meaning of Judaism and also of its doctrine of the law is the requirement of the encounter with Y.H.W.H. But extraordinarily and characteristically enough—in line with the structure of Judaism—it seems to me this *actual encounter is only*

---

[207] Essenes, a Jewish sect from the time of the Second Temple. Accounts exist of Philo, Pliny the Elder, and Josephus telling of their particularly ascetic way of living. Some scholars link the Dead Sea Scroll community of Qumran with the Essenes.

possible for the introvert, in its religious essence perhaps only for the introverted intuitive, for only he is in a position to experience everything external, everything of the law, as pointing to Y.H.W.H. who has pitched his seat in the center of the internal.

(Now I am very sorry that I have not inquired whether I can give a lecture on Hasidism in the Club, as I wanted to do before Zurich. I felt too new and strange there. In Hasidism, the last breakthrough of actual introverted Judaism, all these problems broadly came of age. The redemption of the "sparks" out of matter, for example, is, put psychologically, arguably the taking back of the world into internal space. In this way, everything, every action, every fulfillment of the law can lead to "higher union," to the encounter with Y.H.W.H., and so the structure of the world can be experienced as one that is at the same time "unified" and that is full of Y.H.W.H.)

When I said before that Judaism, in my opinion, hinders individuation, this does not perhaps apply fully to the introv. Int. By the way, I do not mean here this type exactly, but the introvert with strong intuition in general, the combinations can of course vary. The problem of individuation seems to me here again infinitely difficult. Is the path via the inferior function only a contemporary one? For example, the prophets, even Jesus, are arguably typologically psychologically developed in a one-sided way. Despite this, it is indisputable that their center is the Self and not the ego, which, indeed, is what characterizes the central point of individuation.

The first obvious hypothesis is that the *prophet* has simply subordinated his ego to the collective unconscious and its center, Y.H.W.H. This does not conform to facts, for it is a matter not only of a constantly new conscious confrontation with Y.H.W.H., as the changing theophany[208] of the Old Testament demonstrates, but also of a specific direction that is constantly adhered to. Y.H.W.H. is constantly changing his manifestation, but at the same time he is always the same, but this absolutely assumes a tradition of the contents of consciousness out of which Y.H.W.H.'s manifestations are assimilated. The ego of the prophet never plays a primary role, but it is always the crucial place of the shift. Before I return to the problem of *individuation*, which is ob-

---

[208] *Theophany*, from Greek *theophaneia*, meaning the appearance of God; the term describes the manifestation of a deity in sensible form.

scure to me in this context, I would like to bring in another question that it is important to resolve first. Although I consider the patriarchs and the prophets to be the first "individuals," i.e., the first Jewish people not to live in *participation mystique*, a peculiar connection exists between them and the people. The prophets clearly have a compensatory role in relation to the people. They always represent the introverted side, i.e., the people's unconscious—in contrast to the extraverted life of the people—every life of a people *is* extraverted, especially in the case of primitive peoples. So still today, the *individual*, even inasmuch as he individuates, stands in the closest relationship, namely, in a *compensatory relationship to the community*. At the same time then, individuation is characterized by the emergence out of the collective unconscious and on the other hand derives its legitimacy in a certain sense from conformity with the collective unconscious. (In the sense in which you explained the Tao[209] to me.) This is identical with the fact that the Self is both the most private thing and the most general, so that its place is as indefinable as that of Y.H.W.H. It is absolutely still not clear to me whether individuation as a development toward the Self is constructed on the typological idiosyncrasy of the individual (ascendant = Self), or whether it is not right here that the typological and its idiosyncrasies become absolutely irrelevant. The processing of the life "proffered" by the collective unconscious is at best autonomous. But what does this mean?—Without question, the critical stance of consciousness is crucial here, but it seems to me, if I am not mistaken, that a *clarification of the term "collective"* is necessary. Firstly, collective stands in contrast to individual, in which collective is almost identical to "conventional" as far as it refers to collective opinions, feelings, ideas, affects, etc., but on the other hand it seems to me that in this case the binary vision of the collective unconscious that also belongs to the concept of the collective is not taken into account. The overcoming of the collective for the purpose of individuation extends in both directions of the collective (persona-anima), but at a certain point the confrontation is no longer unambiguous. The more the center of the personality moves in the direction from the ego toward the Self, the more "unindividual" does the personality become in a

---

[209] For Jung and Taoism, see n. 297.

certain sense, and the more a center appears in the place of the ego that stands in close connection with the collective. Indeed, the *Self* is in a certain sense a *center in the collective*, it seemed to me anyway that one could infer from this that, for it, conformity with the entities that stand behind all things, events and people arises as Tao. It does not fully satisfy me that prophetic foreknowledge can be explained by its "reference to the archetypes that portray the regular course of all tangible things,"[210] as in that case the "here and now" of the situation is not taken into consideration and yet it is precisely this that constitutes the crucial prophetic task. Perhaps the dominance of an archetype can be substantiated *in the most general way* over a course of time (Platonic year), but the respective *prophetic situational task* seems to me as little resolvable by the act of an archetype as a moral problem can be resolved by the application of the categorical imperative. Precisely the casuistry of prophecy aims at a psychological dynamic in which the prophet's center makes some sort of contact with the center of the course of the event (once again c./f., Tao). This center is, in its general formulation, Y.H.W.H. I must confess the fact that the prophet and the individuated person have a compensatory function in relation to the people or the respective community makes it all the more probable to me that the general center of the happening and the Self stand in the closest connection. (Here belongs the Jewish notion that the existence of the world is guaranteed by the thirty-six righteous men.)

Dear Dr. Jung, perhaps you are annoyed by the apparently speculative character of my deliberations. But as this is about the generic terms of psychology, I believe one must allow oneself to be seduced into investigations that appear speculative, even at the risk of being misunderstood.

The substantial difference between the prophets and the individuated man appears to me a historical one, namely, it is inferable from the progressive dissolution of primitive *participation mystique* and from the emergence of the individual in human history. This historical difference has occupied me greatly as far as it relates to the Jewish problem, and perhaps I can make some headway by means of this

---

[210] Jung, 1921, § 660.

personal participation. (I am absolutely aware of a basic error or at least of a basic limitation that is becoming evident in these notes. I have no—or only very little—understanding of the individuation of the extravert. In Goethe I see something similar, but still do not know what could correspond to Paul's "Christ in me" experience in his case. The introversion of age certainly bridges this. For the extravert, is the crucial thing perhaps the circling of the ego around the Self as something objective?)

The significance of the last 150 years for Judaism is something that most people, especially non-Jews, make false assumptions about for obvious reasons. One must not forget that the Christian peoples have never deemed the Jews worthy of their conscious interest, but that the Jews are not only an interesting phenomenon but also that one can only reach a correct assessment of the individual if one includes their historical situation. By the way, I am also absolutely of the opinion that it is the task of the Jews to engage the interest of other peoples if they value their interest. It is indeed the case that as far as the Jew and Judaism are concerned, the entire Occidental world is still completely unconscious that is declared by the fact that it is still a "Christian" Occident. It looks as if the decline of Christianity will also have its correlation in, among other things, the awareness of the Jewish problem.

Up to 150 years ago one could still speak of the Jews as one people. There existed an absolutely dominant religious-collective bond and a *participation mystique* strengthened by consciousness and history. The particular structure of Judaism had led, alongside the belief in being a chosen race, to an exceptionally negative world aspect. The awareness of living in exile was absolutely not only a historical fact, and did not only gather its evidence from the fully realized historical prophecy of Y.H.W.H. laid down in the Pentateuch, but was based in the same way on the fundamental introverted basis. Being with Y.H.W.H., being chosen, and being *in bona fide* are identical, just as being without Y.H.W.H. was identical with God-forsaken abandonment to the world. Within *Judaism*, an unimaginable *inner tension* gradually developed that I would like to voice some conjectures about. The structure of Judaism as "introverted" unfailingly compelled all opposing types into its framework with terrible violence.

The tension of opposites of "extravert-introvert" that Rosenthal mentions grew particularly great because an extraverted Judaism (the sequence of priests up until rabbinism) also inevitably emerged and became official, but due to the structure of Judaism itself it could never achieve authentic fulfillment because the extravert needs "world," but Judaism stands against the world in favor of Y.H.W.H.

The *repression of the opposing types* by means of the concept of purity and sin was further strengthened by the historical development that cast the Jews ever "inward" and thus that also led to an amalgamated introversion, as it were, i.e., to extraverts with undeveloped, inferior, disregarded and sinful extraversion that asserted itself negatively. The amalgamation was further strengthened by the inferior extraversion of the introverted Jews. The shadow-Jew, the "godless" Jew, clearly shows the characteristics of the authentic Jew with negative omens. Above all stands the great *drift from the Self to the ego*, indeed perhaps from an unconscious conformity with the Self via the consciousness of chosenness to the inflation of the ego that developed with this awareness. The introvert's fear of the object in authentic formulation as a trend: Y.H.W.H., the inner one, must conquer the world, indeed for this purpose he chooses the people, becomes exaggerated adaptation to the object, cowardice, servility, and hypocritical characterlessness. This emphasis on the subject, an authentic task of chosenness: Y.H.W.H. is in us, in our midst—becomes will to power, conceit, and arrogance. The critical stance of consciousness, authentic as Y.H.W.H.'s head, as a conscious critic of him, becomes a reductive stance, intellectualism, skepticism, and nihilism. The energetic aspect with its authentic metaphysical rootlessness leads to revolution for revolution's sake, to the bypassing of concreteness, to groundlessness, to the inflated dreamer.

Without question, all these shadow-sides of the Jew had always been activated from time to time during his historical existence, but the general religious commitment prevented, at least in part, the negative extraversion. But the hate of the nations will not only come from their intuitive recognition of the shadow-Jew, but, without question, also from the fact that they came to sense this shadow. I believe that one cannot deny this, even when one knows how the nations have always compelled the Jews to their shadow-extraversion.

The inner tension in Judaism was exceptionally strengthened by the fact that the development of the Occidental world advanced ever further toward cultural secularization and individualization,[211] whereas the Jews continued to exist as an original people in *participation mystique* with magical customs and with all the positives and negatives of a primitive metaphysical time. Religious collectivism existed as the basis of the people, while on the other hand, the Jews' lasting decisive and significant emphasis on consciousness developed further. A religious people at the time of the enlightenment, living among it. As an inner Jewish problem: fully developed rationality of the clearest definition and alignment with religious-collective life that, while rationally conceived of, it had not lost its original religious character as a folk religion.

With the advent of emancipation, it seems a very improbable result is reached, the *decline of Judaism*. The magnificent and violent introversion of a people ceases across all typological dispositions. Y.H.W.H. speaks no more, and Balaam's sentence: "Lo, the people shall dwell alone and shall not be reckoned among the nations" begins to be untrue (Numbers 22–24 is, by the way, of particular psychological and metaphysical importance). The collective bond disintegrates and, in a magnificent effort, the Jews attempt to catch up with the Occident's development toward the individual in two generations. This process, the conquest and assimilation of the Occidental world in all areas, led to an extraversion of such great magnitude that all libido was withdrawn from the inner world. This leads to complete "forgetting," to de-semitization, to the disintegration into traditionlessness, to exceedingly isolated individuals without foundations, without historical, cultural, and psychic or spiritual continuity. This is the Jew you know, the Jew of today, of this historical situation. The emancipation from the religious-collective foundation with its complete unconsciousness had then to and must now lead via rationalism, materialism, and all the relevant childhood diseases of the opposing situation. This is necessary, cannot be avoided, and

[211] Neumann uses the term *Individualisierung*, which is translated here and in the following as *individualization*. The term *individuation* in German has the English counterpart: *individuation*. In his letter 15 J he makes a clear distinction between the two terms.

awkward for the individual concerned. This Jewish development was, of course, also accelerated by the fact that at the same time the West was going through a corresponding phase on another level—positivism, science, technology that reinforced not insubstantially the illusory feeling of "brotherliness" between Jews and non-Jews.

The *counter-development* that mobilized in a compensatory way, now faces a situation that has never existed before. The direction leads, of course, back to the "foundation," this means, misconceiving in a concrete way, a crazily extraverted Zionism with "territory," while the "good" sees territory and foundation in unison—a return to Judaism before the return to the Jewish homeland (Herzl)—and demands a self-realization of Judaism. But this self-reflection will no longer be required of a people, but of the individual, this is the result of emancipation. In the cauldron of today's Judaism much is brewing. All types are represented here, from the unconscious member of a tribe to the isolated rationalist to the types for which the return to the foundation signifies a substantial life's mission. One of the substantial opportunities that the Judaism of the future has is the exceptional influx of energy that will flow to it out of the free development of individuals. The liberation from the oppressive compulsion of the old Judaism into which, without exception, the types were straitjacketed may lead temporarily to a grotesquely distorted image, to a not unperilous witches' coven in which every Jew leads his "own life" without direction and without continuity, but the gain will be the later abundance of individuations that has only now become possible. (I well know that there was individuation earlier, but actual individuation seems to me to be interwoven with a developed ego as only the emancipation has made possible for the Jews.)

The difficulty of the Jewish problematic lies in no small part in the fact that the *self-realization of Judaism* has hardly yet begun, an individual's consciousness is only of dubious competence. Everyone who speaks about this problematic must start from his own great isolation and cannot speak on any one's account, except one's own.

Palestine represents on the one hand a part of the return of Judaism, but on the other hand its construction still necessarily falls under the sign of the world-conquering extraversion of the previous century. Hence the great contradictions. The atmosphere of freedom that arises here through the missing internal pressure of the law and the missing external pressure of exile can easily lead to chaos with its release of the shadow. But even in this possible chaos it is precisely individuals who will have to keep their cool and to develop. Through the assimilation of the shadow and individuation, a regeneration of Judaism can take place that the world badly needs, after all. I believe that the experience of the Self as a middle point of individuation—as far as I intuit anything at all of these events—could be the living reconnection to Y.H.W.H. as he lives in the religious experience of the Jewish people. Only through this authentic personal encounter do I see a regeneration of the people, if there is such a thing. But it seems to me once again that it is precisely in this connection that the compensatory function of the individuated individual has become evident, and so the apparently unbridgeable contradiction between individuation and Y.H.W.H. as center of the collective unconscious has been removed. (Here I would like to emphasize that—as the energetic point of view already intimates—for me, Y.H.W.H. is not an archetype, but the "God" archetype is only an interchangeable theophany of Y.H.W.H. about which there is nothing more to be said, other than how he appears and what form his "so-called energetic structure" takes, being superior to the appearance itself.)

As far as it is possible to me, I would like to go one more time into the whole group of problems that the Jewish psychology of the individual offers today. Thus, the Christ problem belongs to the problem of Jewish individuation, as I believe its resolution has only become possible through the individual development of the Jew on the one hand, and the development of the people as far as Hasidism, on the other. A great deal of problems, like the question of the "dynamite in the Jewish cellar," the alleged collective neurosis of Judaism (Kirsch), of the Y.H.W.H complex and others could be discussed here. As a basic motto, the conflict of the Jews seems to me to be characterized by the fact that his individual development is split off from the collective development of the people. This discontinuity seems to me to yield a substantial disposition toward neurosis. In any case, I believe that the disproportionately great number of mental illnesses among

Jews does not seem to indicate that there is no tension reigning in the unconscious. Moreover, the basic tension seems to me to be located crucially not *in* the unconscious but between the conscious and the unconscious. But it is precisely this normative tension that again constitutes the relationship of the individual consciousness to Y.H.W.H.

Küsnacht, Zurich,
Seestrasse 228
12th August 1934

Dr. E. Neumann

Dear Doctor,

First and foremost please forgive the fact that I have made you wait such a long time for my reply. At the end of the summer semester I was so exhausted that I had to take a break from all work for a while. Then followed a pressing task—that of formulating two lectures on "The Archetypes of the Collective Unconscious."[212] Then I had to read your comprehensive manuscripts![213] No small matter!

Above all, be reassured that there is no secret society of Jungian disciples—the Word has been freely given to all. I thank you particularly for your intelligent and proper elucidation of Kirsch's article. You have acted completely correctly. I do not believe that the Jews suffered from a collective neurosis until their emancipation. However, whether the emancipation itself did not have a neurotic effect seems questionable to me, and the matter requires some serious consideration. The social cohesiveness of the entire Jewish people was a parallel phenomenon to that of the spiritual and political situation of the Christian Middle Ages. With the emancipation of Christians from the authority of the Catholic church, unconscious archetypes

---

[212] At the second Eranos conference from 20 August to 1 September 1934 Jung gave a paper on the "Archetypes of the Collective Unconscious" (Jung, 1935). It was custom that every speaker would deliver a morning and an afternoon lecture.

[213] Neumann sent Jung the extended version of his rejoinder to Kirsch (see his letter to Jung, 5 N)—the abridged version had been published in the *Jüdische Rundschau* (Neumann, 1934)—the manuscript "Anmerkungen" (5 N [A]), a text based on his review of Rosenthal's article (Rosenthal, 1934) for the *Jüdische Rundschau* (Neumann, 1934a), and the manuscript "Anwendungen und Fragen" (6 N [A]).

were activated in the Christian unconscious that we are still process-ing—it is a type of digestive process that still continues and that has given rise to so-called neopagan developments[214] in Germany that have obvious roots in the distant past and that are concessions to the power of pagan archetypes. I believe, therefore, that the emancipated Jew is equally threatened by an activation of the collective uncon-scious. For sure, one archetype is linked to the soil, and from this emerges the psychic necessity of Zionism; another archetype, having a compensatory relationship with rationalism, is connected with re-ligious archetypes, hence the renewal of Hasidism in its more liberal cosmopolitan form, pretty much represented by Martin Buber.[215] In-

[214] Jung refers to those spiritual and religious movements in Nazi-Germany that tried to re-place Christianity with a new pagan belief system. The most prominent of these groups was the German Faith Movement (Deutsche Glaubensbewegung), which was founded and led by the German indologist Jakob Wilhelm Hauer (1881–1962), who held a seminar on Kundalini yoga at the Psychological Club Zurich from 3 to 8 October 1932. Jung commented on Hauer's lectures in the following four weeks of the same year (Jung, 1932). Hauer and Jung were on good terms with each other despite Hauer's engagement with the Nazis (see the forthcoming publication of the correspondence between Jung and Hauer, edited by Giovanni Sorge as part of the Philemon series). The aim of the German Faith Movement was to establish a specific Germanic faith firmly rooted in the Germanic and Nordic traditions, a religious rebirth from the inherited base of the Germanic race. In his article "Wotan," Jung comments on the German Faith Movement and praises it for being in accordance with the psychological developments in Nazi Germany (Jung, 1936, § 397). On the neo-pagan movements in Nazi Germany, see Poewe (2006).

[215] Martin Buber (1878–1965): Vienna-born Jewish philosopher, essayist, translator, and edi-tor; raised by his grandparents in Lemberg (Lvov). His grandfather Solomon produced the first modern editions of rabbinic Midrash literature and introduced Buber to the Hasidic tradition. This would trigger a lifelong interest in Hasidism and the pursuit to record the Hasidic leg-ends (*The Tales of Rabbi Nachman*, 1906; *The Legend of Baal-Shem*, 1907; *Tales of the Hasidim*, 1949). Neumann's seminar on Hasidism (Neumann, 1939–40) is based on Buber's collection *Die chassidischen Bücher* (1928). In addition to philosophy and history Buber studied psychol-ogy and clinical psychiatry among others with Wilhelm Wundt in Leizpig, Emanuel Mendel in Berlin, and Eugen Bleuler in Zurich. From early on Buber was involved in the Zionist movement. His concept of Zionism was based on cultural renewal and brought him at odds with Herzl territorial Zionism, which led to a breakaway of Buber's Democratic Faction at the Fifth Zionist Congress in 1901. Buber's philosophy of dialogue found its expression in his main philosophical work, *I and Thou* (Buber, 1923) (*Ich und Du*). Together with Franz Rosen-zweig he translated the Tanach, the Hebrew bible, into modern German (Buber and Rosen-zweig, 1991). When the Nazis came to power in 1933, Buber stepped down as professor for social science at the University of Frankfurt. He left Germany for Palestine in 1938. He died in Jerusalem in 1965. His relations to the Zurich school and analytical psychology are manifold: invited by psychiatrist Hans Trüb, Buber lectured at the Psychological Club Zurich in 1920 on "The Psychologizing of the World" (Buber, 1967). In 1934 Buber spoke at the second Eranos conference on "Sinnbildliche und sakramentale Existenz des Judentums" (Buber, 1934). In 1952 Buber launched an attack on Jung in the journal *Merkur* titled "Religion and Modern

sofar as these activated archetypes are not consciously assimilated, a neurotic condition can easily arise. In the Christian West, neurotic unrest is evident. In this sense I would also assume that the Jew has a modern collective neurosis, albeit in a different form from that of the so-called Christian—(not to use the term Aryan).

I know that the Jewish problem is, for you, a matter of the utmost seriousness—just as, for me, our spiritual condition and the psychic life of the individual's soul is the most important thing. You can therefore be sure that I will give my attention to this problematic issue using all available means, as it is for me of the utmost value to discuss the complex intricacies of modern culture and its psychic situation with a Jew who is expressly familiar with the European context and who is coming at this issue from a slightly different perspective, while residing on his own archetypal soil.

I can well imagine that it is challenging for you to adapt to Jewish Palestine with all its many complexities. I too have my own impressions of Tel Aviv and of the country itself.[216] I was extremely interested

Thinking" (republished in *Eclipse of God*) (Buber, 1952). Referring to *Septem Sermones ad Mortuos* (Jung, 1916) Buber labeled Jung a Gnostic and criticized him for overstepping the boundaries of psychology into the metaphysical realm. Jung defends his position in a letter to the editor of the *Merkur* stating that his conclusions are based on empirical facts such as clinical and mythological material, and he asks Buber to read "an analysis of mythological material, such as the excellent work of Dr. Erich Neumann, his neighbor in Tel Aviv: Apuleius's *Amor and Psyche*" (Jung, 1952, § 1510). Neumann had been in contact with Buber in 1935 when he sent the unpublished manuscript of his Kafka interpretation to Buber, who replied in a letter of 13 November 1935 praising Neumann's text for its clear and precise method (Buber and Neumann, 1935). In 1955 Neumann was asked by the editor of the *Merkur* to publish an article on the occasion of Jung's eightieth birthday. In his text Neumann puts in a critical remark on Buber and is consequently asked by the editors to remove or change it in order not to put salt in open wounds (Merkur to Neumann, 20 May 1955, DLA). Neumann replied: "I am aware of the controversy in the Merkur, and the remark is my short contribution to it, and I fully intended your readers to consider it a reference to Buber. Should a 'wound' still exist, I would be delighted to act as a soothing ointment for Jung" (Neumann and Merkur, 23 May 1956, DLA) At the end Neumann agreed to change the Buber reference for the offer to publish an open letter on the Buber-Jung debate in the journal. On Buber and psychology, see Agassi (1999); on Jung and Buber see Stephens (2001).

[216] In 1933, Jung traveled with his friend Hans Eduard Fierz through the Aegean Sea and visited Palestine on this occasion. Their steamboat, the *General von Steuben*, went past Catania on 17 March. They arrived in Haifa on 25 March and traveled the following day by train to Jerusalem, where they took residence in the King David Hotel. On 26 March Jung and Fierz visited the Church of the Nativity in Bethlehem as well as the Dome of the Rock and St. Anne's Church in Jerusalem. They made a trip to the Dead Sea where Jung was especially impressed by the tectonic formation of the rift valley. On 27 March Jung did not attend the visit to the Church of the Holy Sepulchre, as he had sprained his ankle. In general, he seemed rather

to hear about your dreams and of the transformations of the anima.
A psychic blood transfusion!

Now to your "Annotations"![217] Rosenthal remains, indeed, on the
surface of the problem, since everything outside of the area of typology is unknown to him. You should develop what you say in your
"Annotations" into an essay in its own right.[218] Your elaborations are
new to me and *very* interesting. It is in fact unfortunate to treat a
mythical figure such as Jacob in a personal way.[219] It can only be done
"as if." In reality, it seems to me, Jacob is the *quintessence* of the Jew
and therefore a symbolic attempt at a collective individuation, or
rather at individuation on a collective level. (Like, for example, historically, Hitler represents the same for the Germans, or mythically,
we have Jesus, Mithras, Attis, Osiris, etc.) So you are quite right in
conceiving of the problem completely from the side of the collective
unconscious and in understanding Jacob entirely as a symbolic exponent of folk psychology. This way of thinking takes you furthest.

---

disappointed by the manifestations of the Christian confessions in Palestine, which, according
to his opinion, could not match the Islamic devotion. Jung was deeply impressed by the Dome
of the Rock. The very same day the group traveled by car to Jaffa, where they embarked on a ship
for Port Said, which they reached on 28 March. The following day the *General von Steuben* was
already in Athens, from where it headed toward the Black Sea (information from Andreas Jung,
JFA). See also Jung's letter to Neumann from 19 December 1938 (28 J).

[217] See 5 N (A).

[218] Inspired by Jung's suggestion Neumann started to elaborate on his "Anmerkungen" and
wrote a text on the Jacob-Esau myth. The text was finished by the end of the year (see Neumann's letter to Jung, 10 December 1934 [10 N]). After some hesitation Neumann sent the
manuscript to Jung in spring 1935 (see letters from 9 February 1935 [12 N] and [14 N]).

[219] "The notion that Jacob is born simultaneously with the daimon (i.e., Esau; ML) with
whom he must then wrestle in decisive phases of his life suggests the assumption that this
daimon is a part of his own self. It is the *evil* (as the Midrash says) that exists before the good.
But not evil as a general principle, but as Jacob's individual wickedness" (Rosenthal, 1934, p.
390). Jung refers to the myth of Jacob in a footnote to *Transformations and Symbols of the Libido*
as an exapmple of the hero myth and the overcoming of the regressive aspect of the unconscious: "Jacob wrestled with the angel during the night at the ford of Jabbok, after he had
crossed the water with all that he possessed. (Night journey on the sea, battle with the night
snake, combat at the ford like Hiawatha.) In this combat, Jacob dislocated his thigh. (Motive of
the twisting out of the arm. Castration on account of the overpowering of the mother.)" (Jung,
1916, p. 322, n. 61; *CW*, supplementary volume B, p. 337, n. 61) The footnote has been omitted
in *Symbols of Transformations*, though there is a reference in the text: "The struggle has its parallel in Jacob's wrestling with the angel at the ford Jabbok. The onslaught of instinct then becomes an experience of divinity, provided that man does not succumb to it and follow it
blindly, but defends his humanity against the animal nature of the divine power" (Jung, 1952a,
§ 524).

Figure 4. Jung with Hans Fierz in front of the Dome of the Rock, 26 March 1933 (photo courtesy of Andreas Jung; JFA).

The whole bearing of the historical Jew is undoubtedly intro-verted, intuitive, with an opposite tension toward the extraverted, sensing shadow. Unlike for other peoples, this tension is *conscious*. This is where the Jew has his "dynamite," not "in the basement." As you rightly say, *the tension is located between conscious and unconscious*. The Jews strike one to a high degree as a people who are *led*, i.e., ed-ucated and formed by mana personalities[220] who, in turn, are intro-verted and intuitive to a high degree. These are always prime exam-ples of the vital necessities of tribal life that seem to require introversion and intuition. This requirement prevails in the place where repression threatens. The geographical situation must have

---

[220] Jung elaborates on the concept of the mana personality in chapter 8 of "The Relations between the Ego and the Unconscious" (1928): "I therefore call such a personality simply the mana personality. It corresponds to a dominant of the collective unconscious, to an archetype that has taken shape in the human psyche through untold ages of just that kind of experience. Primitive man does not analyze and does not work out why another is superior to him. If an-other is cleverer and stronger than he, then he has mana, he is possessed of a stronger power" (Jung, 1928, § 388).

something to do with this: Palestine—located between the two large population centers of the Nile valley and Mesopotamia—who threaten annihilation from every side (i.e., with terrors of war and extermination). Intuition is vital, especially where the food supply is precarious. Palestine—between the sea and the desert—is no rich land. Primitive tribes in this setting nearly always show a strong dependence on intelligent leaders who provide protection and food— through foreknowledge. The leader of leaders is the true dream, the vision, on a higher level, God. The Jew, spurred on by historic adversities, has retained and defended this original order. And where things are going alarmingly well for him, he antagonizes those surrounding him with aggravations that unfortunately have not befallen him, so as to maintain the order of things. To this immeasurably old primitive structure belongs the early "imagelessness" of God that is not a philosophical abstraction, but rather, to my mind, a primitive relic. I discovered a tribe at Mount Elgon[221] who worshipped God in the moment of the sun's rising and in the new moon, but who did not identify with the sun or the moon.[222] For them, God has no form. The night-god Ayík[223] equally has no form. He is *like* the wind, but is not the wind. At the same time, the "imagelessness" is exceedingly important for the free exercising of intuition that would be prejudiced by a fixed image, and thereby rendered unusable. It is, however, vitally necessary—because of the precarious situation— which is also, for its part, equally necessary, to preserve the original attitude (introverted—intuitive), for through this, thanks to its *inter-*

[221] On his second journey to Africa from October 1925 to April 1926, Jung visited, together with Helton Godwin "Peter" Baynes (1882–1943) and George Beckwith (1896–1931)—they were joined in Nairobi by Ruth Bailey—Mount Elgon (14,177 feet), which lies at today's border of Kenya with Uganda. They stayed for a while with the local tribe of the Elgonyis, in order for Jung to study the "primitive" psychology. See Jung (1961, pp. 253–70) and Bailey (1969–70).

[222] The sun worship of the Elgonyi is also described in *Memories, Dreams, Reflections* (Jung, 1961, p. 267) "The old man said that this was the true religion of all peoples, that [. . .] all tribes [. . .] worshiped *adhísta* that is, the sun at the moment of rising. Only then was sun *mungu*, God. The first delicate golden crescent oft he new moon in the purple oft he western sky was also God. But only at that time, otherwise not."

[223] *Memories, Dreams, Reflections* (Jung, 1961, p. 267): "Besides *adhísta* the Elgonyi—we were further informed—also venerate *ayík*, the spirit who dwells in the earth and is *sheitan* (devil). He is the creator of fear, a cold wind who lies in wait for the nocturnal traveler. The old man whistled a kind of Loki motif to convey vividly how the *ayík* creeps through the tall, mysterious grass of the bush."

nal reference point, a powerful counterbalance to global dangers is guaranteed.

The non-Jews as "world population" cannot fall into an "external" because they are already in it. They inhabit the centers of mass population in the fertile regions. Their number and their possession of the land are a counterweight to the "internal danger." Through his mere existence, the Jew draws attention to these inconveniences. So he falls into the shadow realm of the mass populations. These latter need no self-defense (except in emergencies) and little intuition; rather, they need more sensation and aesthetic feeling (to be able to take advantage of a secure life). In this way, they fall into the shadow of the Jews and can be sure of his secret contempt, for they live in immoral peace with all that the Jew illicitly desires. This ancient tranquility has been sensitively upset by Jewish Christianity that, as far as the fateful development of consciousness is concerned, was plainly necessary. Only with the liberalization—i.e., with the decline of Christianity—as a consequence of the enlightenment, did the Jew receive the reciprocal gift of the Danaans:[224] the emancipation, and with it the enjoyment of the world that goes against tradition and is alienating from God, and that is always the fruit of a secure life.

To banish the dangerous "internal world" the non-Jew employs "images" of a dogmatic nature because otherwise his sensation function would be dissipated in the diversity of objects.

The Jacob-Esau motif appears to me to be Persian. In Ahura Mazda, there were originally present in undivided form Ahura Mazda—the good word or the good disposition, and Ahriman—the evil one.[225]

---

[224] Virgil, *Aeneid* (II, 48–49): "Equo ne credite, Teucri! Quidquid id est, timeo Danaos et dona ferentes."—"Do not trust the horse, Trojans! Whatever it is, I fear the Danaans [Greeks], even when bringing gifts." The priest Laocoön's warning not to accept the wooden horse offered by the Greeks is ignored by the Trojans. When they roll the horse, in which the Greeks are hiding, into Troy, it leads to the fall and destruction of the city. Laocoön and his two sons are slain by giant twin serpents sent by Minerva (Athena).

[225] Ahura Mazda (Ohrmazd in Pahlavi, Ormazd in Persian), "The Wise Lord," Indo-Iranian god; with the emergence of Zarathustra's teachings Ahura Mazda becomes the one God who created the world of perfect order ("Mazdaism"). But the world is also the battleground between the Good Thought ("Vohu Manah") and the Evil ("Angra Mainyu" or "Ahriman"), where the righteous has to choose the side of the Good. The main passage on good and evil in the *Avesta* reads as follows: "Thus in the beginning, the two mental aspects, which are twins, / Mutually disclosed themselves in their thoughts, words and deeds, / The one as the better (of the two) and the other (as) the evil / The wise and intelligent did choose correctly but the

God, in his appearance, becomes antinomy for he is unfathomable, only expressible through antinomy, i.e., to be all encompassing, the expression must be canceled out by its opposite.

The problem of the inferiority of the moon internal world as opposed to the sun external world seems to me to be really human. The complaint of the introvert who is inescapably wedded to his principle but who remains unable to captivate the entire world although he would dearly like to. The solar day is, despite all light, only half day, the other half is sometimes moonless, cloud-covered, dreadful night, and where, then, is the splendor and power of the sun? The complaint of the extravert: why can one not always be happy and active? Why isn't everything good and fine as it should be?

All in the external is sun world and the power of the sun is, without doubt, great. The internal is invisible and *seems* always to be impotent. In reality though, it reigns secretly and pervasively and its power is as great as the sun's. The moon is only the "external" representation of the internal world. The power struggle between internal and external is a projection of anthropomorphic uncertainty.

Your material is very fine and interesting. It would be worth developing the symbolic contributions further.

The Jacob-Esau problem is a clash of opposites as part of an initiation process that concludes with the resolution of the opposites. As in the manifestation of God, the opposites are necessarily revealed, and thus the alienation of men from God accomplishes his breaking down into opposites. This conflict is practically overcome by *one-sidedness*, i.e., man departs from the state of paradise into the world full of suffering opposites and seeks there to create, through the sacrifice of his one half (Esau), a *singular* unity. This *singular* unity is the divine prerogative of absoluteness. Man, by producing, or by believing he reveals, a unity, creates a type of *God-equivalent* and thereby induces inflation by becoming a "little God of the world." In this

---

ignorant and unwise did not" (Yasna 30, 3). Jung gives an introduction to Zoroastrian belief at the beginning of his seminar on Nietzsche's Zarathustra on 2 May 1934 (Jung, 1934–39, pp. 4–14; see also n. 269). There he argues along the same lines as in the letter to Neumann: "Those two spirits, Vohu Manō and Angrō Mainyush, were together in the original Ahura Mazda, showing that in the beginning there was no separation of good and evil. But after a while they began to quarrel with each other, and a fight ensued, and then the creation of the world became necessary" (Jung, 1934–39, p. 7).

state, he encounters his own "other" (Jacob versus Esau) and so recommences the formerly vanquished conflict all over again. The "other" reinstates the divinity of God in contrast to human inflation and thereby establishes the "initiation," i.e., the path of redemption, until the final revocation of the separateness of man from God. I do not mean by this that the Jacob legend has ever been a part of an initiation ritual, but that, it seems to me, it belongs much more to the "redemptive images" that existed before all initiation rites as word and numina of divinity. It could well be part of the old tribal doctrines that extend back far into Neolithic times[226] and thus into a time of remarkable spiritual pregnancy and tension that dissolved only with the invention of the written word.

I am sending this letter via Dr. Kirsch because, firstly, I don't have your address to hand and secondly, because I am not sure if it is indeed really called SIRKIUS street.

What is the meaning of "Galut"[227] psychology? A puzzle.

Warm wishes from your always loyal,
C. G. Jung

---

[226] Neolithic age or New Stone era, term coined by John Lubbock in his influential book *Pre-Historic Times*: "The later or polished Stone age; a period characterized by beautiful weapons and instruments made of flint and other kinds of stone, in which, however, we find no trace of the knowledge of any metal, excepting gold, which seems to have been sometimes used for ornaments. This we may call the 'Neolithic' period" (Lubbock, 1856, pp. 2–3). This stage of mankind's development was characterized through the sometimes so-called Neolithic revolution, the switch from hunting and gathering to agriculture and settlement. First forms of settlements can be traced back to 11550 BCE in the Levantine region, whereas for most of Europe the New Stone age is usually dated from 5500 BCE to 2200 BCE.

[227] See n. 31.

[undated]²²⁸

Dear Dr. Jung,

Our "letter exchange" is starting to oppress me a little as I can see it is making perhaps excessive demands on you. I cannot change the fact that my letters develop into such long excursions and thus demand so much of your time. My excuse is that months always elapse between the letters, and you know how important the contents are to me. Even if all sorts of "attacks" arise in the "typed" letter—I don't like to bother you with my barely legible handwriting—I know very well, of course, that it is impossible for you to meet my "demands," as you certainly have plenty of other things to do. All the same, I had to get this off my chest and I believe myself to have been free from resentment. It is a different matter with the things²²⁹ that have a purely personal relevance to you, and I am quite sure I have remained objective and am of the opinion that, in such a debate as this, even quite personal matters can hardly be avoided.

Over and over again I wonder if I am demanding too much of your time, and in a certain sense this is thoroughly my intention (not *too* much, all the same), but our agreement was, after all, to "prepare" you in this way for a thoroughgoing elaboration of the Jewish question, so that gives me a certain objective license.

There isn't much news from my private domain. The practice is still only very modest, I'm too inactive, but I am determined to do it in my own way. I'm working quite well, the letters to you take up a certain space too, for much is becoming clear to me in them. I am gradually getting to know people here, but I am still very isolated. For

---

²²⁸ Letter was written before 17 November 1934, the date of Toni Wolff's reply to a letter from Erich Neumann. See n. 230.

²²⁹ This letter exists in a handwritten and a typescript version. Whereas the handwritten letter reads here "Dingen" ("things"), the typescript version gives "Briefen" ("letters").

all that, I have the feeling that I'm making progress and I think I'm gradually and slowly becoming active, also in the external world. My impatience and dissatisfaction with myself give me a hard time, but I know I'm tackling things quite well.

Will your lectures on the archetypes appear soon or could you make them available to me somehow? It is incredibly important to me to keep 'up to date', and I'd be very grateful to you if you could make that possible for me.

I wrote to Miss Wolff—I would be very interested in comments from her about my letters—I hope you won't have anything against this—and would only suggest it on this basis, and only if Miss Wolff has the time and inclination.[230] But since there is no adequate forum for discussion here, I would naturally appreciate any critique very much.

Please don't heap too much anger on my guilty head.

Your grateful,
E. Neumann
Tel Aviv,
37 Sirkin St.

---

[230] Toni Wolff replied to Neumann's letter on 17 November 1934: "What you write interests me very much. But your suggestion that I should read what you are writing to Dr. Jung is unfortunately not practical. It would only work if you write to him on a typewriter and send me a carbon copy—that would also be quite pleasant as your handwriting is not easily legible and it is quite a job to decipher it" (Wolff and Neumann, 1934–52).

8 N (A)[231]

[HANDWRITTEN ADDENDUM:] III

Dear Doctor,

Thank you very much for your letter that has provided so many stimuli and questions regarding the problem I am grappling with that only a certain distance permits me to make an as yet provisional summary and response.

I will pursue your suggestion of elaborating on the "Symbolic Contributions" to the Jacob-Esau problem, perhaps with a general introduction. The great difficulty is the rather depressing impossibility of a publication—but first of all it should be finished.

I don't know whether you are aware that the questions in the second letter of the "Applications" that seem very important to me despite their abstractness were not quite done justice in your reply. I want to try to take them up again in connection with some points from your letter.

I have long been convinced of the *neuroticizing effect of the emancipation*, on the other hand, what is not quite clear to me is what you write of the consequent activation of the archetypes. I have just expressed something perhaps analogous in an article for the *Jüdische Rundschau* ("On the Psychological Situation of Judaism. Assimilation and Zionism"[232]), the publication of which I am admittedly not convinced about. However, I was applying this *archetypal danger* not to the emancipation, but precisely to its compensatory movement, *Zionism*. Here, it seems to me there is a danger of a neo-orthodoxy, a communist collectivism and of revisionist nationalism. Therefore it seems to me that by means of the neuroticizing individualization and rationalization of the assimilation a compensatory counteraction was set in motion in the form of a regenerating Zionism. (Activation of the

---

[231] See introduction, p. xxix–xxx.
[232] Neumann, 1934b.

archetypal symbols: Return—returning home to oneself—rebirth.)
The danger exists that one will undo the individualization process
that I regard as the historically necessary action of the emancipation
and will lurch into this regeneration movement, head over heels,
without any personal processing of it. In this way, Zionism is being
neuroticized. That's roughly how it goes. Does this accord with what
you mean? The only difference is probably, by way of abbreviation,
that you say: rationalism, activation of the unc: danger! I say: rationalism, activation of the unc, regeneration, mindless falling into the
irrational: Danger! Or are we saying the same thing?

It interested me very much that you are making a link between the
intuitive orientation of the Jews and the geographical and historical
situation of Palestine. If one pursues this way of thinking does one
not arrive at historical materialism?[233] If you are explaining the intuitive national structure in such a sociological way—noticeably precisely in the case of the Jews—out of which arises a large number of
fundamental traits as I hinted at to you, then this is the first step toward a *sociology of psychic phenomena*. By the way, this interests me
very much because, as paradoxical as it may sound, I see much in the
materialistic conception of history that corresponds with the in-
sights of your psychology from an extraverted perspective. But I do
not yet wish to take a position in relation to this problem area.

(Some observations: Historical materialism also proceeds from the
collective and its assimilation via consciousness, but from the external perspective. It has always amazed me that you have never seen the
phenomenon of Russia from the side of becoming conscious. Not
only from the modernization of layers that had remained medieval,

---

[233] *Historical Materialism*, Marxist historical and social theory, part of dialectical materialism
(see n. 261): "The new facts rendered necessary a new investigation of all past history. Then it
became evident that *all* past history [with the exceptions of its primitive stages] was the history
of class struggles, and that these mutually conflicting classes are always the products of the
modes of production and exchange, in a word, of the *economic* relations of their epoch; that,
therefore, the economic structure of society furnishes the real foundation, from which, in the
last instance, the entire superstructure of legal and juridical institutions as well as of the religious, philosophical, and other ideas of a given historical period, are to be explained. [Hegel
had freed history from metaphysics, he made it dialectical; but his conception of history was
essentially idealistic.] But now, idealism was driven from its last refuge, from the conception of
history; a materialistic conception of history was propounded, and the way found of explaining the consciousness of man from his being, instead of, as heretofore, explaining his being
from consciousness" (Engels, 1877–78, p. 24).

but from the conscious handling and formation of economic social factors that functioned or did not function in an unconscious way up until then. The impacting of social relationships by collective factors is very evident. Even social life can be unconscious as contemporary economic forms clearly show. Even here there are obsessions, autonomous processes, etc. I know absolutely that materialism is blind because it only sees the external side; I am also not a Marxist. But it interests me very much that confinement to the external aspect seems to get such similar and corresponding results as it does to the inner aspect [dialectic of events, becoming conscious, etc.]. The introverted aspect: "creation" of the collective milieu by the coll.unc. is matched by the extraverted aspect: creation of the coll.unc by the milieu. If one sees the "person" in this way, i.e., if one extends the milieu theory to the coll.unc, it seems to become right. For sure, then the emphasis is again on the ego-Self that assimilates the milieu. But in the arena of the unc., historical materialism resonates just as astrology does.)

It does not seem dubious to me that there is a connection between sociological and psychological structure, but it does seem questionable to me that you prefer to jump to the *external perspective precisely in the case of the Jew* while it is after all a question of the psychic structure in its peculiarity. Sociological disfavor is also certainly not a sufficient motive. In that case, as your *remark* portrays it, poverty and the religious internal aspect would be identical to each other, prosperity, numerousness, and land would preclude it. (I.e., Marxist "religion is the opium of the people,"[234] compensation for the negative external word. If this were the case, one would have to agree with the Marxists that it would be better to change the world.) If you are speaking of "taking pleasure in the world in a way that is alienated from God"

---

[234] Karl Marx (1818–1883) writes in the *Introduction to a Contribution to the Critique of Hegel's Philosophy of Right* (1844): "The wretchedness of religion is at once an expression of and a protest against real wretchedness. Religion is the sigh of the oppressed creature, the heart of a heartless world, and the soul of soulless conditions. It is the opium of the people" (Marx, 1844, p. 131). Marx, thereby, refers to Heinrich Heine, who wrote in 1840: "Hail to a religion that poured sweet, soporific drops into suffering mankind's bitter cup, spiritual opium, a few drops of love, hope, and faith!" (Heine, 1840, p. 95; German: p. 364). The popular version of religion as opium "for the people" ("für's Volk")—here quoted by Neumann—is from Lenin's "Socialism and Religion" (1905): "Religion is opium for the people. Religion is a sort of spiritual booze, in which the slaves of capital drown their human image, their demand for a life more or less worthy of man" (Lenin, 1905, pp. 83–84).

that is "always the fruit of life security" then it belongs in the self-same context.

Are you not identifying here a type of Christianity seen by Goethe and Nietzsche with a Judaism that in reality is completely different? The Old Testament is an incredibly "liberal-minded" book, definitely not written by demeaned and insulted men. The fact that it repeatedly has as its central point the inner aspect, the efficacy of Y.H.W.H., is no revenge for defeats. The emphasis lies on the efficacy of Y.H.W.H. in world history, in world events in general. This is not to be understood in the primitive sense in which the good always win through, it was never intended in this way, but in the way that the structure of the world and of man centrally aims at "meaning." If the destiny of the individual is recognized as meaningful through individuation, then this is the same thing in microcosm. Even here the issue is that there is no dualism for the processing, but that every negative and meaningless thing is made meaningful through its incorporation into the life context that has become meaningful. In this way, "evil" is only a "servant of God." The negative external aspect is precisely being dependent on the world. The real openness to the world seems to me to be only achieved when the inner aspect becomes visible behind the scenes of the world. "Possessing the world" in the sense of prosperity, numerousness, and land does not seem to me to be openness to the world but it is something absolutely indifferent, like happiness, wealth in an individual fate, unassimilated raw material.

Your sentence in your letter to me that, for you, it is about the *soul of the individual* and, for me, about *Judaism*, affected me very deeply. Not that I had misunderstood it, and not that it was surprising for me. On the contrary, I had also always seen it in this way, but all of a sudden it has exposed me to a great inner revolution. It is the case, and it is also not the case. Precisely the reality of the Jews, which I experience here and definitely not in a negative way, makes it clear to me that for me it is about the Jews, but then again actually not about them. I do not sense a type of national connection such that I could say it is about the people, this chosen people, and not about the individual soul. Despite this, I sense that there is something fundamentally correct about this contrast that you postulate. It also is not enough to say, as I first thought, that your stated rootedness in nation and the cultural circle is so self-evident that you can lay it aside, mine is, like the entire Jewish existence, not prescribed but surrendered, therefore more perceptible and more persistent in consciousness. That is not enough.

For me a not unexciting piece of reading came into it. There is an essay in a small volume from the Schocken Press "The House of Israel" from the writings of *David Koigen:*[235] *The Semitic and the Aryan Method of Religious Formation*[236] (a horrible title by the way). Here, a dichotomy is constructed in which I once again absolutely find you to be, in very crucial things, a representative of the "Aryan spirit," a fact that was self-evident to me in a certain sense, whereas I stand in no way so clearly on the opposite Semitic side but again, ominously or unominously, in between the two.

"Glorification of the face of the earth," "supreme reality" as the goal of Semitism—Liberation and redemption from reality: goal of the Aryans.

Semitic passion in the actual transformation—metaphysical interpretation, symbol, myth of the Aryans.

Coming into being of man, tribe, people, state, of humanity, of the universe. Creation in time, unifying goal: God. God's dependency on the actualization of man: Semitic.

From becoming to being, notion of two worlds, from the All to nihilism. Soul, not hoodwinked by human history, comprises the world, deification. Visible world, simply a superstructure on the wide fundament of unconscious soul being: Aryan.

Extensive-intensive, God-Soul, etc. etc.

In brief, an abundance of opposites (I will send you the book),[237] I must now hold my own between these two pincers. This antithesis is seductive, and without question the "Aryan side" in part pivotally corresponds with your basic concepts and even the "Semitic" in some

---

[235] David Koigen (1877–1933): Jewish philosopher and sociologist; born in Starokostiantyniv (Russia, today Ukraine). Koigen fled from Bolshevik terror to Berlin in 1921. He published the journal *Ethos* from 1925 to 1927. One of his most influential theories was the concept of the "Kulturakt" according to which culture or civilization is a form of social act. His late works touched on Hasidic thinking.

[236] Koigen (1934), pp. 37–59.

[237] There is copy of *Das Haus Israel* (1934), an anthology of Koigen's work, in Jung's library in Küsnacht.

things with the direction of my objections. Despite this it is not correct, it seems to me.

Learning from the pair of opposites set up by Koigen, I could say that my "reproaches" of your not understanding, even of your not being interested in the Bible as well as your probably intentional ignoring of the questions I posed in "Applications" could be based on the fact that you do not see the other Semitic side of the world, i.e., that you remain with your Aryan archetypes. But if this is perhaps even true in some things, even so a plethora of statements by you contradict this. If I may say so, I certainly have the impression that you privately hold this Aryan basic conception,—but this does not mean in the merely personal domain—but that your modus operandi, the responsibility and historicity of your existence belongs to the other, to the so-called Semitic side of which you have full knowledge. Amazingly, I also find this in the part of your sentence: "our spiritual situation." By saying that for you the crucial thing is "our spiritual situation *and* the life of the soul of the individual" it seems to me precisely this mutuality is assumed.

Much from the seminars belongs here also: Tao = Path = Time; the role of growing consciousness as God's becoming conscious (from a speculative hour with you), this would probably belong to the Semitic side.

Before I go on with this "probably," I would just like to say that this contrast seems to shed light on some "contradictions" that I could not quite get to grips with. E.g., I well recall having once pitted the development of consciousness against your cultural pessimism, thus making myself seem rather ridiculous, something that you knew better than I did. But overall, purely intuitively, the Platonic year with its eternal return seemed to me to be sometimes stalking behind all the emphasized development of consciousness. But on the other hand, the spiral is a symbol of development that you consider to be fundamental.

The alternative: *Development of the individual's soul* toward the Self, toward the point of immortality as the saving reality in the chaos of the world seems to me now no longer to contradict the *realization of God in the historical life of the world*, recognized psychologically e.g., in the symptom of the development of consciousness.

Not only that the "chaos of the world" must emerge out of the individual's worm's eye view, out of the inadequacy of human life toward the realization of God in time. The acceptance of life for which the term *amor fati* is only partly suitable since it assumes a higher level of activity of the Self, transforms the chaos into meaning, chance into destiny, and precisely this process shifts the center of the personality toward the Self. The Jews as a people discovered this exact same process in history that you discovered for the individual, which they have experienced as a destiny of the people, and as their purpose. Just as in the case of the individual, this is identical with the shift of the center toward the Self, the destiny is experienced as formed by the Self or as Self-realization, just as for the *Jews as a people*, whose center has shifted out of their consciousness toward Y.H.W.H., destiny is experienced as formed by Y.H.W.H. and as a realization of Y.H.W.H. This has always been the case and remains so today, I do not know of this of any other people of the earth, this is where the *chosenness* seems to me to be located.

Some questions belong in this context that I touched on in my second letter ("Applications," pp. 6 and 7) and that I would now like to pose again from a rather different angle. Individuation is, on the one hand, an emergence out of the coll.unc., on the other hand the individuated person stands in a productive, perhaps compensatory relationship to the collective, to humanity; in a certain sense he knows himself to be an exponent of this coll.unc., "plays his role," is in "Tao," he *does the necessary thing for now*. (This extends from the prophet right up to the coincidences of the typologies as experienced by you that developed independently of each other.) The shift of the center of the personality from the ego to the Self corresponds *at the same time to a depersonalization*, and the center of the personality coincides with and approximates itself at least to the center that seems to direct what takes place collectively. The *individual experiences* this in his destiny, the Jews in history. Thus, we arrive at my question ("Applications," p. 7): Is not the *Self* therefore, in a certain sense, a *center in or behind the collective*? For it is a ruling authority there, behind things, events and processes of history. In any case, individuation, the being in Tao, do seem to give rise to an agreement with the background of what takes place. Does this not also give rise to the identification of the Self with the center of what takes place as your principle of coincidence expresses it? It seems to me necessary here to clarify the concept of the collective.

Imagelessness is also in my opinion not identical with any old ancient tribal tradition, is certainly also not a "philosophical abstraction," this is thus due to my inadequate expressive abilities. The tribe at Elgon[238] did not make spiritual world history and that is not a matter of chance. Imagelessness established itself among the Jews, as you know, only later and under terrible resistances. The diverse theophanies of God are definitely not imageless in the usual sense, but they have a decisive feature that in all cases something is being "expressed," *consciousness* always experiences something fundamental about the God-Man-World structure, on the other hand it is a current experience of destiny and later of history. The ever new and different theophany, the "I am that I am" (a rather popularizing interpretation of the Ehejeh asher ehejeh revelation, Exodus 3)[239] leads to formlessness, to a superiority over every theophany. Y.H.W.H.'s imagelessness is not a primitive legacy, or in any case, the continuity between such a very conjectured tradition and the inner development in Judaism that tended toward imagelessness is so close that they can hardly be further differentiated. In any case, the composition of the texts takes as its starting point the later imagelessness, already accomplished. In this way I would like to make my comments ("Applications." pp. 2–3) more intelligible. When you are speaking of the paradox and nonformulatability of the Self, then this corresponds exactly to the principle of imagelessness.

One makes a great *mistake* if you consider the *Jews* to be a "*tribe*," as you are doing secretly or not so secretly, quite in contrast to the Indians or the Chinese. For the Jews, there is no abstract philosophy because they have concretized their philosophy in the recording of history in writing, in the interpretation of life as a happening between God, man, and the world. This synchrony of life and interpretation as a basic experience has however become conscious in the Bible for it knows itself to be an expression of this experience. This recognition of the God-Man-World structure is deducible from biblical

[238] See 7 J, nn. 221 and 223.
[239] Exodus 3:14. See also n. 158.

events (not from the law, ritual, etc.). A host of conscious formulations, which can be augmented from the Jewish literature, proves this immanent philosophy, this expression of experiences as adequate to our consciousness if not superior to it, as is the case in the "wisdom of the East." I believe one must free oneself here from Christian prejudices, which in a ridiculous way, see the *Old Testament as a precursor of the New*. It seems to me sometimes that even you have not fully freed yourself from the belief in progress on this point: from primitive tribe to developed Christendom, as the Church teaches. This is simply laziness. E.g., the children's nightmare of Y.H.W.H. as a God of vengeance and many other remnants of protestant theology and biblical criticism still haunt the Club.[240] One could almost say that although the prophet Elijah has appeared to you,[241] you deliberately ignore the monstrous "material" of the Bible, of the theophanies, of the prophets and their history.

It is quite certain that the existence of the Jews is a paradoxical fact and I know how difficult it is to make things capable of rationality here when they are so little visible. The fact of the Jewish people with its historical experience of the Self and the rudiments of a collective individuation that seem to be very far-reaching when one regards the efficacy of Judaism, not the Jews; that is something so mysteriously auspicious for of the future that, as history teaches, even the other

[240] Psychological Club Zurich, founded in 1916.

[241] Elijah is a prophet of the Old Testament (I Kings 17). Neumann refers here to Jung's vision of 21 December 1913, which Jung described in *The Red Book* as follows: "On the night when I considered the essence of God, I became aware of an image: I lay in the dark depth. An old man stood before me. He looked like one of the old prophets. [...] We step outside and the old man says to me, 'Do you know where you are?' I: 'I am a stranger here and everything seems strange to me, anxious as in a dream. Who are you?' E: 'I am Elijah and this is my daughter Salome'" (Jung, 2009, p. 245). Elijah accompanies Jung through his imaginative journey of the *Liber Novus*. Through the course of Jung's visions the character of Philemon emerges from Elijah. Jung also narrated his encounter with Elijah and Salome to the audience of the 1925 seminar: "I could see two people, an old man with a white beard and a young girl who was very beautiful. I assumed them to be real and listened to what they were saying. The old man said he was Elijah and I was quite shocked, but she was even more upsetting because she was Salome" (Jung, 1925, p. 68). Also in *Memories, Dreams, Reflections*: "Near the steep slope of a rock I caught sight of two figures, an old man with a white beard and a beautiful young girl. I summoned up my courage and approached them as though they were real people, and listened attentively to what they told me. The old man explained that he was Elijah, and that gave me a shock. But the girl staggered me even more, for she called herself Salome!" (Jung, 1961, p. 181). On Jung's understanding of Elijah and Salome, see appendix B "Commentaries" of Jung (2009).

peoples cannot free themselves from the hope placed on this people. It was precisely the collective goal that precluded, I believe, the individuation of the individual in a far-reaching way ("Applications," pp. 4–5), at least individuation in the sense of an *entelechial*[242] unfolding, not in the sense of a shift in willingness toward the suprapersonal as far as the identification with it (I and the father are one). This question about the character of individuation ("Applications," p. 6) is closely linked with this.

I am aware that this situation of Judaism is terribly dangerous as the temptation exists of slipping into the unconscious and that the individuation of the individual is the now unavoidable requirement of future achievements as far as the metaphysical task is concerned. The exceedingly difficult question about the psychological significance of the Galut must be at least broached here. A substantial characteristic of the Galut seems to me to be the fundamental and existential "provisionality." Its correlate is a growing messianism that only gripped the entire people in the Galut. But with the absence of all soil, landscape, and historical-cultural attachments, this means a reorientation of the entire people toward what is yet to come, and a radical repudiation and disregard of all that is. (The nonsettling of the Jews was originally intentional even if it was later prevented or hindered by the environment. Without doubt, this reinforced the Jews' love of money as a transportable possession. Both are linked with the radicalism of the messianic hopes, the concreteness of which it is difficult to form a correct picture.) This detachedness of the Jews absolutely relocated their psychological structure in the direction of an emphasis on the impersonal (a subvariety is the spiritual-intellectual abstractness). But this impersonalness was experienced in connection with the collective as an actual subject of history; this is the decisive continuity of the Jewish being. The individual lived a provisional existence within a provisional existence of the whole, hence also the ancestral solidarity and the quasi-substitution by the son (subvariety of the Jewish family life). But this *provisionality* leads inevitably actually to a preliminarity, to a unity with all coming things,

---

[242] *entelechial, entelechy*, from Greek *entelecheia*: denotes the condition of a thing whose essence is fully realized (Aristotle); also used to describe the process of inner self-determined activity (Leibniz; Driesch).

thus the historically strongly present and already further developed structure of intuition in Judaism is reinforced. A Midrash says very characteristically: "Why did God create the world with the letters Beth (Beginning of the word Bereschith and of the first word in the Bible)? It has the form ב. This means you may not investigate what is above and below, and not what was before the beginning. From the beginning of the world until the future world, this is where you shall investigate."[243] It is gradually becoming clearer that it is for this reason that there is so little among the Jews of what exists as "personality" in Europe, and in the East as a "wise man," only the prophet corresponds with this role for us, or the man who functions in the image of God, on a smaller level the one who is collectively led.

Without doubt there exists in this "provisionality" not only a characteristic structure but also a considerable danger. Everything you say against longing and its consequences applies here. But the actual difficulty is, as I have already stressed ("Applications," p. 5), that among the Jews a sovereignty, a "culture," a characteristic form was never intended at all, and that this, in the end, contradicts the central commandment: *Thou shalt not make a graven image.*" Only the absolute indeterminacy, which represents the actual prophetic task, in absolute contrast to the determinacy of traditional Judaism, guarantees that the suprapersonal in this people finds the ever-willing herald of the new message.

Now I know that you can object that the Judaism of which I speak does not exist, that it is not, as it were, historically verified and that this is merely a question of "intuitions" on my part. But even if I reproach myself with this, it still seems to me to be correct. One can measure the Jews precisely because of the peculiarity of their "provisional" structure not by their necessarily always inadequate reality, if one must even demand this of them. Precisely for them, history only

[243] Midrash Bereshith Rabba, I, 10: "R. Jonah said in R. Levi's name: Why was the world created with a *beth*? Just as the *beth* is closed at the sides but open in the front, so you are not permitted to investigate what is above and what is below, what is before and what is behind. Bar Kappara quoted: *For ask now of the days past, which were before thee, since the day that God created man upon the earth* (Deuteronomy 4:32): you may speculate from the day that days were created, but you may not speculate on what was before that. *And from one end of heaven unto the other (ib.)* you may investigate, but you may not investigate what was before this" (*Middrash Rabbah*, 1939, p. 9).

ever gives the yes or no of their being accepted or of their being banished. For sure, this appears as *"being a fugitive and a wanderer"* for the individual and, to him who looks from the outside, a *curse*, but this curse is very similar to the one in which the Son of Man will have nowhere to lay his head. The condemnation of all too many Jews who have this overwhelming burden placed on them by the other peoples, the people of this earth, is all too easy. They all grow and stand on a natural soil, *the Jews are contra-nature, they are Yahweh's people*, the other peoples are "of the earth," and the Jews have always known this. The Torah was offered to all peoples, but this implies an existence completely ruled by Y.H.W.H., all rejected it, so they say. Only the Jews accepted it and thereby took on an unending burden. You have stated many times both the against-nature-ness and the suffering that dominates such an existence in the individuation process of the individual. The decayed appearances of Judaism must be particularly terrible because the people who have lost the umbilical connection to what is to come and who, at the same time, are devoid of the naturalness linked to the soil are really appalling existences. The better ones are impractical dreamers; the worse are scum without any possibility of regeneration.

I sadly cannot credit myself with a great historical perspective because I know too little of world and cultural history, but it seems to me—especially when one takes the present spiritual situation into consideration—as if practically all supranational, i.e., suprapersonal aspirations and efforts toward the "personal" of the peoples are strongly connected with Jewish cultural heritage. I conclude this not only from the fact that clearly the entire world's barbaric and disgust-arousing anti-Judaism goes hand in hand with a wave of autarchic-nationalistic national individualism and that one apparently faces an official explanation in which the unity of the human race is nailed as a Jewish lie amid the renaissance of heathen national cults. Jewish-Christian chiliasm[244] that strives for the thousand year kingdom of developed consciousness, i.e., not only an individual but a collective consciousness that changes the face of the earth is threatened by an

---

[244] *chiliasm*: belief of some Christian denominations that Jesus will reign the earth for one thousand years before the final judgment; there exist similar ideas in Jewish eschatology about the coming of the messiah.

onslaught of heathen, settled, and soil-bound archetypes, accommo-
dated to the world, and of being partly swallowed up by them.

Taking up again the long lost threads that were interwoven into
Koigen's pairs of opposites, I must say that precisely with regard to
your spiritual attitude, I cannot see any contrast to such positions,
which, as it were, "would be distributed according to race," although
probably the starting points of such a difference could be. This would
imply that *both standpoints are compensating* for each other, therefore
each one would have to progress toward the other. Is this a lazy
compromise?

From my side, the protestantization of Judaism seems to me to be
necessary despite its collective ambitions. For me, Palestine is in this
regard only a sort of transition because individuation seems to require, even for a people, the responsible and critical engagement
with the reality of the world, and moreover not as a provisionality to
jump over, but a reality to be overcome.

On the other hand though, and perhaps you have a completely
different opinion about this, it seems to me necessary that individuation that starts from the individual soul must somehow broaden
itself into a world-shaping potency and must be able to consciously
blast through the character of separateness. While this seems to be
fully evident in your reality, I mean again your consciously stated and
desired historical responsibility and effectiveness, this aspect seems
to me to be not yet developed in your theory that may be due in part
to the medical-individual starting point. But the big interpretation of
visions ultimately contains what I mean.[245] It is difficult to formulate
this, but it seems to me that a quite crucial venture lies in this direction, the foundation for a new formation through the becoming
conscious of the collective human basis. The collective unconscious
must not only have individual relevance, but also a collective one,
i.e., the developed consciousness of the individuated person is responsible for the shaping of the collective of this world. (Here the

---

[245] Neumann refers to Jung's interpretation of Christiana Morgan's visions in the seminar
Jung held in the Psychological Club Zurich from 1930 to 1934 (Jung, 1930–34).

future age of Aquarius will probably also go on building with both lines of collective reality.)[246]

The difficulty of finding one's bearings is, for me, no small thing, as you can imagine. A sentence from the Spring Seminar 32 reads: "But in as much one is trying that historical connection one cannot experience Tao."[247] I understand this very deeply as far as it relates to collective bonds. But how can I lose my historical contact, when precisely my isolation, my "singling out" is a central content of this historical tradition and when my notion of individuation as the experience of the Self in destiny and as its realization again constitutes the actual history of my people?

I know absolutely that here lies a danger but the psychic emancipation from which I come with its neuroticizing groundlessness doubtless demands a retrospective connection. I believe I should be able to find a balance between the two polarities: retrospective connection to the collective and thereby to the historical task of the Jews, and on the other hand protestantization, i.e., independence of the soul's own development. But it seems to me, in any case, that no ahistorical attitude of the "wise man" is required. You, for example, stand fully conscious in a historical development that precisely constitutes your German history.

So, if I say, for me, it is not about the people then again this is only correct in this sense that, for me, it is only about what is expressing itself in this people, what apparently wishes to be expressed in this people. As long as this people exists, it offers a possibility of expression

---

[246] The Age of Aquarius refers to the Platonic month that follows the Age of Pisces. A Platonic month is the time that the vernal equinox spends in one sign of the Zodiac while traveling through the entire ecliptic. Jung, calculating with the length of the month as 2134 years, dated the beginning of the Age of Aquarius between 1997 and 2154 (Jung, 1951, § 149, n. 88). See also n. 358.

[247] Jung in the visions seminar on 18 May 1932: "You see, before she can realize the nature of Tao, she must destroy all the ideas behind which she has been sheltered hinterto, because only he who is able to deliver himself over entirely to the river of life can experience Tao. As long as he maintains traditional convictions he remains cut off from nature. He might find peace for his soul within the traditional symbol inasmuch as the symbol works, that is not to be denied—practically everybody does try to make a connection with the past in the secret hope that it may work. But as long as one is trying to make that historical connection, one cannot experience Tao" (Jung, 1930–34, p. 695).

like no other. It has been bred for this experience for nearly 4,000 years and has formed its inner structure according to this. And so finally, I believe once again that I am a good Jew, by which I do not mean the people. I do not know whether this is a negative collective bond, but it almost seems to me not to be.

9 N

Dear Doctor,

My last letter left me with something of a nasty aftertaste, and I now believe I know why. I got far too caught up in "praise of the Jews" and did not take into account nearly enough the fact that, at the same time, the Jews are always the most disappointing people of world history. And indeed not only that—all too many are willing to pay for the attitude toward the future with an impoverishment of the present. There's a nice, relevant Hasidic story about this. "After a Sabbath meal at which many Jewish fathers were present, Yehudi[248] speaks: 'Well, people, if any of you are asked what is your purpose on earth, each one of you answers, "to raise my son to learn and to serve God." And when the son has grown up, he forgets his father's purpose on earth, and strives for exactly the same thing himself. And if you ask him the point of all this strife, he will tell you: "I have to raise my son in the doctrine and for good works." And thus it is, you people, from generation to generation. But when, finally, will we get to see the rightful child?'"[249]

---

[248] Yaakov Yitzchak Rabinowicz (1766–1813), also called Jacob Isaac of Przysucha, byname Ha-Yehudi ("the Jew"), or Ha-Yehudi Ha-Kadosh ("the Holy Jew"), taught a distinct form of Hasidism, which centred on Talmudic study and differed from the hitherto prevalent miracle-based Hasidic teachings.

[249] "Das rechte Kind" from *Der große Maggid und seine Nachfolge* in Martin Buber's *Die chassidischen Bücher* (Buber, 1928, p. 528). English translation as "the right child" in *Tales of the Hasidim: The Later Masters* (Buber, 1949, p. 231): "After a sabbath meal at which many fathers of families were present, the Yehudi said: 'You people! If any of you is asked why he toils so on earth, he replies: "To bring up my son to study and serve God." And after the son is grown up, he forgets why his father toiled on earth, and toils in his turn, and if you ask him why, he will say: "I must bring up my son to be studious and do good works." And so it goes on, you people, from generation to generation. But when shall we get to see the right child?'" Neumann quotes this story also in the second volume of *On the Origins and History of Jewish Consciousness* (*Ursprungsgeschichte des jüdischen Bewusstseins*) (Neumann, 1934–40, vol. 2, p. 24).

We are not only living off the interest of old capital but now that this has been largely devalued by the inflation of emancipation, we are inclined to live on credit, while hoping for an upturn or even invoking one. This won't do, of course.

I do not mean to say that what I wrote to you is wrong—I see quite factually the Jews are in a quite peculiar situation that is calculated to force them to find new and groundbreaking solutions, but one should not be awarding them laurels in advance, while it is still so terribly questionable whether they will succeed or whether they won't just fail as they nearly always do. No real disappointment in the failure of the Jews could dissuade me from believing in them because, out of the making conscious of their failure, a step forward has always emerged, but I wouldn't want to be "a gushing enthusiast in Israel"[250]—that is not my role but rather my danger. I just wanted to write this to you in haste—that I have understood this in something of a new way again. I believe my opposition to some of your objections or alleged underestimations led me to overcompensate rather.

With best wishes,
E. Neumann

---

[250] "Ein Schwärmer in Israel." From a song text by the Zionist rabbi, poet, and playwright Emil (Bernhard) Cohn (1881–1948) titled "Die anderen sorgen für gestern und heut," that was printed in the songbook of the Zionist Berlin youth organization Jüdischer Wanderbund Blau-Weiss (*Blau-Weiss Liederbuch*, 1914, pp. 6–7). Erich and Julie Neumann met each other for the first time as members of the Blau-Weiss.

[10. XII. 1934]

Dear Dr. Jung,

I am turning to you with a request this time. It is about the following: I did not bother about a medical license as I do not need one as a psychotherapist, and I believed that I could not get one. As you know, I have no qualifying certificate, as I could not do my practical year as a Jew.[251] Now—with a slowly growing hold on reality—I learned that it is actually possible to get a license. For this purpose, it is essential that I have a certificate from you confirming that I worked with you for six months—I think you should formulate it as "practical psycho-analytic" or something like that, and that would be accurate as well. I would be very grateful for such a document, and if you could possibly embellish it with an official stamp, that would be impressive—they set a lot of store by titles and such things.

The license would not only be important for work with homes and similar institutions but would also protect me from future regulations only permitting doctors to practice psychotherapy. I am told that although this is not probable, it is not ruled out.

Otherwise, as far as reality is concerned, things are gradually getting better, the practice is getting more lively—although still small—the introductory courses in analytical psychology (12 x 1.5 hours including discussion) that I am doing here and in Jerusalem are relatively well attended (15–20 people in each) and so things are starting to take shape.

---

[251] Erich Neumann studied medicine at the Charité, which is part of the Friedrich-Wilhelms-University Berlin (today: Humboldt University). He completed his studies in 1933 but was not allowed to undertake the required practical internship due to the racial laws implemented by the National Socialists.

The work on Jacob and Esau and symbolism[252] is also nearly ready and just needs typing up, other things are already showing signs of life so that bodes well. Especially now that our young son is restored to health after overcoming fantastically well life-threatening atypical diphtheria after a last minute tracheotomy.[253] All the same, it has been a rather distressing time. After he had come through the operation with glowing colors, he had another suffocation attack two days later that nearly did for him. The terrible "reality" of a thick membrane, upon which so much horrifically depended, has once again given me a lot to think about.

But for today I am only bothering you with my request—I would be so grateful if you could send me such a certificate as soon as possible.

With best wishes,
Your E. Neumann

---

[252] See n. 218.
[253] Tracheotomy, surgical incision on the anterior aspect of the neck and opening a direct airway through an incision in the trachea.

11 J

Dr. E. Neumann,
37 Sirkin Street,
Tel Aviv,
Palestine.

My dear colleague,

Enclosed is the certificate.

Unfortunately I have not yet managed to continue our correspondence as I have had much to do. On top of everything else I have been called as an expert witness to a very complicated court case—a murder.[254]

---

[254] Jung wrote a psychiatric expertise for the jury trial of Hans Näf, which took place in Zurich from 19 to 28 November 1934 (Jung, 1937b). Näf was accused of murdering his wife Luise, who had been found dead of gas poisoning in their flat on 22 February 1934. He was found guilty of murder and sentenced to lifelong imprisonment. The application for revision of 28 February was rejected by the High Court but overruled by the court of cassation (Baechi, 1936). The retrial took place from 14 to 28 November 1938 and resulted in Näf's acquittal of the murder charge (Baechi, 1940). Besides Jung, psychiatric expertise was given by Hans W. Maier, the director of the Burghölzli clinic, and Franz Riklin. Jung gave his witness statement at the retrial on 23 November 1938: "The well-known psychiatrist Dr. C. G. Jung firstly describes his method of character analysis. By the use of 'stimulus words' he examines the reaction of the candidate. He explains that he carried out the test without prejudice and he would be more likely to be favorably disposed toward the defendant since he was called upon by the defense. Näf's reaction time was even above the average for uneducated people. A third of the stimulus words which refered to the crime in question called forth 'maximal disturbances,' a further third were disturbed; indifferent words elicited no disturbances. The expert has the impression that Näf's behavior was attributable to his 'defensive attitude.' He has always lived more or less outside of society. In his case, there must exist a considerable sense of guilt. This can be explained by his generally asocial attitude or to some particular guilt. Reference points for 'harassed innocence' cannot be demonstrated" (*NZZ*, 24 November 1938, no. 2067). The defense brought forward a counter expertise by Hans Kunz, who criticized Jung's method and explained Näf's reaction as caused by fear rather than guilt. The acquittal was certainly an embarrassment to Jung, who was firmly convinced of Näf's guilt as an interview with the *Daily Mail* in 1935 showed: "Dr. Jung also recalled a murder case in which a man found his wife dead in a room filled with gas, and everything at first pointed to suicide. 'But I reasoned like this,' the

I would like to draw your attention to Kurt Gauger's book: *Politische Medizin, Grundriss einer deutschen Psychotherapie (Political Medicine: An Outline of a German Psychotherapy).*[255] It is worth taking a look at this mentality more closely. Gauger is something like the General Doctor to the SA.[256]

I send my best wishes to your son. Adapting to a strange land often causes particularly virulent infections, but hopefully it has immunized him against Palestine now.

I have now begun my winter break and hope to be able to write to you more fully soon.

With warm greetings,
Your always devoted,
C. G. Jung

---

doctor went on. 'What would be a man's immediate instincts in such a case?' 'He would fling open the window and then rush to pick up his wife. He would not notice details, such as the position of the furniture, or even which way his wife was lying.' 'When I questioned the husband in the case, while he reacted normally to general questions I noticed that he remembered perfectly minute details about the scene of his discovery.' 'At his trial I pointed out my suspicions to the jury, and the Public Prosecutor produced, in the handwriting of the accused man, a list of positions of different objects in the room.' 'Anticipating that he would be questioned, the man had written them down, intending to memorize them.' 'He was, of course, convicted and sentenced'" ("Word Clues to Crime," *Daily Mail*, 9 October 1935). Neumann kept a copy of the illustrated report in the *Zürcher Illustrierte* (No. 49, 2 December 1938, p. 1498).

[255] Kurt Gauger (1899–1959): National Socialistic psychotherapist and author. Studied psychology, philosophy, pedagogy, literature, and history; wrote his thesis about Eduard von Hartmann in 1922. From 1925 to 1931 Gauger studied medicine in Berlin and Rostock. During the Weimar republic Gauger was an active member of a right-wing terror organization. In 1926 he went into psychotherapy with Milla von Prosch. Gauger was assistant director of the Institut für psychologische Forschung and Psychotherapie, which was founded in 1936. He was also in a leading position of the Reichsstelle für den Unterrichtsfilm. As a writer he was mainly known for his seaman's tales (*Christoph: Roman einer Seefahrt*, 1941; *Herz und Anker: Seemannsgeschichten*, 1943). His psychotherapeutic writings were mainly occupied with the creation of a specific Aryan psychotherapy and include *Politische Medizin: Grundriß einer deutschen Psychotherapie* (1934). On Gauger see Cocks (1975, pp. 93–107) and Lockot (2002, p. 336).

[256] SA, short for "Sturmabteilung," paramilitary organization of the NSDAP (Nazi Party) founded in 1921. In 1934, the SA had around 3.5 million members and became increasingly dangerous to Hitler, who subsequently accused the SA chief, Ernst Röhm, of plotting against him. On 30 June and 1 July 1934, the leading commanders of the SA were arrested and executed by SS troops. The public was informed about the successful action taken against Röhm's attempted plot ("Röhm-Putsch"). In the aftermath, Röhm's homosexuality was used to discredit his reputation. The SA never again regained its power in the NS state.

11 J (A)[257]

[Zurich, Küsnacht], 21 December 1934.

CERTIFICATE

In 1933–34 Dr. Erich Neumann worked for six months under my direction in theoretical and practical psychotherapy and acquired the skills for the practical implementation of the psychic methods of treatment.

---

[257] In possession of the Stiftung der Werke C. G. Jungs.

12 N

9. II. 1935

My dear Doctor, dear Professor,

Although I can imagine that the Professorship[258] comes all rather late in the day and elicits only an ironic smile from you, I would still like to say something to you in this regard. Certainly, despite everything, this Professorship is a signal—even to you—that the 20 years are complete that are needed for something to make an impact in the collective. As always, it is probably the case, even for you, that you have forged so far on in these 20 years that your solitude is barely touched by this signal, but all the same, you will take some pleasure in it, even if only because your voice will perhaps now be heard by people who are easily impressed by such a title. Certainly you do not need it, but the others do, and if one now happily begins to notice that the psychoanalysis of 1914 has forged ahead with you, one may finally end up, in 1935, at your door, and be able to notice much that is new. I know this from my own experience. I thought I was very well acquainted with what you have published, but a new exploration that I undertook for my course brought an infinite amount into a completely new and clear light once again. The coherence of analytical psychology is in part so well hidden in a plethora of single remarks that I for one am surprised over and over again. Your Professorship is, then, more a signal to us than to you yourself that the world seems ready to allow itself to be surprised by you.

I regret very much of course that our correspondence that was and is very important to me has not been added to by another letter from you, but I know the demands of work that you are under and am now beginning, though with a heavy heart, to come to terms with

---

[258] Jung lectured at the ETH, the Swiss Federal Institute of Technology, from 1933 to 1941. He gave his inaugural lecture on 5 May 1934 (Jung, 1934b). In 1935, the year of his sixtieth birthday, Jung was appointed professor at the ETH.

writing fewer questions and working on more answers. But what about your book on the Jewish question?[259] Was that only accepted by you in the heat of the moment or even only as a therapeutic ruse? I am very against such ploys, and have never experienced any with you—so I would like both urgently and diffidently (a difficult combination) to recommend anew this correspondence to your attention: Please have compassion for the huge pressure of being far away from which I suffer. Every "club lady"[260] can extract more time from you than I can, so I recommend myself and the Jewish problem to your sense of fairness and magnanimity.

Apart from this, things are going well for me and mine. My practice is growing slowly and consistently. You will have noticed as well as I have that I am outgrowing my introversion, this is the motto of the Jacob-Esau work that I have not dared to send to you, and also of my activity here as well as of my interest, for example, in "materialism" as it is called. Precisely there, much is becoming clear anew to me about you. If dialectical materialism regards consciousness as a late blooming of living substance as opposed to the primacy of consciousness of solipsistic idealism, then all of a sudden your connection with science has become clearer to me.[261] The relativization of consciousness stands in this historic line, just as the origin of the collective unconscious emerges—and I had not fully enough recognized this—out of the reaction of the human being to the object

---

[259] Neumann wrongly assumed that Jung intended to write a book on Judaism and psychotherapy. See Jung's reply from 19 February 1935 (13 J).

[260] "Klubdamen" or "Jungfrauen" were used as belittling references to the predominantly female members of the the Psychology Club Zurich.

[261] *dialectical materialism*: general philosophical teaching of Marxism to explain the developmental laws of nature and society. This understanding of reality, which derived from the teachings of Marx and Engels, is based on Hegel's dialectics, according to which reason (consciousness) enfolds in dialectical steps of thesis, antithesis, and synthesis. Reality is, for Hegel, the result of the enfolding spirit of the world ("Weltgeist") that reaches its highest form of self-realization in absolute reason. Hence, for *idealism* the materialist world results from the consciousness of the spirit. *Solipsistic idealism* goes further than that by restricting the entire reality to ego consciousness. In giving the material reality a primacy over consciousness, Marx and Engels turned Hegel's position around: "It is not the consciousness of men that determines their existence, but their social existence that determines their consciousness" (Marx, 1961, p. 20). Ideas and consciousness are seen as mere reflexes of the material reality. For Jung's psychological position between materialism and idealism, see his letter of 10 March 1959 (119 J), where he writes that the world without a reflecting consciousness would be of a "gigantic meaninglessness."

world. On the other hand though, I believe that one cannot misunderstand you more drastically than Gauger does, whose positive findings nearly all stem from you, but who then dares to speak of your "Catholicism" and your "underestimation of consciousness."[262] My contrast with Kirsch seems to me to be most clear in that, in my opinion, he undervalues the role of consciousness. If I now write something about Kirsch, please do not misunderstand me—I really want to learn if I am seeing things incorrectly. I found Kirsch pleasant enough if with some reservations—when I visited him after hearing of his decision to go away the first time. Mind you, he seemed to me quite at risk and very threatened by his unconscious. He told me he could not explain his personal reasons to me—fine. Much that he gossiped about my connection with his alteration remained quite unclear. But he is only pretending to have awareness of what is happening to him without actually having it. Even the panicky breaking away and denial is lazy, and his confusion remains unchanged, it seems to me. The worst thing is that he is always posing. He looks quite ragged, crushed would be more correct, and as far as I could see it had a positive effect on me, but I can't get rid of the feeling that here a chieftain is "lurking" in maiden's clothes. Am I incorrect if, with all due respect to this chieftain, I regard him as a primitive who misunderstands concretistically just like Socrates. I.e.,—as far as he is concerned he is not misunderstanding, as far as he is concerned it may be correct, but not for us?

Kirsch and his wife distinguish themselves in this situation by constantly changing their point of view. She proudly proclaims that she is quite individualistic and egotistic, which should be a hallmark of individuation, and after she has just explained that she has come here firmly decided to remain, she continues—when I advised him against rushing into developments—"James, you stay here and the children and I will go back." Without pausing for breath. I also find her attempts to wash her hands in innocence undignified; even if they separate there is enough of a connection between them for her to have to answer for. It is terribly confused, and please believe me in my most honorable effort to do justice to the Kirsches, but I consider

[262] Gauger (1934).

both to be not harmless in their impact. And though for this reason, Kirsch can in some cases be excellent, I also noticed repeatedly in conversations how he considers the communications and signals from the unconscious to be commands, without moving the debate of the unconscious with *consciousness* into center stage, and, moreover, the limited consciousness of the human being. That is precisely something that I learned from you, and it was not easy for me to see that the unconscious is an "opponent" in exactly the same way as the external world is, although it represents the mother of consciousness and the superiority of the divine. From this false evaluation arises inflation, lack of clarity and pomposity. It is not simply this. In his seminar he discussed the return of the Jews to Palestine, to their soil, to the original homeland, etc.; he declared in an open letter to the *Jüd. Rundschau*—embarrassingly enough for me—"the Shekinah can only be redeemed in Erez Israel"[263] (I am more cautious about this), and suddenly everything is not true. In response to the understandable question of an enraged female audience member and patient: "What will happen to the soil now?" he exclaimed that he had had the experience of the soil. You just can't make things so simple. As far as he is doing something that he must do—and there is something of that going on—I have every respect for him, but there is so much spin and half truth in it all. I attempt to defend him when such and such people ask how "something like this" is possible after a Jungian analysis, but I can't grasp it fully myself. Please don't take this as impertinence or similar, but this seriously concerns me. I know that you are not responsible for your pupils, but perhaps you can clarify something for me. Is this really to do with me? It makes me shudder when I place Mrs. Kirsch's pretensions alongside your modesty, and then am aware that she is practicing analysis. Is this sort of thing really so harmless? I can only say of myself that I feel my own inadequacy ever more strongly that does not make me despondent in any way but rather more cautious, and I am simply not willing to contradict my conscious mind and my intuition that do not accept that Mrs. K., for example, has achieved such a high level of individuation

---

[263] Neumann refers probably to "Die Judenfrage in der Psychotherapie" ("The Jewish Question in Psychotherapy") (Kirsch, 1934), though the open letter does not contain the exact words that Neumann attributed to Kirsch.

as she constantly announces. It has been my experience until now that people who have achieved something close to what I believe you describe as individuation, that such people have become quieter and not louder.

Now I must confess the following. In Zurich, I became aware that my debate with the collective unconscious has not yet taken place. I am only now starting to confront the anima and I see that my position regarding things Jewish, for example, is not yet finished, but has much transformed itself. My worldview looks very different after Zurich and I am just at the beginning. But I have never been manically obsessed with trivia and do not feel myself to be in disarray, but rather half way to being on the right path. Is my assessment of the Kirsches incorrect (which I do not believe), am I really not capable of being objective here?

I urge you, dear Doctor, to respond to this not insignificant question, if possible.

Many thanks for your certificate and for the endorsement of Gauger. Gauger is often very likeable in his attitudes, also cleverer than many other psychotherapists. His intellectual impurity, though, disturbs me violently. He has you, Adler, and socialism to thank for almost everything he says, does he not know it? Or does he not wish to know? Such dishonesty is abhorrent. I am sad not to be able to say something in person to the "Professor" in Zurich.

Ever yours,
E. Neumann

13 J

Dr. Erich Neumann,
37 Sirkin St.,
Tel Aviv,
Palestine

My dear Neumann,

Actually I began a long letter to you some time ago now. Due to other work I have been interrupted again and therefore I am sending you today just a brief sign of life and a reply to your kind letter. The big letter will follow.

When I promised to conduct a correspondence with you about the Jewish question, I was in all seriousness about it and continue to be so. However, I hadn't taken into consideration just how much was going to come raining down upon me, even eating into my holidays. The Professorship you heard about is only a distant sounding echo of all that has been happening. So I must make you wait for my next letter that will be very thorough. I don't think I went so far as to promise a book on the Jewish question, as that would seem personally rather too presumptuous. I know too little about it. Our correspondence is evolving in a very idiosyncratic way, as you will see from my reply.

What you write about Kirsch sounds not unfamiliar to me, unfortunately. I really have the impression that you are seeing this all too correctly. I have such an awkward feeling about both of them that for a long time I could hardly touch the Kirsches' letter[s] from Tel Aviv. It is indeed a very pathetic story. I can only tell you how glad I am, firstly that I have not started a religion, and secondly that I have not founded a church. People may cast out devils in my name all they like or even send themselves into the Gergesene swine![264] I just have to put up with it and also have my hands full trying to do my own work as properly as possible.

I wrote Gauger a long letter containing a fundamental critique and have had no reply. I don't know if that is connected with too much "Heil Hitler" or with too few[265] good manners.

Finally I want tell you that your letter left me with a favorable impression. This seems to promise good things for the future.

With best wishes in the meantime,
Your always loyal,
C. G. Jung

[handwritten addition] You will also receive a couple of manuscripts (*Complex Theory* and *Archetypes*).[266]

---

[264] Matthew 8:28–34; Mark 5:1–20; Luke 8:26–39. According to the manuscript tradition the name of the given locations varies between "Gergesenes" and "Gadarenes" in Matthew, and between "Gerasenes," "Gadarenes," and "Gergesenes" in Mark and Luke.

[265] In the copy, which Jung kept for the archive, "too little" ("zu wenig") has been deleted and replaced by "too much" ("zu viel").

[266] Jung (1934b); Jung (1935).

14 N

[undated][267]

Dear Professor,

If I have not written to you for a long time for reasons of abstinence and out of respect for your more than busy schedule, the price to pay for this is that material has been accumulating and the avalanche is about to break over you. Firstly, I thank you for your letter that tempered my feeling that "[i]n the wide field I am alone."[268] Humanly that is in no way the case, and the practice is going very well too, as are the courses, etc. All the same, my "detachment" is often a problem in the meantime; I am the opposite of a self-publicist, perhaps too much so. But as far as my inner development and my "actual" existence and work are concerned, I am, of course, very much left to my own devices, in fact completely, and so I thank you most particularly for sending the manuscripts that provided much that is new to me. These, your Nietzsche seminar,[269] and the Eranos Yearbook[270] brought a real torrent of new and important material.

---

[267] Typescript letter with the handwritten date of 23.4.1935 on top of the page. It is not certain if the date was added by Neumann or someone else.

[268] Proverbial saying that goes back to Ludwig Uhland's poem "The Shepherd's Sabbath Song" ("Schäfers Sonntagslied'") (1805).

[269] Jung held a weekly seminar on Nietzsche's *Thus Spoke Zarathustra* at the Psychological Club Zurich. The first seminar took place on 2 May 1934—around the time of Neumann's departure from Zurich—and lasted with interruptions until 1939. When Neumann returned one more time to Zurich before the war in May/June 1936 he attended the seminar. On 24 June 1936, Jung replies to the following two questions of Neumann: "Dr. Neumann asks whether Zarathustra's negative attitude in reference to the mob is not really the rejection of the inferior function, or 'the ugliest man,' to use Nietzsche's terms" (Jung, 1934–39, p. 1021); "Then Dr. Neumann asks whether the church, by catching the mob through her forms, doesn't suppress the creative will which can manifest in the mob" (Jung, 1934–39, p. 1022). The seminars were compiled by Mary Foote from stenographic notes by her secretary, Emily Köppel, and distributed among students of Jungian psychology. However, Jung did not see them fit for publication and in order to study the manuscript one would need Jung's personal permission. See Jung's letter to Piloo Nanavutty, 11 November 1948 (Jung, 1973, vol. 2, p. 137).

[270] This, presumably, refers to the Eranos Yearbook 1934 *Ostwestliche Symbolik und Seelen-führung* (see Jung's handwritten addendum to his letter from 19 February 1935 [13 J]). Jung's

If I ask you some further questions in connection to these works, please feel as little pressurized by this as by my sending you the Jacob/Esau manuscript that I have been working on at your suggestion. The "big letter" that you promised me is the most important matter at the moment. I understand it completely when it speaks of the natural psychic life, but, it seems to me, in analysis, for all its fateful naturalness, free will and "the attitude of a leader" are essential—in contrast to "morally spruced-up humiliation."

To speak of myself, if I now fully or approximately understand the breaking in of the anima experience into my life (and my marriage), and keep seeing, for example, from my analysis, how things in Zurich happened in such sovereign independence and fateful certainty of which my ego-consciousness then only grasped a few edges or only saw and sucked dry—the feeling of "psychosis" is missing both then and now. Even if I now understand things that then I "painted," or earlier I "wrote poetry about," the feeling of being taken over by an "enemy" is still missing. With regard to events, I am full of astonishment, perhaps I am too "aesthetic" and only "intuitive," but I have always had an uncertain feeling of meaningfulness and of the possibility of giving meaning to the apparently meaningless, and also the awareness of being my own invisible partner in what is happening to me.

Whereas in life the "leading" mostly comes "afterward," the "voluntary psychosis" of analysis seemed to me to distinguish itself in that the constant attempt is made to be the "leader" at the same time. A problem of analysis itself, of technique, if you like. I was very careful to make transferences to myself conscious straightaway. Is that actually correct? I don't mean that as a general rule, but in such a way that from the very beginning, I pay attention to the autonomy of the patient (if they are not all too autonomous individuals naturally). Up till now that has never had a negative result as far as I can tell, mostly a very positive one in that the collective unconscious became clearly more evident, while, at the same time, consciousness was strengthened. Is that correct or am I preventing something in this way? In my analysis with you, you seemed to work in this way also.

---

contribution was titled "Über die Archetypen des kollektiven Unbewussten" ("Archetypes of the Collective Unconscious") (Jung, 1935).

There would be all kinds of things to report of my "internal" world, and a visit to Zurich would be very nice. In the middle of a mandala that evidently cannot be suppressed any longer is a man on his knees with a lion who is putting a crown on his own head.[271] The anima no longer disguises him from me, that much is clear along with much more. The eagle-snake problem[272] from Zarathustra is exactly present in my Zurich drawings, and that has helped me get further as well.

As far as the Jewish problem is concerned, things are happening there too. Y.H.W.H. as an archetype as an "opposite" to the self. But not quite as an opposite but as a later unprojected form. But the golden Man-Self and Y.H.W.H. as creator of the world are, for me, not actually opposites as they are in fact the same, but the approach is different and becoming conscious of the archetypal is, here, just at the beginning in me.

---

[271] *Mandala*: Sanskrit for "circle" or "orb," a circular arrangement that serves as a tool of concentration; it represents a consecrated space and is meant to be the body of a chosen deity. The mandala is of special importance in Tibetan Buddhism (see Brauen, 1998). Jung regarded the mandala as symbolic representation of the Self that would appear in dreams during the process of individuation. In his Eranos lecture of 1933, "Zur Empirie des Individuationsprozesses" ("A Study in the Process of Individuation"), Jung spoke about the significance of the mandalas as part of the individuation process using the drawings of a female patient (Jung, 1934d). See also Jung (1950a; 1955a).

[272] In Nietzsche's *Thus Spoke Zarathustra* the eagle and the serpent are the animals that accompany Zarathustra: "An eagle cut broad circles through the air, and upon it hung a snake, not as prey but as friend, for the snake curled itself around the eagle's neck. 'It is my animals!' said Zarathustra, and his heart was delighted. 'The proudest animal under the sun and the wisest animal under the sun—they have gone forth to scout'" (Nietzsche, *Zarathustra*, 1980, p. 15). Nietzsche used the image of the serpent curling around the eagle's neck as a symbol for the eternal recurrence of the same (on the eagle and the serpent in Nietzsche, see Thatcher, 1977). In his seminar on Nietzsche's Zarathustra (see n. 269) Jung discussed the animals in the first meeting on 2 May 1934, interpreting the eagle as spirit (intuition) and the serpent as chtonic (sensation) powers: "So the eagle would be the spirit and the serpent would be the body, because the serpent is the age-old representative of the lower worlds, of the belly with its contents and the intestines, for instance. [. . .] On the other hand, the eagle soars high; it is near the sun. It is a son of the sun—marvelous" (Jung, 1934–39, p. 18). For Jung the intertwining of the animals meant the reconciliation of two opposite forces (on the union of opposites in Nietzsche and Jung, see Dixon, 1999, and Huskison, 2004). Their appearance in *Zarathustra* indicates the instinctual and unconscious side warning of an overemphasis of consciousness: "So when the text says that Zarathustra is with his serpent and his eagle, it means, as in dreams, that he is going parallel with his instincts; he is right, looked from a spiritual as well as chtonic point of view. In this case, he is right in what he is actually doing, telling his consciousness that he is getting tired of it; he ought to detach from too much consciousness" (Jung, 1934–39, p. 19).

I hope my future work on Hasidism[273] will develop this. (By the way, "the Jews, the most unknown people"; did I read correctly Zarath. II p. 45, "Talmud, the Jewish book of mysteries?"[274] As ever, such a sentence would not have been possible in the Club[275] about a Chinese, Indian, or Persian content, to say nothing of Gnosis, but the Jews are positioned apparently too elementally in close proximity.) How do I get hold of the "Moon Paper" by Dr. Harding[276] by the way? Hasn't it been included in a seminar collection?

[273] *Ursprungsgeschichte des jüdischen Bewusstseins* (*On the Origins and History of Jewish Consciousness*) (Neumann, 1934–40), unpublished. Neumann wrote these two volumes between 1934 and 1940. Volume one is titled *Beiträge zur Tiefenpsychologie des jüdischen Menschen und der Offenbarung* (*Contributions to the Depth Psychology of the Jewish Man and to the Problem of Revelation*) and volume two *Der Chassidismus und seine psychologische Bedeutung für das Judentum* (*Hasidism and Its Psychological Relevance for the Jewry*). In his study Neumann demands that the depth psychology of modern Jewry needs to be aware of its historical preconditions. Whereas the first volume deals with the apocalyptic prophetism around the time of the destruction of the Second Temple, the second volume is dedicted to Hasidism. According to Neumann, Hasidism is able to bridge the gap between the ancient JHWH and the earth principle (Neumann, 1934–40, vol 2, p. 217). This link brings with it a new set of values: a joyful affirmation of creation and, at the same time, a rejection of melancholy and depression as world-denying emotions (p. 118); an antipathy toward Jewish intellectualism (p. 114); and a new appreciation of the female principle through a deeper understanding of the Shekhinah (p. 123). But, according to Neumann at the end of the second part, Hasidism failed to renew the Jewish psychological condition by giving in to the rabbinate (p. 226). When asked by Gustav Dreifuss in the 1950s why he would not publish the manuscript, Neumann replied that it was not close enough to the primary sources and too much orientated around Buber (see Dreifuss, 1980, p. 68).

[274] Neumann refers to Jung's seminar on Nietzsche's Zarathustra (see n. 269). According to the seminar manuscript the passage from 24 October 1934 read as: "The traditions concerning those books are post-Christian because there are two chapters in which Jesus is mentioned, but he is there always called 'Jesus ben Miriam,' the son of Miriam. And he is called 'the deceiver' because he betrayed the mysteries, which is also the tradition in the Talmud, the Jewish book of mysteries" (Jung, 1934–39, p. 185).

[275] See n. 240.

[276] In the seminar on Nietzsche's Zarathustra Jung refers on 17 October 1934 to a presentation by Esther Harding (1888–1971), delivered in the seminar on dream analysis (1928–30) on 13 November 1929: "You remember perhaps the very excellent 'Moon' paper of Dr. Harding and her committee worked out. The moon is of course the archetype of the inner mother, the faint light of the dark earth. We encountered that figure of the earth mother in the Visions also. Since that is a predominant, prevailing archetype of the woman's unconscious, the ruling aspect, it is characteristic for the particular development of fantasies; therefore, we made a special investigation into the archetype of the mother aspect of the moon" (Jung, 1934–39, p. 166). The exact title of Harding's presentation was "The Symbolism of the Crescent and Its Psychological Meanings" (Jung, 1928–30, pp. 367–81). The contents of the presentation were included in Harding's book *Woman's Mysteries, Ancient and Modern: A Psychological Interpretation of the Feminine Principle as Portrayed in Myth, Story, and Dreams* (Harding, 1935).

Another question: In the *Complex Theory* lecture[277] p. 18. The term "psychic constitution" is unclear to me and rather threatening. Analysis is anticonstitutional inasmuch as it leads to the individuation process by the development of the inferior function. Its transformative, recasting effect changes the "psychic constitution" fundamentally. Of course I understand if one speaks of complexes as of the tendency to prejudices,[278] but that they are "absolute" and not "relative" prejudices, I do not fully comprehend. The sentence: "The constitution decides irrevocably which psychological perception will emerge from a specific observer"[279] evokes my fullest opposition. Not to mention that it applies to me in particular because I have portrayed in my course the development from Charcot through to Jung under the maxim "Abandoning the constitution concept."[280] And I still think this is correct. The concept of individuation as a unified concept contradicts completely, it seems to me, that of an immutable constitution. In the end it is the collective unconscious that is prejudiced, but not the personal unconscious. Even the typological structure is not immutable as it relativizes itself or dissolves in the individuation process.

I understand here again that the absolute prejudicedness is only valid for unconscious people. To the same degree, though, that individuation implies autonomy, this "compulsion" of the complexes and the stars falls away. I am fully clear that this process is an approximate one—and about whether one must say that the cognitive faculty of humanity is prejudiced by the unconscious, but one must not go as far as your sentence goes. It stands, it seems to me at least, in contrast to the fact, well demonstrated by you, that, in the individuation process, an increase in objectivity and truth is learned. The form here is always individual, like that of the whole process, but the content is superindividual, one would have to speak of it being structural.

If I see this correctly, this is the same point in another form that I have already brought to this discussion many times. What stood

---

[277] Jung (1934b).

[278] Jung (1934b), § 213: "Complexes are very much a part of the psychic constitution, which is the most absolutely prejudiced thing in every individual."

[279] Jung (1934b), § 213.

[280] Neumann held introductory seminars on analytical psychology in Jerusalem and Tel Aviv.

behind my question is that the Self as the center of the individual process is also something general, not only suprapersonal but also structurally real.

Certainly, in this opposition, which you emphasize in contrast with Freud, the fact of the individual stands in the foreground, but the individuation process is, after all, something both particular *and* typical at the same time. Otherwise it would not be comprehensible. But not typical in the sense of typology but in the sense of general psychic structure. The proposition that one can attribute the psychological perception of an individual to the constellation of his unconscious (reductive) has become a negative formula in this sentence that I am hostile to and that contradicts or strongly endangers the essentially constructive substance of analytical psychology.

In my experience, which is negligible when compared with yours, the expansion of psychic capacity leads to a general perception of the world, and this exceeds all individually conditioned formulas. An extraverted Indian and an introverted Jew will hold more in common or even identically after the individuation process than typologically different unconscious individuals from one race. Certainly not an identity in the sense of *participation mystique*, but in the sense of individually different nuanced structural experience of a common nature. Thus individuation leads to something no longer and not only private, which transcends the psychic constitution.

Dear Professor, I would like to draw this to a close now as this letter is so full of questions that I don't quite like it. It is rather unfortunate that there is no scientific discussion for Jungian students. What there is too much of in the case of the Freudians—journals always repeating the same thing—in your case there is too little. The not insignificant number of your students ought to have something to say about analytical psychology, even about new things. Or—which I would sadly be able to understand—maybe you prefer not to have your own material associated and confused with that of others about whose form and quality you are more or less in doubt? Your anonymous influence is certainly growing (look at the Eranos Yearbook), but the systematic penetration of analytical psychology is too small even so. The richness of your seminars is quite unexploited. Will you do this in fact? There are often rumors about your book on the dream—will you publish something comprehensive and conclusive in the foreseeable future?[281] I have the feeling that this letter might seem too insistent once again, but please believe me, dear Professor Jung, the matter concerns me very much, so there is nothing to be done about it by you or me.

With best wishes,
Always yours,
E. Neumann

---

[281] At that time Jung intended to write a comprehensive study on dreams, but the project did not exceed the initial stages. In a letter to Cary Baynes on 5 April 1929 he wrote: "I have not yet begun, to write about dreams. I imagine I am not up to such an enterprise yet" (CFB). See Shamdasani (2003), p. 157.

15 J

Küsnacht, Zurich,
Seestrasse 228
27th April 1935[282]

Dr. E. Neumann,
37 Sirkin St.,
Tel Aviv

My dear Neumann,

First and foremost my full apologies for tardy replies and such like.[283]
I gathered your correspondence together in order to reply *in globo*
and then of course I did not have the time to do it. Recently there has
been too much going on as well. However you must not assume that
you make too many demands on my time. Sooner or later the moment will come when I can reply. I have promised you that after all.
It would be advisable though if you could mark your "private" letters
"urgent" or similar so that they can be dealt with in current correspondence. The other letters regarding the Jewish question must be
responded to with some thought and consideration and therefore
need longer.

Now to your general questions:

Each fundamental change in the psychological situation disposes
of one psychological system of adaptation and requires a new one.
Without conscious regard to this, archetypes arise in the intermedi-

---

[282] A handwritten version of this letter (A) dated 17 February 1935. The final typescript version (B)—which includes some handwritten corrections and amendments—was sent to Neumann on 27 April 1935 and is printed here. Differences between the two versions (apart from
spelling) and the corrections in version B will be highlighted in the footnotes.

[283] Version A and B include the sentence: "The certificate is enclosed herewith." But in typescript version B the sentence is crossed out by hand.

ate arena that, as a rule, remain unconscious.[284] They do not remain without influence on the subsequent events. Thus Zionism contains not a little from Jewish history, the reestablishment of Israel as a nation, perhaps fantasies about national kingship, etc. The archetypes become visible only indirectly, such as in the belligerent affectations of the Jewish National Socialists[285] or in the corresponding fantasies of individuals, or in the revival of Hebrew as an everyday language. Now, the archetypes can be a danger in that they bring about an archaization of social and political events, or in that they arouse rationalistic and utopian reaction phenomena that are precisely designed to suppress the effect of the archetypes. The archaization reveals itself in Europe in the form of dictatorships with lictor bundles,[286] roman greetings on the one hand, swastikas, Führer, heroism, the German race, etc., on the other hand. The reactive compensation in Marxism, Communism *et al*. We are thinking the same in essence. I have just abbreviated somewhat.

The apparent influence of the homeland and its characteristics on the psyche is only one half materialism, as, for me, the psyche is something fundamentally existent, upon which the material conditions can have an influence, but which for its part is also at the mercy of

---

[284] Version A continues as follows—which was crossed out: "which lead to a compensation or to a modern application. Both possibilities can have a favorable or an unfavorable effect, in other words Zionism."

[285] Jung refers here to the passage in Neumann's letter 8 N (A), where Neumann warns of the archetypal dangers of Zionism, which would overcompensate for the Jewish emancipation with a new orthodoxy, a communist collectivism, and a revisionary nationalism. Jung's ambiguous usage of the term "Jewish National Socialists" seems to refer to the latter. These revisionist forces were politically organized in the Revisionist Zionist Alliance, founded by Zeév (Vladimir) Jabotinsky in 1925. Already in 1923 Jabotinsky had founded the Betar youth movement in Riga, Latvia. The movement quickly became the principal advocate of militant Zionism and gained a large following in Jewish communities around the world. Initially, the Betar leaned politically toward Mussolini's fascism, admiring its anticommunist agenda, and was even adopting the fascist uniforms and rituals. Despite its right-wing nationalist and military agenda, the Betar was firmly opposed to National Socialism and formed a major force in the resistance movement in Nazi Germany and the occupied territories. Members of the Betar were instrumental in the organization and realization of the Warsaw Ghetto Uprising.

[286] Lictor bundle or fasces, lat. *fasces lictorae*: A bundle of wooden sticks with an ax blade emerging from the center; a symbol of power of the magistrates in ancient Rome. The bundles were carried by the Lictors. Although the fasces were used as symbols by many divergent political movements and governments, they are mainly associated with Italian fascism, which derived its name from the fasces.

psychic effects, so is in the end effect, subject to the reality of ideas. Once again it is the Jews who offer the best example of this!

Regarding Russia, an American whose name I have forgotten, observes: "If nothing came out of the entire revolution than the awakening of the Muzhik,[287] then this alone would be an achievement." By the way, the Muzhik is in fact beginning to argue.

Without doubt you are correct if you reject my judgment of the Jews as I am only basing this on the external aspect. Every judgment, if it is to hold, must be one sided at first in order to be moderated later by more general observation. Everything that you criticize is therefore correct and I would have to feel most deeply affected on account of my one-sidedness if I had not been constantly conscious of this. Before I defend myself, I'd like quickly to take another few steps on the sinful path and add that even the Marxist discovery (and I in no way love Marxism) of religion as the "opium of the people"[288] unfortunately hits the nail on the head in a certain aspect. Every religion is in danger of becoming a narcotic, even Marxism, in other words the gigantic lethargy and lazy thinking of human beings can make each and everything serviceable—and from a certain point on, also not. From this certain point on, the opposite of everything is true, then the spirit is generative despite social circumstances, then it is a matter neither security nor insecurity of life, neither collectivism nor individualism. Such preoccupations apply only as long as humanity is not being afflicted by the spirit. This spirit becomes evident in the king's palace as well as in the hovel of the beggar. I am addressed *personally* by the spirit, not as a member of a people or as a race or as humanity. I could just as well be an animal or a plant. But I am only one single "is," the most extraordinary and imperative counterpart of the Godhead, for which I am so fundamental, as it is for me. This dialogue in limitless eternity is a bigger thing than any millions of facets and gradations of so-called reality—when I am located there. If I am not there, then I am "slave to worldliness," disguised in the fateful role of a human being in a particular time, in a particular place, indissolubly bound to roots in history, nation, blood,

---

[287] Mujik or Muzhik, Russian for peasant, usually associated with Imperial Russia.
[288] See Neumann 8 N (A), n. 234.

soil, and collective opinions. In the face of this bond something in me seems to cry for redemption.

But this voice is an inability to forget the primordial world of pre-conscious existence, a yearning for a redissolution of all superstructures in the All that is the only true being. The Indian *neti-neti*[289] expresses this most strongly. But what Koigen[290] writes about Semites seems to my mind to be characteristic: Not to look back, but to take up the role that is waiting for me and to allow myself to be named as the President of the Society for Psychotherapy and to be appointed Professor by the Swiss Federal Council, if that's the way it must be, because these, and many other certainties less worthy of mention, make me skilled at becoming dissimilar from God, for it is His will that I become an "is," that I become His counterpart. I promise myself no glorification of earth out of it, for I know that my mere existence tears the bread out of the hands of the other. "Ultimate reality" is my goal, for sure, my laboriously hard-won decision that drives me away into infinite distance from God. I may not look back, not even to God, for otherwise I miss my goal, which is, namely, to find myself in my most extraordinary, most intense "suchness" where the Godhead can finally speak to me. Everything useful and so-called good that I can then do is only harmless inasmuch that I never thereby forget myself.

Koigen's differentiations are, on the whole, correct. Internally determined, prophetic, spirit-filled yearning and externally determined need that arouses the desire to take hold of the world and reshape it, is characteristic of Semitic religious feeling. Equally typical for the "Indo-Germanic" is the feeling that resides in the world and its fullness that intuits higher being in the symbolization of becoming and passing away. ("All that must disappear is but a parable."[291]) However

---

[289] neti-neti (composed of *na iti*, "not thus"): Saying that originated from the Upanishads, especially the Avadhuta Gita, and is a response to the student's attempt to gain a positive description of the transcendent self or Brahman, meaning "neither this, nor that." Vedantic Jnana yoga uses neti-neti vichara (neti-neti research) in order to reach a higher state of consciousness through conscious nonidentification with the worldly realm.

[290] See Neumann 8 N (A), n. 235.

[291] Last lines of Goethe's *Faust: Part Two*: "All things corruptible / Are but a parable; / Earth's insufficiency / Here finds fulfillment; / Here the ineffable / Wins life through love; / Eternal Womenhood / Leads as above" (Goethe, 1833; p. 288). For Jung's discussion of Faust's redemption at the end of *Faust: Part Two* see Bishop (2009, pp. 122–23).

one wishes to formulate this contrast, the main thing is that is exists and it expresses a peculiarly different temperament.

If you find that you are standing ominously and auspiciously in the middle of an antithesis, what is implied is that you are on the point of seeing the one as well as the other. This undoubtedly has to do with your psychological activity that has accustomed you to seeing and thinking in antitheses. But whoever has discovered his own inner contrast is lost for the exclusive redemptive sole truth. The basic question of all knowledge is not the true or the untrue, but the true untruth or the untrue truth. It no longer amazes us that the "glorification" of the earth is a disastrous utopia, and the symbolization of events is a beautiful dream, and that both are vital truths without which a conscious life would be pure folly.

It seems to be a fact that has repeated itself many times in the course of history that an idea emerges first of all as an unconscious action of a group or a people, and only much later becomes a "conscious" conception. The emergence of the manhood of God from the kingdom of God of the ancient empires through the transformation that is portrayed in the account of the temptation of Christ must be such a case in the extreme. One could draw the conclusion from this that every movement that grips an entire people is such an unconscious action whose concept becomes a subject of consciousness only at a much later moment. It seems now as if this insight came to the Jews earlier than to other races, which to my mind is explained by their feeling of a covenant with Y.H.W.H. and of their being a chosen people. In fact, it is out of Israel that Christ also emerged, the herald of the idea. It is well known that nothing binds compatriots together more than a shared (spiritual) movement. And nothing strengthens faith in invisible providence more than the invisibility and obscurity of the origin of the movement in the unconscious. The chosenness of the people and their bond with Y.H.W.H. represents the social intermediate stage between pharaohhood and the God-man, so a realization of the idea of the manhood of God at an initially collective and still unconscious level. One could describe this level as the "object level" of the Christian idea. With Christ, the "subject level" of the idea is achieved, for Christ is the only begotten (unigenitus) son of God who represents the summation of that which constitutes the chosenness in ancient Israel. With psychological accuracy, he considers himself therefore to be the one who fulfills the "law and the prophets." Christianity as a spiritual movement, which, for its part, was initiated by the appearance of the *"filius unigenitus,"*[292] could also be considered as the object level of a new, as yet unconscious idea, namely, that of individuation. In ancient Egypt itself, the idea of Osiris ran symbolically through this development from the ancient empire to the Ptolemaic era in anticipation, as the God Osiris gradually evolved from the Osiris of the Pharaoh to the Osiris of all better people. We should therefore expect, if everything does not deceive, such manifestations in the later course of the psychological history of humanity as, say, National Socialism which, with the abundance of power of the "Führer," the total power of the state, the almost religious veneration of the swastika symbol and certain anti-Christian tendencies, to say nothing of the enthusiastic mass movement, demonstrates all the characteristics of an intermediate stage in Christ's original *process of becoming human*. That Hitler has been celebrated more than once as a "savior," indeed that his picture occasionally even adorned an altar, and that the swastika[293] has not stopped even

---

[292] *Filius unigenitus*, lat. for "only begotten son."

[293] *Svastika*, from Sanskrit *su*, "well," and *asti*, "'it is," meaning "fortunate" or "auspicious": An ancient symbol of the sun, first archaeological findings can be dated back to the Indus Valley civilization; mainly associated with the Indian religions of Hinduism, Buddhism, and Jainism; in Hinduism the swastika is meant to evoke the energies of Shakti; its usage as a lucky charm is widespread in Asia. Hitler adapted a right-facing swastika as an emblem for the NSDAP symbolizing the alleged supremacy of the Aryan race. Jung talks about the swastika symbol and its adaptation through the NSDAP in his seminar on Nietzsche's Zarathustra on 13 February 1935: "And those rather competent National Socialists to whom I talked in Germany did not know that their swastika was turning the wrong way. Somebody called their attention to it rather indelicately, and they suddenly said, 'Dr. Jung, do explain to us why the swastika is turning the wrong way.' A most embarrassing question! Sure enough, they hoped to get me into a fix. But you see, though it moves the wrong way when you look at it, if you put yourself *into* the National Socialist swastika, it moves the right way. The symbol is far-reaching; it has a certain psychological meaning, of whatever kind it is. So I think it really means something that the swastika is moving the wrong way" (Jung, 1934–39, pp. 372–73); also, in his 1935 presentation to the Medical Society in Zurich titled "Grundsätzliches zur Psychotherapie" ("Principles of Practical Psychotherapy"), where the swastika is used as an example for political confessions seeking refuge in mythological symbolism (Jung, 1935a, § 20), and in his Eranos lecture 1934: "If thirty years ago anyone had dared to predict that our psychological development was tending toward a revival of the medieval persecutions of the Jews, that Europe would again tremble before the Roman fasces and the tramp of legions, that people would once more give the Roman salute, as two thousand years ago, and that instead of the Christian cross an archaic swastika would lure onward millions of warriors ready for death, that man would have been

in front of church doors, proves the expansion or the descent of the God-manhood into the regions of humanization or the rise of a new notion in the German, which he anyway experiences falsely—or psychologically correctly—in fatal dependence on Jewish priority (*hinc illae lacrimae*)[294] as the chosenness of the blond and blue-eyed race. The temptation episode and the confession: "My kingdom is not of this world"[295] are as yet absent. (For the time being, the social and political movement hopes, like certain expectations from the Old Testament, that all heathens will worship in Jerusalem or like the ancient Christian expectation of *parousia*.[296])

Nothing can become conscious that has not first been sacrificed, hence the sacrifice symbol of Christ. His ignominious death on the cross proves that the idea of the God-man has arisen out of the unconsciousness of the entire race. And from here on, the path to universality is open.

I think you do me an injustice when you assume that I regard the New Testament per se as a development of the Old Testament. The Old Testament is, apart from a few late texts, a self-contained world of such a strong and specific character that it could only decline or continue to exist. The NT (including Job, Ecclesiastes, and the Book of Wisdom) seems to me, to a large extent, to be Greek rather than Hebrew. This seems to have no small thing to do with the language

---

hooted at as a mystical fool" (Jung, 1935, § 98). In a letter to Mary Mellon of 24 September 1945 Jung states that he had "challenged the Nazis already in 1934 at a great reception in Frankfurt in the house of Baron von Schnitzler, the director of the I. G. Farben concern. I told them, that their anticlockwise swastika is whirling down into the abyss of unconsciousness and evil" (JA). In his Eranos lecture of 1933 he interprets the rotation of the left-facing swastika as a movement toward the unconscious, whereas the right-facing swastika rotates toward consciousness and liberation from the chaos of the unconscious (Jung, 1934d, § 564). Vis-à-vis his audience at the Institute of Medical Psychology (Tavistock Clinic, London), on 14 October 1936, Jung explains the psychological meaning of the swastika as a mandala: "Mandalas often have the character of *rotating* figures. One such figure is the swastika. We may therefore interpret it as a projection of an unconscious collective attempt at the formation of a compensatory unified personality" (Jung, 1936c, § 1332).

[294] Latin for "Hence those tears," idiom used to indicate that the actual cause for an action or an event has been detected. First used by Terence in his comedy *Andria*: "hinc illae lacrumae, haec illast misericordia" ("Hence those tears, that is his compassion").

[295] John 18:36: "Jesus answered, My kingdom is not of this world: if my kingdom were of this world, then would my servants fight, that I should not be delivered to the Jews: but now is my kingdom not from hence" (KJB).

[296] *Parousia*, Greek, the second coming; for Christians the return of Jesus Christ at the last judgment and the setup of his Millennial Kingdom.

in which the NT is formulated. It is no longer conceived as Hebrew but rather Greek. In this sense I am also speaking as of a "tribe" (if you like, of 12 tribes). Quite apart from the fact that the OT itself insists on the "Chosenness of the people" and their tribal structure, the unity of the OT speaks for the seclusion of a largely unitary people—of *a small people* that one might describe as a "tribe," at least psychologically. I am not speculating here with the concept of race because one might easily imagine that the original "Jews" were a mixed race of the first order.

I am in no way "intentionally" ignoring the historical "material" of the OT. I acknowledge it as the inestimable and sacrosanct spiritual inheritance of an ancient people that, for me, however, can be considered only indirectly, as comparative material as it were. I look at this like the *Tao Te Ching*[297] and the Upanishads.[298] It is only Chris-

---

[297] *Tao Te Ching*, Chinese text, attributed to the (mythical) author Lao-t'zu; originally passed on as part of an oral tradition the text was first written down around 400 BCE. The teachings of Lao-t'zu are an essential cornerstone of the philosophical foundations of Taoism. Jung's interest in Taoism was first aroused during his work on *Psychological Types* between the years 1915 and 1920. There Jung writes about the unifying symbol in Chinese philosophy and quotes extensively from the *Tao Te Ching* (Jung, 1921, §§ 358–69). He links the Tao as the middle way between the opposites to his concept of psychological wholeness. In the 1920s the contact and friendship with Richard Wilhelm (1873–1930), who had translated the *Tao Te Ching* (Wilhelm, 1911), further increased his interest in Taoism. The *I Ching*, translated by Wilhelm in 1924 (Wilhelm, 1924), inspired Jung's concept of synchronicity (see Jung's eulogy to Wilhelm [Jung, 1930]). He asked Cary F. Baynes to provide an English translation, which was finally published in 1950, and to which Jung provided a foreword (Jung, 1948/1950). The highlight of Jung's collaboration with Wilhelm was his psychological commentary on a book on Taoist yoga titled *The Secret of the Golden Flower*—also translated by Wilhelm (Wilhelm and Jung, 1929; Jung, 1929). As recent commentators have pointed out, Taoist thinking has been instrumental to the development of Jungian concepts such as the "Self" and "synchronicity" (Coward, 1996). Jung's library contained several editions of the *Tao Te Ching*: (1.) *Lao-Tse: Le Tao Te King. Le Livre de la Voie et de la vertu.* (1842); (2.) *Lao-Tze's Tao-Teh-King. Chinese-English* (1898); (3.) *Lao-Tzu: Tao Teh King* (1922); and (4.) *Tao Te Ching: A new translation by Ch'u Ta-Kao* (1937). Jung also owned a copy of Wilhelm's *Lao-Tse und der Taoismus* (Wilhelm, 1925). For further reading on Jung and Taoism see Khong and Thompson (1997).

[298] *Upanishads*, from Sanskrit *sat* "to sit," prefixed with *upa* and *ni*, meaning "to sit down close to (one's teacher)," collection of more than two hundred Indian texts (though traditionally 108 are mentioned according to the holy Hindu number), the earliest dating back to the second millennium BCE. They were regarded as secret teachings that were orally rendered from teacher to student. The Upanishads can be seen as commentaries to and refinements of the teachings of the ancient four Vedas, hence they are also referred to as Vedanta (the end of the Veda). Jung's first written engagement with the Upanishads can be found in *Psychology of the Unconscious* (*Wandlungen und Symbole der Libido*) (1912), where he gives a psychological reading of passages from the Upanishads and the *Rig Veda* (Jung, 1912, §§ 243–45). On Jung and Indian thought, see Coward (1985), Shamdasani (1996), and Sengupta (2013).

tianity with which I am concerned directly and most directly in its most modern problematic that points toward something that is beyond all historical causality. Should there be a substantial difference from the Jews in this? The change and development in the dogma within the Catholic church (for example the emergence of the infallibility,[299] of the Sacred Heart cult,[300] etc.) appears to me to be a durable growth, as is the expulsion of Protestantism and its hundredfold splinter groups. Am I mistaken if it seems to me as if, for the Jews, it is a question of either a perpetuation of the ancient covenant with God or of a tearing up of roots?

What you say about the collectivity of the goal that excludes the individuation of the individual applies not only to the Jews but also to the *churches*. The church is an ideal substitute for the chosenness of the people and because spiritual, therefore universal, in contrast to the racial ties of the Jews "in the circumcision." Inasmuch as you regard individuation as a "universal" metaphysical task even for the Jews, you concur with my view, but you put yourself at odds with your historical determinedness. I do the same, however, but in line with my expositions above with less historical discrepancy, as I am "only" attached to the confession of an *idea*, but not historically to the "people within me." The "tribal" national bonds with their secluded character seem to me—quite separately from their historical-psychological significance[301]—to be a primitive relic, in comparison to the constantly evolving development in the Christian world of ideas, which only gives the impression of being still identical with the worldviews of early Christianity and which, in any case, was never a national bond, but was, from the very beginning, principally universal.

[299] The dogma of papal infallibility was defined at the First Vatican Council of 1869–70 under the leadership of Pope Pius IX.

[300] The devotion to the Sacred Heart of Christ goes back to medieval times, but is mainly associated with the visions of Saint Margaret Mary Alacoque (1647–1690). At the center of this devotion is the belief that the physical heart of Jesus Christ represents his divine love for mankind. In the encyclical letter *Annum Sacrum* Pope Leo XIII decreed the consecration of the entire human race to the Sacred Heart of Jesus for 11 June 1899. This consecration was then implemented by Pope Pius X as an annual practice. The high point of the Sacred Heart devotion came with encyclical letter *Miserentissimus Redemptor* (8 May 1928), in which Pius XI affirmed the truth of Saint Margaret Mary's vision of Christ and decreed that those devoted to the Heart of Jesus would be endowed with heavenly graces.

[301] Version A: "as an achievement of collective individuation."

Contemporary events in Germany are in a certain sense a counter-movement to the world-weariness of the German, which he certainly used to be quite proud of—not quite without good reason—, and, at the same time, it is a return to this same primitive relic, the tribal bond, which wishes to draw religion once again into its circle of influence. But this is taking place back to front: the Jewish racial bond was a result of the covenant with God, whereas the political racial bond would even like to nationalize God. The spiritual secularization of the Germans stood in contradiction to its actual national and physical bonds; therefore, sooner or later something had to happen to show him what's what. The Heavenly Father has long since known this and this is why it is completely superfluous to annex him to the German nation. The wheels of history cannot be reversed.

What you say about the "detachedness" of the Jews has my full agreement. This has always struck me about the Jews, their ability to recognize or intuitively to grasp values or possibilities and to promote them. A *forerunner* is always one step ahead. This Jewish characteristic is certainly a danger, but also an invaluable advantage that will grant the Jew his place in society time and again. Things do not go well for the forerunner if a people—or even humanity—must fall into the spokes of the all-too-quickly turning wheel of events because they might become too uprooted from the earth.

It in no way can be denied that Jewish cultural inheritance is absolutely interspersed everywhere. The prophetic nature of the Jewish spirit has dotted the "i" everywhere. Hellenism, with its infinite fullness of thought, would not have reached its peak without the Jewish contribution. It was even well on the way to drowning in its own waters, had it been deprived of the Jewish initiative.

The Jew can best be understood as a sourdough whose effect must not go too far. If the nations of the earth were to be so cut off from their history and their link with the soil by Jewish fermentation as has happened to the German, then a reaction sets in and then the entire nation does what every single individual should have done. This "should" is a trivial anthropomorphism, for "should" is incommensurate with a conception of history. The historical current of events is a succession of irrational facts, for which one invents, only retrospectively, a fitting causality through which one then believes one can prove that everything had to happen in this way. In this way, we can only determine that a tendency toward national "individuation" runs through the world, and that anti-Semitic moods arise from this—not only in Germany. Of course, I put individuation in quotation marks here, for "collective individuality" is a *contradictio in adjecto*. It would be better to say "individualization" which finds its clearest expression in Italy and Germany through the most dominant Führer figure that towers above [all else].

Now concerning the very great difficulty that you are wrestling with, I will attempt to let you briefly know my thoughts about it. Individuation is the opposite of any historical or ethnic conditionality inasmuch as this gives rise to collective bonds that outweigh the decisions of the Self. This conditionality is always the tragic given situation in which we are irredeemably immersed at first. But the "kingdom" is never "of this world." The "Self" is and remains a mysterious, otherworldly matter that insists on becoming visible with or against the conditionality or situation, to a certain individual and fatefully different degree. The evolving of the Self is the *secret* and absolute goal on the transpersonal level. We, the people, are its *object* (or, as medieval wisdom said very well: *philosophus non est magister lapidis, sed potius minister*[302]). However, where we are subjects, we can do nothing but use those means that are given to us. I.e., where we are only an "ego," we are also completely bound up in people and history. This is why "individuation" can never be realized by "egos" and their intentions. I participate only so much in the course of history as it appears to me to be insignificant and inasmuch as I believe that there are still others who are capable of a higher achievement of consciousness, namely, of the consciousness that events are an irrational current in which, through which, and against which the Self manifests in space and time. Whether we *wish* to erect a kingdom of God on earth or a heavenly realm after death seems to me to be only significant because, in this way, good intentions are announced—a

---

[302]"Et sic Philosophus non est Magister lapidis, sed potius minister" ("And so the philosopher is not the master of the *lapis*, but rather the servant") (*Rosarium philosophorum*, p. 356). Jung quotes the line in his 1935 Eranos lecture "Dream Symbols of the Individuation Process" (Jung, 1936a, German: p. 57; English: p. 136). He reworked the material for *Psychology and Alchemy* (Jung, 1944, § 142). The quote appears again in "Die Psychologie der Übertragung" (Jung, 1945, §531).

human decency that one cannot get around without damage. We have to do something after all, for only in our strongest action does the Self appear.

Yes—to the lazy, one may not betray the secret and equally as little to the evil-minded and the well-intentioned idiots. One of the old masters says very correctly that if God reveals a secret to you, He also gives the grace of proper discretion.[303]

Hopefully I have succeeded in conveying my views to you to some degree. The theme is so difficult that no small doubts grip me about my inability to make such a dark matter somewhat clear. We circum-ambulate a meaningful center in bows and spirals, and must not be afraid to swim into the depths.

I certainly haven't replied to everything. I am too often thwarted in my writing. But I hope you will make me aware of my omissions in your reply.

Your always faithful,
C. G. Jung[304]

---

[303] Version B has the handwritten addendum: "gloria dei est celare verbum" (Proverbs 25:2 [Vulgate]: "gloria Dei celare verbum"; "It is the glory of God to conceal a matter" [KJB]).

[304] Version B includes a handwritten annotation: "I will report later on your very interesting work."

16 N

27. VI. [1935]

Dear Professor,

I am very much indebted to you as I have not yet thanked you for your long and exceedingly important letter and for sending me your work on archetypes.[305] A letter from me has crossed with yours and I hope to be able to make a suitable response but my busyness, along with the heat, has prevented me from getting down to it. Even today I am only sending a brief note, nothing more. I am now in the early stages of a work on Hasidism[306] that I want to work much into so that there is not much "power" left over at the moment, and besides, much has to be "taken forward" before one can talk about it.

I have finished my course for the summer; my "effectiveness" is limited to a strongly growing practice and private work. I will only go on the offensive gradually with analytical psychology here, at the moment I have to keep quiet anyway as the Kirsch matter unfortunately created much resistance to analytical psychology and strengthened the status quo. That the Freudians are having a field day would not be so bad, but it is embarrassing that even qualified people have become more than suspect. The most embarrassing thing is that one can say so little against them. I am extremely sorry not to be able to discuss with you thoroughly the question of the analysis of analysts, this is my biggest interest, practically and theoretically. There is a lot to be said for the methods of the Freudian school with its training and supervisory analyses although I know that this is more difficult in the case of analytical psychology with its fundamental emphasis on the being of the analyst. Please do not misunderstand me, every analyst makes mistakes and I notice every day how much more difficult, responsible, and important every analysis is, especially here in

---

[305] Jung (1935).
[306] Neumann (1934–40), see n. 273.

Palestine. I now have a certain insight into Kirsch's work and I am quite speechless. (About half a dozen patients of his are now with me, those that terminated and others.)

Could he not be helped by an analysis? Please be so good as to tell me, as far as it is possible for you, whether my impression is false. He has not learned enough from an analytical psychological perspective, it seems to me. The fact that he has not understood the types is only bad in the way he applies them and persuades a reality-shy intuitive that he is a sensation type, for example. (I am fully aware of the unreliability of patients' testimonies. Only consensus makes me more sure.) The worst thing, aside from inflation and curiosity, seems to me to be his lack of psychological sensitivity that amazes me because he is actually quite a warm human being. Personally his cluelessness around the "religious problem" affects me the most. Perhaps he is extraverted and it comes from that. He "goes on" constantly about a "religious problem" and convinces people they have one and thus he scares them off their center. Precisely for Palestine this is a disaster because, for the Jews, the central problem is the religious one. It is possessed by the strongest resistance. K. can really frighten one off this.

If I am now posing some questions, then the response to them is completely clear, thanks to you, but even so I would like this confirmation, since after all Kirsch is your pupil, and, if you listen to him and his wife, your star pupil.

I refuse to impose the religious problem on someone, but I see it as the main purpose of analysis in many cases, that it becomes evident as the center, "of its own accord," i.e., within the experience of the analysis—which corresponds to the structure of the unconscious, it seems to me. One should not speak much of religion in front of people here, or generally people of our time, but should allow them to have an experience of it. One may only speak about so-called theological problems, i.e., you have to use thinking.

I do not interpret dreams by lumping them all together, lock, stock and barrel, using it as an opportunity to voice *my* associations, but rather as you set about it in the seminars[307]—by establishing the context, very precisely, very much using a reductive method in the case of

---

[307] Neumann might be referring to Jung's English seminar on Nietzsche's Zarathustra (Jung, 1934–39). See 14 N, n. 269.

the personal unconscious, i.e., rather reductive within the context of a constructive methodology. Where it falters, I risk "oiling" things very cautiously with my own associations with constant readiness to revise. It is different in the case of collective dreams and symbols if the personal material is exhausted; here I bring the collective material and its meaning into the picture. Dr. Adler told me once that you were abandoning the use of association more and more, that was the case in my own analysis too, but I do not think it is right to generalize about methodology, but rather adhere to your view in the Seminars.

Kirsch once spoke of "reading dreams," not to me by the way. I do not do this, I work at them, I can only—rarely—read very collective dreams. In my work with you[308]—and this was my particular case—it depended, I believe, not on the personal unconscious but, as you also said, on the breaking open of the perspective onto the Self and the collective unconscious, and this consequently thrust me simultaneously into the world and out of myself. With Miss Wolff, the personal unconscious came more into its own, in both good and bad aspects. If you work in this way in an individual case and perhaps are more interested in so doing (seminars),—due to the central position held in your work and life by the discovery of the collective unconscious—firstly because others can do the other thing, secondly because these problems come to you and are supposed to come to you, this does not, to me, justify turning this into a methodology. Of course, the scientific problem is situated here, which is by no means always the case in the personal material of the patient.* [Annotated with: * as far as it is ascertainable to him] It seems wrong to me to "talk" someone with a sexual problem into a religious problem, the religious problem and the patient just don't need this. (It is also of no use by the way; I tried it often in my early beginnings.) Despite this, the religious problem can be structurally central and the sexual problem secondary, but this must slowly become evident to the patient from the inside through the analysis of dreams, not because he hears it out of my mouth. Only the Self must speak in this language, I must, I fear, be unassuming.

---

[308] For details on Neumann's time in Zurich and his therapeutical work with Jung in 1933–34, see introduction, pp. xiii–xiv.

I hope, dear Professor, that it will be clear to you that the Kirsch case is important to me not for his sake, but

1. For my sake, as there are contradictions in the way of working, yet both identify as: Jung's pupils
2. For the sake of analytical psychology—another way of saying for my sake, as this is now the medium of my life
3. For the sake of the Jews—so once again for my sake, as you know perhaps more than anyone, that they are the opposition to my life

For these three big "for my sakes," I request a response. K. is only secondary in this. Things are going well for me. My wife and son also. There is much work.

With best wishes,
Ever yours,
E. Neumann

17 N

29. X. 35

Dear Professor,

If I am sending you this brief note from me after a long gap, I am doing this with mixed feelings. I have the need to reestablish contact with you with these few lines, but a certain embarrassment befalls me all the same. If I was not able to write to you on the occasion of your 60th birthday, this was certainly not only a tendency to do my own thing, but more the attempt to hide the empty hands I would have had to come with. An excessive but perhaps understandable ambition makes it difficult for me always only to take, but I am now ready to be able to say to you without bitterness that I must wait, and that even the date of your birthday has not been able to speed up my internal process. I would have gladly laid before you some small piece of work as a private continuation of what the volume "Complex Psychology"[309] broadly intended and achieved, but I did not succeed. My isolated work here makes the slow but not interminable rhythm of my life more audible to me, so you must, please, not lose patience with me as I will also not do. The practice and my daily life require their dues, which I pay them, but it is not that, but the work on the Jewish material that is slow and difficult. Gropingly I feel for contours, difficult because I am myself only gradually starting to grasp where analytical psychology cannot fully be the ground on which I stand. That does not mean that I am not standing on the ground of analytical psychology, more than ever I believe I sense its central significance for me. What is self-evident is becoming clearer to me—that analytical psychology itself has a foundation that is in part so self-evident that it can only become conscious of itself in part. Switzerland—Germany, the West, Christianity. Not a discovery, and

---

[309] *Die kulturelle Bedeutung der komplexen Psychologie* was a festschrift for Jung's sixtieth birthday published by the Psychologischer Club Zurich (1935).

yet it is one after all. I must learn to distinguish. It is difficult when so much weight lies on the other side, it is certainly easier to do as "your Jews" do and to assimilate, such as Westmann,[310] Kirsch, but this would only mean avoiding one's own individuation that must be achieved, despite everything, on the collective-archetypally different foundation. The understandable (to me) anti-Jewish thrust of the entire West, from Marcion to Harnack,[311] from theology to psychology, has the effect on instinctless Jews—and many Jews are instinctless, as you know,—of a Jewish self-poisoning process that was always characteristic of the tendency of the Jews to avoid the bitter path of individuation through the path of being a parasite. Analytical psychology, not yet fully realized, also holds this danger—that of the betrayal of one's own foundation in favor of a "nicer," "more advanced" and "more modern" one. Such ignorance is lent support, it seems to me, in a certain sense by the historical-natural disinterestedness of analytical psychology in the individual, which represents, from the Christian point of view, a superseded primitive stage. It stands to reason that one would charge with utmost haste out of this primitive stage into the "up-to-date" point of view of the individual of the Christian West, a psychological correspondence with baptism. Westmann's glorification of the golden calf against evil Y.H.W.H. follows this trend, regression instead of individuation. You have not

---

[310] Heinz Westmann (also Westman) (1902–1986): Jungian analyst from Berlin. Left Germany for Switzerland in 1935. Westmann participated in the Eranos meeting 1936 speaking on "Die Erlösungsidee im Judentum" (Westmann, 1936). Due to political reasons his presentation (together with Paul Tillich's) were not included in the original publication. In 1937 he came to England, where he cofounded the Society of Analytical Psychology. He moved to the United States in 1955. His main publications include *The Springs of Creativity* (1961) and *The Structure of Biblical Myths: The Ontogenesis of the Psyche* (1984). On Westmann see Reis and Harrod (1987).

[311] Marcion of Sinope (ca. 85–160), founder of a Christian movement, which led to a schism of the church in the year 144 CE. Subsequently, his teachings were declared as heretical and Marcion was excommunicated. In the center of Marcionism stands the belief that the God of the Old Testament, the demiurge, was the creator of the material world and its evils. According to Marcion, this Jewish God is not identical with the Christian God of the Gospels who—in his love and compassion for humankind—sacrificed his son Jesus to absolve humanity of its sins. Marcion's teachings were often said to be close to the Gnostic belief system. Karl Gustav Adolf von Harnack (1851–1930): German Lutheran theologian and church historian, best known for the *History of Dogma* (*Lehrbuch der Dogmengeschichte*, 1886–90), published a monograph on Marcion in 1921, titled *Marcion: Das Evangelium vom fremden Gott* (*Marcion: The Gospel of the Alien God*), followed by *Neuen Studien zu Marcion* (*New Studies on Marcion*) in 1923. On Harnack and Marcion, see Kinzig (2004) and Williams (1994).

worked through the whole of Christianity in vain—I still think that Judaism is missing. Elijah proves it to me—no Jew came out of the collective being of the Jew without a struggle, one cannot get out, one must go through. The final problem in Judaism cannot be affected, it seems to me, and not theorized. I for one must realize it in a Jewish reality, as filthy and as beautiful as it is and will be. A theoretical occupation of the earth is really Jewish, intellectual with goodwill. I am beginning to understand what it means that you said to me that I needed to get into the collective, begin to understand, what, in my "myth," is known as the valley of the buried, which perhaps for the zodiac level 1º (I am 0º) is: "Such a life may be closely bound with the life of the people among whom he lives and works so that it gets lost for a while."

The way in which your being Swiss, Christian, and a Western man is self-evident differentiates you centrally, and not only you, from the way in which it is not self-evident that Jews are Jews. Do you, in fact, underestimate the significance of this point in the analysis of Jews? You did express to me once your abhorrence toward this phenomenon of self-betrayal but I have not noticed anywhere that you have tangibly nailed it down. Please do not misunderstand this to be impudence; as a question it is important to me. I don't know if you are familiar with Westmann's lecture,[312] which, by the way is, in many ways very interesting, but it makes *me* howl with pity. Clueless in things Jewish—not once is the fundamental problem of Gentileism-Judaism "hinted at"—but ready with shameless self-abandonment to "sacrifice the collective bond" which is, after all, a symptom of individuation. The likes of him now puts himself forward as a Jewish representative but this is a "convert" in the simple sense of the word. As has become clearly evident to me though, individuation does not belong to the category of confession but to that of growth. Of course I knew this and everyone "knows" it, but the elemental fact of Jewish soil equating to Jewish reality is only just dawning on me. It belongs to the "becoming dissimilar to God" of your last letter. Every attempt to evade the bitter reality of land profiteering and Arab issues, mili-

---

[312] It is not quite clear to which lecture Neumann refers here. But in his Eranos lecture of the following year, "Die Erlösungsidee im Judentum" (Westmann, 1936) Westmann's arguments are not so different from those of Neumann.

tary service problems and individuation is fruitless. Even you would like to "make use of" the ideology of the Jews being leaven for the European culture. They are indeed quite serviceable in this way, but there remain protected Jews in the psychological sense, without foundation, i.e., without the possibility of individuation. The relationship of the Jews to the "earth" is, in a fundamental way, the same as for the Gentiles and Christians on a Gentile basis, but this problem can be resolved neither by a simple return to the soil (political Zionism) nor by only a psychical return to the soil (the Galut Jew with analytical psychology). Both of these must be achieved together. The environment of the Jew in Europe is the collective unconscious of the non-Jews, and with this, his individuation is impossible. Only among Jews was it and is it possible, for only there does he encounter his archetypal foundation in the world and only in collision with this, can he—at best—achieve individuation. All these problems keep me occupied and will not allow me respite from this incessant work. So, I am well. I only wish to write this to you one more time. It would make me very happy to hear something from you.

With best wishes,
Your grateful,
E. Neumann.

18 J

Prof. C. G. Jung

KÜSNACHT, ZURICH,
SEESTRASSE 228

22. XII. 1935

My dear Neumann,

Do not allow yourself to go gray over missing my 60th birthday. The abstract number 60[313] means nothing at all to me. I much prefer to know, through hearing from you, what you are doing. What the European Jews are doing I already know, but what the Jews are doing on archetypal soil—that interests me extraordinarily. Analytical Psychology (or as it is now called: Complex Psychology) is deeply rooted in Europe, in the Christian Middle Ages and, in the last analysis, in Greek philosophy. The connecting link that eluded me for so long has now been found, it is alchemy, as Silberer[314] already correctly suspected. Sadly he broke his neck on rational psychologism.

---

[313] This letter was—an abridged version—included in Aniela Jaffé's edition of Jung's letters (Jung, 1973, vol. 1, pp. 265–66). Jaffé misread the number "60" for "so."

[314] Herbert Silberer (1882–1923): Austrian psychotherapist, member of the Freud circle from 1907 onward. Freud writes to Jung on 19 July 1909: "Silberer is an unknown young man, probably a better-class degenerate; his father is a well-known figure in Vienna, a member of the city council and an 'operator'" (Jung and Freud, 1974, p. 242). Silberer published his main study, *Problems of Mysticism and Its Symbolism (Probleme der Mystik und ihre Symbolik)*, in 1914. His categorization of dreams into psychoanalytic and anagogic was rejected by Freud and led to an alienation of the two men. Silberer committed suicide in January 1923. Jung, in contrast to Freud, emphasized the importance of the book as the first psychological interpretation of alchemy: "Herbert Silberer has the merit of being the first to discover the secret threads that lead from alchemy to the psychology of the unconscious" (Jung, 1955–56, § 792), In his Tel Aviv seminar on alchemy in 1941/42 Neumann said about Silberer: "Silberer not only discovered alchemy but also the essential concepts of the psychological principles which have been developed in analytical psychology—archetypes are infinitely many things. On the one hand, he interpreted the *Parabola* analytically according to the old analytical school, on the other hand, anagogically, synthetically. His problem was: how can the same thing be interpreted psychoanalytically and anagogically? He interpreted the entire *Parabola* psychoanalytically (Oedipus, Incest, Castration) but then managed to interpret every symbol both analytically and anagogically." (Neumann, 1941–42, p. 66).

I saw G. Adler recently. He's going to England, which he regards as the intermediate station on the way to Palestine.

The "Culture Jews" are always en route to being "non-Jews"; you are completely right, the route does not go from the good to the better, but first downhill to historical actuality. I routinely draw the attention of most of my Jewish patients to the fact that they are self-evidently Jews. I would not do this if I had not so frequently seen Jews who imagined that they were something else. To such as these "being Jewish" is a form of personal insult.

I have heard of Westmann's essay but have not yet read it. I'm told it is *very good*. Your disparaging assessment is valuable to me as is your very positive conviction that the Palestinian soil is essential to Jewish individuation. How does the fact that the Jew in general has lived in other countries than in Palestine for *much longer* relate to this? Even Moses Maimonides[315] preferred Cairo (Fostat) even though he had the possibility of living in Jerusalem.

Is it then that the Jew is so accustomed to being a non-Jew that he requires the Palestinian soil *in concreto* in order to be reminded of his being Jewish? I find it hard to comprehend a soul that has grown up in no soil.

With sincere wishes for your ongoing well-being,
Your always loyal,
C. G. Jung

---

[315] Moses Maimonides (also Rabbi Mosheh ben Maimon) (ca. 1135–1204): Important Jewish philosopher, theologian, legal scholar, and physician; born in Córdoba as part of the Almoravid Empire, Maimonides had to leave the Iberian Peninsula when the Almohad dynasty took over and put pressure on Jews to convert to Islam. He finally settled down in Fostat (today a part of Cairo). He is renowned for compiling the fourteen books of the *Mishneh Torah* ("Repetition of the Torah"), subtitled *Sefer Yad HaHazaka* ("Book of the Strong Hand"), which is a code of Jewish religious law (Halakha).

30. Jan. 36

Most dear Professor Jung,

I thank you very much for your letter that has shown me once again that you continue to have patience with me and once again have engaged with my problems that I know could not be your own.

I do not even believe that Palestinian soil is so important for the Jew but it will become so if ever this soil absorbs sufficient human beings to be a true ancestral soil once again. Certainly the Jews have lived much longer in other countries but without the contact to the soil that was not accessible to them due to their being rooted in the Torah. Now that this foundation of the law is fractured, and I see in Hasidism the revolution of this fracturing, we must come to a new beginning via a regression to the soil, if at all. Only now that the 2000-year-old law in its role as an artificial psychospiritual root soil is broken, is Palestine starting to become relevant and the history of the spiritual productive time is fused with this. Both Maimonides and Philo[316] are in fact assimilated Jews—but they could afford to be—because the root soil of the law made them independent of mere natural national limitations to which we had to return after the emancipation, while consciously repudiating our sole cosmopolitan supranational stance.

I do not wish to write any more about these matters as things have taken a strong and radical turn for me, which has forced me back into my own problems. Nothing has happened in the external world,

[316] Philo Judaeus, also known as Philo of Alexandria (15–10 BCE–40–45 CE): Hellenistic Jewish philosopher, born in Alexandria. Philo brings together Greek philosophical thinking such as Platonism, Aristotelianism, Cynicism, and Stoicism with the Jewish exegesis of the bible. As he combines religious revelation and philosophical reason he has also been seen as a forerunner of Christian theology.

my position on Palestine and on the Jewish problem has remained the same, but this has been put aside because I first need to make some progress myself. My analytical work is making great demands of me, problems are mounting up that I am grappling with without resolving them, and it is becoming evident to me more often that I urgently need to do some more work with you and Miss Wolff. The two years of independently accountable work, completely alone, establishing a practice, actually my very first one, an evident transformation that has been set in motion here, all these things together justify me in my desire to go to Zurich, without needing to reproach myself that I am out of touch with reality. I would very much like to know if it would be possible for you to give me some time, and when this might be. I would have to bring things to a close here for two months, perhaps May/June, or if absolutely necessary in the autumn— ever in the hope that you could arrange it and I ask you to bear in mind that it will and must certainly be as crucial for me as the time was back then. My late resolve will be especially comprehensible to you because of my introverted hesitation when I confess to you that, from a practical perspective that I discipline myself to achieve, this Europe trip must seem rather audacious, if not crazy. The economic situation here is extremely uncertain, my family and my wife's have partially been blown apart, despite this I have the feeling it is the right thing to do. My wife would urgently like to work with Miss Wolff and I consider this also to be crucially important, after that it must be decided whether she will work more in this direction. In short, I believe I have presented the situation to you as it is and would like to now leave it up to you whether you will be able to take this into account. I will sadly not be able to allocate more than 6 weeks to my visit, but I think I could achieve a decent amount of work even in this time. When I was with you back then, you said to me "Widen your horizons!" To a certain degree I think this has happened. I would have to contradict you today if you said to me that, for me, it was all about the Jewish problem, it is beginning to be about me, the Jewish aspect is the obvious location of my debate. Europe, Asia, Primitives, there the Jewish part is a small point, albeit an important one for me, and, as I still believe, also one of general importance, but:

"Before the end, Rabbi Sussja spoke: 'In the coming world I will not have to answer for the fact that I was not Moses; I must answer for the fact that I have not been Sussja.'"[317]

With gratitude,
Your E. Neumann

I would be very grateful to you, dear Professor, if you could let me have your reply quite quickly since I must naturally organize everything here well in advance.

Even if I am vacillating, I still have the feeling that I should act in this way, precisely the "actual" risky thing about this seems to me to be absolutely important. By the way—there are other risks—possible aspects that probably lie dormant in the background.

---

[317] Neumann quotes from Buber's *Die chassidischen Bücher* (Buber, 1927, p. 446). In *Die Erzählungen der Chassidim* (*Tales of the Hasidim*) from 1949 Buber tells this tale of Rabbi Sussja's in a slightly different way: "In the coming world, they will not ask me: 'Why were you not Moses?' They will ask me: 'Why were you not Zusya?'" (Buber, 1949, p. 251). Neumann also quotes the story in his unpublished volume on Hasidism (Neumann, 1934–40, vol. 2, p. 17).

10. III. 36

Dear Professor,

Since I do not know whether a letter from me to you or one from you to me has gone astray, I would like to briefly ask the following. I wrote to you some time ago that my internal situation was compelling me to work with you again and I requested you to let me know if this would be possible now, i.e., in May/June, or in the autumn. Unfortunately I have had no word from you as yet, but the necessity of going to Zurich has proved unshakeably firm. I would ask you to please reply to me as soon as possible. All economic considerations that I discussed in my letter are still important but they have become absolutely secondary as I have reached a point in my development from which I cannot make decent progress on my own, it seems to me.

I am extremely grateful to you for sending me your work from the Eranos conference.[318] This work seems to me to be unique in its evidence, significance, and simplicity.

I have become rather unsettled due to the lack of response to my letter, so I do ask you not to forget me.

In a curious way—quite in the spirit of your inquiry into the collective symbolism of the Jews—some material has emerged in the meantime that I would desperately like to discuss with you, along with countless other things. In the foreground, though, remain my

---

[318] The Eranos Yearbook 1935 was dedicated to *Westöstliche Seelenführung*. Jung's contribution was titled "Traumsymbole des Individuationsprozesses: Ein Beitrag zur Kenntnis der in den Träumen sich kundgebenden Vorgängen des Unbewussten" ("Dream Symbols of the Process of Individuation") (Jung, 1936a); the extended version is known as "Individual Dream Symbolism in Relation to Alchemy" and was later published as part of *Psychology and Alchemy* (Jung, 1944).

own difficulties, the absolute necessity of making a shift from "knowing" to "being," a path for which I very much need your help.

With gratitude,
Your E. Neumann
10. III

PROF. DR. C. G. JUNG　　　　**KÜSNACHT, ZURICH**
SEESTRASSE 228

21 March 1936

Dr. E. Neumann,
1 Gordon St.,
Tel Aviv,
Palästina.

My dear Neumann,

I am sorry that I have not replied to your letter for so long. My time in May and June is unfortunately a very uncertain matter. In reality I am fully occupied. If you do the majority of your work with Miss Wolff and can put up with being squeezed in with me here and there, you can come in May. I would not recommend the autumn as my work will start late due to preceding lectures in America and England.[319] I intend to largely stop my work with patients in the winter anyway in order to get further with some work that has become urgent. As a result of my lectures at the E.T.H.[320] my available time has

---

[319] In autumn 1936, Jung was invited by Harvard University to lecture on the occasion of its tercentenary celebrations, where he was awarded an honorary degree. He left Zurich together with Emma in August 1936 and arrived by steamliner in New York in early September. Jung's Harvard lecture was titled "Psychological Factors Determining Human Behavior" (Jung, 1937a). Jung left Harvard for Bailey Island, Maine, to deliver a seminar on dream analysis. On 3 October he embarked on a ship for England, where he lectured at the St. Bartholomew Hospital London on 19 October. The title of his presentation was "The Concept of the Collective Unconscious" (Jung, 1936–37).

[320] From the winter semester 1933 on, Jung lectured on a weekly basis at the ETH Zurich (Swiss Federal Institute of Technology). With the exception of the semesters 1936/37 and 1937/38 he held his lectures until 1941. Topics ranged from History of Psychology, Dream Psychology, Typology, Eastern and Western Spiritualism, to the Psychology of Alchemy. During his first stay in Zurich in 1933–34 Neumann visited Jung's lectures (see also n. 258). (The lectures are being prepared for publication by Ernst Falzeder and Martin Liebscher as part of the Philemon series.)

been whittled away even more, while even more people wish to come to see me. Furthermore I'm not getting any younger, rather older.

But I believe I understand the compelling nature of your problem and will do my utmost not to let you down.

In the meantime, with best wishes,
Your always devoted,
C. G. Jung

22 N

Dr. Erich Neumann,
Analytical Psychologist,
Tel Aviv

20. I. 37

Dear Professor Jung,

In contrast to my overlong early letters I have now intentionally become very taciturn as I do not wish to detract from your very valuable work and rest times.

Today I would like only to send you a short greeting to maintain the feeling that I have not lost the contact with you. The time in Zurich was eminently fruitful, the development initiated then is ongoing, even if it has been pushed into the background by a strong—i.e., therefore welcome—professional demand. This development, together with the work for my course: Soul problems of the modern Jew,[321] stand at the center for me and the work on the book on which you have already given a mortgage is resting externally at the moment, precisely because internally it has entered a new phase that I would like to wait upon.

As you will be able to imagine, I had a mountain of inquiries, but I will not bother you with them but simply wait until the answers have formed themselves for myself.

---

[321] In 1937–38 and 1938–39 Neumann held a weekly seminar series in Tel Aviv titled "Soul Problems of the Modern Jew: An Analysis of a Series of Dreams, Images, and Phantasies" ("Seelenproblem des modernen Juden: Eine Reihenanalyse von Träumen, Bildern und Phantasien") in which he discussed a series of dreams of a Jewish woman in the first half of her life. Asked on 19 January 1939 why the Jewish theme does not feature more prominently, Neumann reflected on the seminar series: "Besides, something has become clear that was not fully known to me, that the Jewish problem is so deeply integrated into the collective problem that one can not treat them separately. Two years ago we started with the problems of the Jew and have now provided evidence for them with individual material" (Neumann 1938–39, p. 152).

Things are fairly good with us. The situation is however quite dark. Where is light today.

As I have heard, you have retreated somewhat in the service of a larger work, I would be grateful to you if you could let me know if it is the work on symbols you once mentioned or something else. You can hardly believe how important such anticipation is for me, as I know that every one of your works has revealed something crucial to me in one or more regards.

In wishing you and also us a good year and successful endeavors, I am your ever grateful,

E. Neumann
Tel Aviv,
1 Gordon St.,
Palestine
20. I.

23 J

PROF. DR. C. G. JUNG　　　　　　**KÜSNACHT, ZURICH,**
SEESTRASSE 228

25th January 1937

Dr. Erich Neumann,
1 Gordon St.,
Tel Aviv

Dear Colleague,

I am pleased to hear that you are well and that you are busy.

The work that all conceivable external demands seek to keep me from refers to a far-reaching representation of the individuation process.[322] This is at least a reasonably accurate description, although I don't yet have a title.

I wish you likewise a good new year and hope that your activities will be even more fruitful than in the old one.

With best wishes,
Your always loyal,
C. G. Jung

---

[322] Jung was probably reworking his Eranos lectures from 1935 and 1936 (see n. 323), which would eventually form the base of *Psychology and Alchemy* (Jung, 1944).

Dr. Erich Neumann,
Analytical Psychologist

Tel Aviv, 23. VII. [1937]

Dear Professor,

I do not want to let the occasion of your birthday pass—especially as you have not heard from me for so long, without sending you a brief note with my good wishes testifying to my lasting and ever growing bond with you.

(I have selected the strange and unfamiliar typed script for "social" reasons, albeit with a heavy heart, so as not to torment you with my handwriting.)

I particularly wish to thank you for sending me your works, from which the lectures on alchemy,[323] especially, have given me a great deal. Mind you, they do not seem easy to me even after a second reading, probably because here, even more than in your other works, the background of the meanings and the underlying material is so unfamiliar that one must make do at times with interposing the little of one's own experience into these huge contexts and allowing it to be stimulated by them.

I am very much in your debt for not even having delivered the beginnings of the much-vaunted Hasidism work[324] to you as yet. In this letter I do not wish to simply justify myself, but to attempt to give a broad outline of my whole situation so that this "failure," as I

---

[323] Jung's Eranos lectures in 1935 and 1936 were dedicated to the topic of psychology and alchemy: "Traumsymbole des Individuationsprozesses: Ein Beitrag zur Kenntnis der in den Träumen sich kundgebenden Vorgängen des Unbewussten" ("Dream Symbols of the Process of Individuation") (1936a); "Die Erlösungsvorstellungen in der Alchemie" ("Religious Ideas in Alchemy: An Historical Survey of Religious Ideas") (Jung, 1937).

[324] Cf. Neumann's letter to Jung, 27 June [1935] (16 N). On Neumann's work on Hasidism (Neumann, 1934–40), see n. 273.

saw it for a long time, is accorded its due significance. My practice quickly became much more lively after my return from Zurich, i.e., I have constantly had an extraordinary amount to do, and that is saying a lot for local standards. As I was also teaching two private courses in the winter, and I had much work to do on the advanced "Soul Problems of the Modern Jew"[325]—quite apart from private and business matters—I was hugely stretched and had no possibility of doing any further work alongside.

However, something else has been decisive in this. Perhaps you will recall that when I was in Zurich a "rush" of archetypal material broke through in me, both images and voices. This development has continued and, alongside my professional work, has taken priority in this last year. I cannot put into words what this development has given me in every regard, and continues to do so, but without an external reference point, this work has its dangers, despite the assistance of my wife. A big difficulty is my skepticism about what is being so well represented from my internal world, but the relentless criticism on other occasions has reassured me on this score. Besides, the flow of images is so absolutely surprising and initially incomprehensible to me that I am now convinced of the authenticity of the phenomena. I am obviously expressing this in far too restrained a manner, as I am shattered by the superiority and unambiguity of the trajectory of the images up to the Zurich trip that have well and truly revealed themselves to me and whose object-subject I was.

At the moment I am standing, it seems, at a place of waiting, but have the certain feeling of being on the move. This is confirmed to me by my great internal equanimity and decreasing desolation. This may sound overly positive, but it would be ungrateful not to admit to the lighter colors, the appearance of something firm, new. The experience is also very present to me that much that is already in the picture is only being actualized very slowly.

All of this creates an isolation that is only barely compensated for by work. Apart from my wife, who is going through something similar in her own way, no one here understands anything of these things, and it is precisely Palestine, as it faces threats on a daily basis,

---

[325] See n. 321.

and the unrest of Jews who are stirred up both internally and externally, which stands in a peculiarly stark contrast to my internal world whose horizon is, for me, no longer Jewish in the self-evident way it once was. Without succumbing to the danger of an internal syncretism of all external certainty of perspective, it seems to be all the more difficult as the more the internal world emerges, the more the most private matters show themselves to be bound up with universal human symbolism. On the other hand, I feel myself fully recompensed by this often-overwhelming sense of connection. The contrast of my situation with the concreteness of historical and contemporary Judaism is grotesque. More grotesque than you could ever imagine, since the rootlessness and spiritual mania of the Jewish people is experiencing a dangerous upsurge here in what is, for us, an eminently significant historic moment. So, precisely in my remoteness I seem to be in the right place, and the often-pressing smallness of the causal world is counterbalanced by its bigger permeability, by the bigger significance of the individual. Beside this, we live very close to the sea, have it constantly before us, and what this and the landscape means for me as a metropolitan Jew, cannot, I believe, be fully comprehended by you.

The end spirit—earth spirit problem stood in the center of what I have experienced and of my spiritual work. End spirit—Asmodeus;[326] earth spirit, a contrasting principle that arises from below. Transformation of the anima, the red one; the earth spirit with the diamond in the breast; earth spirit arising, pregnant, blue, candle-holding anima in an arc between the trees and an angel air-like being coming from above.[327] Then came—and I could do nothing to stop it—something

[326] Asmodeus, also Asmodai (Hebrew: Ashmedai), from the Avestan language *aēšma-daēva, aēšma meaning "wrath" and daēva "demon": in the deuterocanonical Book of Tobit an evil spirit, that killed the first seven husbands of Sara, "before they had lain with her" [Tob. 3.8]. In the Talmudic story of the Testament of Solomon the demon is tricked in helping to construct the Temple in Jerusalem (Testament of Solomon, 21–25). According to some kabbalistic schools he is a succubus that mated with King David and bore a cambion (half-human, half-demon) son. Asmodeus is generally regarded as the demon of lust and is, according to Christian belief, one of the kings of hell.

[327] As suggested earlier (see 8 N, n. 230) Neumann sent copies of his Jung letters to Toni Wolff. Regarding the passage above she replied to him on 30 December 1937: "What you say about Asmodeus interested me very much. This is a very good point of view and allows conclusions to be drawn about the strongly eschatological attitude of the Jewish spirit, from which

like an altar image. Mary (?) on the bed holding Jesus (?) in a golden moon bowl holding the diamond up high. To the left, in a beautiful southern landscape is the satyr-like but quite human-formed earth spirit with a bunch of grapes, to the right a type of John of Patmos[328] with a bowl of fire, lightning, apocalyptic. This is just an allusion; I do not know whether this is familiar symbolism for you, I write it because I assume so. I do not understand everything by any means, but it is exceptionally rich, and forms, together with the relevant conversations, substantial material for my thought.

In this way, Hasidism has retreated, but I must simply learn more patience and subordinate my will and ambition.

In the work, my greatest challenge is this, that I find it very difficult to reconcile the experience that things come to people when they are ready with my work, which has to stimulate or accelerate this process that is independent from me. I sometimes feel like a superfluous fool. For sure, success and my work can be linked in a certain way, but must it be so? Perhaps one has success with those who are ready and failure with the others? A comment from you about this would be very necessary and important for me.

Dream from a patient, apart from the neurotic things, menstrual disturbances treated successfully with hormones: "She sees lots of small worms through a microscope. A doctor tells her: that is your illness. She sees the worms are bloated full of red blood." Nothing is found organically, the dream stands out in a series on another theme. What should one pay attention to?

Hopefully, dear Professor, you will excuse the scope of this letter that is only about me, but, as I do not write very often so as not to burden you too much, you must forgive my expansiveness. I hope the winter break has done you good and refreshed you somewhat,

---

it may then follow that 'materialism' is more a consequence, a type of attempt at compensation" (Wolff and Neumann, 1934–52).

[328] John of Patmos, author of the book of Revelation, lived on the Greek island of Patmos where he was seized by the apocalyptic vision, which informed the book of Revelation. Traditionally he is identified with John the Apostle, the author of the Gospel of John, as well as the first, second, and third epistles of John. Many modern scholars do not support this theory and regard John of Patmos as a separate author. In the book of Revelation 9:11 Abaddon (Greek: Apollyon), the angel of the abyss, is the leader of an army of locusts that torment those without the sign of God on their forehead. Some commentators identify Abaddon with Asmodeus (see n. 326).

and that things are well with you so far. Did the Zarat. seminar continue or have you used the time for the book? What is your theme for the Eranos conference?

For this year, my wish for you is only that you will get back a fraction of what you give to others, and that not too much will come back to you in the sense that a Zaddiki once spoke of: Every word one speaks which finds no home among the people returns to the speaker and he sometimes feels the powerful force of its return.

I wish you all good wishes and a robust recovery.

Your ever grateful,
Erich Neumann,

Tel Aviv,
1, Gordon Street,
Palestine.

Zurich, 27th September 1937

Dr. Erich Neumann,
1 Gordon Street,
Tel Aviv

Dear Doctor,

Prior to his departure for Berlin (Copenhagen–New York),[329] Professor Jung asked me to thank you for your kind letter. He asks you to excuse the fact that he has not replied to you as his "holidays" were so burdened with work that he was not able to reply to all correspondence.

With best wishes,
Yours truly,
[Marie-Jeanne Schmid][330]

---

[329] Jung was invited to Yale University in October 1937 to deliver the fifteenth series of "Lectures on Religion in the Light of Science and Philosophy" under the auspices of the Dwight Harrington Terry Foundation. The lecture series was published under the title "Psychology and Religion" (Jung, 1938a).

[330] Marie-Jeanne Schmid (later Boller-Schmid) (1911–1984): Jung's secretary from 1932 until her marriage in 1952. She was the daughter of Jung's friend and colleague Hans Schmid-Guisan (1881–1932, see Jung and Schmid-Guisan), who unexpectedly died in 1932 leaving Marie-Jeanne to find a position to augment the family income. Marie-Jeanne filled the position after several attempts of Jung to find a suitable private secretary had failed.

PROF. DR. C. G. JUNG   **KÜSNACHT, ZURICH**
                                            SEESTRASSE 228

4th April 1938

Dr. Erich Neumann,
1 Gordon St.,
Tel Aviv

Dear Colleague,

As I thank you very much for your kind letter of July last year, I must apologize that I have not replied until now. Your letter came shortly before my departure for America where I was giving lectures at Yale University.[331] On my return I had to set off almost immediately for India[332] where I was invited to the 25th anniversary of the Indian Science Congress Association.[333] I have only recently returned.

I was interested to hear of your condition. The images you describe seem very familiar to me. I have the feeling that this is in no way a question of syncretism but rather a recapitulated genuine historical

---

[331] See n. 329.

[332] Jung was invited by the British government to take part in the celebrations of the twenty-fifth anniversary of the founding of the Indian Science Congress Association at the University of Calcutta. He left Zurich at the beginning of December 1937 with Harold Fowler McCormick (1872–1941) and traveled in India for three months. On this occasion he received honorary doctorates from the Universities of Hyderabad, Allahabad, Benares (20 December 1937), and Calcutta (7 January 1938). See letters from the universities' registrars in 1967 to Henry F. Ellenberger (Ellenberger archives, Hôpital Sainte-Anne, Paris); also Shamdasani (1996), pp. xxvii–xxviii, and Sengupta (2013).

[333] The Indian Science Congress Association was founded in 1914 to enhance scientific research in India. The association meets every January. At the Silver Jubilee in Calcutta in 1938 the participation of foreign researchers was first introduced. The meeting was organized in conjunction with the British Association for the Advancement of Science and held under the presidency of Lord Rutherford of Nelson. After his premature death the presidential address on "Researches in India and Great Britain" was given by Sir James Hopwood Jeans. The opening session took place on 3 January 1938.

development that comprises the modern problem at the same time. The internal work and the external run in parallel in a remarkable fashion. I do not wish to raise the matter of therapeutic success in connection with this, at least not directly.

The dream you reported to me in which a patient sees lots of small worms through a microscope which are supposed to be the cause of the illness means that there is a disturbance in the sympathetic nervous system, an abnormal charge, which has abnormally autonomized the smallest parts (worms) of the sympathetic nervous system. In my experience, it is related to contents that are unconscious at this level, but that, due to their creative character, would be synthesizable at least in theory. Whether it will come to this depends on fate and giftedness and equally on a proficiently led internal development. I have always found that drawing and painting serve especially well in such cases. When a person is dreaming in this way, the problem is still located in the physical, organic state and cannot be distinguished from either one of these. Only when the worms coalesce into a snake, for example, is there the prospect of becoming conscious. Parallel symbols are bacteria, small insects, and similar.

When I compare the content of your letter with what one reads in the papers about Palestine, I can well imagine what kind of a fantastic tension of opposites must exist for you. But, for the flourishing of internal development, such a tension is extremely advantageous because through it meaning emerges with particular clarity.

I have learned from Doctor Braband[334]—whom you probably know, that attempts are being made to gather together all those interested

[334] Margarete Braband, later Braband-Isaac (1892–1986): German-born Jewish psychiatrist and psychotherapist. Her interest in analytical psychology was first triggered by a presentation of Jung at the University of Zurich in 1928. She later participated in Jung's Berlin seminar in 1933, which was also attended by Erich Neumann. She met Jung again at the congress of Bad Nauheim in 1934, where he wrote a recommendation for her to the Frankfurt patron of the arts Lilly von Schnitzler (1889–1981). Braband worked in Frankfurt until 1936, when she left Germany with her two children. On her way to Palestine she met Jung in Zurich at the end of March 1936. She settled down in Haifa, where she opened a clinical practice. Once in Palestine she also established contact with Neumann in Tel Aviv. As she wrote to Jung: "I often experience my being alone here in Haifa as very difficult and was glad to be able to finally go back to Tel Aviv once again and to be able to discuss all kinds of professional matters with Dr. Neumann from time to time" (Braband to Jung, 4 May 1937 [JA]). One of the participants of her seminar series in Jerusalem in 1938 wrote to Alice Lewisohn Crowley asking for a donation of Jewish Jungians in Zurich in order to acquire Jung's books for the university library of

in analytical psychology. I have therefore sent some of my books and papers to the University Library in Jerusalem in support of these efforts.

It pleased me very much to hear that you have much to do. Hopefully it will continue in this way.

With best greetings and wishes,
Your ever loyal,
C. G. Jung

Jerusalem. Jung promised to help her by sending available copies of his books: "I will send some texts and books of which I still have duplicates to the Jerusalem University Library" (Jung to Braband, 2 April 1938 [JA]). In 1939 Mrs. Crowley sent $100, which was used for the support of destitute patients of Braband. In 1938 Braband visited Zurich again, met Jung at the Eranos conference in Ascona, and did some psychotherapeutic work with Jung. After the war she moved to Tel Aviv, where she was in regular contact with Neumann and discussed her work with him. In 1953 Braband-Isaac, now married again, received a grant to undertake research with schizophrenic patients in the Friedmatt clinic of Basel. She intended to continue her project in the Burghölzli with Manfred Bleuler (1903–1994), for the purpose of which Jung wrote a recommendation. In 1956 she worked as a visiting medical doctor in Frankfurt, Washington (National Institutes of Health in Bethesda), and Oxford. Her research was mainly concerned with the psychotherapeutic treatment of schizophrenic patients experimenting with physical exercise, music, and chiromancy. She came to Switzerland on a regular basis to see Jung, attend the Eranos conference, and give seminars and lectures in Zurich and Basel. In 1951 she started the treatment of a psychotic patient, who had been referred to her by Neumann. While she was in Basel in 1953, the mental condition of the patient deteriorated. After her return the patient lived with her and her family, and she wrote a number of extensive letters about this case to Jung. The patient had several dreams about Neumann, and Braband asked Neumann for his opinion. Although they agreed on the diagnosis of borderline schizophrenia, there was disagreement about Neumann's interpretation of the patient's drawings and Braband's use of music in the course of the treatment: "Interestingly, Dr. Neumann immediately said without prompting that the church is an apparition like the primitives make it, and he did not at all want to go into the fact that the patient had himself depicted it as church. [...] Also Dr. Neumann found that I should rather have told him a dirty joke at the first dream about me and my mother with a kepi and tomato, I could have triggered an inflation with the music. I explained to him that the patient's dream showed some months later that, through the 'Song of the Earth' he had arrived back in his childhood, at the scent and at his conceitedness which had existed even back then. But we could absolutely not agree and I soon kept my mouth shut as always" (Braband-Isaac to Jung, 17 October 1953 [JA]). Notes on Braband's letters—apparently not written by Jung—found in the ETH archive speak of her resistance toward Neumann, the danger of her method, and her false assumption to be a representative of Jungian psychology. The same commentator judged her short unpublished text "C. G. Jung and Israel," which she had written in 1947 and sent to Jung in 1953, as proof of her inflated attitude. Braband collaborated with John Layard (see n. 455) and Hugo Debrunner. In 1946 she met Martin Buber in Tel Aviv and had a discussion on Jung and "Abraxas." Articles by Braband-Isaac are "Psychotherapie und Gymnastik" ("Psychotherapy and Gymnastic") (1949) and "Musik in der Psychotherapie" ("Music in Psychotherapy") (1952).

Dr. Erich Neumann,
Analytical Psychologist

Tel Aviv, 5th Dec.-'38

Dear Professor Jung,

Since I have written you such a large number of unwritten letters, I am resolving—now that it is doubly difficult—to finally get around to writing to you for real. I don't know if you can imagine how difficult it is today to maintain inner contact with someone like you who has inevitably been touched at best once by the events that are affecting us Jews. It is fully obvious and natural to me to know you live on a completely different plane from ours. Yes, I must say, it is almost a comfort to me to know that your age, if one might put it this way, has removed you some degrees from these horrific world events.

On the other hand, this naturally impedes access a little, for I am most deeply convinced one should not bother you too much, as you, as I know and daily experience for myself, are already "fully immersed," as you once put it, in this world through your practice. Despite all this, it is a necessity for me to write to you once again if only to preserve the feeling that there is still a piece of Europe left, even for a Jew. Please do not misunderstand me. Although I, like all of us, am most deeply affected by the events in Germany[335] that give me

[335] In the night of 9 to 10 November 1938 a pogrom against Jews took place throughout Nazi Germany. The atrocities were organized and carried out by SA paramilitary and the Hitler Youth. During the riots at least ninety-one Jews were murdered, a further 30,000 were arrested by the SS and Gestapo and deported to concentrations camps. Shops and buildings owned by Jews were destroyed, Jewish homes, schools and hospitals ransacked, Jewish cemeteries desecrated, and numerous synagogues were burned to the ground. This all happened under the eyes of the German authorities, who were told only to intervene in case non-Jewish lives or property were endangered. The pogrom is also known as "Crystal Night" ("Kristallnacht"), referring to the shattered glass paving the streets in the wake of the destruction. The attacks were presented by the Nazis as retaliation for the assassination of the German diplomat Ernst vom

constant grounds to be glad that at least my father died before they happened[336]—in my heart of hearts I cannot break free from a sense of sympathy with or even compassion for this "German event." This often seems to be an indication of my insufficiently developed feeling, but I don't even know if this is correct. My experience with individuals has too often taught me that such states of confusion are necessary for their development to be able to simply pass a judgment about it here when it concerns me and my race.

Despite all this, I have too great a debt of gratitude to this nation to be able to identify this simply as the symptoms of its schizophrenic episode. Added to this is the fact that I believe that these entire events will be, in brief, the salvation of Judaism, while at the same time I'm clear that I do not know if I will be among the survivors of this upheaval or not. The enormous extraversion of Judaism that has led it to the brink of its grave will be cut off with the inexorable consistency of our destiny, and the terrible state of emergency that has gripped the entire people and will continue to do so will inevitably force the inner source energies to be called either into action or to their peril. It is both as clear to me that we will not be wiped out, as it is also that immeasurable numbers of us must perish in the process. And to watch this from the sidelines is a terrible torture. The reports that crowd in on one on a daily or hourly basis, and, sadly, the reports of eyewitnesses, make one glad to experience firsthand the terrible propensity of human beings to dissociate from overwhelmingly bad feelings.

Alongside this, in contrast with this, and to some degree also for its sake, I am attempting to write up the work I planned with you in 1933–34 that I have been working on ever since. This is very difficult alongside the thriving practice, the courses, and my "private life."

It is, to some extent, an attempt to demonstrate the collective pre-

---

Rath by Herschel Grynszpan, a seventeen-year-old German-born Polish Jew. The Crystal Night is widely regarded among historians as a turning point of the anti-Semitic policy of the Nazis, from political suppression and anti-Jewish agitation to forced emigration, deportation, and the organized mass murder of European Jews. On the Crystal Night, see Gilbert (2006), Pehle (1991), and Read (1989).

[336] Erich's father, Eduard Neumann, died in 1937 in Berlin from the effects of a brain hemorrhage, an injury sutained from a savage beating by Nazis. See Lori (2005).

determinedness of a part of the problem of the modern Jew. It centers on the problem of internal revelation.[337]

In the first section I want to represent how, in Jewish antiquity, the
principle of direct revelation applied, and how it stood in productive
dialogue with the strong earth and reality bonds of the race.[338] The
Law as a secularization of the traumatic experience of exile whereby,
in apparent acceptance of theocratic prophets, the earth-principle asserted itself to the exclusion of direct revelation.

Apocalypse, eschatological Messianism (Early Christianity), Gnosis as the emergence of direct inner revelation that had been suppressed into a sideline.

(This is as far as I have got in the first draft.)

After a short chapter on the repression of direct revelation in the
Talmud and the countermovement in kabbalah, there follows a comprehensive chapter on Hasidism.[339]

The religious renaissance of Judaism with the individual as the
central phenomenon but in a collective bond through the lasting
adoption of the law as a binding cage of direct revelation.

(A course on this is already prepared in note form.[340])

Assimilation and emancipation as a necessary de-collectivization
of the Jewish consciousness. Uprooting and the loss of memory.

On the problem of the modern Jew. Illustration of the historic-
collective contexts in dream and fantasy material. Reemergence of
direct revelation but now in the individual, in direct connection
firstly with individuation and secondly with the collective problem of
revelation in Judaism. Emergence of the earth-side as location of revelation today—the converse of the position of the problem in Jewish

---

[337] *Ursprungsgeschichte des jüdischen Bewusstseins* (*On the Origins and History of Jewish Consciousness*) (Neumann, 1934–40). See n. 273.

[338] *Beiträge zur Tiefenpsychologie des jüdischen Menschen und der Offenbarung* (*Contributions to
the Depth Psychology of the Jewish Man and the Problem of Revelation*), the first volume of *Ursprungsgeschichte des jüdischen Bewusstseins* (*On the Origins and History of Jewish Consciousness*)
(Neumann, 1934–40). See n. 273.

[339] *Der Chassidismus und seine psychologische Bedeutung für das Judentum* (*Hasidism and Its Psychological Relevance for the Jewry*) became the second volume of *Ursprungsgeschichte des jüdischen
Bewusstseins* (*On the Origins and History of Jewish Consciousness*) (Neumann, 1934–40). See n.
273.

[340] From 9 November 1939 to 30 May 1940 Neumann held a seminar series on "Analytische
Psychologie und Judentum: Der Chassidismus" ("Analytical Psychology and Jewry: The Hasidism") (Neumann, 1939–40).

antiquity—in a tension of opposites with the "spirit" principle that seems to hinder revelation. I.e., while the revelation principle used to stand in contrast to the heathen earth principle, now it appears in a positive form, coupled with strongly Near Eastern–Gnostic–pagan symbolism in a strong tension of opposites with the Law.

I have at least preedited this part of the material in several courses,[341] so I hope I am no longer fully groping in the dark. Highly apparent is the strong presence of the religious problem in the first half of life in a strongly collective-toned manifestation, more or less unconnected with one's private problems into which it grows in the course of the work.

You can well imagine how interesting this work is on the one hand, but how ill equipped I am for it on the other. I take the view, however, that I may collect materials for my living psychological work, even as a layman, as far as they are accessible to me and useful. This incursion into theological, religious, and historical areas is of course dillettantist in a certain sense. But the urgency of these problems for the Jewish situation seems so huge to me that even the inevitable arbitrariness of such an attempt is permitted, as long as it is conscious of its preliminariness and relativity.

I slid into these things, firstly, in the pursuit of the Jacob-Esau work into the general collective (I will take the liberty of sending you a supplement to the Jacob-Esau work soon), secondly in my engagement with images from the unconscious that I paint at longer and shorter intervals. A large part of my thought originates in the effort of capturing these images conceptually.

Actually these contents have occupied me incessantly in the last years, only infernal reality makes it extremely difficult to formulate things because I need time to do it and an occasional half day simply is not enough. In future, when a large group of relatives must be provided for and, on top of that, the economy is declining along with the practice, it will be a lot worse for sure. But on the other hand

---

[341] In 1937/38 and 1938/39 Neumann held courses on the "Seelenprobleme des modernen Juden: Eine Reihenanalyse von Träumen, Bildern und Phantasien" ("Soul Problems of the Modern Jew: An Analysis of a Series of Dreams, Images, and Phantasies") (Neumann, 1938–39).

one's concentration increases because of it and a certain despairing—joyful will to come to terms with reality precisely as an introvert and, what is more, as an intuitive.

Thus, the full uncertainty about any future and yet still having the feeling of being in the right place gives me—at least now and again—a remarkably paradoxical inner confidence, from which I believe that there could be a new, lively beginning in the individual and in the collective. And exactly because what has been experienced by the individual has such a strong connection with that experienced collectively and repeatedly with what has been historically effective, this connection between the most individual and the ancient has something strong and almost joyful about it.

Dear Professor, I ask you to forgive both the length of this letter as well as its poor form, but, in my case, badly typed is still better than well handwritten, and the length arises from the great distance from here to there, which, can only be bridged by a certain comprehensiveness, if at all. As a trip to Zurich under the current circumstances has been put back further than ever, you must please tolerate the long letter.

In thanking you very much for the Zosimos work,[342] I would like to take this opportunity to ask whether anything else of yours has appeared since "Psychology and Religion."[343]

With best wishes,
I am your ever grateful,
E. Neumann
[handwritten addendum:]
P.S. By the way, is it true that the dreamer in "Dream Symbols"[344]

---

[342] Jung's lecture at the 1937 Eranos conference titled "Einige Bemerkungen zu den Visionen des Zosimos" (Zurich, 1938).

[343] Jung's lectures at Yale University of autumn 1937 (see n. 329) were published for the Terry Foundation by the Yale University Press (and by Oxford University Press, London) in 1938 (Jung, 1938a).

[344] Jung's Eranos lecture 1935, "Traumsymbole des Individuationsprozesses: Ein Beitrag zur Kenntnis der in den Träumen sich kundgebenden Vorgänge des Unbewussten" ("Dream Symbols of the Process of Individuation") (Jung, 1936a); extended version published as the second part of *Psychology and Alchemy* (Jung, 1944).

and "Psychology and Religion" is a Jew? Will you publish anything on the specifically Jewish features of this development or do you see nothing specific about it. E.g., The "voice." And what about "Jewish material"? If you can say something about this, I would of course be very grateful.

PROF. DR. C. G. JUNG   **KÜSNACHT, ZURICH**
                                 SEESTRASSE 228

19th December 1938

Dr. Erich Neumann,
1 Gordon St.,
Tel Aviv,
Palestine

Dear Colleague,

Please do not be concerned that you have written me such a long letter. It has long interested me to know what you are actually doing. You must not imagine that I have retreated to the snow-clad heights, enthroned high above world events. I am right in the thick of it and am following the Palestinian question on a daily basis in the newspapers, and think often of my acquaintances there who have to live in this chaos. When I was in Palestine in 1933,[345] I was unfortunately able to see what was coming all too clearly. I also foresaw great misfortune for Germany, even quite terrible things, but when it then shows up, it still seems unbelievable. Everyone here is shocked to their core as it were by what is happening in Germany. I have a great deal to do with German refugees and am constantly occupied with accommodating all my Jewish acquaintances in England and America. In this way I am in constant contact with contemporary events.

What you write about your plan of work interests me very much. You are proceeding in parallel with the experiences that I have been having in Europe for many years. I think you must be very careful

---

[345] See n. 216. This letter has been printed in the Jung letter edition (Jung, 1973, pp. 317–18), but in the 1973 edition the year of Jung's visit to Palestine was wrongly rendered as 1923 (p. 317).

when evaluating your specifically Jewish experiences. While there are, for sure, specific Jewish traits in this development, it is at the same time a general one that is also happening among Christians. It is a question of a general and identical revolution of minds. The specifically Christian or Jewish traits have only a secondary meaning. So, for example, while the patient you asked about is a pure Jew raised as a Catholic, I could nowhere describe his symbolism, inasmuch as I could delineate it, as Jewish with any certainty beyond doubt, although certain nuances strike one as Jewish occasionally. If I compare his material with my own or with that of many other academically educated patients, it is only the surprising consistency that strikes one, the difference is negligible. The difference between a typically Protestant and a Jewish psychology is especially small when contemporary events are taken into consideration. The whole problem is itself of paramount importance for humanity that is why individual and racial differences only play a small part. All the same, I can imagine very well that among Jews who live in Palestine the immediate impact of the environment brings the chthonic and old-Jewish into view. It seems to me as if anything specifically Jewish as well as specifically Christian could be best discovered in the way and form that unconscious material is assimilated by the subject. In my experience the resistance of the Jews to this seems more obstinate and thus the defensive effort seems to be much more vehement. But this is nothing more than a purely subjective impression.

The Zosimos essay was the most recently published piece from me. But still to come are an article on India (in English in an American journal),[346] two lectures on the mother complex,[347] which will appear in the 1938 Eranos Yearbook, and a longer commentary on Zen Buddhism,[348] and finally a comprehensive introduction to the individuation process for the American edition of my Eranos lectures.[349]

[346]"The Dreamlike World of India" and "What India Can Teach Us" (Jung, 1939a, 1939b).

[347]"Psychological Aspects of the Mother Archetype" (Jung, 1939). Speakers at the Eranos conference were asked to deliver two lectures.

[348]"Foreword to Suzuki's *Introduction to Zen Buddhism*" (Jung, 1939c).

[349]Text was originally written in English and published as "The Meaning of Individuation" in *The Integration of the Personality* (Jung, 1939/40), an English collection of Jung's Eranos lectures; the editors of the *Collected Works* decided to include the revised German version "Bewusstes, Unbewusstes und Individuation" translated as "Conscious, Unconscious, and Individuation" (1939d).

Dr. Stern[350] has informed me of his comprehensive correspondence with you. It is obvious from this that the devil has stirred things up between you.[351] As soon as one notices this, one must not say any more, but return to oneself.

I was very pleased to hear that you are fully employed although it would be even better if you had time to realize your big plan. In the hope that your health is good, with good wishes, I remain your always loyal,

[C. G. Jung]

[350] Max M. Stern (1895–1982): German-born Jewish psychoanalyst; a severe ailment contracted in World War I led to a partial disability and years of hospitalization. Once recovered, he studied medicine and became interested in analytical psychology. He took part in the IV General Medical Congress for Psychotherapy in Bad Nauheim (11–14 April 1929). In 1935 he left Frankfurt first for Paris, where he trained among others with Elisabeth de Sury, and later that year for Tel Aviv. In Palestine he continued his training with Erich Neumann until 1937. On Neumann's recommendation he started working independently in 1936. Due to his ill health Stern left Palestine for America where he became a respected member of the psychoanalytical community. Since the 1950s he was a training and supervising analyst at the Psychoanalytic Institute of the New York University Medical Center (formerly the Downstate Psychoanalytic Institute). His main work, posthumously published, is titled *Repetition and Trauma: Toward a Teleonomic Theory of Psychoanalysis* (1988). On Stern see Abrams (1983).

[351] Max Stern wrote to Jung on 6 November 1938 (JA). In his letter he referred to an argument with Neumann that had arisen after a presentation in October 1937. During the argument Neumann declared himself as the only representative of analytical psychology in Palestine and denied Stern any right to publicly represent Jung's psychology. In the aftermath a letter exchange between Neumann and Stern developed, which Stern sent together with the text of his presentation to Jung. Stern accused Neumann, who was his training analyst at the time, of breaking analytic confidentiality, of being ignorant of fundamental analytical concepts such as resistance and affect, and of deviating from Jung's psychological theory. Jung replied to Stern on 19 December 1938 (JA) confirming that his presentation had been in line with Jung's psychological understanding and that Neumann's remark about the unconscious character of affects would have been ambiguous. He finished his letter with a declaration of impartiality: "Therefore: where dispute arises, the wise man remains silent" ("Darum: wo sich Streit erhebt, schweigt der Verständige"). For Neumann's reply to Jung, see 29 N.

Dr. Erich Neumann,
Analytical Psychologist

Tel Aviv, 15th November 1939

Dear Professor Jung,

The fact that I have been so absent and that I have not written to you
for so long, against my own best intention, has a familiar internal explanation, I'm afraid. To some degree, I have also been absent to myself and have not come back to myself fully even now. Of course, it
does not look like this from the outside, i.e., I am working, but am
more or less swallowed up by the work with individuals and the private work on the Jewish. At the same time neither the one thing nor
the other any longer seems as important as it did, say, a year ago. I do
it as well as I can and as badly as I must, but I always have the feeling
that I am playing a role as a Jew, mindful of the Gods, while a quiet
ironic feeling—battle of Thermopylae[352]—resonates at the same time.

Two things are colliding in me that cannot easily be reconciled, the
one namely the consciousness of belonging to a dying people, and
the other is the knowledge that something new is emerging—not
Palestine—that is quite secondary—and that I am co-responsible for
this. That this new thing should be done precisely to the impossible
object,—to the Jews—seems to me to be a paradox that strikes me as
really Y.H.W.H.-like and Jewish. Please do not misunderstand me, I
don't mean anything to do with chosenness or the prophetic, indeed
it seems to me that it is precisely the sacrifice of these principles that

[352] Battle of Thermopylae ("The Hot Gates"), 480 BCE, fought between an alliance of Greek
city-states and the army of the Persian Empire under Xerxes I. Despite being vastly outnum-
bered the Greek troops led by King Leonidas of Sparta were able to hold the narrow pass for
three days until they were betrayed by a local resident. Most of the Greeks were killed in the
final standoff, and the Persian army advanced toward Athens. The name is synonymous for
bravery and heroism in defending ones homeland, even when the odds are against one.

is what we face today and that is so difficult for me. It is indeed characteristic that I tried to portray the danger of the intuitive type as part of the first, separate section of my work on the revelation problem in Jewish antiquity. Overall I have not at all lost an accompanying and supervisory consciousness, but I see myself over and over again so collectively imprisoned, in a nonprimitive sense, that I am afflicted with self-limitation and know that I must suffer from it.

Sacrifice of intuition is my own problem, but I think it is also a central Jewish problem that is most closely linked with the rootlessness of the Jewish structure and exactly this link between the collective and individual seems to me also to be Jewish.

In the meantime, I have also recognized that Jewish symbolism—at least that of Western Jews—is consistent with that of European people, that here something secular is taking place. Of course, I knew this before, but the problem of the singularity of the Jews would have been simpler if a specific symbolism could have been demonstrated. I have abandoned this and stand without preconceptions before something that is incomprehensible to me. In the course of history, individuation is the consequence of Jewish development; at the same time it seems to be the abolition of the Jewish. My slogan: it is no longer about Judaism but it is about Jewish people, about the individual as revelation-center and realization-center of the Self—but it seems to me, along with the dissolution of the old Judaism, to require and to signify something like a new Jewish beginning, and how should I believe in it, why must I believe in it?

You see, dear Professor Jung, if I may interweave a very personal confession here, I do not believe in it, everything speaks against it, and I am so tired of the Jews and the Jewish—and every free minute and every thought belongs to these subjects, and I must protect myself from being completely swallowed up by this work. I am after all no "ignoramus," and Moses identification, prophet identification, etc. are not unknown facts to me. But, you see, my position toward Judaism is extremely revolutionary and even my attempt to create the continuity through to the modern Jewish person from the openness to revelation of antiquity via the inner Hasidic revolution is, as I of course will know myself, a new interpretation—how can I help myself in this paradox?

The following dream of mine comes to mind in relation to this:
June '39

I, probably identical to the personality of an old pilgrim.(?)

At first, as if in a pub or similar, with the Nazis (?), not trapped, but suitably threatened. With the help of small pictures that he was showing to them, he did something revolutionary, shows it to the others cautiously; but it was like being among people who half belonged together. When it was time to leave (Journey?) something like father and son stood next to him (Landlord? The father) and he tore up all these pictures all of which were unremarkable, at which the landlord looked at them all but said nothing. The son was favorably disposed, the father became like an old prince. Scene in a big castle. The prince came to the pilgrim and said: "Go." This was preceded by a judgment scene in which the son had protested in vain. (?) He—I—rose, took the wide-brimmed hat and staff, nothing more. There was a wooden hat (begging bowl?) which I was not allowed to take and threw angrily against the ceiling of the castle so that it shattered, and the sound resounded echoingly through the high castle, down the massive stairs. I asked may I not even say goodbye to the son? He shook his head with a mocking smile.

The pilgrim then left, the ship was supposed to collect him. At the foot of the castle the prince asked (something like): So you think I am letting the *pardes*[353] be worked on incorrectly? He, the pilgrim, said humbly, as if excusing himself: No, only I have learned to do it in a different way, you should clear the weeds.

Then it was like the end of a drama. The ship did not dock, but sailed past, upon which the prince scornfully stabbed the pilgrim (Dagger made of gold with a transparent glass-green stone blade).

---

[353] Pardes, meaning orchard; etym. from Persian root, cf. the English word "paradise" or the German word "Paradies." According to the Talmud the exegeses of two biblical texts is not allowed: the "ma'ase bereschit" ("book of creation") and the "ma'ase merkava" ("book of the chariot throne") [Ezekiel 1 and 10]. The explanation of this law is accompanied by the Talmudic story (Babylonian Talmud, Chagigah 14b) about the dangers four sages face by attempting to "enter the pardes": one dies, another one loses his mind, the third one becomes a heretic, and only the fourth one—Rabi Akiba ben Joseph—enters and leaves the garden peacefully. The three concepts of "ma'ase bereschit," "ma'ase merkava," and "pardes" have subsequently become key aspects of many Jewish mystical interpretations and texts. See Dan (2007, p. 14). Pardes also used an acronym for the four methods of the interpretation of the Torah: Peshat, Remez, Derash, Sod (plain or contextual, allegorical, metaphorical, and esoteric meaning).

The pilgrim pronounces the demise of the prince. He had secretly covered the whole ship with needle script beforehand, piercing in the news of the unjust prince. The ship now sails on the open sea to Milan or Boulogna [*sic*] (or similar), where the High Court passes judgment and, with a huge army in its wake, besieges the town of the prince, kills him, destroys his rule and installs a new one.

The end is like a dialogue being read out loud in a drama, last pages of a manuscript. The dying pilgrim rising above the prince in the dialogue, he in an ascending curve, the prince in a descending and sinking curve.

The Gnostic motifs are clear, as is the mystical *pardes* motif. On the whole I would be able to say much about the dream. Pilgrim—Wotan—Intuition, Prince-Landlord-Sensation. New order, the son, the inner work that calls forth the new: needle script, etc. Despite this, the link between the personal and the collective is once again obscure. Especially, the "sacral" killing of my pilgrim soul by the prince is rather sinister, just as the pilgrimage is all in all rather surprising. I would ask you very much, if it is possible for you, to say something about this. My cohesion with reality seemed gradually so strong that I did not have *so* much to do with the wide-brimmed hat of Wotan any more. If I understand the dream correctly, the revolutionary part triumphs only and precisely because it is killed by its opposite. This seems to be most tragic, as the whole has something mythopoetic about it that moves me deeply, but that I cannot properly grasp. It has something of epoch change about it that I keep finding in my pictures and understand passably, but whose connection with myself is disconcerting to me.

I'd like to take this opportunity to ask you something else. My last picture shows me a huge hermaphrodite of such comical size that I become dizzy. But what is striking is its division into the male upper half and lower female whereas the whole of space with its starry sky resides in the unconscious water part,* which, in feminine form reaches as far as the navel. Out of the navel as the connection point grows a botanical unifying symbol. But this whole figure stands, as it were, in a world space, as we do in ours. Naturally, I know that you can only say something about this to me when this being is what it purports to be, an archetype. Now my Jewish work circles around the

Y.H.W.H. earth opposite, the positive tension between these poles, their contraction, destruction, and reconstellation. I understand this image, among other things, as the unity aspect of this opposite and the development that emerges from it, but it has such a strange and ghostly character that all of this is not enough for me by a long way. I even understand the feminine as Godhead of the world and the Y.H.W.H. life in his being, which breaks in from above. At least as an aspect of unity, i.e., no longer in the tension of opposites, it is a matter for my consideration. I would like to know only whether another quite different collective matter is behind it and that can be expressed.

I take the fact that the war prevents me from sending you my just completed German manuscript (part one)[354] as a commission to write the Hasidism section for its duration. Everything here is extremely serious and difficult. My "worries" tell you enough about my situation that, surrounded by much work and many "nice" people, is naturally very isolated.

*[handwritten insertion: There is air space everywhere, but to the side, a water lily blossoms at the height of the navel, so that the lower space is "water space" after all.]

We are all well; my closest family, though destitute, are in England,[355] so we must not complain. Zurich would have been very important for me and it is more unattainable than ever, but if things become too pressing, ways will be found.

---

[354] *Beiträge zur Tiefenpsychologie des jüdischen Menschen und der Offenbarung* (*Contributions to the Depth Psychology of the Jewish Man and the Problem of Revelation*), the first volume of *Ursprungsgeschichte des jüdischen Bewusstseins* (*On the Origins and History of Jewish Consciousness*) (Neumann, 1934–40). See n. 273.

[355] Most of Julie Neumann's family fled to London after 1933. Erich's brother Franz also immigrated to England. Their mother Zelma Neumann was in London on her way to Tel Aviv when the war broke out and stayed with Franz and his family. She joined Erich and Julie in Tel Aviv in 1947. Julie's youngest sister Ruth Goldstone (neé Blumenfeld) described the fate her family: "Martin and his family immigrated to Australia, Julie and Erich went to Palestine, I went to England where I married my cousin Salo. Finally I succeeded in finding a job for my sister Lotte, and my parents were soon able to come after her. I was able to get a transit visa for Argentina for my brother Paul. As the war broke out shortly after that he was no longer able to use the visa. So he stayed here in London with his wife. [. . .] Julie visited us several times in London and had good contact with my children. At the end she visited me in London with her husband in order to see our mother who was over 90 years old. Erich was already very ill on this visit and wanted to visit his brother Franz who was a doctor. Very soon when he was back home he died from cancer" (letter from Ruth Goldstone to Angelica Löwe, 3 June 2007; Löwe, 2008, p. 42).

I do beg you, dear Professor, not to take this letter and its inquiries as a claim on your time. If you do happen to find the time to say something to me, I will be very happy, but you know better than I that these things take a long time anyway and much becomes clearer gradually in the process of development, so there is no hurry. The lack of shape in this letter corresponds to the certain blockedness in me and my long silence. The fact of only ever "developing" myself alongside work and not being finally able to present either to you or to myself any "achievement" makes me more silent than is good for me.

Very many thanks for the last Eranos work that has clarified much for me. One more remark about Dr. Stern.[356] Without question, the devil has stirred things up there, the affair has taught me a great deal, also about myself. Anyway, the fact that he has become a passionate Freudian with all the accessories in the meantime confirms to me that his analysis with me was abysmal, but it has also shown me that my skepticism toward him that he did not "experience" and realize the contents was not completely incorrect. I understand that one cannot always reach Jung from Freud, but to regress from Jung to Freud seems to me to be a moral defect, perhaps I am wrong, or better said to correspond to a Jewish-destructive nature. Anyway. My complex to feel too responsible still exists in any case, at least in part.

I wish you and all who belong to you that these momentous times will pass you by as much as possible without putting you in harm's way, and am,

In old gratitude,
Your E. Neumann

[handwritten addendum] P.S. I am not as completely swallowed up as this somehow rather inhuman impersonal letter strikes me at this time. Please believe me about the personal matters. It is almost unhealthy to almost only have oneself to check things out with, so that this letter is a bit too much like an "analytic session."

---

[356] See nn. 350 and 351.

PROF. DR. C. G. JUNG   **KÜSNACHT, ZURICH**
                                            SEESTRASSE 228

16th December 1939

Dr. Erich Neumann,
1 Gordon St.,
Tel Aviv

Dear Colleague,

It pleased me to hear something from you again. You obviously
waited rather too long before writing to me again for your letter is so
concentrated that a complete response to it is absolutely impossible
in writing.

With your dream I had the need of a dilution or an elaboration.
When dreams assume this legendary form, content is present for
elaboration, which should be taken up and developed through active
imagination. I would have needed to dramatize the dream even more
so that it would reveal its secrets sooner. The Wotan association does
not refer to the Germanic regression in Germany, but is a symbol for
a spiritual development that involves the entire cultural world
(Wotan as the wind God = Pneuma).[357] This also explains why Wotan
also makes an appearance with the Jews, albeit only with German
ones, as I have seen many times.

The hermaphrodite is indeed an archetype. It represents a unity of
the pairs of opposites and is probably a symbol of duality that

[357] Jung talks about Wotan as a storm god in his article "Wotan" (Jung, 1936) and in his seminars on Nietzsche's *Thus Spoke Zarathustra*. According to Jung the seizure of Nietzsche's consciousness through the Wotan archetype is indicated by the image of the wind and can be seen
as a foreboding of Nietzsche's insanity (see Jung, 1934–39, pp. 1073–75, 1227–28). Nietzsche's
fate, Jung concludes, anticipated the development in the Germanic unconscious in the 1930s.
See also introduction, pp. xxxi.

corresponds to Aquarius and would thus roughly equate to the same value as the fish symbolism at the beginning of our era.[358] As the alchemical symbolism already sets forth, it means the Self whose Indian symbols are also male-female. (C./f., e.g,. the Atman figure at the beginning of the *B[ri]hadaranyaka Upanishads*.)[359] This problematic transcends racial differences and emerges from the spiritual wind that blows over Europe or probably over the whole world, for even in the far East all of these things are in a rapid flux.

We are naturally very impacted by the immediate danger of war in our own land but for the time being everything is on hold.

In my lectures I am dealing with the Eastern orientation linked with yoga philosophy and the Western orientation linked to the Ignatian Spiritual Exercises.[360]

Please accept my best wishes,
Your always loyal,
C. G. Jung

---

[358] Cf. *Aion* (Jung, 1951, § 142): "If, as it seems probable, the aeon of the fishes is ruled by the archetypal motif of the hostile brothers, then the approach of the next Platonic month, namely Aquarius, will constellate the problem of the union of opposites." For a commentary on *Aion* see Edinger (1996). On Jung's understanding of the Age of Aquarius in regard to *Aion* and *Liber Novus* see Owens (2011).

[359] *Bṛhadāraṇyaka Upaniṣad*, I, iv, 3: "He was not at all happy. Therefore people (still) are not happy when alone. He desired a mate. He became as big as man and wife embracing each other. He parted this very body into two. From that came husband and wife. Therefore, said Vājñavalkya, this (body) is one-half of oneself, like one of the two halves of a split pea. Therefore this space is indeed filled by the wife. He was united with her. From that men were born." (Mādhavānanda, 1965, p. 99).

[360] In his weekly lectures at the ETH Jung (cf. n. 320) dedicated the winter semester 1938/39 and summer semester 1939 to the philosophy of yoga interpreting Patanjali's *Yoga Sutra*, the *Amitāyur-Dhyāna-Sūtra*, and the *Shrī-Chakra-Sambhāra Tantra* (see Hannah 1934–41, vol. 2 (= Modern Psychology, vols. 3 and 4], pp. 11–143). In the summer semester 1939 and the winter semester 1939/40 he contrasted this view on Eastern spiritualism with a psychological reading of St. Ignatius of Loyola's *Exercitia Spiritualia* (see Hannah 1934–41, vol. 2 (= Modern Psychology, vols. 3 and 4], pp. 149–264). (Theses lectures will be published as part of the Philemon series by Martin Liebscher and Ernst Falzeder.)

31 N

Dr. Erich Neumann,
Analytical Psychologist

Tel Aviv,
1, Gordon St.

11 May 1940

Dear Professor Jung,

Precisely now that uncertainty about the future has grown greater than ever I want to send you a sign of life and to leave all my extensive but unfinished letters to you to one side.

It seems to me that the everyday is taking a back seat right now and only the most personal matters still have the right to be perhaps worthy of communication. Please understand my sending you my talk in this vein. I gave it here in relative privacy, i.e., to a quite small circle. It would be important for me to know whether you could identify at least to some degree with its formulations, or whether this way of seeing things is foreign to you.

The talk belongs to a certain extent in the third section of my book: *On the Depth Psychology of the Modern Jew*, whose second section, "The Psychological Meaning of Hasidism," I am now writing, and whose first section, "The Problem of Revelation in Jewish Antiquity," happily needs only now—after the umpteenth reworking—, to be typed up.[361]

If it is technically possible I will permit myself to send you this section shortly.

I hope very much that the contact with you, dear Professor, will not be interrupted, even through the passage of time; I am pretty much out on a limb and know very well that my work on the Jewish

---

[361] Neumann (1934–40). See n. 273.

is very incomprehensible and untimely even for the Jews. All the more important, then, is "Zurich" if I may call it something so impersonal when I mean something so personal. It is not so much about consensus as about the feeling of solidarity beyond what is different, of this you may be sure.

I remain, in old gratitude,
Your E. Neumann
   [handwritten addendum] The Manuscript is being sent under separate cover,—hopefully you will get it.

PROF. DR. C. G. JUNG   **KÜSNACHT, ZURICH**
                                      SEESTRASSE 228

7th December 1940

1, Gordon St.,
Tel Aviv

Dear Colleague,

Your letter of the 11th May 1940 has just arrived, along with the manuscript: *Religious Experience in Depth Analysis*.[362] So it has taken a very long time to get here, as you can see.

I thank you very much for your letter. Naturally I have not yet read the manuscript, but will report to you as soon as I have.

I hope things are going well otherwise. As you know, we live here in Switzerland on an island with reduced heating. Otherwise, there is nothing new to report.

With best wishes,
Your always devoted,
C. G. Jung

[362] This might be the first draft of the unpublished typescript "Zur religiösen Bedeutung des tiefenpsychologischen Weges" ("On the Religious Significance of the Way of Depth Psychology"), dated "Tel Aviv, 1942" (Neumann, 1942). During the war Neumann also wrote a text titled "Die Bedeutung des Bewusstseins für die tiefenpsychologische Erfahrung" ("The Significance of Consciousness for Depth-Psychological Experience") (Neumann, 1943), dated "Tel Aviv, 1943," which was divided into four parts: 1. "Symbole und Stadien der Bewusstseinsentwicklung" ("Symbols and Stages in the Development of Consciousness"), 2. "Bewusstseins-Entwicklung und Psychologie der Lebensalter" ("Development of Consciousness and the Psychology of the Life Stages"), 3. "Der tiefenpsychologische Weg und das Bewusstseins" ("The Way of Depth Psychology and Consciousness"), and 4. "Stadien religiöser Erfahrung auf dem tiefenpsychologischen Weg" ("Stages in Religious Experience on the Way of Depth Psychology"). Neumann's typescript from 1942, which was probably based on his 1940 presentation, is very likely to have been intended for use as a fourth part of this project.

Dr. Erich Neumann,
Analytical Psychologist

Tel Aviv, 1st October 1945
1, Gordon St.

Dear Professor,

For a long time I have felt the urge to write to you and to renew the connection that means so much to me. But as the date shows, the inner difficulties that had to be overcome were not small. The years in between in which I did not dare to write to you so as not to endanger you were no small thing. I very much hope that you, your family, and all individuals close to you have withstood this time without serious damage, inside or out. Fate has wrapped a tight bow around us, we are healthy and are working, and all close family members of my wife and myself managed to get out in time. That means a great deal and yet in such a time as ours is not very conclusive.

I would like to briefly update you about myself. I can well imagine how you are being showered with updates from all over the world, but the contact to you and Miss Wolff is—even symbolically—the most precious thing, but also the only thing that is left to me of Europe. I know and affirm it so that I may also remain linked to the German cultural circle in this way, more than with all else.

My inner life is moving in a certain dialectical opposition to the times we live in. This is conditioned by my intuition, but I could hardly say that I suffer because of it. My relationship to the external world is amply (for me anyway) engaged through my large practice, the courses and a few close people, otherwise I am substantially taken up with the continuum of my internal work and the writing that flows from it, regardless of what may come out of it. But right now that is starting to change, as I would like to tell you later. But to return to my dialectic. After I had completed the large work on Jewish antiquity—on the Soul History of the Jew—(it is now obsolete and only useable as source material), I wrote a book on the psychological meaning of Hasidism for the modern Jew, which I still stand by.[363] But then, after I had arrived at my current internal state, the Jewish problem and the work on it was ended as far as I was concerned, precisely at a time when it was becoming palpable in the world in an indescribably horrific way. I, meanwhile, was coming back to "pure" psychology. Firstly in essays and lectures from which I took the liberty of sending you the larger work on *Depth Psychology and a New Ethic*.[364] All these things are unpublished, of course, some of them have been made public in courses, a few in lectures. The practice and the local community are predominantly almost exclusively German. Psychologically, psychoanalysis reigns in blinkered, dogmatic proponents with around 25 registered members in the country, a free polyclinic, training, etc. It is understandable both from the social, rational, and national situation, they are about 50 years behind here intellectually, but much is made more difficult because of this, even when I disregard my own personal unsuitedness to publicity.

But now I am in the middle of a large work and I would like to arouse your interest in it, i.e., I'd like to briefly tell you about it. "Archetypal Stages of the Development of Consciousness."[365] Myth, childhood, science of neurosis. The first book, "Psychology of Myth," is almost complete,—I'm writing the last chapter of it. Mythology as a projection of the ego—and the development of consciousness. The individual stages with their symbols as mythological cycles through which the "ego" passes in its development. The archetypal stages as transpersonal preconditions that are passed through in the course of the history of humanity and in the individual's own childhood history. What is important for me here is, for example, the debate with Freud—that is essential. E.g., when, in the "Life of Childhood," Ford-

---

[363] Neumann (1934–40). See n. 273.
[364] Neumann (1949b).
[365] This later develops into *The Origins and History of Consciousness* (Neumann, 1949a).

ham[366] simply accedes to or takes for granted the Oedipus complex,[367] that simply will not do. Primal parents instead of Oedipus complex, the clarification of the incest stage, the concepts of castration, building on the transformations, that I believe, were superseded by you later. Stages: Uroboros, Great Mother, separation of the primal parental couple, fight with the dragon. From the creation myth to the hero myth. Matricide, patricide, etc., auto conception of the spirit in the Osiris myth and the kings' ritual. Much is old, summarizing, clarifying, some seems to me to be important as a completion. Represented deductively because it is the only possible way to do it if it is to be clear. Important, among other things, for a transpersonal psychology of childhood and for a therapy that can first refer to stages and cycles of symbols but that acquires an orientation in this way. In a sense, a history of the development of the libido in the sense of transpersonal analytical psychology. For sure, it can only be an attempt at something, but perhaps a helpful one. Both for remedial teachers or the child analysts, who work, I say, in a "Jungish" way, as well as for us Jungians ourselves, the lack of such clarifications in the work was always very troubling. I must say though that *child analysis* has extremely frequently proved itself to me to be important and decisive in the work. Also in the analyses of the second half of life. Do you

[366] Michael Scott Montague Fordham (1905–1995): English analytical psychologist and child psychiatrist, coeditor of Jung's *Collected Works* in English. The beginnings of Fordham's interest in Jungian psychology dates back to 1933. He enters analysis with Helton Godwin ("Peter") Baynes (see nn. 221 and 372), followed by an analysis with Hilde Kirsch (see nn. 172 and 178). In 1945 he is appointed editor of the *Collected Works* and a year later is one of the instigators of setting up the Society of Analytical Psychology. He was the first editor of the *Journal of Analytical Psychology*. His lifelong interest in the works of Melanie Klein led him to undertake a Kleinian analysis in the 1980s. Fordham's works include *New Developments in Analytical Psychology* (1957), *The Objective Psyche* (1958), and *The Self and Autism* (1976). His memoirs are titled *The Making of an Analyst: A Memoir* (1993). *The Life of Childhood: A Contribution to Analytical Psychology* was published in 1944. Fordham sent a copy to Jung, who replied in a letter of 14 September 1945: "Thank you for your kind letter. I have received your interesting book about 'The Life of Childhood.' It arrived during my illness and that is the reason why I never thanked you for it" (MFP). On Fordham see Astor (1995), on Fordham's relation to Neumann and his critique of Neumann's child psychology (Fordham, 1981), see introduction, p. lvi–lviii.

[367] In *The Life of Childhood* (1944) Fordham cites the Oedipus myth as the classic example of the process of identification, which would occur universally in childhood (p. 20), and uses it to describe the relationship between the parents and their effect on children: "The development of the child differs according to sex owing to the functioning of the Oedipus and Electra myth, whereby the boy has a negative attitude to the father and a positive erotic one to his mother, while the reverse holds good for the girl" (p. 47).

have a different opinion about this? The fact that in your publications, the work on the discovery of the archetypes and on the individuation process is center-staged does not seem to me to be proof of the contrary. It seems to me that problems such as that of the stability of the ego and the possibility of its realization have their roots in childhood experiences. For example, an unsuccessful dragon fight in which the transpersonal contest takes place with the personal parents onto whom the primal parental couple is projected. So, when the first section is finished, the Psychology of Myth, I will allow myself to send you one "for inspection" and would, of course, be exceptionally grateful to you for any comments on it, all the more as it is crucially important for me to know what your take is on this. My experience is so terribly inferior to yours; the foundations of the work reside in your psychology, so that in a certain sense your approval of my efforts is of essential importance.

As you can imagine, I am very busy with my writing, which must be done alongside 8–9 hours of practice, courses, etc. This has its disadvantages, but on the whole I am balancing it and it me, so that it works. Those that feel hard done by announce themselves sorrowfully, whether it is my wife, I myself, or someone else, but as I have learned quite well to put up with myself, I am managing to get others to tolerate me also. Working under these conditions of time and climate is, at times, inevitably consuming, but when it gets too bad and I don't notice, my wife lets me know, sometimes even my own unconscious too. This is really quiet. Times of making pictures[368] and imaginative series alternate for me with productive times of writing, they rarely overlap. Mostly I live off the images, etc., for years and never actually manage to be done with them. I really should work through much of this with you, overall I am faced with all these contents *unfortunately pretty much alone*, i.e., no one is there who can correct me in my general processing. But dear old reality prevents

---

[368] In 2006, eighty-one of Neumann's dream paintings were sold at an auction at Sotheby's London (see Sotheby's, 2006, p. 150). The paintings dated from 1933 to 1948, annotations were added until 1959. Drawings can also be found in Neumann's two dream books titled *Buch der Einweihung* (*The Book of Initiation*) written between 1940 and 1959, which were auctioned as well (Neumann, 1940–59; Sotheby's, 2006, pp. 148–49). In the 1930s Neumann also drew three books for his children, one of which depicts the biblical story of Jacob (NP; see the cover of *Harvest*, 2006).

one from slipping too far inward, which I am not always thankful about, as my work compels me. With my large practice and a very big and growing practice on the part of my wife we are still managing to keep up with inflation "elegantly." I.e., we can take 4–6 weeks holiday per year, which I need for my work, my wife—who is very overstretched, needs it to relax.

You see, dear Professor, I am writing nothing about the times, nothing about Palestine. My inner dialectic indicates the only possible path for me. At these times, the general human condition moves me, and this only. How else could one bear it. This "passionate intensity," if I may say so, makes life meaningful for me. And although I often check this out in myself, it does not seem to be a flight from the reality of the day. My practical work extends into this everyday reality, perhaps my other work will also do in future. The fact that, on the whole, I live in such an insular way here I regard as a requirement for my development and my work, which I must accept. I do not know where in the world I could have gone on working and maintaining my family in the last decade as I have been able to here. Much here is dangerous, absurd, and almost unbearable, but everything remains comprehensible at the same time, all too comprehensible. My distance will, I fear, and must, remain. But where in the world would I have less distance than here?

I hope very much that this letter—which has become all too long,—finds you well and fully employed. G. Adler sent me your work on the child archetype recently,[369] which I like very much. You can imagine how important it would be for me and how much I would enjoy hearing what you are working on. I think your illness of which Adler wrote to me[370] is long since overcome and has remained without aftereffects. It is good that your 70th birthday fell in peacetime at least.

You will forgive me that, apart from the "official greeting," I did not write to you on that occasion. This letter of reconnection had to be

---

[369] *The Psychology of the Child Archetype* in Jung and Kerényi (1941); see also Jung (1941).

[370] Gerhard Adler's letter to Neumann is missing. On 11 February 1944 Jung slipped and broke his ankle. Twelve days later, probably due to the immobilization following the injury, he developed a pulmonary embolism and suffered a heart attack. During three weeks of a semiconscious state Jung had a series of visions that he describes in *Memories, Dreams, Reflections* (Jung, 1961, pp. 293–301). After a year of convalescence Jung suffered a second heart attack in 4 November 1946. See also n. 393.

written first, and I am not very good at writing formal things. Is your great alchemy work[371] of which Adler wrote now complete? We are up to date with all the English works, only Baynes's bombed-out book[372]—which would have been very important for me—has not made it to Palestine.

With that, I will end this mammoth letter. I would be very grateful if you would pass on warmest greetings from my wife and me to Miss Wolff. I will write to her soon.

With best wishes to Mrs. Jung, I remain,
Your grateful,
E. Neumann

I wrote the letter on the typewriter out of "consideration" only. I don't like doing it, but my writing is known to be illegible.

---

[371] *Psychology and Alchemy*, published as volume 5 of the *Psychologische Abhandlungen* (Jung, 1944), is the extended version of Jung's Eranos lectures from 1935, "Dream Symbols of the Process of Individuation" (Jung, 1936a), and 1936, "Religious Ideas in Alchemy" (Jung, 1937).

[372] Helton Godwin "Peter" Baynes (1882–1943): Analytical psychologist, Jung's assistant and translator of his work. London-born Baynes studied medicine. Because of the breakdown of his first marriage with Rosalind Thornycroft (1891–1973) he came to Zurich for therapy with Jung shortly after the end of World War I. Over time he formed a friendship with Jung and became his first assistant. He organized and joined Jung's journey to Mount Elgon in 1925 (see n. 221), shortly after the tragic suicide of his second wife, Hilda (née Davidson). English translations of Jung's writings by Baynes include *Psychological Types* (1926) and *Two Essays on Analytical Psychology* (1928), which he translated with his third wife, Cary F. Baynes (née Fink). Despite reservations by Jung and Toni Wolff, Baynes left Zurich in 1931 in order to marry Agnes Sarah "Anne" Leay and settled down in England. Baynes became the leading figure of Jungian psychology in England. He wrote two influential books, *Mythology of the Soul: A Research into the Unconscious from Schizophrenic Dreams and Drawings* (1940), which used material from two cases, one of them being Michael Fordham (see n. 366), and *Germany Possessed* (1941), a psycho-biography of Hitler. During the days of the blitz, Reed House, in West Byfleet near London, where Peter, his wife, and their three children lived, was frequently endangered by bombs and doodlebugs. At one time three incendiary bombs landed in the garden, one on the roof of the house, and two on the lawn (Baynes-Jansen, p. 9). In a letter to Jung he describes the pressure of the situation: "We had a streak of bombs straddle the house last night; one fell among the trees just beyond the ditch at the bottom of the field and one on the wood the other side of the road. But the only damage was a couple of window casements blown out by the blast in the summer-house, and some glass in the greenhouse. That was at 8:30 in the evening. So now we all sleep down in the hall" (unpublished letter, quoted in Baynes-Jansen, pp. 312–13). The book Neumann refers to in his letter might be *Mythology of the Soul*, as he seemed to have a copy of *Germany Possessed* as a quote in the unpublished typescript "Die Bedeutung des Bewusstseins für die tiefenpsychologische Erfahrung" ("The Significance of Consciousness for Depth-Psychological Experience") (Neumann, 1943) indicates.

Küsnacht, Zurich,
Seestrasse 228

8th January 1946

Dr. Erich Neumann,
1, Gordon St.,
Tel Aviv

Dear Doctor,

As Professor Jung is still away on holiday I would like to let you know that your work on the occasion of his 70th birthday[373] has arrived here safely. Your work on *Depth Psychology and a New Ethic* as well as your letter of 1st October have also reached Professor Jung. I am sorry that I did not let you know of their safe arrival immediately, as Prof. Jung intended to do so himself personally. Unfortunately in the last year there has been so much urgent work to attend to that he has not yet got round to reading your works. Since his illness, he must use his energy sparingly and this means sadly that some things have to be laid to one side. I know, however, that he hopes very much to be able to write to you at length very soon.

I don't know whether you will remember me. As you will see, I have remained faithfully in my post since you were last in Switzerland.[374]

With belated best wishes for the New Year and best regards,
Your,
[Marie-Jeanne Schmid]

---

[373] It is not clear to which text Schmid refers. Neumann did not contribute to the festschrift for Jung's seventieth birthday. Probably he sent an unpublished typescript. No matching text could be found in the ETH archive, the Jung family archive, or in the Neumann papers in Jerusalem.

[374] Marie-Jeanne Schmid worked as Jung's secretary from 1932 to 1952 (see n. 330). The last time she had met Neumann was when he visited Zurich in May/June 1936 (see letters 19 N, 20 N, and 21 J).

Dr. Erich Neumann,
Analytical Psychologist

Tel Aviv, 4. VI. 46
1, Gordon St.

Dear Professor Jung,

In the last post I have sent you the first section of my book on the archetypal stages of the development of consciousness, which deals with the psychology of myth. The second section will follow very soon; I am just rewriting some elements of it. As you can imagine, this work is very important to me and I would like to publish this work this time. I think it is now ready to come out. The isolation of my existence in Palestine is probably greater than you imagine, and I fear a part of the deficiencies of which I was fully conscious on sending the manuscript to you has to do with this basic fact of my life. I have virtually no opportunity of discussing any scientific matters with peers, and this may be evident. How much my work is damaged by this and where its errors lie I expect to learn from you, dear Professor. Although I have, I think, achieved a certain degree of personal equilibrium, at least as much as my affective and "marslike" nature will allow, I am quite shaky in my self-evaluation as well as in the evaluation of my work. Sometimes, especially when I am caught up in the work, I find it important, at other times everything becomes doubtful once again. I.e., my presentation and my ability to formulate adequately what I have to say becomes problematic, but not the matter itself. Even here, of course, I come up against the limitations of my nature, that I expect too much from the material that I am starting from and I distance myself too far from it.

The fact that I have heard absolutely nothing from you apart from the confirmation of receipt from Miss Schmidt [*sic*] is naturally rather disappointing, but I hope that only the best reasons were behind this, namely, copious and productive work, but not over exertion or illness. The *Alchemy*,[375] *Paracelsica*,[376] and the *Mythology*[377]—this unfortunately only very recently—are the latest works of yours that are in my possession, I do not yet have the book on contemporary events[378] and the Eranos essay on the mass.[379]

The alchemy book is, it seems to me, the most important book since *Transformations*, for me anyway, though I must also say that for me, as remarkable as that may sound, it is a type of "West-East Divan"[380] in which I browse to repeatedly discover something new. As the third in the league I love, by the way, Mann's *Joseph* novel.[381] I express a quiet wish that I would love to read something from you about it. Jung-Kerényi, Mann-Kerényi,[382] but why not Jung-Mann?[383]

---

[375] See n. 318.

[376] Two lectures given in 1941 on the occasion of the four hundredth anniversary of the death of Paracelsus: "Paracelsus als Arzt" and "Paracelsus als geistige Erscheinung" (Jung, 1942).

[377] *Essays on a Science of Mythology* (Jung and Kerényi, 1941).

[378] *Essays on Contemporary Events* (Jung, 1946) includes 'Wotan,' 'After the catastrophe,' 'The fight with the shadow,' and 'Psychotherapy and a Philosophy of Life.'

[379] Jung's Eranos lecture of 1941, "Transformation Symbolism in the Mass" (Jung, 1942).

[380] Collection of lyrical poems by Johann Wolfgang von Goethe, inspired by the Persian poet Hafis, first published in 1819.

[381] Thomas Mann (1875–1955): German literary Nobel laureate (1929), wrote a four-part novel on the biblical stories of Genesis titled *Joseph and His Brothers*. The four volumes retell the biblical stories from Jacob to Joseph and were written between 1926 and 1943 (Mann, 1933–43). Paul Bishop argues that Jung's archetypal theory played a significant role in the development of Mann's novel (Bishop, 1996). In 1952 Neumann sent a copy of his commentary on Apuleius's *Amor and Psyche* to Mann, who replied: "I am reading the small book with the greatest attention and feel very at home in it. An eternally charming story and a brilliant, deeply lively commentary" (Mann to Neumann, 31 May 1952 [NP]).

[382] Karl Kerényi and Thomas Mann were in correspondence with each other from 1934 to 1955. In 1945 Kerényi published the volume *Romandichtung und Mythologie: Ein Briefwechsel mit Thomas Mann* on the occasion of Mann's seventieth birthday (Kerényi, 1945), which is most likely the collaboration to which Neumann refers in the letter. The entire correspondence was published in 1960 (Mann and Kerényi, 1960).

[383] Although Mann spent his first years in exile from 1933 to 1938 near Jung in Küsnacht there was almost no personal contact between the two men. On the relationship between Mann and Jung and an alleged meeting in the 1940s, see Paul Bishop (1999). After having read Jung's "The State of Psychotherapy Today" (Jung, 1934a), Mann noted in his diaries on 16 March 1935: "Another one [sc. article; ML] about psychoanalysis in Germany and the revolting conduct of Jung has caused me to reflect on the ambiguousness of human and intellectual phenomena. If a highly intelligent man like Jung takes the wrong stand, there will naturally be traces of truth in his position that will strike a sympathetic note even in his opponents. Jung is correct when he insists that only a kind of 'soulless rationality' would overlook the fact that there is something positive about neurosis. [. . .] Jung's thought and his utterances tend to

To my mind, Mann has been confusing Freud with you for a long time,[384] but, anyway, the history of ideas will not be disturbed by that. For me, these two names are most closely interwoven with each other as discoverers of the mythical world. Please do not be angry with me because of this, I do know, of course, that it is not my job to demand even more of your already overstretched energies.

So now to return to me and my book. I once dreamed, almost three years ago, that you said to me: "I would like to eat some more fruit with you." This sentence got into me in its own or in my own way, and independently of the complexity of its meaning, it has been a strong incentive for me. For, as paradoxical as it may be, it was a challenge to me, and for me, the book is a fruit, which, I am sending you herewith "to eat." Should you have a taste for it, it would be a great pleasure for me, and if "eating together" could find expression in an introduction from you, my egotistic interpretation of the dream would come fully true. But, of course, I withdraw this request in the first instance because your response cannot be predicted. But I do not withdraw my request that you read this book and write something about it for me.

It is my plan to come to Zurich next year, but its viability is still uncertain. It would be highly significant for me to discuss very deep seated fantasies and images that it will take a very long time to come to terms with otherwise.

Although I don't like not writing by hand, I have typed this because of the illegibility of my handwriting, as well as I can, I hope you will value my now writing a few lines. I hope very much that you are well; here we are "physically" well, psychically there is too much to process that is difficult, collectively more than individually.

---

glorify nazism and its 'neurosis.' He is an example of the irresistible tendency of people's thinking to bend itself to the times—a higher class example. He is *not* a loner in the sense of the *Schlamm* article, is not one of those who remain true to the eternal laws of good sense and morality and thereby find themselves to be rebels in their time. He swims with the current. He is intelligent, but not admirable" (Mann, 1983, p. 235).

[384] Mann read Sigmund Freud extensively in 1926 and held two speeches on Freud: In his 1929 speech, "Freud's Position in the History of Modern Thought" ("Die Stellung Freuds in der modernen Geistesgeschichte"), Mann depicts Freud's antirationalism as a radicalization of the enlightenment. In 1936, Mann was invited to hold a speech in Vienna on the occasions of Freud's eightieth birthday. His presentation was titled "Freud and the Future." On 14 June 1936 Mann visited Freud in order to present his speech to Freud in person (see Hummel, 2006).

I hope that both letter and manuscript arrive before your holidays. As soon as the second section is ready—I think in about 6 weeks—I will send it to you too.

With best wishes and greetings,
I am your,
E. Neumann

Küsnacht, Zch, 11th July 1946,
Seestrasse 228

Dr. Erich Neumann,
1, Gordon St.,
Tel Aviv

Dear Doctor,

I would just like to let you know that your letter of 4. VI. has arrived safely as well as your manuscript a little later. Professor Jung has taken your manuscript and your earlier works to Bollingen with him where he hopes he will soon be able to read them. Unfortunately he has been so overloaded with work and all kinds of obligations this semester that he could only deal superficially with correspondence and, besides that, is now in urgent need of some relaxation.

With best wishes and greetings,
Your devoted,
[Marie-Jeanne Schmid]

37 J

PROF. DR. C. G. JUNG

KÜSNACHT, ZURICH
SEESTRASSE 228

5 Aug. 1946

Dear Doctor,

I must not keep you waiting any longer, although I am by no means finished with all the reading you have sent me. In particular, your *magnum opus*[385] gives me much to do. I am especially impressed by the clarity and precision of your formulations. I must tarry with any further impressions and ask you for corresponding patience. You can hardly imagine how overloaded with work I am, predominantly with letters. Recently I had to deal with around 100 letters in 14 days. The post connections with other countries were barely reinstated and the floods of letters began. It is also hailing manuscripts that are especially onerous. Alongside this, I must see patients and take care of my own writing. Since my illness I am no longer as capable as I was and must conserve my energy somewhat. In consequence I am not keeping up with demands anywhere. I always wanted to write to you, but each time a matter got in the way that needed to be dealt with immediately so that I never found the space to write you in a substantial way. I have also been giving some thought to how we can get you back to Europe again. But for the time being I can't see any way this can be done. The situation here is extremely difficult and everything is uncertain. While we are still living on our cultural island as before, everything around us is nothing but destruction, physically as well as morally. To do something reasonable oneself, you have to close your eyes. Germany is indescribably rotten. Letters I receive from there are, with a few exceptions, part childish, part obstinate,

---

[385] Jung refers to the manuscript of *The Origins and History of Consciousness*. See Neumann's letter from 4 June 1946 (35 N).

part hysterical, which convinces me more than everything that my diagnosis of the state of the German psyche was correct. In France, England, and Switzerland it is now Catholic scholars[386] who are engaged with my psychology. By the way, a book has just come out by a reformed Theologian, Dr. H. Schär: *Religion and the Cure of Souls in the Psychology of C. G. Jung* (Rascher, Zurich).[387] That should interest you. It is very good and positive. The author is a lecturer in the psychology of religion at the University of Bern. I have just formulated 2 lectures on the *Spirit of Psychology* for Eranos.[388] It is a matter of fundamental explanations. I am sending you off-prints. In the near future my small book on the *Transference* will appear.[389] It is a risky

[386] Since August 1945 Jung had been in contact with the Dominican priest and professor for Dogmatic Theology in Oxford Victor White (1902–1960). In his first letter to White Jung wrote: "I am highly interested in the point of view the church takes with reference to my work. I had many discussions with catholic priests in this country too and it is on my instigation that catholic scholars have been invited to the Eranos lectures of which you presumably have heard. We enjoy the collaboration of an extremely competent scholar of the patristic literature, Professor Hugo Rahner S.J. of Innsbruck University. Quite a number of of catholic publications have been occupied with my psychology in this country too and there are some among them, which are really very understanding" (Jung to White, 26 September 1945; Jung and White, pp. 4–5). Next to Hugo Rahner (1900–1968), Catholic theologians attending the Eranos meetings until 1946 included Ernesto Buonaiuti (1881–1946), professor for Church History, excommunicated in 1924; and Henri-Charles Puech (1902–1986), professor for History of Religion at the College de France. Via Jolande Jacobi, Jung got in contact with Père Bruno de Jésus-Marie (1892–1962), the editor of the *Etudes Carmélitaines*, who came to see Jung with Hans Schnyder von Wartensee (1895–1987) in June 1946 (Jacobi to Jung 13 June 1949, Jung to Jacobi, 2 July 1946; see Jung and Jacobi [JA]).

[387] Hans (a.k.a. Johann Friedrich) Schär (1910–1967): Protestant theologian, professor of Science of Religion, Psychology of Religion, and Pastoral Theology at the University of Bern. *Religion and the Cure of Souls in Jung's Psychology* (*Religion und Seele in der Psychologie C. G. Jungs*) was published in 1946. Jung praised the book in his inaugural speech of the C. G. Jung Institute on 24 April 1948: "Of particular interest are the repercussions of complex psychology in the psychology of religion. The authors here are not my personal pupils. I would draw attention to the excellent book by Hans Schär on the Protestant side, and to the writings of W. P. Witcutt and Father Victor White" (Jung, 1948, § 1135). His book *Erlösungsvorstellungen und ihre psychologischen Aspekte* (*The Idea of Salvation and Its Psychological Aspects*) (1950) was the second volume of the publication series of the C. G. Jung Institute Zurich. Schär, among others, delivered a eulogy at Jung's funeral service.

[388] The topic of the Eranos conference 1946 was *Geist und Natur* (*Spirit and Nature*). In accordance with the tradition of the conference Jung delivered two lectures titled "Der Geist der Psychologie" ("The Spirit of Psychology") (Jung, 1947). The text was later reworked and republished under the title "Theoretische Überlegungen zum Wesen des Psychischen" ("On the Nature of the Psyche").

[389] *The Psychology of the Transference* (*Die Psychologie der Übertragung*) (Jung, 1946).

Figure 5. Neumann talking to Gershom Scholem, Adolf Portmann (right), and Olga Fröbe-Kapteyn at Eranos (Eranos Archive; courtesy of Paul Kugler).

matter but when one is old one can say more than when one has life still ahead of one.

The situation in Palestine seems to be very difficult. The new age is announcing itself with endless birth pains.

Recently I met Scholem[390] here at the home of one of my kabbalist

[390] Gershom (Gerhard) Scholem (1897–1982): German-born Jewish scholar of Jewish mysticism; born in Berlin, Scholem, a dedicated Zionist from 1911 onward, immigrated to Palestine in 1923. He knew Martin Buber and Walter Benjamin from his Berlin years. As part of his dissertation he translated and commented on the kabbalistic books *Sefer ha-Bahir* (Book of Illumination) (Scholem, 1923). In Jerusalem he first worked as a librarian, before he obtained a position at the Hebrew University, which he served until the end of his life. Scholem was arguably the most important scholar of the kabbalah in the twentieth century. He published numerous books and articles, including *Major Trends in Jewish Mysticism* (1941) and *Sabbatei Sevi: The Mystical Messiah, 1626–1676* (1973). Scholem's name is inseparably linked with the Eranos conference, which he first attended in 1949. In a letter to Olga Fröbe-Kapteyn from 3 April 1948 Neumann expressed his disappointment that Scholem would not attend the conference. In a letter from 14 April (probably 1949) he urged Fröbe-Kapteyn to put money together for Scholem's attendance: "Please see to it that you get the money together for Scholem, it would be very nice and important" (Neumann to Olga Fröbe-Kapteyn [EA]). The relationship between Neumann and Scholem was on good terms and based on mutual respect (private conversation with Rali Loewenthal-Neumann). Neumann reviewed the German edition of *Major Trends in Jewish Mysticism* (Neumann, 1958a). Scholem wrote an obituary for Neumann (Scholem, 1960), which he sent to Olga Fröbe-Kapteyn "with sad greetings. Dr. G. Scholem"

pupils.[391] He is an interesting phenomenon. He's plunging into the unconscious from the roof and since the corns on the feet are blind, he can't see what he's getting into.

In the meantime with best greetings and wishes,
Your always devoted,
C. G. Jung

(EA). In the obituary Scholem wrote: "He [Neumann] came from C. G. Jung's school of Analytical Psychology and was among its most respected and gifted representatives in the world. He was an autonomous man who thought through the Jungian ideas in his own way and sought to develop them further. I often heard him described as the logician of the Jungian school" (Scholem, 1960).

[391] Probably Rivkah Schärf (see n. 398) or Siegmund Hurwitz (see n. 500).

38 MJS

2 January 1947

Dr. Erich Neumann,
1, Gordon St.,
Tel Aviv

Dear Doctor,

I don't know whether you have now heard about Prof. Jung's illness but, so that you do not remain too long without news in response to your letter of 14th December 1946,[392] I would at least like to tell you that this latter arrived safely.

Prof. Jung had another serious heart attack[393] about seven weeks ago from which he is recovering only slowly and with great effort. Although he is feeling quite a lot better—for the last week he has been able to sit for about an hour a day in an armchair—he is still very weak in every regard, and, since he must be spared all exertion, I have to keep all weightier correspondence from him. Unfortunately

---

[392] Neumann's letter is missing.

[393] Jung's second heart attack happened on 4 November 1946. Barbara Hannah recalled the incident: "Altogether, Jung's health seemed to be particularly good in the autumn of 1946. [...] It was, therefore, a completely unexpected shock to hear two days later that he had had another heart attack the night before and was again very ill. This time, refusing to go to the hospital, he had to have two nurses to look after him, day and night, in his own house. This illness was even more unexpected, especially to Jung himself, than the one in 1944. He had the feeling then that 'there was something wrong with my attitude' and at first felt in some way responsible for having broken his leg. But this time it was a real bolt from the blue. [...] Jung remained ill for three months. About December 16 he sent me a message that he was still suspended over the abyss and warning me against optimism; he added that the real trouble was in the sympathicus. After his illness he told me that he was doubtful if he really had a heart infarct. At all events, it was mainly a disturbance of the vegetative nervous system that had the effect of giving him tachycardia (racing of the pulse). He again found himself confronted, like medicine men all over the world, with curing himself. The doctors insisted it was another heart infarct; and he was thus forced to find out for himself what was really the matter and how it should be met. Once again he said that he had an illness because he was faced with the mysterious problem of the *hieros gamos* (the *mysterium coniunctionis*)" (Hannah, pp. 293–94). Cf. n. 370.

it cannot be predicted how long it will take until he can take up his work again and concern himself with his correspondence. So I have to ask you for your patience.

With best wishes and greetings for the New Year, I remain your devoted,
[Marie-Jeanne Schmid]

39 MJS

[Küsnacht, Zurich] 8th January 1947

Dr. Erich Neumann,
1, Gordon St.,
Tel Aviv

Dear Doctor,

Just to inform you that your manuscript Part II has also arrived safely.[394]
I have sent the second copy on to Miss Wolff who is currently in the
Rigi.[395] She has not been very well for a while now, which may well
be the reason you have not heard from her for a long time.
    Professor Jung continues to be fairly well.

With best wishes,
Yours truly,
[Marie-Jeanne Schmid]

---

[394] Second part of *The Origins and History of Consciousness.* See Neumann's letter from 4 June
1946 (35 N) and Jung's letter from 5 August 1946 (37 J).
    [395] The Rigi is a mountain range in central Switzerland, located between the Vierwaldstätter
Lake, the Zuger Lake, and the Lake Lauerz.

Dr. Erich Neumann,
Analytical Psychologist

Tel Aviv, 1st February 1947

Dear Miss Schmid,

Firstly I would like to thank you very much indeed for your communications, which, as unpleasant and oppressive as they were, at least brought the unpleasant uncertainty to an end. No one knows how torturous the isolation is in which we live here and I would make a big request of you to keep me up to date if the time allows you to do so. To hear so belatedly about Prof Jung's being taken ill is actually, as you will understand, an unbearable state. I have already received a letter from Miss Wolff, which pleased me very much, and who, having received the second section from you, has now read it, but I would very much like to ask you to write to me about the nature of Miss Wolff's illness, if you can, as she only alludes to it and I don't like to inquire about it to her. I hope it is nothing serious. She wrote to me that Prof. Jung is recovering well, but of course I am very concerned and would be glad to be briefed further.

It is obvious that my manuscript must be kept back, in any case I thank you once again for the trouble the manuscript gives you but all the same, I request you to keep me up to date with news. I hope you are well yourself, but can imagine how demanding the current situation is for you both inwardly and externally.

Once again many thanks and best wishes,
I am your,
E. Neumann
Tel Aviv, 1 Gordon St.,
Palestine

41 MJS

Küsnacht, Zch, 25th February 1947

Dr. Erich Neumann,
1, Gordon St.,
Tel Aviv

Dear Doctor,

I'm sorry I could not reply to your letter of 1. II. immediately as I had been wiped out by the flu, which is widespread here at the moment.

Prof. Jung's progress continues to be encouraging. He can now spend the larger part of the day in the library and has even been able to undertake short walks as far as the garden gate. Now and then he receives brief visits, but he is not seeing any patients at all—and this will have to continue to be the case in order to avoid another catastrophe. But he has started to work on his own studies again, albeit at a very slow pace. He has revised last year's Eranos lectures and is now working on his explorations into the Trinity.[396] It's not looking good for his correspondence, as he has neither the time nor inclination to bring to it, or only in very limited measure. I have, though, brought it to his attention that a letter from you was awaiting him and a second part of your manuscript. He remembered immediately that he had a read a part of section 1 and commented that he will read the second section whenever possible.

As far as Miss Wolff is concerned, she has been suffering for nearly two years now from a difficult arthritis. This has worsened so much in the course of this winter that she can now hardly walk—unfortunately the cure in the Rigi has also not helped in fact, although she

---

[396] Jung revised his Eranos lecture of 1940–41 "Zur Psychologie der Trinitätsidee." The extended version, "Versuch einer psychologischen Deutung des Trinätsdogmas" ("A Psychological Approach to the Dogma of the Trinity"), was first published in 1948 in *Symbolik des Geistes* (Jung, 1942a).

has felt stronger on the whole since then. As you can imagine she is exceptionally brave, goes on working as always and takes part in all the Club evenings, etc. It is really painful to see her in this condition, mostly because one can't actually hope for any improvement.

And—as you were kind enough to inquire about me—in general I am quite well. Only, as you rightly guess, the longer this goes on, the clearer it is that I feel like a policeman who has to hold back a huge crowd, and that is tiring in the long run. That, and the adaptation to the irrational in Prof Jung's life and way of operating that is coming ever more strongly into the foreground. One can do nothing other than fulfill one's role to the best of one's knowledge and conscience.

In wishing you all good regards I remain your,
[Marie-Jeanne Schmid]

42 J

Küsnacht, Zch, 21st April 1947

Dr. Erich Neumann,
1, Gordon St.,
Tel Aviv

Dear Colleague,

I have just seen Dr. Adler who was in Zurich. He informed me that you were asking after me. You have evidently not received the hand-written letter. According to my not entirely reliable memory it was written either in November or in February when I was gradually getting a guilty conscience that I had not finished reading your man-uscripts, although they interest me very much. But so much has hap-pened here that I can hardly find the time to take care of my corre-spondence, let alone the uninterrupted reading of manuscripts.

I asked you in my earlier letter whether you would be willing to have your manuscript printed here—I mean your great book. If you wish to publish it in this form, I would gladly recommend it to my publisher, Rascher. By the way, I have already hinted at this to him. In this book you have done a great deal better than I have and you have further developed much, where I got stuck in the difficulties of be-ginnings.[397] I must tell you more about this—God willing. At the moment it is simply impossible for me as I am occupied with some things that are also to be published,—to be precise, with the work

---

[397] Jung reiterates that argument in his foreword to Neumann's *The Origins and History of Consciousness*: "It [sc. the book; ML] begins just where I, too, if I were granted a second lease of life, would start to gather up the *disjecta membra* of my own writings, to sift out all those 'be-ginnings without continuations' and knead them into a whole" (Jung, 1949, § 1234).

that will be published along with Rivkah Schärf's[398] dissertation that is now gradually taking shape.

In the meantime, best wishes, in anticipation of your reply,
Your always loyal,
C. G. Jung

---

[398] Rivkah Schärf Kluger (1907–1987): Religious scholar and Jungian psychotherapist; born in Bern, grew up in Zurich; received her doctoral degree in Semitic Languages and Religious History from the University of Zurich. Her doctoral thesis "Die Gestalt des Satans im Alten Testament" (1948) (English: "Satan in the Old Testament" [1967]) was published together with several essays by Jung "Zur Pänomenologie des Geistes im Märchen" ("The Phenomenology of the Spirit in Fairytales"), "Der Geist Mercurius" ("The Spirit Mercurius"), "Versuch zu einer psychologischen Deutung des Trinitätsdogmas" ("A Psychological Approach to the Dogma of the Trinity"), "Zur Psychologie östlicher Meditation" ("The Psychology of Eastern Meditation") in volume 6 of *Psychologische Abhandlungen* (*Psychological Treatises*) titled *Symbolik des Geistes* (*Symbolism of the Spirit*) (Jung, 1948a). Rivkah Schärf underwent a longtime analysis with Jung and became a close collaborator of his. After its foundation in 1948 she regularly held courses at the C. G. Jung Institute on mythological and religious topics until the early 1980s. After her marriage to Yehezkel Kluger the couple moved to Los Angeles in 1955 and to Haifa in 1969. In Israel they were instrumental in the further development of the Israel Association of Analytical Psychology, founded by Erich Neumann. Schärf Kluger and Neumann shared a common interest in Hasidism. Her works include *Psyche and Bible: Three Old Testament Themes* (1974) and *The Archetypal Significance of Gilgamesh: A Modern Ancient Hero* (1991, published posthumously by Yehezkel Kluger). On Schärf Kluger see Dreifuss (1988) and the recorded interview *Remembering Jung: Rivkah and Yehezkel Kluger* (2003).

Dr. Erich Neumann,
Analytical Psychologist

Tel Aviv, 23. IV. [1947]
1, Gordon St.

My dear Professor Jung,

I have just received a letter from Gerhard Adler from which I learn that, to my greatest regret, a letter from you to me must have gone astray. It is possible that it will arrive belatedly, although that seldom happens, but even this is not ruled out at the moment in the chaotic circumstances that prevail here.

With great pleasure, I gather from Adler's letter that you like my book, that you want to offer it to Rascher and are even willing to write an introduction for him—and for me. It goes without saying that I am exceptionally pleased about this, and especially, as you can imagine, about the introduction, and I am not only in agreement but, far beyond that, I am most gratefully obliged to you. For I know what each new additional demand means for you that diverts you from the "main business," your own work.

Would you be so kind as to inform me whether I have to wait for a response from Rascher, or whether I should write to Rascher myself.

I am just revising the *Ethic* that you have also now read and that you also like—which I am very pleased about—because it has become too abstract and I feared it would be rather too "philosophical" for you. I think it ought to be published in England. But, of course, that is not as important as the publication of the book.

Now I have a further request, but it is one that, I hope, will be a job for Miss Schmid more than for you. My wife and I wish to come to

Switzerland, if possible, in August. I would like to speak to you in person once again after such a long time, come to the Ascona conference, and possibly see Rascher. Since we're all considered "terrorists" here now and find it hard to get a visa, it would be exceptionally important if you could request our attendance at the Ascona conference. I would attempt to arrange everything else so that we could be there in August. Such an attendance request would certainly be important both for here and for Bern.

I heard from Miss Schmid and also from G. Adler that you are quite recovered and already immersed once again in your work. I wish very much to be able to see this for myself in not too long a time. The distances make all contact so difficult, and besides it is now more than ten years since I have been able to speak to anyone. It is high time to speak with you, Miss Wolff, and Adler once again.

The situation here is desperate, not worse than in the whole of the Western world to which we belong apparently more for the worse than the better. But some time even this will reach a positive outcome, with and/or without us. In the meantime, I am working a great deal. Practice, course and the next book on the developmental stages of woman. The joy of writing and working is comparable now with little else.

Once again, dear Professor Jung, my thanks for your willingness. In the hope of hearing from you soon, I am
Your grateful,
E. Neumann

Küsnacht, Zch, 30th April 47

Dr. Erich Neumann,
1, Gordon St.,
Tel Aviv

Dear Colleague,

I was very pleased to receive your letter that arrived in about 4 days. I only hope that my letter of 21 April has also now reached you.

As I gather from your letter that you are willing to give me a free hand regarding the publication of your writings, I will now speak to Rascher in order to see what can be done. I will therefore attempt, in the first instance, to get your book out. After that, it might be possible to accommodate one or other of your essays in my *Psychological Treatises*. I will write a short foreword to your book as soon as we know it can be printed. The situation in this regard is quite difficult here as the printing presses are enormously overloaded. A further question will be the revisions. With the uncertainty of the post, this question is not completely straightforward.

I enclose the requested letter of invitation to Ascona. I'm looking forward to seeing you again after such a long time. I will however not be speaking at this conference as I must grant myself necessary peace and quiet. But I will be there whatever happens.

The things one reads in the papers about Palestine are not pleasant, for sure, but life elsewhere in Europe (with very few exceptions) is also not very pretty. I can't ward off a certain deep pessimism. I can only compensate for it by studying atomic physics, which promises to become very interesting for psychology.

As soon as I have got things clear with Rascher I will write to you again. Meanwhile, with best greetings and wishes,

Your loyal,
C. G. Jung

45 J[399]

Küsnacht, Zurich, April 30th 1947
Seestr. 228.

Dr. E. Neumann,
1 Gordon St.,
Tel Aviv.

Dear Dr. Neumann,

As you know, there is another Eranos meeting to be held as usual in Ascona this summer. It will take place from August 18th to August 26th. There will be a number of very interesting lectures to be discussed, among them lectures by Prof. Erwin Schrödinger (Dublin), Prof. Charles Virolleaud (Paris), Prof. H. Leisegang (Jena), Prof. Erik Peterson (Rome), Dr. Leo Baeck (London), and others.[400]

The purpose of my letter is to invite you to this meeting and I hope very much that you are able to attend it. It would be of [the] greatest interest to us to hear of your own experiences in the field of medical psychology.

Hoping to see you in Ascona,
I remain,
Yours sincerely,
[C. G. Jung]

[399] English invitation to Eranos meeting, Ascona 1947; first version; attached to Jung's letter of 30 April 1947 (44 J).

[400] Erwin Schrödinger (1887–1961): Austrian/Irish physicist, Nobel laureate (1933); founder and director of the Dublin Institute of Advanced Studies (1940–55). Charles Virolleaud (1879–1968): French archaeologist and religious historian; helped in deciphering the inscriptions of ancient Ugarit. Hans Leisegang (1890–1951): German philosopher and physicist, author of *Die Gnosis* (1924); lost his chair for philosophy in Jena in 1948 because of his political criticism. Erik Peterson (1890–1960): German theologian; converted from Lutheran protestantism to Catholicism and moved to Rome in 1930; in 1947 he became assistant professor for Patristics at the Papal Institute for Christian Archaeology in Rome. Leo Baeck (1873–1956): German rabbi, highest Jewish representative during the Nazi period in Germany; was deported to the concentration camp Theriesienstadt in 1943, which he survived; after the war he settled down in London. Baeck was the only one of those mentioned in Jung's invitation who lectured at Eranos in 1947.

Dr. Erich Neumann,
Analytical Psychologist

Tel Aviv, II. V. 47
1 Gordon St.

Dear Miss Schmid,

I'm afraid I must come to you with another request even though I already have so much to thank you for. The difficulties of getting to Switzerland from here are very great because of the current anxiety about terrorists, and you will understand that both my wife and I are very keen to be able to come to the Ascona conference this year. My need to speak with Dr. Jung again after so many years is understandably very great, especially now in connection with my book.

First request: The enclosed letter from Mrs. Fröbe-Kapteyn[401] needs to be redrafted in such a way that it also applies to my wife who, as you probably know, has been working as an analyst for ten years. It would perhaps be good to insert a sentence to the effect that the renewing of our cultural collaboration is very important precisely for Palestine and precisely at this time. (Which, by the way, is the truth.)

---

[401] Olga Fröbe-Kapteyn (1881–1962): spiritualist, theosophist, and scholar, founder of the Eranos conference. Born in England to Dutch parents she first attended school in London and later the art school in Zurich. In 1909 she married Iwan Fröbe, an Austrian musician and conductor, who tragically died in a plane crash six years later. She moved to Ascona in 1920, where she developed her interest in Indian philosophy and theosophy. In 1928 she had a conference building, the Casa Eranos, built next to her house (Casa Gabriella). There she held annual conferences from 1933 on that were dedicated to dialogue between East and West. Neumann, who first attended the Eranos conference in 1947, gave presentations from 1948 until 1960. Fröbe-Kapteyn, who shared with Neumann the role of an outsider in the Zurich Jungian circles, became one of the closest friends and allies of Neumann in Switzerland. In 1954 she traveled with Erich and Julie Neumann to the Netherlands and England. Her collection of archetypal imagery formed the basis of the Archive for Research in Archetypal Symbolism in New York. On Jung, Neumann, and the Eranos conference, see introduction, pp. xv, xxxvii–xli, lii.

Second request: Please would you request Prof. Jung to write a separate letter to me and my wife in which he urgently requests us to come to the conference in Switzerland. It would be good to mention in it that we traveled from Palestine to Switzerland in 1936 and that we ought to do this again after such a long time. Perhaps to reinforce this, a remark about the book and Rascher.

I'm afraid that all this is very necessary, as without such letters, etc., the application for a visa is pointless.

Thirdly, I request permission to nominate Prof. Jung and Miss Wolff as Swiss referees.

The granting of a visa mostly takes longer than two months, and as I can only apply for it when I have these letters, I'm afraid I must ask you to speed things up as much as possible so that there is at least the possibility that this trip will come to something.

Dear Miss Schmid, Please forgive all this pestering, but I'm afraid I have no choice.

With many thanks in advance,
Your E. Neumann
PS Dear Miss Schmid! I have just received Prof. Jung's letter with the "invitation" to me to which I will reply straightaway. Unfortunately though [missing][402]

---

[402] Line is missing. Neumann asks to rewrite and extend the invitation to his wife Julie. See 48 J.

19th May

Dr. Erich Neumann,
1, Gordon St.,
Tel Aviv

Dear Doctor,

Enclosed the amended letter of invitation. I hope it achieves the desired outcome. I have sent the letter from Mrs. Fröbe to her with details of how you would like it amended. I hope she will send you the new draft straightaway too.

Prof. Jung is, of course, willing to serve as a referee, and Miss Wolff whom I have also called is willing to do so as long as this means only a "private" reference. (She has had difficulties because of patients of late.) But I am sure only Prof. Jung will be interviewed by the immigration authorities so she will not have any sort of unpleasantness so you can readily put her down for this.

In haste, with best wishes,
Your,
[Marie-Jeanne Schmid]

48 J[403]

May 19th 1947.

Dr. E. Neumann,
1, Gordon St.,
Tel Aviv.

Dear Dr. Neumann,

As you know there is another Eranos meeting to be held as usual in Ascona this summer. It will take place from August 18th to August 26th. There will be a number of very interesting lectures to be discussed, among them lectures by Prof. Erwin Schrödinger (Dublin), Prof. Charles Virolleaud (Paris), Prof. H. Leisegang (Jena), Prof. Erik Peterson (Rome), Dr. Leo Baeck (London), and others.

The purpose of my letter is to invite you and your wife to this meeting and I hope very much that you are able to attend it. It would be of greatest interest to us to hear of both your experiences in the field of medical psychology.—At the same time it would be most important to be able to discuss the publication of your book, a thing that can hardly be done by letters.

Hoping to see you in Ascona,
I remain,
Yours sincerely,
[C. G. Jung]

[403] Invitation to Eranos meeting, Ascona 1947; second version; attached to Marie-Jeanne Schmid's letter of 19 May 1947 (47 MJS).

Dr. Erich Neumann,
Analytical Psychologist

Tel Aviv, 24. V. 47
1 Gordon St.

My dear Professor Jung,

I do apologize very much for my rather late reply to both your letters, but a mild illness and subsequent increased workload are to
blame for this. So firstly, many thanks that you want to attend to my
book and, beyond that, maybe other works. I hope very much that
the book can be released by Rascher. It belongs, it seems to me absolutely with this publisher. I would have the technical matters arranged, I think, it would just be a shame if everything drags on a long
time. With time, even if it goes against my temperament, I have become patient. I have shortened the *Ethic* work and completed it too,
it dates back to 1942–43; I have also outlined the links with my book.
I will send you them shortly, please then dispose of the old copy. I
fear the work would be too long for *Psychological Treatises*—I would
personally be very pleased and in agreement. Only 2 come into question from among my other works, the *Stages of Religious Experience*,
which I consider good (and which has been extended in the meantime) and *The Depth-Psychological Way and Consciousness*.[404] Which
needs to be revised. The other has been superseded by the book.

---

[404] "Der tiefenpsychologische Weg und das Bewusstseins" ("The Depth-Psychological Way and
Consciousness") is the title of the third part the unpublished typescript *Die Bedeutung des Bewusstseins für die tiefenpsychologische Erfahrung* ("The Significance of Consciousness for Depth-
Psychological Experience") (Neumann, 1943), whereas "Stadien religiöser Erfahrung auf dem
tiefenpsychologischen Weg" ("Stages of Religious Experience on the Depth-Psychological Way")
is the title of the fourth part. This final part could not be located among Neumann's unpublished material, but might be identical with the typescript "Zur religiösen Bedeutung des tiefenpsychologischen Weges" (Neumann, 1942).

G. Adler wrote, to my great joy, of how well you have recovered and how deeply you are immersed once again in your work.[405] This has made me very happy even if it also, on the other hand, gives me a guilty conscience to pester you once again with my affairs. This is one of the yardsticks of my life here that much could be said about. The political is not as bad as it sounds and is made to sound, but bad enough. Your pessimism is, I fear, all too justified. But apart from the stark isolation,—where would it be better?—the life here is nice and healthy for the children. It is better for them to grow up in freedom among Jews, everywhere the "end" is uncertain.

It interested me very much to hear that you're taking comfort in "atomic physics." I've just been reading a book about *The Inner World of Atoms* by Z. Bucher,[406] which is very stimulating although I can't yet recognize anything other than important analogies. It is remarkable for me that I am being thrust toward these analogical images in the second part of my book that you're not yet familiar with. "Splitting of the archetype," etc., appeared to me long since as a correlation with the physical event without losing sight of the symbolic nature of it. Your image of the crystallized nature of archetypes belongs naturally very much in this context, but—unmathematical as I am—the decisive thing for me is the image that distinguishes the psychical,— and the energetics, as legitimate as they are, are only an abstract approximation. If you would have a look at the second section, your critique would be very necessary and desirable, specifically on the issue of the energetic conceptions.

Our trip to Switzerland—many thanks for your help with this—is still hanging very much in the air, but I still hope it will be feasible and I will be able to talk with you "face to face" about some matters. It would be necessary and it would be very nice. Hopefully everything here will remain peaceful.

As I close for today, with best wishes and greetings for your ongoing recovery and work, I remain as ever in gratitude,
Your E. Neumann

---

[405] The letters from Adler to Neumann are missing.
[406] Bucher (1946).

Erich Neumann,
Analytical Psychologist

Tel Aviv, 14 June
1 Gordon St.

Dear Miss Schmid,

Firstly I thank you very much for the prompt fulfillment of my requests; I'm afraid I must burden you one more time. I have been told at the consulate here that it would be desirable and useful if we could apply directly to Bern from Switzerland as it can take up to 3 months to sort out. As it would not be very sensible to acquire the visa for the Eranos conference after it had finished, I would now like to ask you to write in Professor Jung's name to Bern on behalf of myself and my wife. Request, invitation, dates of conference, and petition would be accelerated in this way. Once again many thanks from my wife too.

Your,
E. Neumann

51 J

20th June 1947
To the Federal Immigration Authorities, Bern

Dr. Erich Neumann, Tel Aviv, and his wife and colleague have been invited to take part in this year's Eranos conference. The conference runs from 18th–26th August in Ascona. Dr. Neumann is a student of mine, and it is a matter of personal importance to be able to see him at the conference as, among other matters, I wish to discuss the publication of various of his works. I can recommend Dr. and Mrs. Neumann in every regard and would ask you most courteously to grant them the entry visa for Switzerland as soon as possible.

With best respects,
[C. G. Jung]

Küsnacht, Zch, 1st July 1947.

Dr. Erich Neumann,
1, Gordon St.,
Tel Aviv

Dear Colleague,

Having read your first volume, the only troubling terminology to strike me was that of the "castration complex." I consider the use of this term to be not only an aesthetic error, but also an erroneous overvaluation of the sexual symbolism. This complex is a matter of the archetype of sacrifice, a term that is much more comprehensive, and that takes into account the fact that, for the primitive, sex does not have, by far, the same significance as it does for the modern individual. We must always keep in mind that in the psychology of the primitive the search for food in relation to hunger plays a sometimes decisive role. Thus the symbols of sacrifice are by far not only castration or its derivatives, that is particularly plausible if you take the taboos into consideration that all signify sacrifice, each and every one. The prohibition of words or syllables, for example, can only be derived from castration by really stretching the point. We must much more regard the occurrences of real or hinted castration in the spirit of the archetype of sacrifice, from which all of these multifarious forms can be much better understood, without difficulty. The expression "castration complex" is, to my taste, much too concretistic and therefore one-sided, even though it definitely proves to be applicable in a whole series of phenomena. But I would like to have avoided everything that would amount in the end to allowing psychic events to appear as a derivative of a specific instinct. We must place the existence of the psyche as a sui generis phenomenon in the first place and understand the instincts as being in a specific relationship to this. If one does not do this, then all psychic differentiation is basically nothing but. . . . What does one do with a castrated Origen?[407]

That is the only point that I must take issue with. Otherwise, I must say that I admire your clear and rich portrayal to a high degree. I have spoken with Rascher and he has said he is willing to take on the book, but not until next year for economic reasons. In fact, an unavoidable drop in prices is expected, which has made all publishers cautious. If I come across anything else, I will let you know. I will now subject your smaller writings to a closer inspection, as it is possible that Rascher may publish them as a collection. But this question has not been clarified adequately. So you see, since I have been better, I have been engaged with your affairs and am doing my best to facilitate publication. With such extensive things, this is of course not all too easy.

In the meantime, with best wishes,
Your always devoted,
C. G. Jung

[407] Origen of Alexandria (185–245 BCE), also Origen Adamantius: Early Christian theologian and philosopher, well known for his neo-Platonic treatise *On First Principles*. According to Eusebius's *Church History* Origen castrated himself in his youth: "At this time while Origen was conducting catechetical instruction at Alexandria, a deed was done by him which evidenced an immature and youthful mind, but at the same time gave the highest proof of faith and continence. For he took the words, 'There are eunuchs who have made themselves eunuchs for the kingdom of heaven's sake,' Matthew 19:12 in too literal and extreme a sense. And in order to fulfill the Saviour's word, and at the same time to take away from the unbelievers all opportunity for scandal,—for, although young, he met for the study of divine things with women as well as men,—he carried out in action the word of the Saviour" (Book 6, 8,1; Eusebius, 1890). To what extend this account is true or the repitition of rumors by adversatories has been subject of debates in scholarship. Jung's library contains *The Writings of Origen* (1910–11) and a volume of selected texts by Eusebius (1913).

Dr. Erich Neumann,
Analytical Psychologist

Tel Aviv, 8th July 47
1, Gordon St.

Dear Professor Jung,

You can imagine how I pleased I was about your letter letting me know that Rascher has accepted my book. What is more, I am really touched by the active engagement you are showing toward me and my productions. I find myself in the rather precarious position of begging you really and seriously not[408] to overburden yourself with my things on the one hand—you see this Freudian slip sums it up best—so after saying "not" to overburden you—and, then following on from this request, I dive right into the discussion of my works again straightaway. You will, I hope, make an allowance for my slip and for me, as the egotism of the drive to produce is very strong, and as you yourself know only too well, it knows how to defend itself with great violence against the attempts by consciousness to contain it.

I think by now you will have received the partly shortened, partly extended *Ethic* that would form the main part of a book of smaller works, should it come to the of publication such a volume. This has now been "brought into line with" the "Stages book,"[409] which it predates, abbreviated, and illustrated in parts three and four with some dreams, but is otherwise unchanged. Of the essays you already have, I consider both the first two to have been superseded, as their essential contents have been worked into the second part of the book. My question to you concerns this. If it comes to a volume of essays and *Ethic* did not come out as a single publication, which I could well

---

[408] not" ("nicht") has been crossed through and then inserted again.
[409] *The Origins and History of Consciousness* (Neumann, 1949a).

imagine, would further material still be needed? I still have a paper on the *Personal and Transpersonal Psychology of Childhood*[410] and a work: *Prolegomena to the Psychology of the Feminine*,[411] which is actually an introduction to the book on the psychological stages of woman that I am currently working on. It could absolutely appear as an essay in its own right. In any case, I will complete both and have them typed up.

But now to the other important point of your letter, the objection to the "castration complex" terminology. You will excuse me if I elaborate at length here, but it is a matter for substantial discussion.

Firstly, it goes without saying that I am in full agreement with you in this as we must avoid "everything that would amount in the end to allowing psychic events to appear as a derivative of a specific instinct." You write: "I consider this term not only an aesthetic error but also an erroneous overestimation of the sexual symbolism. . . . The expression 'castration complex' is, for my taste, much too concretistic and therefore too one-sided."

I have looked through the first section once again in response to this and I would like to make the following remarks:

1) That the term castration as it is implemented and employed can hardly be misunderstood in a concrete way.
2) That I—up till now—have found no term that could replace it, the reasons for this I will explain.
3) That—and why—the "archetype of sacrifice" in connection with the first section does not express what is meant by the castration symbol.

All these possibly relevant arguments change nothing in regard to the fact that you believe that my remarks could be misunderstood in this manner; the question is, whether this is helped by an annotation.

---

[410] Among Neumann's unpublished material is the fragment of a text dated April 1939 titled "Bemerkungen zur Psychologie des Kindes und der Paedagogik" ("Observations on the Psychology of the Child and Pedagogy") (Neumann, 1939).

[411] On 7 October 1950 Neumann held a lecture at the Psychological Club Zurich titled "Zur Psychologie des Weiblichen im Patriarchat" ("Toward a Psychology of the Feminine in the Patriarchy"), which he repeated in Basel and Tel Aviv. This lecture was published together with "Die Urbeziehung zur Mutter" ("The Primordial Relation to the Mother") (1951) as "Die psychologischen Stadien der weiblichen Entwicklung" ("The Psychological Stages of Woman's Development") (1953). See also letter 73 N, n. 457.

Re 1) On pages 63f., 66, 69, 80, 92, 100, etc., the equivalence of castration, death, dismemberment, madness, and delirium is repeatedly formulated in such a way that a "genital" misunderstanding of castration would have to be impossible, especially as the symbolic meaning of the sexual is explored at length in chapter one, pp. 18, 21. It seems to me absolutely necessary to retain the sexual symbols that are interpreted in a personal way by psychoanalysis. For this reason, I have also consciously retained "incest," once because the transpersonal makes use of these symbols, and then by emphasizing its factual symbolic meaning.[412]

But why is it so hard for me to forego the castration symbol?

Re 2) The debate between the ego-consciousness and the unconscious proceeds substantially along symbolic lines: masculine opposed to feminine (C./f. "Prolegomena" above), Uroboros incest, matriarchal incest, matriarchal castration, the associated cycle of symbols of the fertility rituals, of the gorgon, of the phallic adolescent stage (p. 66), they all revolve around the symbol of the phallus. The entire Osiris chapter with djed-pillars, the sed festival, as well as the concept of the lower and higher masculinity stands and falls with the fact that the conscious ego-hero has the masculine character that he, however, only gradually achieves in stages in the course of his development (pp. 110, 140ff.).

In this sense, "castration" is the thing that threatens this masculinity at the varying stages and in different ways. Hence "higher castration" equates to blinding as castration of the "higher" masculinity, hence "patriarchal" castration as "annihilation by the spirit" (p. 212).

---

[412] The page numbers here and in the following refer to typescript version of *The Orgins and History of Consciousness* and do not match the printed version. In his introduction to the published version Neumann clarifies his understanding of the castration motif and emphasizes its transpersonal symbolical character: "The castration motif, for instance, is not the result of the inheritance of an endlessly repeated threat of castration by a primordial father, or rather by an infinity of primordial fathers. Science has discovered nothing that could possibly support such a theory, which moreover presupposes the inheritance of acquired characteristics. Any reduction of the castration threat, parricide, the 'primal scene' of parental intercourse, and so on, to historical and personalistic data, which presumes to paint the early history of humanity in the likeness of a patriarchal bourgeois family of the nineteenth century, is scientifically impossible. It is one of the tasks of this book to show that, in regard to these and similar 'complexes,' we are really dealing with symbols, ideal forms, psychic categories, and basic structural patterns whose infinitely varied modes of operation govern the history of mankind and the individual" (Neumann, 1949a, pp. xxi–xxii). See also introduction, p. lviii.

I cannot imagine that one could misunderstand this in a concrete way where "castration" is used in such a symbolic way as are creative potency and impotency (c./f., p. 177, p. 105).

Re 3) In my opinion, for this reason, the castration symbol in the "Psychology of Myth" cannot be substituted by the notion of sacrifice, because the "sacrifice" is only a subsuming concept, but not a symbol. In castration, there is the threat to the ego and consciousness by the terrible mother of the unconscious. The ego is supposed to be sacrificed, against which it defends itself. This dramatization of the situation, as an expression of the conflict tension of psyche is not in any way denoted by the concept of sacrifice, but it is very much so by the castration symbol. Not until the hero stage does the sacrifice archetype become relevant, it seems to me, as a fulfilled act assumed by the ego (c./f., *Transformations*). But this situation is not to be subsumed with the other into one concept in which it is precisely the task of the ego to resist, to make itself independent and to sacrifice itself, i.e., to allow itself to be castrated.

I hope to have persuaded you, or else I would be grateful to you for a suggestion. In any case my "resistance" is not a matter of obstinacy. The concept of sacrifice belongs, just like the taboos, etc., to the "offering" in the sense of a positive relationship of the ego to the Self and belongs thereby on the side of consciousness—strengthening—expansion, etc., the castration symbol stands in the first part where it is a question of a disempowerment of the ego-consciousness and of a danger of violation by the unconscious.

Dear Professor Jung, I do hope that I have not bored you too much with my deliberations, but they do seem to me perhaps appropriate in such a fundamental problem of terminology whose significance was clear to me from the beginning.

I have in no way given up hope of being able to see you and speak to you personally. So far, the Swiss visa is still not here, but it could still arrive. The uncertainty of all dispositions is disturbing, but what can one do. The restoration of your health permits you now to get on with your own intensive work, thank God, so G. Adler wrote to me,[413] and as I am only too much aware how indispensable everything is

---

[413] Letter is missing.

that you have to do, I would like to ask you once again not to waste too much time on my matters, "going over my mistakes." Your efforts for my book, which is really important to me, is already almost filling me with feelings of guilt, I really could not expect of you any extra burden from the smaller works. In case I do get to Switzerland, I could probably do some things myself there.

Once again with the warmest of thanks,
I am always,
Your E. Neumann
  [Remark:] Replied!

54 J

PROF. DR. C. G. JUNG

KÜSNACHT, ZURICH
SEESTRASSE 228

19 July 1947

Dear Colleague,

Whatever I can do toward publication of your highly valuable works, I do with pleasure. Unfortunately everything is very delayed due to my illness, which has cost me a good half year. In old age, one feels the pressure of time, and the years become fewer, i.e., one now sees it palpably: *utendum est aetate, cito pede labitur aetas—Nec bona tam sequitur quam bona prima fuit!*[414]

I cannot repudiate the justification of "castration complex" terminology and even less its symbolism, but I must take issue with "sacrifice" not being a symbol. In the Christian sense it is even one of the most significant symbols. The etymology is unclear: as many say *offerre* as they do *operari.* "Sacrifice" is active and passive: one *brings* a "sacrifice" and one *is* a "sacrifice." (Both of these together in the sacrifice symbolism of the mass!) With incest it is the same thing, which is why I had to use the additional term *hierosgamos.* Just as only the twin concepts "Incest-Hierosgamos" describe the whole situation, so also "castration-sacrifice." Could one say *castration symbol* instead of castration complex, to be on the safe side? Or castration *motif* (like incest motif)?

You still have to gain experience for yourself as far as being misunderstood goes. The possibilities exceed all terminology. Perhaps you had better insert a short explanation in the text on the negative and the positive aspect of the symbol and, indeed, right at the beginning where you speak of the castration complex.

---

[414]"Life's to be used: life slips by on swift feet, what was good at first, nothing as good will follow" (Ovid, *Ars Amatoria* III, 65–66; trans. A. S. Kline).

I hope very much that it will be possible for you to come to Switzerland. At the moment I am in my tower on the Obersee enjoying my holidays, which were most urgently needed. Our club wants to start a "C. G. Jung Institute for Complex Psychology."[415] The preparations are already underway. Mrs. Jaffé will be the secretary.[416] She has written a magnificent work on E.T.A. Hoffmann, which I will also publish in my *Psychological Treatises*.[417]

I am very well again, but the weight of 73 years is palpable.

With best wishes,
Your always loyal,
C. G. Jung

[415] The foundation of the C. G. Jung Institute Zurich took place on 24 April 1948. On this occasion Jung gave an address outlining the direction and goals of the new institute (Jung, 1948). Although, officially, the institute began its courses on 25 October, the teaching had already started in the previous term.

[416] Aniela Jaffé (1903–1991): German-born Jewish psychotherapist, Jung's secretary from 1955 to 1961. Orginally from Berlin Jaffé studied medicine in Hamburg. She did not finish her studies as she fled Nazi Germany for Switzerland in 1933. She underwent analysis with Liliane Frey and Jung. Jaffé was the secretary of the C. G. Jung Institute from 1948 until 1955, when she became Jung's full-time secretary. In the last years of Jung's life she recorded and edited his biographical account *Memories, Dreams, Reflections* (Jung, 1961; cf. Jaffé, 1968). Jaffé was a close confidante of the Neumanns. The friendship between Jaffé and Julie Neumann lasted until Julie's death in 1985. Jaffé was the editor of the three-volume German edition of Jung's letters and collaborated with Gerhard Adler on the English edition (Jung, 1973). Her own work includes *Apparitions and Precognition: A Study from the Point of View of C. G. Jung's Analytical Psychology* (1958), *The Myth of Meaning in the Work of C. G. Jung* (1967), *From the Life and Work of C. G. Jung* (1968), and *C. G. Jung: Word and Image* (1977). She was also one of the contributors to *Man and His Symbols* (1961).

[417] Aniela Jaffé's *Bilder und Symbole aus E.T.A. Hoffmanns Märchen "Der goldne Topf"* (*Images and Symbols in E.T.A. Hoffmann's Fairy Tale "The Golden Pot"*) was published in Jung's *Gestaltungen des Unbewussten* in 1950 (Jaffé, 1950).

Dr. Erich Neumann,
Analytical Psychologist

Tel Aviv, 21. VII. [47]
1 Gordon St.

Dear Professor Jung,

I would like to send you my most heartfelt greetings for your birthday and hope that you will spend this year in the best of health and work. This last year brought me renewed and deepened contact with you and your lively interest, and I can only hope that the next years and my work will take further what has begun to be a great enrichment for me. I do hope that you know how much your interest means to me, and what a necessary affirmation it is for me in an intellectual situation that often comes dangerously close to splendid isolation.

I hope still that we will soon be able to speak to you in person. So far the Swiss visa has not yet arrived and it is high time it had. (By the way, has Mrs. Schmid applied to Bern in your name to telegraph the visa as I asked her to do in writing?)[418]

Here, it is beginning to be very unsettled again, the future is very bleak here as it is everywhere, and it will be difficult for us to leave the children on their own in Palestine while we are in Switzerland. But first of all it would be good to know what's going to happen.

I hope you are now restored to the best of health and recovery, and am, once again with all those hard to express wishes that are in me,

In gratitude,
Your
E. Neumann

---

[418] See Neumann's letter to Marie-Jeanne Schmid, 14 June 1947 (50 N).

now: Bollingen, Kt. St. Gallen
24. 7. 1947

Tit.
Federal Immigration Authorities Bern

At the beginning of July I took the liberty of making an application to you to arrange, soonest, a visa for Dr. med. Erich Neumann, 1 Gordon St., Tel Aviv, to enable him to participate in this year's Eranos Conference that begins on 18th VIII. I am very concerned to resume international scientific relationships. These efforts are of great importance for Switzerland. Dr. Neumann now informs me that on 15th. VII he was still not in possession of a visa and that the Swiss Consulate in Jerusalem is refusing to inquire about this by telegraph in Bern. I would be very obliged to you if you could expedite the granting of the visa as quickly as possible.

Yours faithfully,
[C. G. Jung]

57 J

9th August 1947
To the Federal Immigration Authorities,
Bern

I write to express my thanks to you for granting the visa to Dr. and Mrs. Neumann in Tel Aviv. My second letter has crossed with yours. I have since received direct news from Dr. Neumann.

In the meantime I have been asked to endorse an application from England. It is for Dr. Lotte Paulsen[419] (145 Fellows Road, London, NW3), who has been recommended to me as a member of the Society of Analytical Psychology, London. This lady is a well-known psychologist who would like to take part in this year's Eranos Conference, which runs from 18th–26th August.

I can warmly support this application and would request you to grant the visa as quickly as possible to enable her arrival in good time.

With many thanks in advance,
Yours truly,
C. G. Jung

---

[419] Lotte ("Lola") Paulsen (1902–1994), née Fulda: German-born psychotherapist, founding member of the Society of Analytical Psychology; studied in Leipzig where she went into analysis with Ruth Benedict; after her immigration to England in 1937 she continued her analysis with Michael Fordham. See Plaut (1995).

Dr. Erich Neumann,
Analytical Psychologist

27th Sept. 47
Geneva

Dear Professor Jung,

As I actually wanted to write to you in detail, I kept waiting for a peaceful hour only now to find myself writing to you at the last minute, very belatedly and quite briefly.

I have much to thank you for from my stay in Europe, not only for your time that you gave to me and for your efforts with Rascher to which I attribute "substantially" the fact that he has taken on my book and *Ethic*.

I had the impression of being strongly accepted and permitted into your midst and I very well have this to thank for the fact that now the central question—which I never actually asked you and which is also difficult to ask—seems to me, in hindsight, to have been answered. It is like in the—rationally hard to grasp—Hasidic stories where the Zaddik knows the question already and answers it in his sermon or in his conversation. But this is precisely one of the "last things" which I had to ask and it has become almost "unaskable," now that a new window, if not even a door has been opened to me once again.

If the significance of my rather isolated self-sufficiency in Palestine has also become very clear to me once again, precisely because of Zurich, you will therefore understand how terribly much the possibility of meeting with you means and must mean.

Tomorrow my wife and I fly back to Palestine, back to work. But if you understand the depth of my gratitude and my attachment to you, you will also believe me that I will do everything in my power to bring this "impersonal-personal" into a living reality.

With old gratitude,
Your E. Neumann

Please will you give your wife my best wishes. Should your wife have any comments on my manuscript, I am, of course, very grateful for them.

Dr. Erich Neumann,
Analytical Psychologist

Tel Aviv, 17th Dec. 47

Dear Professor Jung,

So once again not weeks but months have past before I have got around to writing to you. But you will understand that after the holidays, my practice demanded my full attention first of all, and then the corrections of *Ethic*, the preparation of the great book, course preparations and, not least, political events[420] have very much laid claim to me.

In the meantime, though, much that is new has constellated—very much with your gracious help. I received the invitation to speak at the Eranos conference on the "Mystic"[421] and to write the introduction to the Great Mother publication of the Eranos archives.[422] Mrs.

---

[420] Under increasing international and domestic pressure because of its anti-immigration policy to Palestine, the constant combating of violence inside the territory, and the increasing economical problems at home, Britain, which had held the League of Nations (forerunner of the United Nations) mandate over Palestine since 1922, asked the United Nations in February 1947 to find a solution to end the conflict between Palestinian Arabs and Jews. A report issued on 1 September recommended the foundation of two separate states. The plan was discussed and accepted by the UN General Assembly on 29 November. The Jewish celebrations were immediately followed by Palestinian attacks against Jews and looting of Jewish shops. In the twelve days following the UN voting eighty Jews were killed, the number was even higher in Arabic cities outside Palestine. See Gilbert (2008), pp. 141–55.

[421] In 1948 Neumann gave his first Eranos lecture, "Der mystische Mensch" ("Mystical Man") (Neumann, 1949).

[422] Neumann was asked by Olga Fröbe-Kapteyn and Jung to write an introductory text to the first publication of the *Eranos Archive for Research in Archetypal Symbolism*. The plan for the book was that it would feature symbolic representations of the Great Mother. The material was first shown as an exhibition at the Eranos conference 1938 on the topic of "Gestalt und Kult der Grossen Mutter" ("The Gestalt and Cult of the Great Mother"). But Neumann's introduction grew extensively and became a manuscript in its own right. It was finally published in 1956 under the title *Die große Mutter: Der Archetyp des großen Weiblichen* (*The Great Mother: An Analysis of the Archetype*) illustrated by images of the Eranos collection.

Fröbe-Kapteyn has been corresponding with me about this up till now[423] and I have now received the papers from America to apply for a Bollingen fellowship. If I receive this, as I hope to do, it will finance not only the Swiss trip, which I am already very happy about, as I will see you and speak to you again, but it will also give me the opportunity to limit my practice somewhat that is almost growing over my head, and to get down to my own work in peace.

It is very important to me to first complete the *Psychology of the Feminine* as a completion of the *Origins History*[424] in which the deviations from the masculine stages in the psychology of consciousness will be portrayed. All this costs time, of course, and circumstances are such here that I earn just about what we need with my workload of 50–55 hours per week. The fellowship would be granted for the Eranos lecture and for the introduction to the Great Mother that you proposed me for, as Mrs. Fröbe-Kapteyn wrote to me. I would like to thank you very particularly for this, as this work will be a special pleasure for me since this volume will be highly valuable as an illustration for the Great Mother chapter in my book. You will understand how happy I would be if, in addition to this work, I could get to write my next book in peace and quiet. As I am a difficult author and know that, so far, I have had to write *every* book twice, I dread every new beginning anyway, but especially, of course, if I must always write "on the hoof" and without continuity.

If Mrs. Fröbe-Kapteyn hadn't kindly forewarned me, the questions on the Bollingen form would probably have really terrified me. I rec-

---

[423] Letter from Olga Fröbe-Kapteyn to Erich Neumann, 30 October 1947: "We would like to invite you to speak on the *'Mystic' from the Perspective of Psychology*. Jung considered that this theme would appeal to you and we would be delighted if you would accept this invitation." Travel expenses should be covered by Bollingen; a fellowship should be offered. [. . .] Even before the war, the Bollingen Foundation planned to publish a series of publications from the Eranos picture archive. They will each consist of around 100 images in large format with a foreword. All images of each volume must relate to a single archetype or primitive image. I have proposed that we commence with the archetype of the Great Mother" (Neumann and Fröbe-Kepteyn [NP]).

[424] See nn. 411 and 457. Although Neumann did not write a monograph on the psychology of the feminine, he used the title "Psychologie des Weiblichen" for the second volume of his collection of essays, *Umkreisung der Mitte* (*Circling the Midpoint*) (Neumann, 1953b). This volume consisted of the articles "Die psychologischen Stadien der weiblichen Entwicklung" ("The Psychological Stages of Woman's Development") (Neumann, 1953), "Über den Mond und das matriarchalische Bewusstsein" ("The Moon and Martriarchal Consciousness") (1950b), and "Zu Mozarts Zauberflöte" ("On Mozart's Magic Flute") (Neumann, 1950a).

ognize contritely everything that I am not and everything that I cannot offer. I am not a member of a "scientific, artistic, or other learned society" and even with the "complete list" of my publications, it is an ugly business. So I urgently need your help once again, dear Professor Jung. Would you be so kind as to write me a letter of recommendation for the foundation that bears the name of your tower that is so dear to me?[425] I think that with two further letters of recommendation from Miss Wolff and G. Adler, I'll manage it.[426] But beside that it says in the form: "Give names and present addresses of three persons from whom the foundation can obtain further information with regard to your qualifications, and who can give expert opinion concerning the value of your project as a contribution to knowledge." Here I need to put three other names. If that is really necessary, it would be a bad thing, for who can assess my highly unfamiliar qualifications and offer an expert opinion about the value of the matter? Since Mrs. Fröbe-Kapteyn requested that I did not speak with anyone about the Eranos book apart from with you, I ask you for your advice in this matter that is certainly only a formality. I have the intention of simply putting your name a second time instead of the desired three names. It goes against regulations but I think it should suffice.

The time in Switzerland, as I hinted to you from Geneva, has had an effect on me that is palpable more indirectly than directly. The fact that you have now pinned the "mystic" on me, as it were, is closely connected to this for me. Personally, I don't feel fully up to the task, but, of course, precisely that is a big incentive, and I will

---

[425] See 61 J.

[426] Gerhard Adler's letter of recommendation is dated 27 December 1947 and reads: "I have been familiar with Dr. Neumann's work for the last twenty years, and he seems to me to be one of the most distinguished and original psychologists which I have ever met. His work on the development of consciousness ('Stadien der Bewusstseins-Entwicklung') which I have read as manuscript, is undoubtably one of the most important books written by a follower of Professor C. G. Jung, and also in the general field of psychologiocal research." Toni Wolff's reference was written on 2 January 1948: "I should like to recommend Dr. Neumann warmly for obtaining the benefit of a Fellowship of the Bollingen Foundation. His qualifications for the work in question are of the first order. He is about to publish the first part of an extensive book on the origin of the mind. I have read the manuscript and am thrilled at the prospect of a very original contribution to the history and psychology of human consciousness" (NP).

attempt to do it justice. For this reason, too, it would be good to have a bit more space to plunge once again into the sea of mysticism.

There is not much to report from my personal domain. There is the hope that we will get through unscathed. It is impossible to write about this as the events are too close and get to one too closely.

I hope your plans for the institute are shaping up in the meantime, without, dear Professor Jung, your having to invest too much energy and work into it all yourself. I only hope that the exertions of the summer were not too much for you. Please do not make too many demands of yourself, because so much is rightly demanded of you. I would have gladly laid before you the plan for an International Journal of Analytical Psychology, but heard to my regret from G. Adler that you and the Zurichers are not in favor of it.

Despite this, I am of the opinion that a broader publication for analytical psychology is immensely important and is, in no way, substituted by the institute. Such a centralization would be urgently desirable exactly because the circle of colleagues is still scattered in every sense. Could one not affiliate the journal to the institute—alongside the publication of documents that you plan? A selection of the lectures held there, together with other contributions, could well be published in this way. The whole project could almost be financed by the subscriptions of those attending the lectures. I can well see the difficulties, but I consider them easier to overcome than those related to the institute. While large publications from our circle are still appearing in such small numbers, the abundance of smaller pieces not in the club archive or hiding on people's desks should not remain without impact. I think the Zurichers could easily do some more work. Analytical psychology must not be allowed to become a secret doctrine; to some degree it is this inevitably anyway anywhere that it seeks to grasp the essential secret of the psychical. But it means that the possible reach of analytical psychology is curtailed in a dangerous way if even the younger colleagues behave as if—you will forgive my malice—only the third half of life has any significance for humanity. Indeed, Dr. Scherf [sic][427] expressed the suspicion, when I was ranting in this way, that I must be an extravert and you can imagine

---

[427] Neumann refers to Rivkah Schärf, see n. 398.

what sort of a vote of no confidence this implied. But, in the name of all Gods, you know just what a hopeless introvert I am, and despite this, something needs to happen in this direction. Joking aside.

I didn't want to neglect alerting you to the urgent need for a journal, which, by the way, Dr. Meier[428] absolutely appreciated when I spoke to him about it.[429] In my opinion, it is a simply matter of an official "analytical-psychological" duty, and the difficulties that exist must be overcome.

In any case, I am very much looking forward to the fact that in all probability I am returning to the Eranos conference and will be able to speak to you. Please excuse this huge letter; I am already typing it to be on the safe side, so that no deciphering is necessary. I very much hope that in the meantime your health is good and that you are managing at least a part of the massive workload you have planned for yourself. I wish you, dear Professor Jung—and also Mrs. Jung—a joyful Christmas and a good and healthy new year.

With best wishes, I am as ever,
Your grateful,
E. Neumann
My wife also sends you and Mrs. Jung best wishes for the New Year.

---

[428] Carl Alfred Meier (1905–1995): Swiss psychiatrist and Jungian analyst. Born in Schaffhausen Meier studied medicine and psychiatry in Zurich, Paris, and Vienna. He went into analysis with Jung in the late 1920s. Meier was honorary secretary of the International General Medical Society for Psychotherapy during Jung's presidency (1933–39/40). After the war he became the first president of the C. G. Jung institute in 1948 and succeeded Jung as honorary professor of Psychology at the Swiss Federal Institute of Technology in 1949. Meier cofounded and presided over the Clinic and Research Center for Jungian Psychology in Zürichberg (1965–2011) (see Meier, 1964). His works include *Antike Inkubation und Modene Psychotherapie* (*Healing Dream and Ritual: Ancient Incubation and Modern Psychotherapy*) (1949) and *Lehrbuch der Komplexen Psychologie C. G. Jungs* (*The Psychology of C. G. Jung*) in four volumes (1968–77). See also the festschriften *Experiment und Symbol* (Rüf, 1975) and *A Testament to the Wilderness* (Joan Meier, 1985). On Neumann's problematic relationship with Meier see introduction, pp. xxxix–xli, xliii–xlv.

[429] In a press release regarding the foundation of the C. G. Jung Institute C. A. Meier writes on 11 October 1948: "The findings of this scientific study are to be published in a *series* 'Studies from the C. G. Jung Institute Zurich,' which will be brought out in occasional frequency by the Rascher Verlag, Zurich and is already in preparation. It is also the later intention to publish a multilingual Journal as there is a strong need to create a platform and meeting place for Jung's students, scattered throughout the world" (Meier, 1948 [NP]).

60 J

Bollingen, 8th January 48

Dr. Erich Neumann,
1 Gordon St.,
Tel Aviv

Dear Colleague,

I was very pleased to hear from you again. As requested, I enclose a certificate for the attention of the Bollingen Foundation. I really believe that on this occasion my recommendation will suffice. By the way, I have already worked as much as possible on the gentlemen in Ascona about you. Incidentally, you must not take the demands of the Bollingen form too seriously. It is mainly red tape. Despite this, if you do have any difficulties, let me know immediately so that I can approach Mr. Mellon[430] personally in a letter.

You must not stress too much about the "mystic." It is enough, for example, if you treat this problem of mysticism within an area, e.g., that of kabbalah—perhaps historically, as a representation of the history of the main influential symbols in kabbalah.

---

[430] Paul Mellon (1907–1999): American philanthropist and art collector, son of Andrew W. Mellon, US secretary of the treasury from 1921 to 1932. Mellon and his first wife, Mary Conover Mellon (1904–1946), met Jung at the Bailey Island seminars in 1936–37 (Jung, 1936/37a). They attended the Eranos conferences in Ascona and settled down in Zurich in 1939 in order to undergo analysis and take part in Jung's seminars. In 1940 they returned to the United States. On Mary's initiative a foundation, named after Jung's Bollingen retreat, was set up in 1945. It was dedicated to the wider dissemination of Jung's works and ideas and lasted until 1968. After Mary's unexpected death in 1946 Paul carried on with the project in memory of his late wife. He married again in 1948. His contribution as a benefactor to both the art world and the educational sector was recognized through several awards and honors—among those the Honorary Knight Commander of the Most Excellent Order of the British Empire (1974), the National Medal of Arts (1985), and the National Medal of Arts and Humanities (1997). His autobiography is titled *Reflections in a Silver Spoon* (1992). On Jung and the Mellons see also Schoenl (1992).

I fully appreciate what you argue in respect of the journal. Up till now, the difficulty has been with the staffing of it. There were and are too few active people available, and if something like this is to be initiated, we must be certain that someone very responsible will devote themselves to it so that something decent comes out of it. Everything has been so delayed by the war. We are only gradually starting to implement a plan of action that we should really have started years ago. Once the institute gets going and documents are published, then the next point on the action plan will be the journal. But for this, we must have assembled the necessary team. We can only expect real participation from you, from Switzerland, from America, and a bit from Holland. The English are rapidly going daft, and Germany is at ground zero to such a degree that one does not know at all what is going to happen there. France and Italy are not even in the picture as they are at least 50 years behind. As far as the Zurichers are concerned—you are completely right: they are still quite asleep. In this regard, I hope the institute will have an educative function and will awaken people out of this dream state.

I read with great apprehension the news about Palestine in our newspapers[431] and brood on ways and means of ever getting you out of this hornets' nest. I can't see any way at the moment, but I hope that your publication will have an effect.

With best wishes and greetings,
Your always loyal,
C. G. Jung

---

[431] See introduction, pp. xxxiv–xxxv; also nn. 420 and 433.

PROF. DR. C. G. JUNG   **KÜSNACHT, ZURICH**
                                  SEESTRASSE 228

January 8th 1948.

TO WHOM IT MAY CONCERN.[432]

I have known Dr. Erich Neumann for more than ten years. He is a very conscientious and reliable scientific author. Through the most unfavorable contemporaneous circumstances he was forced to leave his country and to settle in Palestine. The war with all its difficulties has hindered the normal publication of his work. But now, since normal connections could be reestablished, the publication of his work becomes possible. Indeed, the contracts for the publication of some of his works have already been signed.

I can very highly recommend Dr. Neumann for a scholarship. He is one of my most gifted pupils who has contributed important researches that are by far the best among the more recent publications in the field of psychology. I have read his work in manuscript form and, because it does not exist hitherto in any other form, Dr. Neumann is unable to produce further references, since I'm the only one who knows of its contents. It is my opinion that Dr. Neumann is most worthy of receiving a scholarship.

C. G. Jung
Prof. Dr. med. et jur. hc C. G. Jung
Seestr. 228 Küsnacht-Zurich

---

[432] Jung's reference for Neumann's application for a scholarship by the Bollingen Foundation. It was written in English.

Dr. Erich Neumann,
Analytical Psychologist

Tel Aviv, 24. 1. 48
1 Gordon St.

Dear Professor Jung,

As I think this letter will only be a short one, I am risking writing it
by hand, although it is unfortunately you who must bear the risk.
Firstly, I would like to thank you warmly for your extremely kind
letter, most especially for your letter of recommendation, which I
hope will do the trick for me in America.

I am really in suspense to hear the outcome on which a great deal
depends. As far as the "mystic" is concerned, I will have to make it
easier and more difficult for myself at the same time. I cannot work
it around a special area as both you and Miss Wolff advised, as I'm
afraid I am lacking the qualifications to do so. This would mean that
only something rather "third hand," as it were, could emerge. But to
interpret psychologically the "mystic as type" seems to me an interesting problem that has, besides, long concerned me. But of course
this leads all too easily into the boundless, i.e., indeed, into the mystical, but not yet by a long way to the Eranos conference, nor to
something with perspective.

Slowly it is getting so uncomfortable here because of the British
betrayal[433] that one cannot fail to see what will come out of it all. As
a minor side issue, the post is in chaos. For this reason, I have already

---

[433] Neumann refers to the civil war between Jewish and Arab communities in British Mandate Palestine in the month after the decision of the United Nations to create two independent
states. The war lasted from 30 November 1947 to 14 May 1948. When Arabic states intervened
on the side of the Palestinian Arabs after the Declaration of the Establishment of the State of
Israel (15 May 1948), the Arab-Israel war, or War of Independence, began, lasted until 10 March
1949, and ended with a victory for the Israeli forces. See also introduction, pp. xxxiv–xxxv.

sent Rascher a larger section of the *Origins* manuscript, and am now coming with another request.

Would you have the time to write the foreword to *Origins* as you proposed back then? I do not believe it is urgent, i.e., I am sure there is no hurry, but since *Origins* is to be preannounced with *The New Ethic* that is actually based on it, I would like to come to you with this request already, esteemed Professor. I hate having to pester you again and again and to rob you of your time, but I must admit that your foreword to my book is the greatest pleasure that the coming year holds before me.

If I can assist you in some way with a summary or such like, I will of course do this very willingly. I do not know, for example, whether the comprehensive contents list to Part 1 has now turned up. In case Rascher can't give it to you, let me know via Miss Schmid, and I will have one typed up.

I hope very much that your health and your strength leave nothing to be desired, and equally, that the institute is taking shape and, as far as possible, without your having to do too much on your part. You will surely know, too, that, if it does get as far as a journal, I am at your disposal to the best of my abilities.

Warm greetings to Mrs. Jung,
And once again very many thanks,
E. Neumann.

Dr. Erich Neumann,
Analytical Psychologist

Tel Aviv, 3rd April 48

Dear Professor Jung,

Although I still do not have any definitive reply from Bollingen and therefore don't know whether my trip will come to anything, quite apart from the fact that no one here can be sure what will happen tomorrow or the day after tomorrow, I am behaving in everything as if all will continue normally, and I would also like to commence my preparations for Switzerland. If I reckon with a stay of about 6–8 weeks, of which a proportion will belong to Ascona and the work in the Eranos archive, I would very much like to know when would suit you best as I hope very much that you will have time for me once again, if your health allows. I was very pleased to hear that you have even given another lecture and that you will speak at Ascona, for this best proves that you are feeling well again. Regarding my trip, it is a question of whether, for example, the second half of July suits you better than the first half of September, excluding August. Would you be kind enough to let me know.

There is not much new to report from me. The practice that has become a bit—not a lot—smaller—(nearly everyone under 35 has been called up)—is, pleasingly, giving me rather more time during which I have for sure enough to do. Since the danger of being without any postal connection looms once again, even with Switzerland by the way, I have urged Rascher to go to print quickly. For this reason, I have prepared *New Ethic* and *Origins* ready for printing, which, as you know, is a ridiculously huge job. I am working on the Eranos lecture in any case, but in the main I am engaged with the *Psychology of the Feminine*, which is promising to become very interesting.[434] I'm doing a course with notes, writing individual sections for it, but the development will still take a long time, hopefully we still have enough.[435] The book will actually be the counterpart to *Origins* but seen from the feminine side, whereas, in *Origins*, it was a matter of the development of the masculine-patriarchal consciousness.

I hope that the institute is now beginning to get going and the world gone crazy does not bury all that has been carefully started with another world war. This is applies everywhere, and one must have the paradoxical faith that the meaning of what one is doing does not need to be obvious for us to be able—and to be allowed—to press on patiently. The difficult thing about this paradoxical position is—for a skeptical nature like mine in any case—that such inner attitudes and "certainties" threaten to be denounced and reduced by the "ego" as an ideal position. This inner dialectic is unquestionably one of my weaknesses and threats, possibly also a drive—which one has to come to terms with, as it enhances the work of the "ego." This is why I have such a strong resistance to the mystical, which is of course very close to me. I will rename the title of my lecture "The Mystical Man" because that gives me more leeway and makes it possible to do away with the subtitle. I am mulling over the subject with difficulty and I'm afraid I can't make it easier for myself by restricting it to a special study as I don't have the time or inclination to do so, but besides I must somehow stay within the bounds of my own and others' experience to be able to say anything at all.

I am sure you will speak to Dr. Braband;[436] as I have the fully ungrounded impression that she wishes to leave Palestine, I would like to urge you not to believe all the negative things she says—if she does so. She does not see the truly hellish shadow problem at all, not in micro or in macro, it seems to me. Possibly we will all perish from

---

[434] See nn. 411, 424, and 457.

[435] Fragments of seminar protocols from February and March 1948 show that Neumann discussed the female aspect in fairy tales such as the brother Grimms' "The Nixie in the Pond" ("Die Nixe im Teich"), Oscar Wilde's "The Fisherman and His Soul," Friedrich de la Motte Fouqué's "Undine," and Hans Christian Andersen's "The Little Mermaid" ("Die kleine Meerjungfrau"). The texts were introduced and interpreted by Dr. J. Mendelssohn, and the discussion was led by Neumann (Neumann, 1948 [NP]).

[436] See n. 334.

it—only we?—but it is terribly overwhelming to see how the acceptance of the shadow, earth and blood all belong together and how obviously, even today, the longing for roots and the offering up of blood sacrifices to the earth belong together. The fact that one has the "evil eye" because one comprehends but is distanced from it does not make it easier, especially as one can only do anything about it in individual work and otherwise one must be silent for the time being.

Dear Professor Jung, would it be possible for you to write the introduction to *Origins* perhaps rather earlier than intended? In this situation, i.e., with these pressures from me, that I ask you to forgive, it is becoming clear to me how uncertain everything seems to me in reality, and how much I would like to have "finished" at least the little that I have done.

Greetings from your ever grateful,
E. Neumann

Please do not be angry with the ugly typed letter, but in my experience my handwriting is barely legible.

Best wishes, by the way, also from my wife, to Mrs. Jung.

14th Apr. 48

Dear Professor Jung,

I'm afraid, unless a miracle happens, which one should not count on, nothing is going to come of my Swiss trip and my Eranos lecture. After a long correspondence, I have today received notice from the Bollingen Foundation,[437] which I must admit to you I consider to be an unsubtle disgrace but at the very least incomprehensible, if one rules out obvious reasons.

The comprehensive and precisely defined offer of a total of $1,100 covers little more than the travel and Swiss residential expenses, i.e., I am supposed to cover myself the preparations for the book that must be written, for which I will lose about 2 months work, and my family must hopefully also continue to live during this time.[438] Therefore, I am supposed to write the Introduction Book to the 100 images for nothing, a fine work that I had been looking forward to, but a difficult work all the same, sandwiched between my practice and the situation in Palestine, and in addition without any certainty of publication. It is a mystery to me what these gentlemen were actually thinking. You will appreciate that, under these circumstances, I will turn this "Fellowship" down and will write my *Psychology of the Feminine* instead.

Mrs. Fröbe-Kapteyn wrote to me exceptionally confidently and seemed to have accepted that such an award would be offered to me

[437] Letter from the Bollingen Foundation (signed by Vice President D. D. Shepard) to Neumann, 5 April 1948 (Neumann and Bollingen [EA]).

[438] Bollingen Foundation to Neumann, 5 April 1948: "You have applied to this Foundation for a grant in aid or fellowship to assist you in the carrying out of a project consisting of research in the Eranos Archive, maintained by the Eranos Foundation at Ascona, Switzerland, and the preparation, upon the basis of the archive material, of an extensive introduction or separate volume, designed to accompany a contemplated illustrated volume designed *The Great Mother*. [...] The fellowship is for the sum of $1100. This sum shall be payable only if you reach Ascona, Switzerland, as planned, during 1948" (Neumann and Bollingen [EA]).

as an intermediary award for the preparatory work, and that the fellowship would follow for the writing of the book.[439] That would have made sense. She wrote that normally a sum of around $150 per month for three years would be granted, and compared with that, this total award that has been granted me is particularly grotesque.

You will understand that I am very disappointed, but there are worse things to deal with these days. But besides the fact that my "lion nature" is wild, which easily amuses me, I am very sad that I will not be able to speak to you in this way. I am sorry about the Eranos lecture, the conference, etc., but the most bitter thing is that the personal contact from the previous year cannot be continued. And this is not for political reasons that have made and make everything uncertain in any case, but because the Americans are. . . .

As there is now no hurry, I will take my time over my reply to America; do you have any advice for me in this matter?

Everything here continues to be terrible and uncertain. One has to simply wait and carry on working, which is what I am doing.

I hope the institute is now open and is working contentedly, the post has been functioning excellently and I would like to ask you to think of me if any of your publications have appeared in the meantime. The *Symbolism of the Spirit* is not yet in Palestine.[440]

At least my work has been going well so far; I am writing individual sections, and am not allowing myself to be deterred by the times we live in, which is not always easy. *I Ching* has been positive so far. Dreams not referenced to the times.

Many thanks for your efforts with the Bollingen matter and very best greetings,

From your grateful,
[E. Neumann]

P.S. Have my letters from January and April arrived? I only ask because of the postal situation.

---

[439] On 24 March 1948 Olga Fröbe-Kapteyn had written to Neumann to reassure him and to inform him that the Bollingen Foundation had asked her to organize the reimbursement (Neumann and Fröbe-Kapteyn [NP]).

[440] Jung (1948a).

65 J

Küsnacht, Zch. 10th May 1948.

Dr. Erich Neumann,
1, Gordon St.,
Tel Aviv.

Dear Colleague,

I am most profoundly disappointed by the (to put it mildly) extraordinary ruling of the Bollingen Foundation. I do not know what is behind it. I'm afraid I am completely powerless in this matter. I have done everything in my power to recommend you and have explained in great detail to Mellon and his representatives why you are important to me. If all this is to no avail, then I really don't know what else can be done.

I have hesitated to write to you as the official postal connections with Palestine have been discontinued. I will now attempt to reach you via Nicosia, as you see.

I will have an interview tomorrow with the chief of the Department of the Interior[441] in relation to the institute and will use this opportunity to attempt to implement my plan to get you to Switzerland, either temporarily or long term. I am writing this more to show you what a concern it is of mine to promote you and your work, but I also have the awkward feeling that I am—as they say—dangling a sausage in front of your nose without any guarantee that you will really be able to catch it. If one is not a public institute, one is re-

---

[441] Philipp Etter (1891–1977): From the Christain Democratic People's Party of Switzerland, Etter presided over the Swiss department of the interior from 1934 to 1959. His positive attitude toward Jung and his psychology also becomes evident through a number of requests for Jung's autograph for his son's collection. (I am grateful for Thomas Fischer from the Stiftung der Werke C. G. Jungs for prvoding me with this information.) On Etter see Kreis (1995).

stricted on every side. By the way, I will write to Barrett[442] and let him know how great my disappointment is. There's nothing to be done with Mellon as he has just got married—and Barrett has damn little influence.

I will do the foreword very soon. I won't be able to write a long piece—it would be quite superfluous anyway as your work speaks for itself. I have a heap to do and can't keep up with anything. My report cards will contain the grade: "Unsatisfactory" to an increasing extent. The comprehensive contents of volume 1 has reappeared and is here with me.

With best greetings and wishes for which one might hope they had magical powers,
Your always loyal,
C. G. Jung
*PS. As we have already discussed together, your book will appear in the monograph series of the institute and moreover as contribution II that I wanted to duly let you know.
*[handwritten addendum]

---

[442] John D. Barrett Jr. (1903–1981): Editor of the Bollingen series from 1946 to 1969 and president of the Bollingen Foundation from 1956 to 1969. See McGuire (1981).

Dr. Erich Neumann,
Analytical Psychologist

Tel Aviv, 12. VII. 48
1 Gordon St.

Dear Professor Jung,

I had just decided to send you good wishes for your birthday and to write to you of how much you have bestowed on us all with your good health, when your letter of 10th May arrived, albeit substantially delayed. You will have an inkling of how things are for us; as far as me and my trip are concerned it looks likes this: Bollingen's strongly improved proposal makes the trip possible; a visa, even if crazily only for 14 days, has arrived and it can be extended. It is uncertain whether I will get the exit permit from here. I hope it will be OK. Everyone under 41 is in the army, I am 43. If, as I believe, there will soon be a cease fire, I could then come. As long as we're being mindlessly bombed all over the place, I am unable to make the decision to travel. Yesterday a bomb dropped next to us, it can happen on every corner and at any time—to travel in this is impossible.[443] But I still hope that it will work. Even so, I will come alone and perhaps for a short time, but all this will sort itself out.

I am very grateful for your efforts for me and for my work, this has nothing to do with the "results" anyway. Sometime something will emerge. I would not wish to remain in Switzerland long-term, a

---

[443] The house next to the Neumanns, Gordon Street 3, was hit and destroyed by a bomb. In his defense of Neumann toward Jolande Jacobi (see introduction, p. xli), Jung mentions Neumann's isolation and endangered situation in Tel Aviv: "Neumann is coming from his hermit's existence in the strange world of Tel Aviv. The house opposite him has been bombed to the ground, and 'Israel' is writhing in birth pangs. N. is strongly infected by the collective because of his fearful rejection of the external world. This attitude is responsible for the lack of empathy and must therefore be taken into consideration" (Jung to Jacobi, 24 September 1948 [JA]).

regular occupation for some months would be the fulfillment of a dream. But I don't fully believe in it. The visa for 14 days, even if I am certain that it will be renewed, speaks a clear language. I will, for sure, always be on the margins in Palestine, sorry—in Israel, even on the most extreme margin, and almost on the outside, but here, there is no protected Judaism as an optimal state, and indeed a dangerous but healthy shadow development that at least makes a healthy and creative nation possible. For me, a paradoxical but apparently beneficial situation.

I am very concerned that *Origins* is apparently in no way in press, as it should have long since been by now. I have received no proofs. What's happening with the monograph series of the institute? Apart from a hint in a conversation with you, I have heard nothing about it. Is everything still as it was with Rascher who has not written a word about it, and there has been airmail from Switzerland for three weeks now? What is Contribution no. 1? I would at least like to get to know the society who are good, I'm sure. What does this mean for the translation into English, which is, of course, very important to me? Please be so kind as to let me know about this. I must get this book—which I have been carrying around far too long—behind me. I am already in the middle of the next one and I know that the corrections will pull me right back. Every book that I read depresses me when I get the impression I need to change something, etc. After all, its latest, I believe, third revision goes back to 1946. You will, I think understand this my "distress." In any case, I am looking forward to your introduction, whether short or long. While it is difficult, it is, despite everything, wonderful that you are unable to get to grips with all your work, as it shows how inexhaustible is what you have been commissioned to do, and what you are still able to manage. When you write that you would get the grade: "unsatisfactory," that does not concern me too much. Certainly not objectively, and subjectively, i.e., applied to you, it does not seem to me that labels can be very damaging to you.

Esteemed Professor Jung, you know so well that I wish you a healthy, peaceful, and creative time that it is not worth wasting time on saying it, therefore I rather wish that we, your pupils, friends, relatives, do not have to rob you of too much energy and time so that you can give yourself a bit more peace and quiet—which you surely need.

I hope very much that I will be able to see you at the Eranos conference and that everything will work out. Otherwise, I will come later in any case when peace has come here and I am healthy—to select the images for Bollingen, i.e., the hope exists of speaking to you this year, despite everything.

Once again my warmest wishes for you with best greetings to Mrs. Jung,
I am your grateful,
E. Neumann

Dr. Erich Neumann,
Analytical Psychologist

Tel Aviv, 14. VII. 48
1, Gordon St.

Dear Professor Jung,

I have just received a letter from Rascher about *Origins*.[444] Since I previously only heard about the plan from you, but have heard nothing more, you will not hold it against me if I ask for some information. Is the institute that will publish my book independent from the Psychology Club, does it stand under your leadership, and who is "publishing"? I assume that it is independent, stands under your leadership and you are publishing. Then everything is in order.

But secondly and most importantly. I have a contract with Rascher stating that he will publish my book by September. I consider this necessary for many external and internal reasons and therefore have fervently fought with Rascher—and successfully. I have to reluctantly accept a small delay because of the situation here. But I am in no way in agreement with Rascher's statement that "it will appear *after* a work by Dr. C. A. Meier-Fritzsche, *Ancient Incubation and Modern Psychotherapy*."[445] I am writing to Rascher by this same post in this vein. Whether my book is no. 2 or no. 5 in the studies has nothing to do with it, I do not want its publication date to be postponed. If I have

---

[444] Rascher to Neumann, 6 July 1948: "Now concerning your second work 'The Origins and History of Consciousness', the C. G. Jung Institute has demanded that this work appear in the series: 'Studies from the C. G. Jung Institute.' This series appears per contractual agreement in the format [. . .]; your second book, which will simultaneously be the second book in the 'Studies' series, must therefore also be in this format [. . .], and not in the same format as 'Depth Psychology.' Apart from this, our contract of 19th September 1947 applies, also for the second work which will appear after a work by Dr. C. A. Meier-Fritzsche, 'Ancient Incubation and Modern Psychotherapy'" (RA).

[445] Meier (1949).

understood this incorrectly, which may be possible, then everything is fine. Otherwise the studies numbers and the publication date would not fall together, which would also not be the worst thing to happen. Therefore I hope very much that the delay is not connected to the adoption of the book into the studies series of the institute. You wrote to me in May that my book was in press, but I'm afraid that was an error. The proofs that were promised me in February still have not arrived as of today, there is another format for the studies, etc. I only hope that Rascher does not achieve the planned postponement of the print in this way.

Please excuse the technical questions, but as I have not even received a communication from the institute of its very existence, let alone one informing me that it wishes to publish my book, I must, for better or for worse, turn to you once again.

So, no hard feelings, as they say …

Best wishes,
Your E. Neumann

Küsnacht, Zch., 30. July 1948.

Dr. Erich Neumann,
1, Gordon St.,
Tel Aviv.

Dear Doctor,

As I do not know whether Prof. Jung will get around to responding to your letters at the moment, I would like to quickly let you know the reasons for the delay. Prof. Jung was ill when your letters arrived and although it fortunately was nothing serious, he was still unable to take care of his correspondence and has now gone to Bollingen to recover, from where he will hopefully write soon.

Since I could only read your letters fleetingly and they are now in Bollingen, I cannot make a response to them, but I am sure that the matter of the publication of your book in the monograph series of the institute will be clarified to your satisfaction. If you would like to see Prof. Jung before Ascona—I very much hope that it will in fact be possible for you to come to Switzerland—I ask you to write directly to Prof. Jung in Bollingen, St. Gallen Canton, as I am myself going away on holiday for 14 days and it is still quite uncertain when Prof. Jung will be back in Küsnacht.

With best wishes and greetings,
Your,
[Marie-Jeanne Schmid]

17. VIII. 1948

Dear Colleague,

I finished reading your lecture yesterday.[446] I can only express my admiration to you for the manner and style in which you have mastered your difficult task. It has turned into a quite excellent representation, as clear as it is thorough, of the problem of the mystic. This has never before been captured in such an extensive way and in such depth as in your work. The saint who bought firewood instead of a fur has found a particular sympathy with me.[447] It is good that you did not say less, and more would have been unwise. τῷ καιρῷ πρόσεστι πάντα τά καλά[448] (everything good rides on the correct quantity). I thank you for the work.

With best greetings and wishes,
Your devoted,
C. G. Jung

[446] Neumann's Eranos lecture 1948 titled "Der mystische Mensch" ("Mystical Man") (Neumann, 1949).

[447] This is the passage from Neumann's lecture: "Not only the heroic character of these mystics' efforts but also the results at which they aim reveal that these mystics are not uroboros nihilists. There is a Hasidic maxim which sums up this problem with popular simplicity. A famous rabbi is said to be a 'Zaddik [a perfectly righteous man] in a fur coat.' The explanation is: 'One man buys a fur coat, another buys firewood. And what is the difference between them?' The first one wants to warm only himself, the second wants to warm others as well.' Just as it is a basic fallacy to confuse individuation with this 'fur-coat Zaddikism,' it is a misunderstanding of the intention of the high mystics to regard them as essentially hostile to the world" (Neumann, 1949/2007, p. 405). The Hasidic tale "Im Pelz" ("In a Fur Coat") can be found in Martin Buber's *Die chassidischen Bücher* (Buber, 1928, pp. 600–601) and in *Die Erzählungen der Chassidim* (*Tales of the Hasidim*): "The rabbi of Kotzk once said of a famous rabbi: 'That's a zaddik in a fur coat.' His disciples asked him what he meant by this. 'Well,' he explained, 'one man buys himself a fur coat in winter, another buys kindling. What is the difference between them? The first wants to keep only himself warm, the second wants to give warmth to others too.'" The story is also quoted in Neumann's volume on Hasidism (1934–40: vol. 2, p. 47).

[448] "καιρῴ πάντα πρόσεστι καλά" ("Nothing too much; all that is good is attached to 'Right Season'") (Diels and Kranz, 1951–53, vol. 2, p. 380/9). Critias of Athens (460–403 BCE) attributed the phrase to the pre-Socratic philosopher, poet, and statesman Chilon of Sparta (sixth century BCE).

Küsnacht, Zch., 27th October 1948.

Dr. Erich Neumann,
1 Gordon St.,
Tel Aviv,
Palestine.

Dear Colleague,

I am afraid I am charged with communicating to you a rather unpleasant development. At the time we agreed that your book should be published under the auspices of the institute's publications, there was as yet no close agreement between Rascher and the institute. Since then, a contract has come into force that states that for texts that appear under the auspices of the institute, 2% of the author's honorarium must be diverted to the institute. Rascher, who actually should have told you of this, has asked me whether I had told you about it, to which I of course replied that this was not the case, but as you see, this is what I am now doing.

However, on the other hand, you must take into consideration that the fact that I am willing to publish your book in the institute's series has been a strong motive for Rascher to venture into the printing of your comprehensive works at all. I had to bring all kinds of persuasive skills to bear in this regard. Besides, the "C. G. Jung Institute" brand carries a certain propaganda value.

I am sending you at the same time an off-print in the usual post. I would have liked to send you my new book, but I am not sure if it would get through. If you are persuaded that one can trust the regular post, please let me know and then I will send it to you.

With kind greetings and best wishes,
Your always loyal,
C. G. Jung

71 N

Dr. Erich Neumann,
Analytical Psychologist

Tel Aviv, 13th Nov. 48
1, Gordon St.

Dear Professor Jung,

Many thanks for your letter. I had already written to Rascher that I was in agreement with the symbolic payment to the institute, and now a letter from Meier declares everything to be invalid and my contract to be the only valid thing.[449] I find it just outrageous that you are being troubled with this nonsense and confusion.

As far as the post is concerned, it arrives late, but it does always arrive and there is no risk involved in sending things here. Naturally I am exceptionally grateful to you for every dispatch. Even if I am generally glad to be here and not in Zurich for many other reasons, envy still naturally grips me when I see the Zurichers referring to manuscripts of yours that are still unknown to me. Would it be possible to have a copy of "Mysterium" for a while, for example? I imagine that working through this could help me with a great deal. Please do not take this as an expression of envy. But as I now know how long it takes from the preparation of a manuscript to its publication, it is naturally difficult for me to have to wait so long. But if this is impossible, as I assume, I would like to approach you once again when I am back in Switzerland. If all goes well, i.e., if Bollingen

---

[449] C. A. Meier's letter is missing. Cf. Neumann to Rascher, 4 November 1948: "Prof. Jung wrote to me that 2% of my honorarium is allocated to the C. G. Jung Institute; I am in agreement with this, but would like to have sight of the usual contract for Institute publications"; Neumann to Rascher, 13 November 1948: "Dr. Meier has since informed me that the inquiry from Prof. Jung is based on an error; nothing from my book is to be paid to the Institute, which I, by the way, also find in order" (RA).

renews, I do hope to be able to come to the next Eranos conference in Switzerland again.

Here things are going well for me and for all of us, with plenty of work, and we are all quite optimistic. Without the world noticing, something remarkable is happening here—and despite everything—it is positive.

Dear Professor, I hope that you find yourself restored to the best of health and that you are enjoying being creative once again, and, with warmest greetings, also to Mrs. Jung, I am

Your ever grateful,
Erich Neumann

Küsnacht, Zch., 10th December 1948

Dear Colleague,

Please excuse my writing to you by hand. I can better concentrate my thoughts in this way. The "Myst. Coniunct." manuscript is not yet ready to travel, and the last chapter has also not yet been written. There are however one or two other manuscripts that are more or less ready for printing of which a copy could be sent to you.

Your text on the *Ethic* has appeared here and is already stirring up the dust and, indeed, in such a way, that it might come to my having to speak out about it.[450] At the institute the question has arisen whether it would now be wise, given the circumstances—and taking advantage of your kind willingness—to bring out your book as part of the institute's series of publications. The fear exists that future discussions would be prejudiced by this, and that the institute would be defining itself by certain formulations, even if only morally, or that it would be giving the appearance of doing so. A small institute, which still stands on weak legs, must not risk too many opponents. (Side glances to university and church!)

I have reread your text and again had a very strong response to it, and I am certain that its effect will be like that of a bomb. Your formulations are brilliant and of incisive sharpness; they are therefore challenging and aggressive, an assault troop in an open field, where there was nothing to be seen in advance, unfortunately. Naturally the opponent concentrates his fire on the unprotected troops. It is precisely the obviously bold but unambiguous formula that is most vulnerable because it has an unprotected side. One cannot fight a war without losses, and one gets nowhere with a static equilibrium. Even

---

[450] See introduction, pp. xlii–xlix.

the title *"New" Ethic* is a trumpet cry: aux armes, citoyens![451] We will get some poison gas in the nose and some dirt on the head. In Tel Aviv you risk occasional Egyptian bombs for it.

I am not quarrelsome, but I am strident by nature and therefore I cannot conceal from you my secret pleasure. But I will have to act concerned and possibly exercise my duty as commandant of the fire brigade. Your writings will be a *petra scandali*,[452] but also the powerful impetus for future developments. For this I am most deeply grateful to you.

With best wishes,
Your very devoted,
C. G. Jung

---

[451] French for "To arms, citizens," from "La Marseillaise," the national anthem of France; the orginal title was "Chant de Guerre pour l'armée du Rhine" ("War Song for the Army of the Rhine"), written and composed by Claude Joseph Rouget de Lisle in 1792, and used as anthem of the First Republic: "Aux armes, citoyens, / Formez vos bataillions, / Marchons, marchons! / Qu'un sang impur / Abreuve nos sillons!" ("To arms, citizens, / Form your battalions, / Let's march, let's march! / Let an impure blood / Water our furrows!").

[452] Latin for "rock of offense," from Greek *petra skandalou* (πέτρα σκανδάλου) in 1 Peter 2:8 "And, a stone of stumbling, and a rock of offense, *even to them* who stumble at the word, being disobedient: to which also they were appointed" (KJB), where this phrase was seen as a reference to the Jews "who rejected the Saviour on account of his humble birth, and whose rejection of him was made the occasion of the destruction of their temple, city, and nation" (*Barnes' Notes on the Bible*).

Tel Aviv, 1. 1. 49
1, Gordon St.

Dr. Erich Neumann,
Analytical Psychologist

My Dear Professor Jung,

Your letter was as much a great joy as a surprise. I must admit to you that I in no way expected to cause a stir or even a scandal in the close-knit circle of Jung students with my *Ethic*. In my opinion I have only summarized, thought through to the end, and formulated in a way that cannot be misunderstood what you yourself have stated or implied countless times. It is absolutely fair enough that the emphasis of your interest did not exactly focus on the ethical consequences, but shifted more and more to the later phases of psychic development, and that seems to me to derive from your own development. You went through the weight of the ethical problematic in your time as student, friend, and opponent of Freud and then grew beyond it. But then the necessary polemic against Freud has caused a section of your students to turn a blind eye to how much blood was spilled in this debate, and how your moral courage in separating from Freud perpetuated Freud's moral courage with which he set himself against his time. Indeed, you have personally emphasized over and over again—at least in many conversations with me—the significance of the moral stance of the "ego" and of the strength of the "ego," but, in your writing, this aspect is often less evident as is the obvious therapeutic aspect in general. My inner "consternation," to formulate it in an exaggerated way—about the condition of the Jung students in Zurich, now evidently to me at least, seems I fear, to be substantiated. If I found something amiss, for example, or not as it should be, there were only two reactions, either they said—in a highly satisfied way—

yes, yes that is just the shadow, or they smiled in a rather superior way about my provincial attitude, which was thought not quite up to it simply because I made a value judgment about where one ought to allow the wisdom of the unconscious to prevail, beyond good and evil. But they seemed to me all too often to mistake the unconsciousness of the ego for the wisdom of the unconscious.

If pure ambition and casting side glances at both "university and church,"—and also power and money—belong to the foundations of the C. G. Jung Institute, then one should let this institute be eradicated, because it is, in fact, abusing your name and endangering your life's work. You know, and I know all too well, that my strong Mars tendency signifies a danger, but my heart rose when you wrote to me that you have a "strident nature." I understand most deeply that it can no longer be your task to get involved in the battle of the day, and for God's sake please do not misunderstand me and think that I am requesting a defense of *Ethic* or even of my person, but I do request you—in your role as "fire brigade commandant"—not to extinguish too enthusiastically, where the fire, that ancient cleansing method of humanity, could possibly eradicate some filth. Some of the reservations against your teaching are based on the unrevolutionary and all too bourgeois stance of your students who always wish to anticipate the wisdom of the "third half of life" before they have the struggles of the first behind them. The synthetic and superior stance of your age, which contains the opposites, conceals from your "heirs," who ogle at the so-called treasures of this world and want to have everything at once, the aggressive and revolutionary character of your work—and despite everything—of your being. I do not wish to conceal from you that it sometimes seems to me that you are yourself rather complicit in this. I know that psychologists are not a "religious order," but I do not understand fully how it can be that the necessary fourth is the devil, and in the patronage of the institute can sit enemies of this devil—legitimate and serious enemies. I confess even that I am naïve enough to consider Mrs. Jacobi's[453] Catholicism as offensive—to put

[453] Jolan[de] Jacobi (1890–1973): Psychotherapist and close collaborator of Jung; born as Jolande Szekacs in Budapest to baptized Jewish parents, she married the lawyer Andor Jacobi in 1909. When the communist Bela Kun came to power in Hungary in 1919, the couple moved with their two sons to Vienna, where she got involved in Karl Rohan's conservative Europäischen

it unkindly etc., etc. Where's the "new ethic" now, you will perhaps ask me, and you could say that what I am attacking, like "Savonarola," is precisely one of their and your conclusions. But I believe that is not the case. In my experience, this acceptance of the fourth is, as the fine German language puts it, a "devilishly difficult"[454] matter, and in no way so pleasant and easy a thing as, say, a compromise. You see, the neutral stance of Switzerland also has its risks alongside all that is good. With the exception of you, of course, they have not experienced the evil that has the whole world by the throat, and this is the bourgeois-ethical inadequacy that endangers your students. (This is what, for example, brings a man like Layard,[455] despite everything, much closer to me than Mrs. Jacobi with her *Shadow Lover and the Rautendelein.*[456])

Please do not misunderstand me. I do not mean one individual thing and I can be mistaken in every detail, but what frightens me is

---

Kulturbund (founded in 1922). In her capacity as executive vice president (1928–38) she got in contact with the cultural and intellectual elite of Europe. Her friendship with the author Albert von Trentini made her convert to Catholicism in 1934. She met Jung for the first time in February 1928, when he gave his lecture "Die Struktur der Seele" ("The Structure of the Psyche") (Jung, 1928a) at the Kulturbund in Vienna. In order to become a student of his she studied psychology at the University of Vienna with Karl and Charlotte Bühler. She wrote a dissertation on the "Das Altern" ("The Aging") (1938) and came back to Vienna, which she had fled after the Anschluss, under the risk of her own life, to sit her final exam. Jacobi settled down in Zurich to work with Jung. Her parents and husband remained in Hungary and fell victim to the Nazis in 1944. After the war Jacobi was pivotal for the creation and development of the Jung Institute (see n. 415). She was a member of its curatorium for years. She taught, practiced, lectured, and wrote several books on Jungian psychology, including *Die Psychologie von C. G. Jung* (*The Psychology of C. G. Jung*) (1940) and *Komplex, Archetypus, Symbol in der Psychologie C. G. Jungs* (*Complex, Archetype, and Symbol in the Psychology of C. G. Jung*) (1957), for both of which Jung wrote an introduction (Jung, 1940; 1956b). Jacobi also contributed to Jung's *Man and His Symbols* (Jacobi, 1964). For Jacobi's difficult relationship with Neumann see introduction, pp. xxxix–xli, xliv, xlix, lii–liii.

[454]"eine [. . .] *teuflisch schwere* Sache"

[455]John Willoughby Layard (1891–1974): English anthropologist and psychotherapist. In 1914 Layard went to the New Hebrides Islands in Melanesia to undertake anthropological studies (*Stone Men of Malekula*, 1942). Initial analysis with Homer Lane, later with Wilhelm Stekel and Fritz Wittels. In 1929 Layard attempted to commit suicide in Berlin. He survived and moved back to England. In the early 1940s he started to see patients as an analyst while continuing his own therapy with H. G. Baynes, Gerhard Adler, and Jung himself in Zurich. His main psychological work is titled *The Lady of the Hare* (1944), which describes the dream series of Mrs. Wright, a countrywoman and devout Christian, whose dream of a hare initiates her psychological healing process. Layard's interpretation reveals his Christian faith, to which Neumann refers in the letter.

[456]Jolande Jacobi, *Der Schattengeliebte und das Rautendelein* (1946). On Jacobi see n. 453.

Figure 6. Erich Neumann with John Layard at the Eranos conference 1958 (Eranos Archive; courtesy of Paul Kugler).

the absence of passion of the spirit that, for example, is suggested in your implied reaction to my text, everywhere seeking reassurances against the truth.

Of course there is nothing I would want less than to damage you or the institute and I can now assure you that I would respond positively to a request from the institute not to publish my book there. At the same time, though, I would like to assure you that my fervent efforts will continue to prove myself worthy of "the hate of the pussyfooters."

I am doing a lot of work—a small text, an interpretation of *Eros and Psyche*.[457] I have taken a chapter from the large book *Psychological Development of the Feminine* and wish to publish it separately.[458] I'm

[457] Published first as commentary to a new edition of Apuleius's *Amor und Psyche* (*Amor and Psyche*) under the title "Eros und Psyche: Ein Beitrag zur seelischen Entwicklung des Weiblichen" ("Eros and Psyche: The Psychic Development of the Feminine: A Commentary on the Tale by Apuleius") (Neumann, 1952). Neumann held a course titled "Zur Psychologie des Weiblichen: Anhand des Märchens *Amor und Psyche*" ("On the Psychology of the Feminine: Based on the Fairy Tale *Amor and Psyche*") at the Zurich institute at the beginning of October 1950 (Protocol, 5 October 1950, AJP.) See n. 518.

[458] The material in question could either have formed part of Neumann's commentary on Apuleius's *Amor and Psyche* or he could have used it for his lecture at the Psychological Club

working on the images volume for the "Great Mother," etc., etc. It gives me much pleasure. For this New Year, I wish for myself that everything will sort itself out and that it will be possible to speak to you this time in connection with the Eranos conference. I hope there will be peace here by then. Anyway, I am eternally grateful that it has always been possible for me to go on working "undisturbed" or, better, unhindered by wars and unrest. But precisely this fact strengthens the feeling of responsibility in me of producing something at least passable. (Many thanks by the way for the help on the index for *Origins*, which is a great vexation.)

In hoping that you understand me when I am possibly overstating things—as is my tendency—I remain,

Your grateful,
E. Neumann

Zurich in the coming year (title "Zur Psychologie des Weiblichen im Patriarchat," 7 October 1950), a presentation he held again in Basel and Tel Aviv. This lecture was later published—together with contents from his article "Die Urbeziehung zur Mutter" ("The Primordial Relation to the Mother") (1951)—under the title "Die psychologischen Stadien der weiblichen Entwicklung" ("The Psychological Stages of Woman's Development") (1953).

10. II. 49

Dear Professor Jung,

It is difficult to get my bearings in the Zurich games of shadows and to differentiate between the "being" and its shadow, and although I should now be an expert in the shadow, it remains difficult. After I had written a letter to the "President" alone, I did the *I Ching* and cast: "Preponderance of the Great transforms into Inner Truth." I wish therefore, against my nature but obedient to the *I Ching*, to "put rushes under it" with the knowledge that it is no flaw if despite this, "the water goes over one's head."[459]

Dear President,

I have been informed by the Curatorium of the institute that bears your name and whose president you are that it is not desirable that my book *The Origins and History of Consciousness* should be published as a publication of the institute.[460] I had not sought this honor, but

---

[459] *"Six at the beginning means: To spread with rushes underneath. No blame.* When a man wishes to undertake an enterprise in extraordinary times, he must be extraordinarily cautious, just as when setting a heavy thing down in the floor, one takes care to put rushes under it, so nothing will break" (Baynes, 1940, p. 120); *"Six at the top means: One must go through the water. It goes over one's head. Misfortune. No blame.* Here is a situation in which the unusual has reached a climax. One is courageous and wishes to accomplish one's task, no matter what happens. This leads into danger. The water rises over one's head. This is the misfortune. But one incurs no blame in giving up one's life that the good and right may prevail. There are things that are more important than life" (Baynes, 1940, p. 121) See also n. 297.

[460] C. A. Meier, vice president of the institute, wrote to Neumann on 3 February 1949 (NP): "Dear Colleague, As you already know from Jung, due to the fierce public and private controversy which has arisen about your *'New Ethic'*, the question has been discussed in the Institute about whether it would be right to publish the 'Origins and History of Consciousness' in the Institute's own series. After a comprehensive discussion in the Curatorium, we came to the decision that it would be better for the young Institute not to expose itself to too much fierce public controversy. For now, we would prefer to publish works which have the character of monographs on questions of Complex Psychology which require a better material and scientific

on the contrary, long after the contract with Rascher was agreed, I gave permission, post hoc, for the book to be taken on by the institute.[461] At that time, following my good intuition, I immediately turned to you with the question regarding whether the institute was under your leadership and made my permission conditional on this (14 July 1948). I hereby lay aside this honor, as I have already communicated with you in my reply to your private letter, into the hands of those who have recalled it, with the requirement that Rascher Press is in agreement with these changes. I regret the decision of the institute exclusively for this reason: that the young institute, which sadly bears your name—in my unauthoritative opinion—has dishonored it out of ill-judged opportunism.

Collegial integrity alone, to say nothing of anything else, would have demanded that when one believes one must take such a step, at least to have admitted the truth that one is operating from opportunism and to declare this. The spurious justification of the vice president that, as the "New Ethic" is an object of controversy, they have decided only to publish monographs, is galling in its inelegant untruth because it seeks to obscure a clear fact. But the fact is that they do not wish to have my—compromising—name associated with the institute. With this, Esteemed President, you have declared yourself in agreement. This is what it is about, because it was, in fact, not *Ethic* but my other book that was to appear in the institute's publications.

This Curatorium, from whom its vice president has distanced himself by saying "I can understand the Curatorium's decision to this effect" and by the president having written me an unambiguous personal letter, is a remarkable institution. (I should not have said "unambiguous"—I had not applied your sentence: "One cannot fight a war without losses"—to myself.)

---

underpinning. Therefore, it also seems to me personally right if your large comprehensive work appears as a publication in its own right, and I can thus understand the decision of the Curatorium to this effect. I hope you will not have any difficulties with this and assure you that we are all very much looking forward to your book coming out. With best wishes, ever yours, C. A. Meier." See also introduction, p. xlv.

[461] Neumann to Rascher, 14 July 1948: "In principle I am completely in agreement with the acceptance of the book into the Studies, but only if it does not then lead to a delay in its publication. I have informed Prof. Jung of the same in a letter" (RA).

Dear Professor Jung,

I would like to call upon you—although I am perhaps not entitled to do so—as the "Commandant of the Fire Brigade" in the old biblical style: "Philistines be upon thee, Samson!"

For two reasons, however, I am grateful for the decision of the Curatorium even though it has cut me off once and for all from your institute and its representatives. It seems to me to be fatefully correct that my book and I myself have been expelled from your institute. On the outside, I find myself quite well and in the best of company, namely, in that of C. G. Jung, provided he is not president. So herewith I accept the honor, dear Professor, of representing the truth of your psychology in the world, for which there is no room in your institute.

The second reason—which I have seen with some consternation—is that the [new] Ethic is much less up to date than I had believed, as the simple values of the old ethic, e.g., integrity, the love of truth, and courage, are still unknown in the circles of people whom I considered to be representatives of the new ethic. So yet again, the church is correct to have banned me—and you—in the name of the institute.

With the same post as the communication from the institute came one from Rascher—that Kegan Paul have accepted *The New Ethic*. Would you fancy writing a foreword for the English edition, dear Professor?

I send warmest greetings and the request that you would inform the board of my decision and my remarks about it,

I remain despite everything,
Your,
[Erich Neumann]

Do you recall the question, dear Professor, about why so few men come to you? It is not easy to accept the things you ask of us. Please imagine your own reaction if this had happened to you with one of your books at a Freudian Institute, moreover, in the case of a book for which Freud himself had written the foreword. But this example is wrong. That would not have been possible.

PROF. DR. C. G. JUNG   **KÜSNACHT, ZURICH,**
                                             SEESTRASSE 228

29th March 1949

Dr. Erich Neumann,
1, Gordon St.,
Tel Aviv.

Dear Colleague,

I can understand your annoyance but I had to marvel at your both mild and acquiescent reply in your last letter but one. I have concluded from this that it is not important to you anyway how your book is published. I have naturally communicated your previous response to Dr. Meier. Now, if you had protested immediately to the degree that you have done so in your recent letter, I would have attempted to push through my original intention of publishing your book in the series. You must understand my current situation somewhat: I have to try to operate under the current circumstances, but I would like to avoid the emergence of some sort of orthodoxy that pushes out other types of individuality. Since your clear reaction to my original proposal, I have now gone back to the Curatorium.

I will gladly fulfill your wish for a foreword to the planned English edition of your *Ethic*, albeit with the condition that you make a few more revisions to the current text. In the last fortnight I have occupied myself by nothing else but reading through your text three times and I have noted down my latest thoughts. I enclose these notes with revision proposals.[462] I would like to comment that, in general, your text strikes me as a chapter from a larger context. This is probably

---

[462] See appendix II.

because it lacks an actual introduction to the extent that you have not defined adequately the position you are writing from, and I fear that the reader cannot get a picture of the situation in which the newer ethical considerations take place. For an English edition, however, such an explanation would be most important, as the English-speaking public is not familiar with debating as it is practiced in Europe, with the exception of the Oxford dons, but they are hidden away in the background of Anglo-Saxon public life.

I am sorry that I am lumbering you with even more work. But it is very important to me that your text on the *Ethic* comes out in an acceptable form for its Anglo-Saxon audience.[463] You can take nothing for granted, especially any knowledge of philosophical or psychological concepts. You must explain it carefully and in the simplest of language, at least the points it particularly depends on or which are particularly significant.

In the meantime, with best wishes,
Your devoted,
C. G. Jung
*P.S. I am also enclosing my foreword to which I have only made revisions that seemed necessary to me. I hope you are in agreement with them.
*[handwritten addendum]

---

[463] See Jung's letter to Cary Baynes from 9 May 1949 (CFB). Quoted in introduction, p. xlvi. See also appendix II.

Dr. Erich Neumann,
Analytical Psychologist

Tel Aviv, 6th April [1949]

My dear Professor Jung,

Your silence in response to both of my letters[464] has rather unsettled me, but I thought perhaps you had too much to do and so I was only a little sad. Now I see—as I have received a letter from Miss Wolff today—that I have "fallen from grace" and that the court has turned away from me.[465] That troubles me little, even if I am astonished to hear from Miss Wolff that all of a sudden my point of view "is not actually that of depth psychology" that had never even once occurred to me, to you, or to Miss Wolff—until recently. However, if I must now accept that you are angry with me or that your silence has arisen from your breaking off your relationship with me—I would in no way be prepared to put up with this. I am willing to defend *The New Ethic*—which apparently no longer has any friends in Switzerland—

---

[464] Jung's letter from 29 March (75 J) did not reach Neumann in time for this letter. See Neumann's letter from 9 April (77 N).

[465] Wolff's letter is missing. Neumann replied to her writing that her letter had triggered "a prompt and so sharp a reaction [...] that I thought it better to hold back my reply and to wait. [...] I am convinced that if your letter had been spoken and not written that my reaction would have looked different, but in any case you will understand that the Zurichers' reaction to my Mystic lecture and to the '*Ethic*' have triggered my surprise and anything but my pleasure" (undated letter, Wolff and Neumann) He hoped that a personal conversation in Zurich would clear out further misunderstandings. Wolff responded in a letter on 27 July 1949 defending her position: "I just do not know if there is any point in talking any more about the *Ethic*. I wrote everything to you that I have to say. Evidently you have mixed me up with all the other. I was not even at Ascona last year, I have nothing to do with the publication of your book, I am just a regular lecturer at the Instiute and, otherwise, other ladies make the decisions. Also, I told everyone I am on personal terms with [you] that is my view that your book should be accepted as a publication of the Institute. I hope you still remember that I am one of those who recommended to you that you should even publish the 'Ethic'" (Wolff and Neumann [NP]).

in open battle against the whole institute, Protestants, Catholics, baptized Jews, unbaptized Jews, and even against Jungian analysts if any should show up, and I pledge to prove from the writings of C. G. Jung that my teaching is the real and unfalsified teaching of Holy Jungian Psychology that I believe myself to represent now, as ever, against friend and foe.

Who would have thought it! Never would I have thought that your droll warning that I had yet to experience how much one can be misunderstood would have to become a reality in this highly surprising way.[466] May I quote you something from Miss Wolff's letter that shows the "revised" position? "You no longer seem to be on good terms with nature, hence with the unconscious and the inner laws of nature. Your old testament perspective is getting in your way. This is why it must indeed be a text on ethics." Dear Professor Jung—now tell me yourself,—it would be laughable if it did not make me cry. Here* one is indignant that I am so anti-Jewish, which I can understand, and all of a sudden one discovers—you must surely have vilified me—I am representing an old testament perspective in the *Ethic*. You see it has come to this, if you let them get away with casting "side glances at university and church" in "only" ethical matters. Why, for God's sake, do you not understand the danger that threatens you and us and your work if such things are possible.

*[in I.]^[467]

Please believe me that this is not about me and not about "being right" and certainly not about an endorsement of me by the—as far as I'm concerned—not very authoritative Jung Institute. I will be able [and will have to]^[468] make my way without that also, but I don't want—through your covering of things with which you are yourself in no way identical for it to now come out—that yes means no and no means yes. Everything I have written is now supposed to be false because I have dared to exercise a critique of your technical position, because I, as has been shown, rightly do not believe that these things can be wielded technically or pragmatically. Of course, all this is

---

[466] See Jung's letter to Neumann, 19 July 1947 (54 J): "You still have to gain experience for yourself as far as being misunderstood goes. The possibilities exceed all terminology."

[467] Handwritten insertion by Neumann.

[468] Handwritten insertion by Neumann.

happening—crazily—only to retrospectively reinforce your position "against" Neumann that, in my opinion was never intended as such by you. What intellectual disingenuous is all this! Can you not now at least understand from the outcome of this "affair" how justified my reaction is? I still dare to hope that if I am additionally roaring like a "lion," shaking my mane and not simply letting my coat be ruffled by holy and unholy dogs, that you must understand this as a "Fellow Lion."

I now have nothing more to say; I hope very much that this unfortunate, crazy, and ugly matter has not taken up your time and energy that you need for other things. I am anyway, now as ever, with and without *Ethic*—

Your grateful,
E. Neumann

9 April 49

Dear and Highly Esteemed Professor Jung,

Your letter that crossed with mine–and for which I am exceedingly grateful—has stunned me, and for reasons that I will explain to you in detail later, moved and upset me. But firstly I would like to sort out the "technical" things. Your reading of my first letter that it was not important to me where *Origins* was published was absolutely correct. My protest and my anger apply not to the fact but to its causes and the background to them, as well as to the manner in which they were carried out. As I am [also] informing the institute at the same time, I have already instructed Rascher in a letter of 1st April[469] (as he had inquired of me regarding this), that publication under the auspices of the institute is definitely not an option. This took place before the letter from the institute that I received on 7th April[470] and I have nothing to add to this.

Here, too, I would almost advise appointing someone to the institute who has some subtlety of perception and something of what declining Europe called "intellect" about them. An institute bearing your name may not permit itself to choose the term "promote" for a foreword from you, and it ought even less to imply that it has made a censorious revision to a foreword of yours, one written for a book that is absolutely not permitted to appear under its auspices. For this is, of course, the background to the otherwise quite inappropriate

[469] Neumann wrote to Rascher on 1 April 1949: "I herewith inform you that I definitely do not grant my permission for publication under the auspices of the Jung Institute. This matter is closed as far as I am concerned. [...] But as I am incidentally curious about whether another decision has been made by the Institute, I would ask you to treat this communication confidentially. [...] The Institute has renounced the right to publish the book, I have declared myself to be in agreement with this" (RA).

[470] This information is confusing as Neumann was already informed about the institute's decision by Meier's letter from 3 February 1949 (see n. 460).

communication of the Institute . . . "so you must let it come out as a book in its own right, with the foreword from Professor Jung that he will send you the final version of directly."

I would never have dared to suggest alterations to your foreword, but you will understand that there is nothing left for me to do, far off the beaten track and at the mercy of all hostilities, than to inform you, my only real counterpart, of the fact that I perceive your revisions as bitter, and where.

It is not about the fact that May '48 shone more favorably on me than April '49, nor about the qualifications to your endorsement of me that seem necessary to you. I have nothing to say about this, although the discrepancy between "creating a unified whole" and "woven his facts into a pattern" is monstrous.[471] The second formulation leaves the question completely open as to whether these contexts are relevant, which the first implies with your all too kind emphasis.

My concerns are about the new inclusions, my bitterness about a change that is at the root of Dr. Meier's fear of a system that scared him off even in Ascona.[472] When you formulated, for the first time, "buildings in which the empirical conceptual forms find their natural living space," you were under the influence of the book itself; "finding a living space," with the new addition about the personal

---

[471] In the final version of his foreword Jung deleted the word "lückenlos": "Es ist ihm [sc. Neumann] geglückt, [*lückenlose*] Zusammenhänge herzustellen und auf diese Weise ein Ganzes zu schaffen, was dem Pionier nie gelungen wäre und an das er sich auch nie hätte wagen können" (Jung, 1949, p. 556). In his 1954 translation R.F.C. Hull rendered: "He has woven his facts into a pattern and created a unified whole" (p. xiii).

[472] C. A. Meier left the room during Neumann's presentation on the "Mystical Man" at Eranos 1948. Jung mentions the incident in a letter to Jacobi, in which he defends Neumann against her criticism: "Neumann is in my view a first class force, and it is up to the proficiency of my students to prove that he is not promulgating any dogma, but is merely seeking to create order. Dr. Meier, for example, would do better to thrash out the connection of his Asklepios with psychotherapy than to run away from a lecture. He would come up against some ticklish problems where some spade work such as Neumann does it would be very welcome" (24 September 1948 [JA]). In an undated letter to Meier from autumn 1948 Neumann refers to this incident: "I was of the opinion that, with the telling of your dream, which seems very clear to me, the complex-laden nature of your reaction to my lecture of which you heard the beginning had become clear to you, and with that, the matter seemed to me to be settled. Now I notice that you evidently believe that you formed a correct picture at that time in a downright anticipatory intuition about its 'future' progression. For this well proves that, after you had become acquainted with the lecture for the first time, you had confirmed your 'fundamental objections' which came to you before you knew what I had to say" (NP).

equivalence and the exclusion of the "textbook sentence" from which I knew immediately that it would heap the enmity of Zurich upon me—that is a total distancing that perhaps is not intended by you in the way it now sounds.[473] Now it sounds like this—to me: What can one do, there are simply some people who, for good or ill, cannot help creating a system and concocting hypotheses about it. Thank God there are other sorts of people too. Of course I am exaggerating. But it seems to me that the completely understandable qualification of your all too strong endorsement—which evokes no sort of "bitterness"—belongs to this. Now, all that remains is the qualification and the endorsement is dubious in decisive points.

I fear that your institute and Mrs. Jacobi, especially, will have to create an orthodoxy for the very reason that nothing of their own occurs to them, and you, dear Professor, will not be able to do anything about this.[474] However, I promise you I won't let them put my back to the wall, as far as it is possible to me. I already know now that I am naturally a bad Jewish-intellectual student of yours, for whom the essential thing evades me. Hence my anger at the sentence in the disloyal letter from Miss Wolff that I quoted to you. I adhere to the sentence from Mrs. von Keller[475] after the incident with Meier, which

[473] The Jung archive at the ETH Zurich contains the different drafts of the foreword (HS 1055: 851,1–3). (HS 1055: 851,1) is the handwritten version of May 1948; (HS 1055: 851,2) is a typescript version of the May 1948 draft—with handwritten changes. The original text, "This book qualifies more than any other as an actual textbook of this new branch of knowledge. I congratulate the author on this achievement," is crossed out and replaced by: "The development of an ordered system can never disregard a total hypothesis which for its part is based on the temperament and the subjective assumptions of the author, alongside the objective principles. This issue is particularly relevant in psychology. The 'personal equation' conditions the way one sees. Relative ultimate truth requires the consonance of many voices. I can only congratulate the author on this achievement." The printed version dated March 1949 sticks to this version with the exception of "Errichtung" ("construction") for "Entwicklung" ("development") and "seiner Leistung" ("on his achievement") for "dieser Leistung" ("on this achievement").

[474] For Jacobi's relationship to Neumann see introduction, p. xxxix–xli, xliv, lii.

[475] Alwine (Alwina) von Keller (1878–1965): New York–born German pedagogue and psychotherapist, close confidante of the reformist pedagogue Paul Geheeb, who in later years would also be analyzed by her. In the 1930s she left Germany for England and Switzerland, where she lived with Emma von Pelet in the Casa Shanti next to Casa Gabriella, where the Eranos meetings took place. Having started her analytical traning in Berlin with Ernst Bernhard, she continued her analysis with Jung, whose student and close collaborator she became. Her ardent fascination with India, which she visited in 1929, led her to translate yogic texts from Sri Aurobindo (1943 and 1945) and Swami Vivekananda (Keller, 1944). On Keller see also Bernardini, Quaglino, and Romano (2011).

was the start of it all: Now you must go on your way like a rhino and not look to the left or the right.

And with that, now let's get down to business.

I am disturbed, exhausted, and unhappy that I have robbed you of 14 days with my small book, which does not deserve it. It is a by-product, a polemical text, and, of course, you hit the nail on the head as usual, it is a chapter from a bigger conceptual framework. For this reason, you have done me a great favor with your comments for which I am very deeply obliged to you, more deeply than ever before. Originally, a second section was supposed to follow the first with some additional content, and this second part contained dreams, fantasies, etc., especially even of my own, for this small book was not really conceived from the head. But it was the all too personal and barely representable part of the material that had to be discarded because of this. To this extent, I confess that I am guilty, but I would not know how to do it any other way, even today. Since your letter, I have again been giving some more thought as to whether I can, may and ought to write this second section—but it just won't work.

Now, in the closest connection with this, I turn to your new critique, which, by the way, I will comply with as far as it is possible to me.

When I wrote this book in a different format and without the second section, I definitely did it in a way that then seemed possible to me because of your endorsement. Conscious of what the title indicates. All your new objections disregard this title, which was altered by you because of this. I have consciously (p. 91) left out the integration process and referred to your works. I.e., I have only been able to go to the very edge of where the religious problem begins. In order to be comprehensible and to get the discussion going, one must eschew constantly pointing to processes that are, in fact, not representable anyway. Besides, I cannot usurp the stance of a person of your stature and age. I will leave that to others. Your latest position is purely religious and is actually no longer interested in ethics. I know only too well that is ultimately valid, and also valid for you regarding what sort of dangers are emerging for the world, including Zurich. I am daring to protest here. The ethical behavior of the personality cannot *only* experience itself as the grain of corn between hammer and anvil. Esteemed Professor Jung, you sin against yourself to pitch this, your last phase, against the new ethic. I mean the following. I am not, as Miss W. assumes all of a sudden, such an idiot to have "forgotten" these things that I have experienced quite strongly and continue to do so. But the ethical stance of the alchemists exists in the preparation and the preservation of the fire, in a plethora of active and responsible operations, he must *do* the Opus, even in the knowledge that ultimately, however, the Opus does itself—but not in a way that violates things of earth. I am not "old protestant," not "old testament," but a Jew, i.e., a person who has experienced in the deepest way possible that ritual and symbol do not protect what is human if no moral "ego" constitutes its counterpart and if no old or new ethical stance forms the counterbalance to the symbol-laden unconscious. Hasidism is not the exponent of Jewish ethics, and Catholicism is, it seems to me, amoral inasmuch as it is not the old ethics, but in no way does it represent the new ethic. Ten years ago, no, in fact 13 years back, you told me that and why you never went to Rome and you pondered that perhaps this is *the* enemy, but I will not take up the fight if it is not required of me. And now? Massacre of the Jews, burning of the witches, all misery and crime of the world can take place with the collective symbols and within its rituals. The church remains the ancient Great Mother whom I know well. Miss Wolff is of the opinion that Faust made it easy for himself and that he does not deserve the Catholic conclusion for that reason. What a misunderstanding. In my experience one must be an anti-Catholic sinner,—that means a suffering and unredeemed person—in order to encounter her.

My shadow is really big enough to always have demanded and deserved my attention. For this reason I know how right you are about everything you say about suffering the shadow. But, it seems to me, one does not need to say this to anyone in a world whose sense of guilt threatens to annihilate them. But that it belongs here, is also inferred, must be included, that is a matter of depth psychology that preoccupied me. This is where the justification lies for having written this book. A Mrs. Jacobi on her knees—that is the danger!, but not an all too belligerent Neumann. Believe me, I suffer from my shadow enough to fully understand every word you wrote. But you have gone on too far ahead, others are too far behind—that is the difficulty. The activist accents are necessary—here a Jewish flame is burning that cannot be refuted by any symbolism because it is the inner life of the symbol. If one really wished to coformulate the whole, one would no longer be able to formulate anything at all. Not even you have managed this, not to speak of me. That is a matter of great art, not one of psychology. An example for many. Your critique of the formulation, "engaging" the Self. But that one can and one must, quite independently of the fact that it is all what one wishes to "make" it. One can also "engage" God, e.g., as the king, which is familiar to you, one can also live it, although it does not need that. In a novel that I wrote when I was 25, I called it giving "his signature."[476] I do not believe that I ever meant by this that even without this signature the contract is valid. Only with it, however, does it take effect humanly.

Dear Professor Jung, I would like to completely relieve you of any inner and outer difficulties that a foreword to this *Ethic* could lumber you with. You have unfortunately already gone above and beyond for this matter. I believe when I take all these things into consideration and perhaps write a postscript to it, it will do. So much about so little, the *Origins* is a thousand times more important to me, I am beginning to accept already that, after that, no cockerel will crow.

If anything else sounds incomprehensible, please believe me that it was not so intended—just as so much of what has happened since was not intended.

With great gratitude,
Your,
[E. Neumann].

---

[476] Neumann wrote a novel titled *Der Anfang* (*The Beginning*). One chapter was published in an anthology of young German Jewish authors, *Zwischen den Zelten* (Neumann, 1932).

Dr. Erich Neumann,
Analytical Psychologist

Tel Aviv, 1. VI. [1949]

Dear Professor Jung,

On this occasion it is just a technical request, in haste, and a query that I'm bothering you with.

We require new passports to exit the country, a matter that remains difficult, and my wife must state her profession in her passport in order to get the exit visa for the conference, etc. Certification is required as we are a young and therefore a particularly bureaucratic state. For obvious reasons I do not wish to issue her with such a "Diploma" personally, so I am asking you to certify that my wife, Julie Neumann, has been working for more than 10 years as an analytical psychologist with your assent. (Training: Adler, Miss Wolff, and my humble self.)

The other thing. The "Living Thoughts L."[477] have approached me to write the volume on you. I had accepted and written to Rascher.[478] R. objected angrily and informed me that you and he had already turned down the publisher's request.[479] Whereupon, I equally angrily

[477] The "Living Thoughts Library" was a book series edited by Alfred O. Mendel. Each volume presented the work of a prominent thinker through excerpts from the primary sources and an introductory explanation by a representative of or scholar in the field. In the first volume of the series Thomas Mann introduced the philosophy of Arthur Schopenhauer (Mann, 1939).

[478] Neumann to Rascher, 24 April 1949: "I have been invited to write and assemble the Volume on Jung for the 'Living Thoughts Library' which I'm sure you know, in which the leading minds of the world are represented. I have naturally accepted and hope that it will be a pleasure for him on the occasion of his 75th birthday next year. However, as the volumes combine an essay on the author with a selection of his writing, I felt it was necessary to ask you for your permission" (RA).

[479] Rascher to Neumann, 7 May 1949: "As far as the compilation volume for The Living Thoughts library is concerned, the publisher has already approached Prof. Dr. Jung and us. We have resolutely declined their request" (RA).

withdrew my agreement. Response from them: you had absolutely not declined etc., etc. I consider the matter closed, but just wanted to put you in the picture anyway, in case you wish to do something about it. In principle, I think it could only be a good thing if something like this came out on the occasion of your 75th and this is why I had accepted it. What's been done for Freud, should also be done for Jung.[480] Of course I did not know that you had been asked and that you had suggested Mrs. Harding.[481] The publisher has only just told me this. I only say it so that no misunderstandings arise.

As I am up to my ears in all sorts of things, you will forgive my brevity. I certainly hope that it all works out and that I will be able to come to Switzerland once again this year and see you and speak with you. The *Ethic* can wait till then. The translation is due in two years and I have contractually agreed upon revisions, etc. At the moment I am torturing myself with the Eranos lecture, the *Great Mother* and the *Psychology of the Feminine*, both internally and externally.

With best wishes, also to Mrs. Jung,
Your grateful,
E. Neumann

---

[480] The editor Alfred O. Mendel wrote to Jung on 26 October 1948 asking him for the permission to edit a volume on Jung. In his letter Mendel mentioned the volume on Freud (Wälder, 1941): "In the book series whose catalogue I enclose, there is a volume on 'Freud.' In keeping with Freud's express wish, it was compiled by his 'right-hand man,' Dr. Wälder" (JA).

[481] In his letter to Mendel from 11 November 1948 Jung wrote: "From among my students, Dr. M. Esther Harding in New York (108 East 38th Street) would be the most obvious person" (JA). On Esther Harding see n. 276.

Küsnacht, Zch., 18th June 1949
Seestr. 228

Dr. Erich Neumann,
1, Gordon St.,
Tel Aviv

Dear Colleague,

Enclosed, the requested certificate.

It was reported to me that this Living Thoughts Library is not a very serious concern.[482] I was under the impression that this is an American outfit. Such things are very frequently of unbelievable superficiality in America. I tentatively suggested Dr. Harding just because I was of the opinion that this was an American matter. It then turned out that it is not actually a biography that is planned but a type of anthology, i.e., 1/3 biographical notes and 2/3 excerpts from my works, so to a certain extent a disloyal competition with my own publications. This was the reason why I declined. If you possess different information and if it really is a question of an original piece and not simply cobbling together an anthology, then this would be a different matter of course. I would naturally be very much in agreement if you wrote something like this, especially if it is for Europe and takes place in German.—But I see from the letter from Mr. Mendel that in fact it is supposed to be "30–40 pages introductory words, the remaining 160–170 pages, a selection from my works."[483]

---

[482] Jung's verdict is somehow contradicted by an impressive number of prominent European and American intellectuals who wrote for the series: John Dewey on Thomas Jefferson, André Gide on Michel de Montaigne, Heinrich Mann on Friedrich Nietzsche, Thomas Mann on Arthur Schopenhauer, Leon Trotsky on Karl Marx, Paul Valéry on René Descartes, Arnold Zweig on Baruch Spinoza, Stefan Zweig on Leo Tolstoy, to mention only a few.

[483] Letter from Alfred O. Mendel to Jung on 13 November 1948 (JA).

I wish you all necessary luck for your big subject at the Eranos conference. It's a huge soup you've landed yourself in there!

I have now happily written—at least in rough—my investigation of synchronicity, which has been weighing on me for a long time. But, for now, I must have it looked over by the physicists.

With best wishes,
Your,
C. G. Jung

79 J (A)[484]

[Küsnacht, Zch.] 18th June 1949

CERTIFICATE.

I hereby confirm that Mrs. Julia Neumann (1 Gordon St., Tel Aviv) has been practicing as an Analytical Psychologist with my authorization for more than ten years.

---

[484] In possession of the Stiftung der Werke von C. G. Jung.

Dr. Erich Neumann,
Analytical Psychologist

Tel Aviv, 16. VII. 49

Highly esteemed and dear Professor Jung,

Firstly I would like to wish you all the best for your birthday, and hope that your health and strength have been restored to you and to us all as in the last few years. You do know that I also hope to be able to see and speak with you personally—as much as indeterminable fate will allow. Alongside the surprising and rather sinister matter of the publications, the last year has bestowed on me, in compensation, so much that is personally unexpected and not easily digestible that my relationship with you, dear Professor Jung, is indeed the firmest link that ties me personally to Europe, despite everything. It goes without saying what this means as there is, for me, no other shore than the Occidental European one. Although we still have not got an exit visa, I hope everything will sort itself out in time. I definitely hope to be able to speak with you even if you are not going to Ascona.

I hope you will understand that I have not touched the burning (in every sense of the word) topic of *New Ethic* again. Not even after G. Adler's long letter in which he reported your conversation to me.[485] Firstly I had to get to grips with the difficult subject of my Eranos lecture in some sort of passable way, which was not easy, and added to this were personal matters that provided striking contributions to the subject and the whole situation, and not least, I wanted some distance. So I hope to be able to speak with you in person about these complicated questions; it seems better to me than writing it all, although, as you perhaps know, I am always caught up in an

---

[485] Letter is missing.

internal compliance in the initial moments of personal contact, which is rather misleading.

In the meantime, *Origins* has finally come out and I am anticipating with some suspense the new surprises that await me. Even here I will not have succeeded in writing in a way that cannot be misconstrued by evil wishers and/or idiots. I do not have the intention or ability of attempting such a thing either, and do not even believe that anyone—you included, dear Professor, can ever write in such way. But, dear Professor Jung, I urgently ask you for one thing. If someone in Switzerland should determine, to your initial amazement, that my book is an attack on you, or on psychology or the church or anything else, then please do *not* read my book once or even several times more in response. (It has become such a thick tome that it rather fills me with horror.) I still cannot ward off the impression that with every book one reads over and over again, one will always be able to find something for "idiots and evil-wishers" to say against it. It is interesting to find where this label sits, but not even *that* is of interest. (Please do not think that, by this, I am saying that I did not agree with substantial parts of your critique.)

I would be grateful to you if you could let me know if you are able to come to Ascona as I would have to arrange my stay a bit differently if not, always provided we can leave here and that it is possible for you to find time for me.

I, too, warmly thank you—especially on behalf of my wife—for the certificate and I wish you once again all the best for the New Year; I am, with best wishes to Mrs. Jung,

In gratitude,
Your,
E. Neumann

Küsnacht, Zch., 23rd July 1949
Seestrasse 228

Dr. Erich Neumann,
1, Gordon St.,
Tel Aviv

Dear Doctor,

Professor Jung who is already in Bollingen and, if possible, wishes to write no letters at the moment, has asked me to write to you and to let you know that he has now made the decision not to go to Ascona as he fears that the associated demands would cancel out the entire benefits of his holidays. Despite this, he very much hopes to be able to see you and asks you to let him know as soon as possible whether you will come to Zurich before or after the conference. He hopes that you would not mind possibly seeing him in Bollingen.

Hopefully you have now received the exit visa, or will do in time.

Professor and Mrs. Jung send you and your wife warm greetings, and I join them in doing so.

Your,
[Marie-Jeanne Schmid]

82 J

Dear Colleague,

As a result of all sorts of interruptions I have up till now only been able to work through a little more than half of your manuscript.[486] Very difficult for a lay audience, even an educated one, as too much is taken for granted. Very interesting for me as exquisitely thought through. Only—you have the tendency of characterizing the unconscious too pessimistically. It would be advisable to immediately place a positive remark after every negative one, otherwise one gets the impression of a catastrophic tragedy without grace from above. That would just not resonate with the experience: "that God helps the brave." Otherwise, I don't have any substantial corrections to report so far. I am especially impressed by how thoroughly you have thought through the problems. But do not forget that behind this cloud of thought sits an audience that will hardly be in a position to follow.

In the meantime, with best wishes,

Your devoted,
C. G. Jung

---

[486] As Jung could not attend the Eranos conference 1949, Neumann seemed to have asked Jung for his opinion about his lecture before the conference. The title of his lecture was "Die mythische Welt und der Einzelne" ("The Mythical World and the Individual") (Neumann, 1950).

83 N

[around] 26th July 1950

Dear Professor Jung,

You will understand how immensely difficult it is to write a birthday letter to you, and especially for your 75th. Such a day prompts me so urgently to reflect and to try to capture what the encounter with you has meant for my life and just how much your life per se has been growing in significance, quite independently from me—how could all this be expressed in a letter.

   In the autumn of '34,[487] I came to you for the first time, then in '36 from Palestine and then finally, after 11 years and the war and many experiences, came the reunion with you in '47. That is a long stretch of life. Of course you don't know what it meant for me that I have always had the impression and retain it to this day, that in your eyes as well my work is meaningfully affiliated with yours, thanks to your investment in me. In my state of remote isolation I naturally did not know whether the trajectory of my development was "consistent" with yours or not; it was only when I got my hands on your and Kerényi's book,[488] many years after its appearance, that I became quite sure that *Origins* could not be completely "wayward." I have tried to burden you as little as possible with my own private development, but it does belong here in this context. In this remote little country, which is diminutive, in many things narrow and barbaric, productive in much, and pregnant with the future, I stand, inwardly of course, completely alone, with a decaying Europe at my back and a dangerously emergent Asia before me. Indeed, in this situation the reconnection with you has always been a vital support.

---

[487] Neumann is wrong. In fact he came to Jung in autumn 1933.
[488] Jung and Kerényi (1941).

And now you are 75 and the next world war, be it cold or very hot, stands once again at the door. Of course one wonders what one is doing actually; has any of it any point. You yourself have embedded your work and its impact in the world, and that will be amplified, less, I believe, in a jaded Switzerland or in the pseudo-certainty of America, than in a place where danger and suffering threaten to extinguish the individual. But what about us? But what about my generation? For us, everything lies in an obscurity of danger, so that it is difficult to always keep an unshaken faith that the choice is located in the individual. In a time when the claim of the collective person is asserting itself externally and internally with violence and with justification, it is often difficult enough to keep on going, because the meaninglessness of keeping the world in order by the individual and from the inside out seems so apparent. But in the meantime I am so convinced of the real paradox of the living that I can brush off these worries, and for this reason I am also certain that your work is not an end but a beginning, even if we do not know where it is actually headed. I hope you will not consider me arrogant if I admit to you that even here my enforced isolation helps. I find it appropriate and keep experiencing that, despite everything, my own vitality is soaring up out of it. My rootedness is not very effective in the sense of the possibility of seeing only the one thing. Even here, your being-more-than-European and your quest through the times and nations have helped me very much. Many remarkable things have happened to me, and I have thus experienced much in other ways and forms, and with hindsight, I know that you have been my inner leader in it all. This has often been a comfort to me, especially as I experience much in a very different and contradictory way from you, as you know. In this way, far beyond these "incidents" and "frivolities," a transcendent sense of belonging to you has always remained inwardly apparent to me and it is possibly stronger than you imagine. Whenever we are together in person, my moon always elicits your sun in the most joyful way, so I would like to assure you of this at any rate on this "festive occasion."

I hope very much that you will spend your birthday without too many stresses and wish you and Mrs. Jung all the best. If my wife and

I come to Switzerland, as we would like to—my wife has been very ill for a long time—we will express our congratulations to you in person. I have heard a rumor that you will come to Ascona, but I fear it will be too great a struggle for you. So we are not going to raise our hopes of that for now.

Ever yours,
E. Neumann

Erich Neumann,
Analytical Psychologist

Tel Aviv,
20. VII. 51

Dear Professor Jung,

I am sending you this birthday greeting as a sign that I have not completely disappeared. I hope very much that you have now recovered from the exhaustion and hope that you will be able to come to Ascona without it being too much for you. But please take good care! Everything else is unimportant. The last year was a difficult one for me—apart from the fact that I did some pretty good work and, among other things, completed the manuscript of the Great Mother for Bollingen. Although I have always made an effort not to burden and pester you with my private matters, this time I cannot spare you, dear Professor. So I hope very much you will have a couple of hours for me—as usual. So for this reason too, I will let you know as soon as I am in Switzerland to find out when it would suit you best to see me.

Otherwise, I thank you very much for allowing me to see the draft of the new *Transformations*[489]—it has not yet arrived—so as not to repeat too many blunders in the *Great Mother*. With many greetings to Mrs. Jung too, and best wishes—you know it goes without saying that I send those—

I am,
Your,
E. Neumann

---

[489] *Symbole der Wandlung* (*Symbols of Transformation*) (1952a) is the revised version of *Wandlungen und Symbole der Libido* (*Psychology of the Unconscious*) (1912).

85 N

[Ascona, no date][490]

Very dear and esteemed C. G. Jung,

A letter that I wrote to you and Mrs. Jung weeks ago, soon after my arrival in Switzerland, has evidently got lost in your mail in Küsnacht. Therefore I am repeating my previous request. I would like to see and speak to you and your wife more than once if at all possible. We are in Zurich from 24th September until 6th October and I would like to know when and where I can visit you as my time in Zurich is occupied with work and I would like to make plans. Would you be so kind as to write to me at the Hotel Seidenhopf, 7–9 Sihl St., Zurich? I hope very much that you and your wife are enjoying good health; my wife and I have recuperated very well, firstly in Sils Maria and now in Ascona. I'm looking forward very much to speaking to you, there is always much more to talk about than we ever manage.

Goodbye, with best wishes to Mrs. Jung from my wife too,
Ever yours,
E. Neumann
We will stay here until the 21st and then go to Zurich via Basel.

[490] No date or year is given. The letter must have been written between 1948, the year Erich Neumann lectured at Eranos, and 1955, the year in which Emma Jung died (27 November 1955).

Dr. Erich Neumann,
Analytical Psychologist

Tel Aviv, 5th Dec. 51

My dear Professor Jung,

You must excuse me that I have selfishly held on to the *Job* until now,[491] but I had to read it a second time after a certain gap before I could send it back to you. I am sure you will not take exception if I make a few comments about it.

Firstly it is a book that grips me deeply, I find it the finest and deepest of your books, and I should also say that it is actually no longer a "book." In a certain sense it is an argument with God, a concern similar to that of Abraham when he argues with God because of the downfall of Sodom. It is—for me personally—especially also an argument against God who allowed 6 million of "His" people to be killed, for Job is precisely also Israel, and I don't mean that in a "small" way, I know we are the paradigm for the whole of humanity in whose name you are speaking, protesting, and consoling. And exactly the conscious one-sidedness, yes, often the inaccuracy of what you are saying is, to me, an inner proof of the necessity and justice of your attack—which is, of course, not one, as I well know.

But for all this, it seems to me that it takes the normal reader too little into account in the intermingling of points of view. In part, it is an interpretation of the Occidental inner history of the soul; in part, it is a dialogue with God; in part, a psychological analysis; in part, a myth or, better, the making conscious of the Occidental myth. For me personally, it is precisely this intertwining and interweaving, this dramatic authenticity of the "document" which is the crucial thing,

---

[491] *Antwort auf Hiob* (*Answer to Job*) was published in 1952 by Rascher in Zurich (Jung, 1952b). For a detailed commentary on Jung's book see Bishop (2002).

but whom do you want to burden with this? For it does not purport to be like the *Sermones*[492] (which I find *Job* to be the continuation of) as a text for the initiated, although it is this in a certain way.

Questions. Could it not be made clearer that Job is a prototype for suffering humanity, just as it is about the analysis of the situation of humanity at the turn of time. But then the confinement to the canonical books is still not comprehensible, why then do Gnosis and the Jewish Midrash not belong here? Is it only about the Western image of God, you do mean the general transformation of the image of God, but can one simply leave out Asia? And if so, is it not even more the God-image of Western humanity? Fine, how should one separate this, but how should one understand that the history of God is contained explicitly in the canonical texts, is it not therefore about the image engendered by these texts?

You imply this problem, but what you write in the last pages (pp. 106–7) belongs at the start, or also at the start.

The oscillation between the theological and the psychological formulation needs to be rather strengthened if it is not to seem unintentional. E.g., pp. 93–94. The problem of the "metaphysical advocate" against Yahweh often sounds too Gnostic, whereby Yahweh—despite your counterassurance—becomes all too similar to the demiurge. (Here it seems to me to be a real unresolved religious problem.) In reality, you believe in the feminine Sophia as the highest authority without admitting it.[493] Perhaps it only seems to me to be so because this is how it is for me personally. Only the matriarchal psychology of the psyche and the Holy Ghost is comprehensible. (??)[494] When you speak of the omniscience of Yahweh, it sounds always ironic. But

---

[492] Jung (1916); see n. 179.

[493] *Sophia*, Greek for wisdom, in Latin *sapaientia dei*, or the wisdom of God. In chapter 3 of *Answer to Job* (Jung, 1952b, §§ 609–24) Jung places the book of Job in the tradition of wisdom literature begining with the book of Proverbs. Other examples, cited by Jung, as texts in which the wisdom of God is expressed, are the Psalms, Song of Songs, Ecclesiastes, Book of Wisdom, and the Wisdom of Sirach. Jung calls her "a coeternal and more or less hypostatized *pneuma of feminine nature* that existed before the Creation" (Jung, 1952b, § 609). According to Jung it is Job's righteousness that reveals Yahweh's unconscious separation from wisdom to himself: "the 'just' God could not go on committing injustices, and the 'Omniscient' could not behave any longer like a clueless and thoughtless human being. Self-reflection becomes an imperative necessity, and for this Wisdom is needed. Yahweh has to remember his absolute knowledge; for, if Job gains knowledge of God, then God must also learn to know himself" (Jung, 1952b, § 617).

[494] The two question marks in brackets were inserted by Neumann.

what if he really possesses it and only gives himself archaically to the archaic because he can only become comprehensible to it in this way and if everything that you say is correct but necessary at the same time. The problem is—why was an unconscious world created, but does not the omniscience that precedes it suggest a meaningful direction though, in which the Godhead can never be manifest in a different way from one that corresponds to humanity.

If one loves people beyond their qualities, how could God's love, which is also supposed to exist beyond his qualities, become conscious in any other way than by God seeming terrible? And if the Godhead "wanted" this, how could it be accomplished in any other way than with help from Satan who is equally necessary? Not as a "test," but as the only situation in which the superiority of the human being—which you have already established—can appear. So, for example, I do not see Psalm 89 as a betrayal.[495] At a lower lever, it is a punishment that is threatened, and on a higher—has Yahweh broken his covenant with David, with the Jews, with humanity? The manifestation of Yahweh is "bound" to the status of man, this is his covenant, your polemic against theology is often not differentiated from that against God. Did God say he is only the summum bonum?

The unity that we Jews confess is precisely the one of the metaphysical advocate *and* the fear- and terror-inspiring God. You portray the transformation of humanity in this numinosum as if there were no problem of transference and projection in it. In the dramatic portrayal of the development, that is fully justified, but at the end a distancing summary that is not any longer trapped in the process itself could be helpful. Of course I know that it is precisely your deep concern to "secure" human existence in this way, so that it contributes so decisively to the fate of the Godhead. Therefore one can only portray this event in a two-sided way, but the meaningful disposition of the

---

[495] Jung writes in *Answer to Job* quoting Psalm 89:13–14: "In view of this intense personal relatedness to his chosen people, it was only to be expected that a regular covenant would develop which also extended to certain individuals, for instance to David. As we learn from the Eighty-ninth Psalm, Yahweh told him: 'My steadfast love I will keep for him for ever, / and my covenant will stand firm for him. / [...] I will not violate my covenant, / or alter the word that went forth from my lips. / Once for all I have sworn by my holiness; / I will not lie to David.' And yet it happened that he, who watched so jealously over the fulfillment of laws and contracts, broke his own oath" (Jung, 1952b, §§ 569–70).

world, or even only the potentially meaningful existence in it, may not be overlaid with a Gnostic sentiment that portrays Job's humility, which is all too justified, as the gagging of a wise man by a monster of a God. (It is striking that the infinite goodness of God is conceptually present, but does not really appear in any one place.)

I am not defending Yahweh but the advocate in heaven whom Job himself calls upon. The analysis of Job is after all only a part, the other side is also present, which, for example, puts this Yahweh on trial in you yourself today. With the manifestation in the storm and thunder, have you not overlooked the one in the rustling of the wind although it has revealed itself as the higher form?

You know well that the question of the new ethic still grips me. What about "washing off the obnoxious darkness"[496] on p. 95 and "the guilty man is selected for incarnation"[497] on p. 99? (May I gently make you aware, by the way, that such a young institute as the C. G. Jung Institute will have to distance itself from you and your writings?)

The terrible trajectory of development: Yahweh, Yahweh-Sophia, Christ, divine child, may not be based on the "random" selection of interpreted places, or this line must at least become visible at the end in its absolute relevance, so that the discussion does not overshadow the [biggest] question of the *Answer* with adequate or inadequate interpretation of individual texts.

I very much hope, dear Professor, you will not take offense at the bluntness of my objections. None of them are central issues; it seems to me, I have only noted what occurred to me. But despite this, I hope that I have understood you, if not, I would be very grateful for details and corrections. My remarks basically tend to deepen the stormy reaction that this book will trigger so that it is not made all too easy for those who do not wish to understand. Especially the "Gnostic misunderstanding" to which Quispel[498] also seems to have

[496]"We therefore need more light, more goodness and moral strength, and must wash off as much of the obnoxious blackness as possible, otherwise we shall not be able to assimilate the dark God who also wants to become man, and at the same time endure him without perishing" (Jung, 1952b, § 742).

[497]"The guilty man is eminently suitable and is therefore chosen to become the vessel for the continuing incarnation" (Jung, 1952b, § 746).

[498]Gilles Quispel (1916–2006): Dutch theologian, professor for the History of the Early Church (Utrecht University), expert on Gnosticism. Studied classical philology and theology and was awarded a PhD degree for his thesis on Tertullian's *Adversus Marcionem* (1943). Quispel

Figure 7. Gerhard Adler, Erich Neumann, and Gilles Quispel at the Eranos
conference 1951 (Eranos Archive; courtesy of Paul Kugler).

succumbed should be prevented as much as possible. In any case, all
this must not be at the cost of the "naïveté" of the portrayal that so
profoundly deepens the impression—to me anyway.

In the *Psyche*,[499] which Rascher will send you as soon as it comes
out (which should happen any day), a similar process of an arche-

---

met Jung for the first time at the 1944 Eranos conference, to which he became the regular con-
tributor on Gnostic topics from 1947 until 1971. It was Quispel who convinced Jung and C. A.
Meier in 1952 to purchase a number of Gnostic scriptures discovered in Nag Hammadi (Egypt)
in 1945. These five scriptures (Codex I) were named after Jung—against his will—and remained
in Zurich until 1975, when they were returned to Egypt (on the "Codex Jung" see n. 543). Quispel became especially known for his research on another scripture from Nag Hammadi's
"Codex II," the Gospel of Thomas. Jung wrote a foreword for an (unpublished) volume of Quis-
pel's Eranos lectures (Jung, 1949a). Quispel's works include *The Jung Codex: A Newly Recovered
Gnostic Papyrus* (together with G. Van Unnik and W. C. Puech) (1955), four lectures held at the
Jung Institute published as *Gnosis als Weltreligion* (1951), *Gnostic Studies* (1974), *Tatian and the
Gospel of Thomas* (1975), and *Gnostica, Judaica, Catholica* (2008). On Quispel see Van den Broek
and Vermaseren (1981). An interview about his relationship with Jung was conducted by James
Kirsch and Suzanne Wagner, titled "Remembering Jung: A Conversation about C. G. Jung and
His Work with Gilles Quispel" (Kirsch and Wagner, 1977).

[499] "Eros and Psyche: The Psychic Development of the Feminine: A Commentary on the Tale
by Apuleius" (Neumann, 1952).

typal nature seems to me to exist. But taking place in the feminine and at the edge of antiquity. But I have only been able to hint at it and for sure it is a problem of apparently smaller numinosity. But who knows, even the divine daughter is not without deep significance. The rebirth of Sophia in ecstasy is still quite puzzling to me, but there is something about it.

I hope very much that my letter will not upset you, but I could not send *Job* back to you without my thanks. That these thanks bring questions with them will not surprise you.

With all warm wishes,
Your,
E. Neumann

Tel Aviv, 11th Dec. [1951]

Dr. Erich Neumann,
Analytical Psychologist

Dear Professor Jung,

I'm coming to you this time with a request. My son is supposed to begin his medical studies in Zurich at the end of next year (at the moment he wants to become a psychotherapist), but it is very difficult to get a place there as a foreigner. I am asking you for a letter of sponsorship in which you say what needs to be said. I will also write myself and try to put my connection with Switzerland through you, Rascher, Ascona into the mix. I very much hope that such a letter from you will be the deciding factor. Miss Schmid will then send it on to Dr. Hurwitz.[500] Very many thanks.

---

[500] Siegmund Hurwitz (1904–1994): Swiss psychotherapist of Jewish descent, medical doctor, Jung's dentist and friend; analytical training with Jung, Toni Wolff, and Marie-Louise von Franz. Hurwitz and his wife Leni, who was one of the editors of Jung's *Gesammelte Werke*, were good friends with the Neumanns. Hurwitz shared with Neumann a common interest in Jewish mysticism. His article on "Archetypische Motive in der chassidischen Mystik" was published in the third volume of *Studien aus dem C. G. Jung Institut "Zeitlose Dokumente der Seele"* (*Timeless Documents of the Soul*) (together with articles by Marie-Louise von Franz and Helmuth Jacobsohn). He presented a copy to Neumann with the dedication "Herrn u. Frau Neumann überreicht vom Verfasser" ("Presented to Mr. and Mrs. Neumann by the author") (GEA). His refusal to join the Psychological Club Zurich was also instrumental in bringing to fall the notorious Jewish clause, which stated that the number of Jewish members should not exceed more than 25 percent. This policy went back to the 1930s and was formalized in a document from 7 December 1944. It was finally withdrawn in 1950 (see Maidenbaum, 1991). His works include *Die Gestalt des sterbenden Messiahs* (*The Figure of the Dying Messiah*) (1958), *Die Erste Eva: Eine Studie über dunkle Aspekte des Weiblichen* (*Lilith—The First Eve*) (1980), and *The Dark Face of God in Judaism* (1994).

I would like to draw your attention to a picture by Blake, in case you do not know it. From the Job series. (World's Masters New Series, Blake, Fig. 43.)[501]

"Job affrighted by a vision of his God. Plate ii of the Series. Job's God is himself with a cloven hoof, which is the Great Selfhood, identified by B. with Satan. He is entwined with the serpent."

Once again many thanks and greetings,
Your,
E. Neumann

At the same time I wish you and Mrs. Jung all the best for the New Year, i.e., especially health and productivity. The first especially for you, the second for us all.

---

[501] William Blake (1757–1827), *With Dreams upon My Bed Thou Scarest Me & Affrightest Me with Visions* (Job 7:14), plate 11 of Blake's *Illustrations of the Book of Job* (1825). The engravings of 1826 were preceded by two series of watercolors (1805/6 and 1821). See cover picture.

Küsnacht, Zch., 12th December 1951

Dear Doctor,

Although I hope that Prof. Jung will answer your letter in the fore-seeable future, I would like to let you know straightaway that the manuscript has just arrived safely (held together by a good spirit, but complete) and I warmly thank you for sending it back.

May I add that your letter not only interests me deeply but has also somehow "redeemed" me, by explaining why I had the feeling in certain points that something was not right without being able to see why. It also interested me to see that your "critique" corresponds in essence with one such by Hans Schär (the clergyman), only the latter has expressed his in a very protestant unskilled way, so that Prof. Jung could not elaborate on it. I am in exceptional suspense about how Prof. Jung will react to your letter.

And now—instead of a Christmas card—I would like to send you and your wife good wishes for the New Year—which will hopefully bring you much joy and happiness, many pleasant surprises and only a strict minimum of unavoidable "bad quarter hours."

Your,
Marie-Jeanne Schmid

89 J

PROF. DR. C. G. JUNG

Pro tem: Bollingen, Ct. St. Gallen

Until 15. 1

Küsnacht, Zurich,
Seestrasse 228
5. 1. 1952[502]

My dear Neumann,

I thank you very much for your kind letter and the way you understand me. This compensates for 1,000 misunderstandings! You have put your finger on the correct spot, one that is painful for me: I was not able to take account of the normal reader.

He must much more make allowances for *me*. I had to pay this tribute to the merciless fact of my age. In the undiluted providence of the most extensive noncomprehension, no persuasion and *no captatio benevolentiae*[503] succeeded, and even the Nuremburg funnel[504] slipped from my hands. Not in my uniform, but "naked and bare must I give up the ghost" in full awareness of the offense that my nakedness will cause. But what will this mean in the face of this arrogance that I had to demonstrate to be able to insult even God? This has caused me greater discomfort than when I had the whole world against

---

[502] The handwritten version dates 5 January 1952; the typescript version (signed C. G. Jung) gives the date of 7 January.

[503] *captatio benevolentiae* (Latin), rhetorical device, in which the speaker addresses the audience at the beginning of his speech in order to ask for the goodwill of the listeners.

[504] *Nürnberger Trichter* ("Funnel of Nuremberg"), proverbial saying; to use a *Nürnberger Trichter* means to use a device that helps drum something into someone's head without any effort on the person's behalf. It goes back to the book *Poetischer Trichter* ("Poetic Funnel") by the Nuremberg poet Georg Philipp Harsdörffer (1607–1658), which claims in its subtitle to "infuse" the German poetry into someone's head within six hours.

me. Of this latter, there is nothing more that is new to me. I have hinted at my grief and my condolence in my motto: *Doleo super te frater mi*.[505]

To your questions: It is about the canonical image of God. This affects us first and foremost, and not a general philosophical concept of God. This latter lives neither in me nor anywhere else. It is merely intellectual. God is always specific and always locally relevant, otherwise he would be ineffectual. For me, the Occidental God-image is relevant, whether I agree intellectually or not. I'm not pushing any philosophy of religion, but I am gripped, almost smitten, and am defending myself to the best of my ability. Nothing of Gnosis and the Midrashim belongs here, because nothing of that is in it. Purusha-Atman[506] and the Tao only have to do with my cognitive knowledge, but not my living emotion. This is local, barbaric, infantile, and inscrutably unscientific.

The "oscillation between the theological and the psychological formulation" is in fact "unintended." Sophia is actually more personable than the demiurge, but in the face of the reality of both, my sympathy does not count.

God himself is a *contradictio in adjecto*,[507] therefore he requires the human being in order to become whole. Sophia is always one step ahead, the demiurge always one step behind. God is an affliction that man should cure. God thrusts himself into man for this purpose.

---

[505] The motto of Jung's *Answer to Job* is from 2 Samuel 1:26: "Doleo super te frater mi Ionathan decore nimis et amabilis super amorem mulierum" (Vulgate); "I am distressed for thee, my brother Jonathan: very pleasant hast thou been unto me: thy love to me was wonderful, passing the love of women" (KJB).

[506] *purusha* [trans. "male"], also *atman* in the Vedanta tradition, the transcendental Self or pure Spirit. "In Classical Yoga the *purusha*, which is styled the 'power of Awareness' (*citishakti*) is conceived as being absolutey distinct from nature (*prakriti*), which lacks all awareness. Yet what we call consciousness is due to a curious correlation (*samyoga*) between the *purusha* and the *prakriti*" (Feuerstein, 1997, p. 236). This is why Sir John Woodroffe (pseud. Arthur Avalon) could describe it as "a center of limited consciousness—limited by the associated Prakrti and its products of Mind and Matter" (Avalon, 1919, p. 49). Jung discusses the *purusha* in the Kundalini seminar on 26 October 1932: "So *purusha* is identical with the psychical substance of thought and value, feeling. In the recognition of feelings and of ideas one sees the *purusha*. That is the first inkling of a being within your psychological or psychical existence that is not yourself—a being in which you are contained, which is greater and more important than you but which has an entirely psychical existence" (Jung, 1932, pp. 45–46).

[507] *contradictio in adjecto* (Latin), "contradiction in itself" or "contradiction in terms"; a contradiction between an adjective and the noun it modifies, e.g., round square.

Why would he do this if he already has everything? For sure, God must manifest his true form to man in order to reach him, otherwise man would eternally praise his goodness and justice and thereby refuse admittance to God. This can only happen through Satan but satanic action is not vindicated otherwise God would not be really recognized.

The "advocate" seems to me to be Sophia or omniscience.[508] Ouranos and Tethys[509] do not sleep together any more, Kether and Malchuth are separated, the Shekinah in exile;[510] that is the reason for the affliction in God. The Mysterium Coniunctionis is the concern of man. He is the *nymphagōgós*[511] of the heavenly marriage. How can man distance himself from this event? He would then be a philosopher, who speaks *about* God, but not *with* him. The former would be easy

---

[508] Reference to Job 19:25: "For I know that my redeemer lives, and that he shall stand at the latter day upon the earth." Jung identifies the "redeemer" or "advocate" with Sophia: "God was now known, and this knowledge went on working not only in Yahweh but in man too. Thus it was the men of the last few centuries before Christ who, at the gentle touch of the pre-existent Sophia, compensate Yahweh and his attitude, and at the same time complete the anamnesis of Wisdom. Taking a highly personified form that is clear proof of her autonomy, Wisdom reveals herself to men as a friendly helper and advocate against Yahweh, and shows them the bright side, the kind, just, and amiable aspect of their God" (Jung, 1952b, § 623).

[509] Jung is wrong here. Ouranos was the father of Tethys, not her spouse. According to Hesiod's *Theogony*, Gaia, the primordial Greek goddess personifying the Earth, was born out of chaos. She created Ouranos, the sky, and Pontos, the sea, by herself. Seduced by the powers of Eros she lay together with Ouranos and created the Cyclopes, the Hekatonkheires, and the Titans, among which were Oceanos, representing the primal river surrounding the world, and his sister and wife Tethys, the nurturing moisture. However, in Homer's *Iliad* (Book XIV, 200–210), Hera deceivingly tells Zeus and Aphrodite that she will see Oceanos, the father of all gods, and mother Tethys, in order to finish their endless strive. The passage attributes the genealogical roots of the Greek gods to Oceanos and Tethys instead of Ouranos and Gaia, which might have led to Jung's mix-up. Jung owned a copy of Johann Heinrich Voss's German translation of *The Iliad*.

[510] *Kether*, also *Keter*, Hebrew for crown, in the kabbalah the highest of the ten sefiroth—the attributes through which the *Ein Sof* ("the endless") reveals itself—of the Great Tree of Azulit; it is the divine will for creation and beyond human comprehension. *Malkuth*, Hebrew for kingdom, is the lowest sefirah, also known as Shekhinah, which is the divine presence (see n. 273). Jung probably means the unity between the Shekhinah and another sefirah, the Tifereth. These two represent the female and the male principle of God, which were separated when the Shekhinah went into exile with the Jewish people. (See Jung's letter to Ernst Fischer, 21 December 1944; Jung, 1973, vol. 1, p. 44 [German]; vol. 1, pp. 355–56 [English].)

[511] *nymphagōgós*, Greek for bridal guide. In ancient Greece the paranymphos accompanied the bride and groom in a carriage from her father's home to her new home, whereas the *nymphagōgós* would guide her on his own, if the groom had already been married before. Jung uses this concept to emphasize the reunion of the female and male side of God in a *unio mystica*.

and would give man false security; the latter is difficult and therefore exceptionally unpopular. Precisely that was my lamented fate; therefore, it needed a powerful illness to break through my resistance. I am supposed to be *beneath and not above* everywhere. How would Job have looked if he had been able to distance himself?

If we are talking of the Occidental, spec. Protestant image of God, then there are no texts whose more or less reliable interpretation can be considered. This is a matter of lock, stock, and barrel where one does not take a sledgehammer to crack a nut, i.e., it is a matter of a *représentation collective* about which everyone knows something.

As far as the nigredo[512] is concerned, it is certain that no one is redeemed from a sin that he has never committed and that one who is standing on a summit cannot scale it. To each one, the precise humiliation that he receives is given along with his character. If he seeks wholeness seriously, then he will fall unawares into the hole designed for him and from this darkness the light will rise for him; but the light cannot be lit for him. If someone feels themselves to be in the light, then I would never persuade him into the darkness, for otherwise he would seek and find something black with his light that he is not. The light cannot see the darkness that is peculiar to him. But if it declines and the human being follows his twilight as he followed his light, he will thus find his way into *his* night. If the light does not decline, he would be a fool if he did not remain in it.

Your *Psyche* has arrived—many thanks—and I have started reading it. I will write to you about it later. So far I have been very impressed by your representation and am enjoying it.

Job and *Synchronicity*[513] are currently in press. For the time being my unfortunately very limited capacity is fully allocated to writing the last chapter of *Mysterium Coniunctionis* that will fill 2 volumes, followed by a third that will contain the *Aurora Consurgens* (attributed

---

[512] *nigredo*, Latin for blackness, used in alchemy to describe the first stage of the alchemical process; psychologically, it equals the confrontation with the shadow as the initial stage of the individuation process.

[513] *Synchronicity: An Acausal Connecting Principle* (*Synchronizität als ein Prinzip akausaler Zusammenhänge*) was published together with Wolfgang Pauli's *The Influence of Archetypal Ideas on the Scientific Theories of Kepler* (*Der Einfluß archetypischer Vorstellungen auf die Bildung naturwissenschaftlicher Theorien bei Kepler*) as volume four of the institute's series titled *Naturerklärung und Psyche* (Jung, 1952c).

to Thomas of Aquinas)[514] as an example of the reciprocal penetration of Christianity and alchemy.

Once again many thanks!
Your devoted,
C. G. Jung

Ps Hopefully you will not take offense at my having taken the liberty of leaving off your title in the address. Please do the same with me.

---

[514] This third volume of *Mysterium Coniunctionis* on the *Aurora Consurgens* was written by Marie-Louise von Franz (1957).

Dr. Erich Neumann,
Analytical Psychologist

Tel Aviv, 6. II. 52

Dear and honored C. G. Jung,

Although your letter was a great gift to me, I was not able to write to
you sooner. Firstly, illness—and before, during and after it, rather too
much dimming of the light. For this reason the part of your letter
where you speak of one needing to follow his own dusk gripped me
especially. I am trying to do it, or better said, there is nothing left for
me to do than this. But there remains, it seems, nothing left but this
generally.

I have written much, would have had much to write, but actually
it seems to me to be only a detour and an excuse. Over and over again
I am drawn to "Zen," only I sense even there the innocuous superficiality of one's own intention. In short, I do not know where to turn,
and precisely that seems to be what is required of me. But I am
ashamed to open my mouth, and that I did open my mouth, and in
addition for not properly seeing what it is like to keep it shut. It is
going on working, is fascinated and I will soon be able to start writing again, I fear. How good it would be to be a Chinese monk. (It
does not look like anima to me, it has nothing affective about it; it is
a sort of quiet despair.)

Do you know Yogananda, the *Autobiography of a Yogi*?[515] This is also
haunting me very much. Exceptionally convincing through the un-

[515] Paramahansa Yogananda (1893–1952): Indian yogi and guru, founder of the Yogoda
Satsanga Society of India (1917) and the Self-Realization Fellowship (1920); born in Gorakh-
pur, Uttar Pradesh, India; moved to the United States in 1920, where, over the next thirty-two
years, he introduced the American audience to the philosophy of yoga and yogic meditation
practices. His autobiographic account titled *Autobiography of a Yogi* (1946) became an international success. Yogananda praises Jung for his contribution to the understanding of yoga in the

mythical and the everyday of the present. I don't even know where to go with it. With it, the problem of "magical causality"—synchronicity—behind all the immeasurably personal. The last *I Ching* was barely assimilable. The increase with 6 in fourth place. I don't understand it any better than that you are the prince to whom I write this letter. The capital city is being relocated?

All the best to you, the year will bring you some storms from the external world, I hope it will not bother you, but please do not over exert yourself, the intensity of your work is overwhelming, but is it not too much? Warm greetings to Mrs. Jung, I hope Rascher has sent you two *Psyches*, as I would like Mrs. Jung to have a memento of that as she was my comfort in the institute.

As ever in gratitude,
Your,
E. Neumann

---

west: "Yoga has been superficially misunderstood by certain Western writers, but its critics have never been practitioners. Among many thoughtful tributes to Yoga may be mentioned one by Dr. C. G. Jung, the famous Swiss psychologist" (Yogananda, 1946, p. 226). He extensively quotes from Jung's article "Yoga and the West" (Jung, 1936b).

PROF. DR. C. G. JUNG   KÜSNACHT, ZURICH,
                                        SEESTRASSE 228

28. II.1952

Dear Neumann,

I should have written to you some considerable time ago but I have
been banished to bed once again with the flu. At 77, this is no longer
such a simple matter as *facilis descensus Averno*, for all the more difficult is *revocare gradum*, i.e., the impetus to return is gradually losing
its plausibility.[516] I have got out of bed again for the first time today
and am writing to you as one does in the three dimensional world.
I must let you know in the proper way how much your *Amor and
Psyche* pleased me.[517] It is brilliant,—and written with the keenest
sympathy. I believe I now understand why you allow the fate of Psyche and her femininity to unfold with Apuleius on the far shores of
the ancient hero world. Thus, you write it in a succinctly dogmatic
way, as an event rooted in an anonymous primeval world, removed
from personal capriciousness, which should and will stand as a clear
example, when Apuleius experiences, *in imitatio* of Psyche, the descent to the under-gods and his consummation as Sol and thereby
achieves the "highest authority of the masculine." This "midday position of the sun" is a triumph with which the hero's journey begins,

---

[516] Virgil, *Aeneid*, VI, 125–29. Asking for the entry to the underworld Aeneas is told by the
Sibyl of Cumae: "sate sanguine divum, / Tros Anchisiade, facilis descensus Averno: / noctes
atque dies patet atri ianua Ditis; / sed revocare gradum superasque evadere ad auras, / hoc opus,
hic labor est" ("Trojan son of Anchises, / sprung from the blood of the gods, the path to hell is
easy: / black Dis's door is open night and day: / but to retrace your steps, and go out to the air
above, / that is work, that is the task.") Jung used this quote as an epigraph for "Dream Symbols
of the Process of Individuation" (Jung, 1936a).
[517] Neumann (1952).

namely, the voluntary abdication before the "human and the feminine" which has "proved its superiority in love."[518]

Your depression seems to me to belong in the Mysterium of the
afternoon. For bad books, it is enough that they have been written.
Good books, however, wish to achieve something above and beyond
this, and begin to pose the question to which one would prefer to
leave the answering to others. It seems to me that the conversation
has already begun. Ten pairs of turtles cannot withstand this. Even
sinister events serve for the best if one is benevolent out of an inner
necessity. After all, one should be represented before God, and there
something will, for sure, become true in one. I have seldom seen a
more fitting oracle. You only have to listen quietly and then you will
hear what is expected of you if you only "hold on to your heart."

Paramahansa Yogananda:[519] *Autobiogr. of a Yogi*: 100% pure coconut
oil, from 40°C in the shade and 100% humidity onward it becomes

---

[518] In the autumn of 1950 Neumann held a course titled "Zur Psychologie des Weiblichen:
Anhand des Märchens Amor und Psyche" ("On the Psychology of the Feminine: Based on the
Fairy Tale Amor and Psyche") at the Zurich institute. Neumann's presentations led to fierce
discussions with staff members who were present, especially with C. A. Meier. On 5 October
1950, in the aftermath of this debate, Jung invited colleagues to Küsnacht in order to discuss
Neumann's presentation. Jaffé's protocol of this meeting mentions the following participants:
Marie-Louise von Franz, Emma Jung, and Liliane Frey. C. A. Meier's absence is noted. Jung
criticized these public attacks on Neumann: "One should not have discussed the problems in
public. It is so finely nuanced that it is not possible to sort it out in a discussion. But above all,
one can't load these things onto N. in public. One can't load them onto Dr. Meier either. [...]
Besides, one must not forget that he has been in Palestine on his own for 9 years. When he
worked with me back then, many things that you are learning today had not even been uttered.
When he left, we did not yet know much that we know today. And besides, we are not dealing
with a theory, but a human being. You cannot do this right in the middle of a course. I would
like to see the animus in you if you were to be corrected in a lecture. If I had been there, I
would have attempted to rectify some things. But I would have said it only once and then shut
up. N. is very sensitive, easily gets upset. But he is a creative man. And one should not upset
such people. Leave him alone" (Protocol, 5 October 1950, AJP). In his discussion Jung states
that if the text were a dream of a man, the figure of Psyche would represent the anima; in the
case of a woman, it would represent the Self. Von Franz criticized Neumann for interpreting
the fairy tale from the female psychological point of view, thereby neglecting the context of the
fairy tale, which is given as a dream of the male character of the novel. In her 1970 study *A
Psychological Study of the Golden Ass of Apuleius* she reiterates that argument in support of her
view that the novel is about the anima problem of Apuleius and not about the female's process
of detachment from the mother. Although not explicitly referenced, she refers to the discussion in 1950 (Marie-Louise von Franz, 1970, English, p. 77, n. 1; German: p. 70, n. 1).

[519] The typescript version (in contrast to the handwritten version) gives here the following
handwritten addendum by Jung: "Höchster Schwan, Yogawonne." The meaning of Paramahansa
is "supreme swan," a title, which was bestowed upon Yogananda by his teacher Sri Yukteswar and
indicates the highest spiritual attainment.

ever more credible, from the latitude of 16° South, the best psychological travel guide, involves rather too much amoebic dysentery[520] and malarial anemia to make bearable the moral change of scene and the high frequency of miraculous interludes; proves itself splendidly alongside Amy McPherson[521] and her ilk as a metaphysical Luna park on the Pacific coast south of San Francisco,[522] is no ordinary *Ersatz*, but authentically Indian to all five senses and offers guaranteed century-long strolls into the great hinterland as the foreground grows increasingly darker, makes all arts of illusion superfluous and offers absolutely everything that one could wish for in the midst of a negative existence, superlatively as an antidote for desperate population growth and traffic density and impending spiritual undernourishment, so rich in vitamins that calcium, carbohydrate, and such banalities become superfluous. Mr. Martin Buber could lengthen his beard by 2 meters with this. Yes, what else could one imagine above and beyond this? Happy India! Blessed coconut-woven elephantitis islands, chapattis smelling of hot oil—aah, my liver cannot bear them any more! Yogananda fills the great void. But I did not want to write any preamble for him![523] This is just what I'm like.

Best wishes and no hard feelings!
Your,
C. G. Jung

[520] *Amoebic dysentery*, type of dysentery caused by the amoebia *Entamoeba histolytica*. The disease is transmitted through contaminated food or water and is very common in developing countries. Jung was diagnosed with amoebic dysentery in India and was admitted to the hospital in Calcutta in January 1938 (see also n. 332). Jung's friend and collaborator, the sinologist Richard Wilhelm (1873–1930), died prematurely from the consequences of the disease in 1930.

[521] Aimee Semple McPherson (1890–1944): Canadian-American evangelist, well-known US celebrity in the 1920s and 1930s through her use of the radio, founder of the International Church of the Foursquare Gospel (1927). The center of the Foursquare Church is the Angelus Temple (built in 1923) in Los Angeles.

[522] After his return from India in 1936 Yogananda resided in a hermitage in Encinitas, California, south of Los Angeles. Besides Encinitas he founded several Self-Realization Fellowship temples, among others in Hollywood and San Diego.

[523] After Jung's rejection the preface was written by W[alter] Y[eeling] Evans-Wentz (1878–1965), anthropologist and scholar of Tibetan Buddhism; best known for the English translation and edition of the *Tibetan Book of the Dead*.

21st June '52

Dear, esteemed C. G. Jung,

Now I am once again so much in your debt! Thanks for your last letter, thanks for the *Job* and for the off-prints! I have wanted to write for a long time but it wouldn't work. Firstly I was too much wrapped up in myself and then in a work that I have been despairingly grappling with. It was in fact supposed to become the Eranos lecture, in the meantime I am writing more and more, comforted only by confirmatory *I Ching* castings when I feel like abandoning it, and God knows what manner of Eranos lecture will emerge from that. But there is simply nothing to be done about it. A highly "meta-psychological" thing, falling between all chairs of all faculties. But I had at least to make the attempt, even if only perhaps for myself, of coming up with a unified model that gives a place to all the phenomena that till now have been rattling around at the edge of our worldview. They are all things that have exercised and bothered me for years with links to the *Spirit of Psychology*[524] and *Synchronicity*,[525] but I wish to make it clear that on my head be it. The parapsychological phenomena as well as the teleological phenomena in psychology and biology. Doubtless the depth psychological picture is rather changed by this, but I am always coming across propositions of yours that point in the same direction, only you are much more careful and scientific than I can ever afford to be. I *must* simply ask myself what consequences it has for our worldview if one of these phenomena is correct. Sometimes it seems to be as if I had to solve all puzzles of the world at once and the fact that all these phenomena take place to the highest degree outside of our awareness, makes the attempt to grasp it and to formulate it somehow adequately so terribly demanding, it

[524] Jung (1947).
[525] Jung (1952c).

seems to me at least; in any case I cannot remember having been gripped by a work to this degree. And at the same time a crazy uncertainty about whether all this is actually crazy, on the other hand though, also the feeling there is something to it—in brief, it's not an edifying situation and you will now understand why I could not write. Actually it should be called: *Towards a Theory of Psyche: A Meta-Psychological Experiment*, the excerpt for Eranos I will naturally describe in a more harmless way.[526] In reality I will only be able to discuss it with you, I fear. But you are lucky that as I won't be finished with the draft manuscript before Eranos, I will unfortunately have to spare you for now.

There is not much to say about your Buber discussion. I find your answer—in contrast to that of Buber—very fine.[527] But, of course, it won't do much good. I too cannot bear him, although in all mendacity he always says something substantial. Admittedly your Gnostic strain, if one does not know you personally, is certainly strongly noticeable in your writings, as is possibly your scientific cautiousness and skepticism confusing for someone who knows you only vaguely and reads without recourse to their own experience. Anyway, it is comical enough that Mr. Glover[528] and Mr. Buber extend these unequal hands to each other.

---

[526] Neumann's Eranos lecture of 1952 was titled "Die Psyche und die Wandlung der Wirklichkeitsebenen" ("The Psyche and the Transformation of the Reality Planes") (Neumann, 1953c).

[527] On the Jung-Buber debate in the journal *Merkur* (Jung, 1952; Buber, 1952) and Neumann's correspondence with its editor (Neumann ad Merkur [DLA]) see n. 215.

[528] Edward George Glover (1888–1972): British psychoanalyst, analyzed by Karl Abraham in Berlin in the 1920s. A leading member of the British Psychoanalytical Society in the 1930s, he opposed the psychological theories of Melanie Klein, whose daughter, Melitta Schmideberg, he analyzed at the same time. Glover resigned from the society in 1944, when the rift between the supporters of Klein and those of Anna Freud led to the development of three separate training groups. Neumann refers here to Glover's attack on Jung in his book *Freud or Jung* (1950). Jung commented on Glover's critique in a letter to Maria Folino Wald from 5 December 1951: "Glover's book—apart from its more venomous qualities—is quite amusing: it is exactly like those pamphlets people used to write against Freud in his early days. It was quite obvious then that they were merely expressing their resentments on account of the fact that Freud had trodden on their toes. The same is true for Glover. A critique like his is always suspect as a compensation for an unconscious inclination in the other direction. He is certainly not stupid enough not to see the point I make, but I touched upon a weak spot in him, namely, where he represses his better insight and his latent criticism of his Freudian superstition. He is a bit too fanatical. Fanaticism always means overcompensated doubt. He merely shouts down his inner criticism and that's why his book is amusing" (Jung, 1973, p. 239 [German]; vol. 2, p. 31 [English]). Other works by Glover include *Psycho-Analysis* (1939) and *The Technique*

In this context, two "confessions" of where I have failed as a propagandist of analytical psychology. America, Pastor. Psychology, the essay on your position on religion. At first hesitatingly accepted when they wrote to me that it should not be too heavy and should be good for use in a sermon, then I sadly had to decline, but I proposed Reverend Schär[529] as the right man to do this.

Furthermore, I have declined the honorable invitation to take on one of three papers for the German Therapist Congress.[530] I am only willing to go to Germany for international matters. The past and the present of the wider and even the closer colleagues (Kranefeldt[531]) is still all too present to me. I hope you will understand my perspective. On the other hand, I will be part of a discussion for a week on cultural psychology in Amersfort in Holland, at a sort of wisdom school.[532]

---

of Psycho-Analysis (1955). On Glover and the Freud-Klein controvery see Roazen (2000) and King and Steiner (1991).

[529] On Hans Schär see n. 387. Schär did not write on Jung in *Pastoral Psychology*. Nevertheless, after the English publication of *Answer to Job* in 1954 Seward Hiltner (1956; 1956a) introduced the book and Jung's understanding of religion to the readers. In the May issue of 1956 Wallace Winchell (1956) and J. Maxwell Chamberlin (1956) commented in the Readers' Forum, to which Hiltner responded in a statement (1956b). Jung himself replied to the journal on the question "Why and how I wrote *Answer to Job*" (Jung, 1956) and responded to Walter Houston Clark's review of *The Undiscovered Self* (Clark, 1958; Jung, 1959). "Psychotherapists or the Clergy," the last chapter of *Modern Man in Search of a Soul* (1933a), was reprinted in the journal in 1956 (Jung, 1956a).

[530] The second congress of the Deutsche Gesellschaft für Psychotherapie und Tiefenpsychologie (German Society for Psychotherapy and Depth Psychology) took place in Stuttgart from 8–11 September 1952. Representatives of different psychological schools were invited to discuss their theoretical differences. After Neumann's refusal to participate, the only Jewish speaker, Alexander Müller—an Adlerian, who survived the concentration camp—was confronted with five former members of the Deutsche Institut für psychologische Forschung und Psychotherapie ("Göring institute"): Carl Müller-Braunschweig, Franz Baumeyer, Edgar Herzog, Wolfgang Hochheimer, and Harald Schultz-Hencke.

[531] Wolfgang Müller Kranefeldt (1892–1950): German psychiatrist and psychotherapist, National Socialist, member of the German Institute for Psychological Research and Psychotherapy ("Göring institute") in Berlin since 1936. Kranefeldt was originally analyzed by Jung and was seen as Jung's main representative in Germany before and during the Nazi era. Jung wrote the introduction to Kranefeldt's book *Psychoanalyse: Psychoanalytische Psychologie* (*Secret Ways of the Mind: A Survey of the Psychological Principles of Freud, Adler, and Jung*) (Kranefeldt, 1930; Jung, 1930). Kranefeldt also published two articles in Jung's *Wirklichkeit der Seele* (Jung, 1934c). An active member of the AÄGP and the IAAGP, he was involved in the editing of the *Zentralblatt*. For Neumann's opinion on Kranefeldt see his letter to Olga Fröbe-Kapteyn, 22 May [1949] (introduction, pp. xlix–l).

[532] The Internationale School voor Wijsbegeerte (ISVW, International School of Philosophy) in Amersfoort was founded in 1916 by the Dutch writer and philosopher Frederik van Eeden, together with Martin Buber and the mathematician L.E.J. Brouwer. Neumann lectured in

They only wanted to discuss the *Ethic*, but I turned that down as it belongs in the large context of cultural psychology. It fills me with horror, but I should perhaps not duck out of all these things. It seems to me that I needed peace and time, and that writing is, if anything, always better than talking. My extremely demanding daily practice is plenty enough people for me.

I am very glad that I am able to see you and your wife. My wife and I both hope to exit here in time. Although I am worried about what will emerge in the work, I am sure you will understand if not the objective then at least the subjective justification of its genesis.

All best wishes,
Ever yours,
[E. Neumann]

Amersfoort on a number of occasions—as did Jung. Unfortunately the archives of the school—containing the details of these representations—were destroyed in World War II (information ISVW, 8 July 2013).

D. Erich Neumann,
Analytical Psychologist

Tel Aviv, 12. XII [1952]

Dear and esteemed C. G. Jung,

As I have sadly heard that you have been seriously ill but that you have now recovered, I would actually only like to write to you of how glad I am about your return to health and how concerned I am that you are still over-exerting yourself so much. When I cast my eyes over your work of the last ten years then I must say that there is something almost shocking about the magnitude of this achievement alone. But I believe that I have learned from you that even being obsessed with work is, in fact, also an obsession. You see, your loyal companions around you should do more to ensure that you have peace and quiet—so that those of us at some distance could have a clearer conscience when we are there. I always nearly have a bad one when I would like to speak to you and I see how many predators you have already fed. But of course I know all too well myself that one can at the most only keep an eye out, and "it" is always much stronger than caution.

So I wish you and Mrs. Jung—also from my wife of course—only peace and health for the time being for the new, hopefully peaceful—year. There is nothing special from my end. After Europe I am now mostly doing smaller works for the time being. One on the *Magic Flute* is almost ready, one on Henry Moore is brewing but as yet unwritten[.][533]

---

[533] "Zu Mozarts Zauberflöte" ("On Mozart's Magic Flute") (Neumann, 1950a); *Die archetypische Welt Henry Moores* (*The Archetypal World of Henry Moore*) (Neumann, 1961).

The "field" work from Eranos will have to stretch over years, it now seems. I cannot rush it. However, I must now finally write up the book on the psychology of the feminine.[534] If the next Eranos conference makes its usual demand, then I am well supplied with work— alongside the current practice. À propos obsession see above. Health-wise I am tolerably well, if also very fragile. You should know that you are actually also a giant as far as health goes, but if it is at all possible, you should no longer allow the storms of the spirits to blow through you. Everyone will just have to get used to it.

All the best,
Ever yours,
E. Neumann
    I will type from now on to spare you my handwriting.

---

[534] Neumann (1953b).

PROF. DR. C. G. JUNG

KÜSNACHT, ZURICH
SEESTRASSE 228

17th December 1952

Dr. Erich Neumann,
1, Gordon St.,
Tel Aviv, Israel

My dear Neumann,

I thank you very much for your kind letter. I am in fact rather better. I can get up again and do a little in my library but only in a very limited way. I all too easily get tachycardia attacks,[535] which subside again after one or two hours, but exhaust me very much. I am not seeing any people any more and lead a rather monastic existence.

Regarding workload, I would though like to remark that one easily spots the splinter in one's brother's eye when one has a beam in one's own. You really have a whole pile on your plate.

My best wishes for that and for the coming year,
Your devoted,
C. G. Jung

---

[535] *Tachycardia*, from Greek *tachys*, rapid or accelerated, and *cardia*, heart, describes a physical condition, where the patient experiences an unusually fast heart rate.

Dr. Erich Neumann,
Analytical Psychologist

Tel Aviv, 15. IV. [1953]

Dear and esteemed C. G. Jung,

It has proved to be as impossible not to write as to write.[536] It is almost 20 years since I came to work with you and Toni Wolff in 1933. How much has changed and developed since then, but for me and for my wife too, Zurich was inconceivable without both of these luminaries joined in recent years by your dear wife too—without whom Switzerland and Zurich would be impoverished for us. Naturally we are at the margin and such an event shows this even more clearly, for the threads of our connection with Europe are in fact these human bonds that signify the important and strong bonds in the texture of our life. So much is going through our minds and our hearts,—for my wife, Toni Wolff was the only person ever with whom she spoke about herself.

I hear better news about your health, thank God, also things are quite good as far as ours goes, I am now keeping the work tempo under stronger control, whether I like it or not. If the time is there, then good, if not, then there's nothing to be done about it.

I would like to ask some things from you, if your strength allows as far as your work on the *Study in the Process of Individuation*[537] is concerned, but there is no hurry. Otherwise I am myself energetically at work, which for me is never ending.

---

[536] Toni Wolff died of a heart attack on 21 March 1953. See n. 145.

[537] "Zur Empirie des Individuationsprozesses" ("A Study in the Process of Individuation") (Jung, 1950) was a revised and amended version of Jung's 1933 Eranos lecture by the same title.

Otherwise, nothing else today. While we, here, always think about Switzerland very much anyway, at the moment it is a rather sad obsession. The comfort is that there are many and grateful memories.

In all loyalty,
Yours,
E. Neumann

PROF. DR. C. G. JUNG

KÜSNACHT, ZURICH
SEESTRASSE 228

12th December 1953

Dr. Erich Neumann,
1, Gordon St.,
Tel Aviv, Israel

My dear Neumann,

Today you have surprised me with 2 new books at once: *On the Psychology of the Feminine* and *Cultural Development and Religion*,[538] which as yet I know nothing about. I am looking forward to them and will let you know what sort of reactions they arouse in me.

At the moment I am constantly being sent books that I must read because they are curiously synchronistically arranged. This, your new book belongs quite evidently in this series. For now, I would like to thank you warmly for both texts and hope that I can soon send you my new publication *On the Roots of Consciousness*.[539] You will find therein some old familiar things and some new. My book on the *Mysterium Coniunctionis* will soon go to print. Otherwise, one muddles through.

With best wishes for the new year, I remain,
Your ever devoted,
C. G. Jung

---

[538] The first two volumes of Neumann's collection of essays *Umkreisung der Mitte I / II* (Neumann, 1953a; 1953b).

[539] Volume 9 of the *Psychologische Abhandlungen* (Jung, 1954).

Dr. Erich Neumann,
Analytical Psychologist

Tel Aviv, 28. XII. 53

Dear and esteemed C. G. Jung,

I wanted to write anyway for the New Year and now your letter has preempted me. As you will have determined by now, there is not much that is new to you in the essay volumes. Only a few works are unknown to you; due to Rascher's technically quite proper suggestion of making three smaller essay volumes out of my one thick tome, it now seems like more. The *Great Mother* that, with God's and Bollingen's help, will come out in America and indeed also with Rascher at the end of the year (c. 400 pages text and about 250 images and tables), might well interest you more.[540]

I am very much looking forward to your new book but I am hoping for the appearance of the *Coniunctio*—of which I have heard so much—with very particular anticipation. I would be very grateful to you if I could possibly see the proofs, otherwise I would have to wait another year, the way things are now going. But I have the conviction that this book is very important for the *Stages of Development of the Feminine*, which I am writing at the moment.

While I frequently detect with amazement how much by you has now been accepted by the Freudians without you noticing, I detect with the same amazement how the Jungians do not recognize me or do not wish to recognize me. I always recall then with pleasure your prophecy about *Origins*: You will see, they will not read you even once, but with time it will come. So I pat my leonine ambition ever reassuringly on the shoulder and comfort myself with the fact that

---

[540] Neumann (1956). See Neumann's letter to Jung, 17 December 1947 (59 N) and n. 422.

production is still going well, which is after all the actual enjoyment of the matter, if one can call this thing enjoyment that on the other hand is an abominable torment.

Although my all too sensitive nature is gradually compelling me to moderation, the discrepancy remains between the intuitive conception and the endless travail of every accomplishment, which then has to extend to the indexes and translations, a true cross. But since I, as a Jew, am a good Christian, it seems to me at least, I find all that perfectly in order—if I am myself in order. On the other hand, I must admit a mild horror grips me at the expanding pile of printed and written paper that rustlingly asserts a connection with me. It is truly a type of compulsion and addiction—I have been writing almost continuously since my twelfth, certainly since my sixteenth year—and while I also know that this is definitely part of my nature and, I hope, of my authentic life task, it sometimes seems to be a true paper hell.

As you will notice, I have a mild winter depression, which is not uncommon for me at this time, but at the same time I am not too bad, only rather unsteady. Besides that, I am on the verge of a writing wave and I am engaged in the solemn rites of resistance and the ultimate surrender to this wave. Are you familiar with anything like this yourself, or does this belong to my individual idiosyncrasies?

Now this has turned into a rather curiously egoistic type of New Year letter, but I think you will understand me. Therefore along with health and peace, I wish for you that the hell fires of writing and paper warm you only in a friendly way, but do not burn, and with warmest greetings to your wife in ancient loyalty, I am,

Your,
E. Neumann

Dr. Erich Neumann,
Analytical Psychologist

Tel Aviv, 24. I. 54

Very dear and esteemed C. G. Jung,

Many thanks for sending your book *The Roots of Consciousness*.[541] I have naturally as yet only briefly glimpsed inside and am looking forward especially to the great work on the tree.[542] Sadly I will no longer be able to use it for the section in the *Great Mother*, as I refuse to spend the long period till a book's appearance on countless post revisions, which then take me quite away from current work. Besides, I am only dealing with the matriarchal aspect there—and that is already saying too much.

I hear that sadly another gastric flu has laid claim to you, but that this too is now recovered from. Belatedly I'd like to congratulate you on the Jung Codex, which seems to have been a great affair.[543] Something quite other pleases me about this, namely, that your deep connection with Gnosticism was celebrated so festively. I have never quite understood your resistance when they wanted to make you a Gnostic like Buber and even Quispel did. Of course, you are not one,

[541] Jung (1954).

[542] "Der philosophische Baum" (Jung, 1954a).

[543] The first five of fifty-three Gnostic scriptures (in thirteen codices) discovered in Nag Hammadi in Upper Egypt in 1945 (*Nag Hammadi Scriptures*, 2007). This Codex I was acquired by Gilles Quispel in 1952 (see n. 498) with the help from C. A. Meier and the financial support of Georg H. Page and presented to Jung as a birthday present. Despite Jung's protest it was named after him. Codex I contains the following scriptures: "The Prayer of the Apostle Paul," "The Apocryphon of James," "The Gospel of Truth," "The Treatise on the Resurrection," and "The Tripartite Tractate." It was returned to Egypt in 1975. Aniela Jaffé sent Neumann a copy of Jung's address on the occasion of the presentation of the codex (Jung, 1953) with the remark: "I am sure I don't have to write my private opinion of the Code affair to you, but if it interests you I can send you C. A's *conterfei* which appeared in local newspapers!" (Jaffé to Erich and Julie Neumann, 13 December 1953 [NP]).

but for people who do not understand what psychology is, it seems to me for the best that they consider you a Gnostic. Doesn't the Gnostic piscatorial ring you wear and which I love so much say something similar? In any case, when I think of my own imagination, the Gnostics always strike me as very close, closer almost than the alchemists, and it pleases me hugely when research increasingly comes upon the Jewish origins of Gnosticism. I have always suspected this, already because of kabbalah, quite apart from myself. For me this is certainly also a primal position out of which originates the Christian in Judaism, which adheres so differently and so much more intimately to the person of Jesus than the church does and what has come out of that in Christendom. This is just a small unofficial excursion on the secret significant event of the Jung Codex.

All the best and once again many thanks. Your dedication has hopefully made an impact; there is still not much evidence of "new light," except that I know much more that I must have patience.

Warmest,
Yours,
E. Neumann

PROF. DR. C. G. JUNG   **KÜSNACHT, ZURICH**
                                            SEESTRASSE 228

30th Jan. 1954

Dr. Erich Neumann,
1 Gordon St.,
Tel Aviv/Israel

Dear Neumann!

Best thanks for your kind letter! I was just occupied with a letter to Hull, who is supposed to insert a passage for me about your works in the English edition of *Symbols of Transformation*.[544]

The transition to the New Year has not gone without some difficulties: liver and intestines have revolted against the too rich hotel cuisine in Locarno, which on the other hand is a good thing as my holiday ended up 1 1/2 weeks longer than planned.

---

[544] Jung to R.F.C. Hull, 29 January 1954: "Dear Mr. Hull, Regarding 'Symbole der Wandlung', may I ask you to add to my foreword, at its end on pag. 8, the following remarks: 'Seitdem meine späteren Arbeiten sich hauptsächlich mit der Frage der historischen und ethnischen Parallelen befasst haben, haben die Untersuchungen Erich Neumann's umfangreiche Beiträge zur Lösung der ebenso zahlreichen wie schwierigen Fragen, die auf diesem bis jezt noch wenig erforschten Gebiete überall auftauchen, gebracht. So ist vor allem sein Hauptwerk, welches die Ideen, die mich seinerzeit zur Abfassung dieses Buches veranlasst haben, weiterführt und in den grossen Rahmen der Bewusstseinsentwicklung überhaupt stellt, nämlich "Die Ursprungsgeschichte des Bewusstseins" (Zurich 1949) zu erwähnen. Seine neuere Schrift "Kulturentwicklung und Religion" (Zurich 1953) gehört ebenfalls in diesen Zusammenhang.' Yours sincerely, C. G. Jung" (LC). Hull's translation reads as follows (*CW* V, p. 6): "In my later writings I have concerned myself chiefly with the question of historical and ethnological parallels, and here the researches of Erich Neumann have made a massive contribution toward solving the countless difficult problems that crop up everywhere in this hitherto little explored territory. I would mention above all his work, *The Origins and History of Consciousness*, which carries forward the ideas that originally impelled me to write this book, and places them in the broad perspective of the evolution of human consciousness in general."

I have penetrated quite far into your *Cultural Development* and will be able to read further as soon as the letter mountain that has collected during my absence is demolished.

I would acknowledge without further ado the description "Gnostic" if it were not a term of abuse in the mouth of a theologian. They accuse me of the same crime of which they make themselves guilty, namely, the pretentious disregard for epistemological limits: when a theologian says "God," then God has to be just that and just like the magician desires it to be without his feeling in the slightest compelled to be accountable to himself and his audience about which term he is making use of. In a bogus way he offers his (limited) notion of God to the naive listener as a special revelation. For example, what sort of a God is Buber talking about? Yahweh? With or without *privatio boni*? If it is Yahweh, where does he say that this God is definitely not the Christian God? I accuse the theologians of all confessions of this tainted way of doing holy business. I do not claim that my "Gnostic" images are a faithful and obligatory rendition of their transcendent background, and that this latter is invoked by the fact that I mention it. That Buber has a bad conscience arises from the fact that he only publishes *his* letters, but does not grant me a fair representation because I am just a Gnostic and at the same time he has no idea about what motivated the Gnostic.

In the meantime best wishes and greetings from
Your devoted,
C. G. Jung

PROF. DR. C. G. JUNG

Pro tem Bollingen,
St. Gallen Canton

22. IX. 1954

Dear Neumann,

I very much apologize that your earlier letter was not replied to. I was no longer keeping up with my correspondence as my secretary was taking an unusually long holiday due to illness. In addition my wife is unwell—with what we at first considered to be sciatica—and has had to interrupt her holidays several times. Now she has been in the Hirslanden clinic for 3 weeks with a crushed vertebral disc due to a fall 8–10 years ago. She is now having traction therapy and must remain in hospital for about another 2 weeks.

Of course I'm not keeping up with anything. I have stayed in Bollingen temporarily, but return home at the end of this month. In any case I can see you on 1st Oct. if this time suits you. If not, I ask you to arrange a suitable time with my secretary. I will of course reserve the necessary time and look forward to being able to speak with you once again.

I am quite well given the circumstances, but I am no longer so productive.

With best regards to your esteemed wife and
Warm greetings,
Your faithful,
C. G. Jung

101 J

Dr. E. Neumann,
c/o van der Mandel,
Middelduin en Dalschweg,
Bloemendaal bei Harlem[545]

Dear Neumann,

A certain Mrs. Blech from Nesher in Israel has produced a Hebrew translation of *Psychology and Education* and would like to have it checked over by me.[546] I have an idea that the thing should be looked over in order to avoid any sort of misconception, but as I am in no way competent I would like to ask you whether you will perhaps have a look at the translation yourself or whether you have someone to whom you could entrust such a task. Please reply by return as I must let Mrs. Blech know soon. In case you have no desire to do it yourself or do not know of anyone who could do it instead of you,

---

[545] From August to November 1954, Erich and Julie Neumann spent three month in Europe. In a letter to Olga Fröbe-Kapteyn, who accompanied them after the Eranos conference on their journey to the Netherlands and England, Neumann outlined his plans: "Request invitations, programmes, communications with the consulate here etc. Strangely enough it is supposed to be difficult at the moment particularly in Switzerland, but certainly not for us, I think. But request three months with two entry visas. We start on the 9th August in Amersf., on the 4th or 5th we will be in Amsterdam. Please also write to v. Waverens, of course I will also write to them very soon. I hope that will be OK until the 15th, not too demanding. Then Zurich-Ascona. Then holidays, probably also at the end with you, then the Jung Institute for a week at the beginning of October. Then England, then Holland again, with individual lectures—not yet certain. Then home directly or again via Zurich" (Neumann to Fröbe-Kapteyn, 27 May [1954] [EA]).

[546] The essays "Über Konflikte der kindlichen Seele" ("Psychic Conflicts in a Child") (1910), "Analytische Psychologie und Erziehung" ("Analytical Psychology and Education") (1926), and "Der Begabte" ("The Gifted Child") (1943) were republished together under the title *Psychologie und Erziehung (Psychology and Education)* (Jung, 1946b). The Hebrew translation by Netta Blech came out in 1958 as *Psykhologiah analytit we-khinukh* (Tel Aviv: Dvir, 1958). Jung wrote a foreword to the Hebrew edition stating that "[n]ot knowing this language, I am unable to appreciate the merits of the translation, so I can only bid it welcome as a 'firstling' that is unique in my experience" (Jung, 1955, § 1822).

Dr. Schärf[547] has expressed a willingness to provide some scrutiny. In any case I wanted to let you know of this matter first, as a translation of this text that should not contain any misconceptions will be distributed in Israel.

I hope you are having a pleasant stay in Holland.

With best wishes,
Your devoted,
[C. G. Jung]

[547] On Rivkah Schärf Kluger see n. 398.

[England, 2nd half of October 1954][548]

Dear and esteemed C. G. Jung,

As I am myself neither timewise nor linguistically in a position to check the translation, Dr. Schärf would certainly be the correct person for it. Of course, I could also find someone to take on this task back home.

I hope Mrs. Jung is keeping well again and that you yourself are healthy and in good spirits. The Holland trip was demanding with all the lectures, but successful; now in England we are only resting.

Best wishes from my wife too,
Yours,
E. Neumann

[548] See n. 545. Erich and Julie visited their relatives in London. See also n. 335.

103 J

PROF. DR. C. G. JUNG   **KÜSNACHT, ZURICH**
                                                                    SEESTRASSE 228

9th July 1955

My dear Neumann,

My forthcoming birthday is being preceded by all sorts of fireworks and, to my astonishment and to my delight, I have found your name among those who are anticipating my celebration. At this impending opportunity that I could easily miss later in the deluge, I would like to sincerely thank you not only that you have taken to the pen for me in such a generous way, but also for that greater thing that you are achieving in your life's work.

So that the shadow also accompanies the fine things, I have received from the world government a little senile diabetes in ideal competition with a little hypertrophy of the prostate, which offers hopeful prospects of further possibilities. I had to accept the honorable doctor of the Federal Technical University with the dignity of a man [line missing] knows, and a "docile, gentle guest" was permitted to sit at a richly considered table, rather constricted by the simultaneous presence of a small diabetes on the one hand and a small liver insufficiency on the other. The entry to the higher and highest stages of age that are not the destiny of every mortal must evidently be paid for. As a prelude to this new epoch, my poor wife had to undergo stomach surgery due to a carcinoma from which, however, she has recovered in a wonderful way and indeed with a very good prognosis. In return I am in a previously unforeseen fix. The sweet cup of joy is not without *the* bitter wormwood. (*The* wormwood is forbidden me because of its sugar content!)[549]

---

[549] In the orginal German letter Jung wrote "Wermuth." As there is no German "die Wermuth" he probably meant "Wehmuth." Jung plays on the similar sound of "die Wehmut" (sadness) and "der Wermuth" (vermouth).

Figure 8. A picture taken on the occasion of Jung's eightieth birthday 1955 (with Carleton Smith) (Verkehrszentrale Schweiz; courtesy of Andreas Jung).

I hear that your health is also under attack. Take care of yourself, thoroughly, please. Men like you are *rarissimae aves*[550] whose perspective the world needs.

Please accept my best wishes,
And greetings,
Your ever devoted,
Jung

[550] Latin for "rare birds."

Dr. Erich Neumann,
Analytical Psychologist

Tel Aviv, 23. VII. 55

Dearest C. G. Jung,

It is terrible that for me it has now come to this, that I need your birthday as a reason to write. But this is how it is now, my ability to write letters has almost completely gone astray. The only good thing is that I at least have the opportunity of speaking with you when I am in Switzerland. That is possible and a good thing, i.e., I am also very much looking forward to it this year. Writing letters, on the other hand, is all too laborious. Of this you can be sure, what I wish for you ranges from health and joy to your remaining eternally creative once again. Every one of your books is a constant surprise! I am already completely wild about the *Coniunctio*!

I was pleased to hear only good things of Mrs. Jaffé and your dear wife's health. (Mine has also been pretty good this year.)

This year I will go to Amersfoort again for a week before Ascona and to Holland for a second time after Zurich for a series of lectures. I am not looking forward to that as much as to Engadin, but the people in Holland understand me particularly well, which is a pleasure.[551] I am doing a lot of work—not including my practice. Psychology of the feminine, of childhood, and on the archetype. On the whole, it is as difficult as ever to keep up with and to accomplish as

---

[551] Neumann was well known in the Netherlands. After his death the *Nieuwe Rotterdamse Courant* published an obituary highlighting Neumann's frequent presentations in the Netherlands: "In het begin van de jaren '50 bezocht hij de Internationale school voor wijsbegeerte te Amersfoort, waar hij een van de drukst bezochte sprekers was. Voorts hield hij referaten aan Nederlandse universiteiten." ("At the beginnings of the 50s he visited the Internationale School voor Wijsbegeerte in Amersfoort, where he gave lectures that were very well attended. Furthermore he gave presentations at Dutch universities.") (26 January 1961.)

there is naturally always a great deal of reading connected with it. But with time, one does manage it after all—*deo concedente*,[552] and it comes together and gives pleasure. A Dutch newspaper that wants to run an article about me has asked me "where I deviate from you, or am of a different opinion." As ever—and I was able to reply in this vein with great delight, I do not see any "deviations" anywhere. Even where I am taking things forward, I am standing, it seems to me, completely on your territory. And I must say, isolated as my position is, both externally and internally, I constantly consider this interweaving with your work as one of the finest gifts of my life. And I know that even where you see accents differently from the way I do that I am someone who, in your eyes, is taking it forward. I have now got used to being this and enjoy being it and I hope this is also true for you. Now this is the only thing that I can give you for your birthday; I see an infinite amount of work before me and I am ready for it.

In this spirit, a good day, a good year to you and your dear wife,

Your grateful,
E. Neumann

---

[552] *deo concedente*, Latin for "so God will," "God yielding."

28 November 1955

Dear Neumanns,

Our dear Mrs. Jung passed away peacefully yesterday (Sunday, at 10.30 am). The pulse had stopped. For the last days she has been fully anesthetized, but despite this, witnessing her departure must have been a torture that even Professor Jung has infinitely suffered from. Even he experiences it as a release. I have not seen him today as yet. The funeral is on Wednesday morning in Küsnacht church. The private family cremation a bit later. The children and grandchildren are forming a close and protective group that is lending strength in these difficult times. This is as it should be.

I will write again later.

Warmest,
Aniela

Dr. Erich Neumann,
Analytical Psychologist

Tel Aviv 10. XII. 55

Very, very dear C. G. Jung,

You will perhaps be surprised that I have not yet written to you. This is for two reasons. For a start, I am slow in such things because it seems to me so pointless in the face of your loss to speak of what we have lost. The second reason was that my mother became seriously ill in these weeks and died two days ago; she has lived with us for almost 9 years. For me all this belongs together, as different as it is also.

Although I only got to know your wife in the last years, from 1948, I think, for me Zurich has been curiously changed without her. She was the conscience, something one could rely on in gloomy Zurich, something solid and full of interest and understanding, with all due distance. (You, yourself, by the way, so that you do not misunderstand, belong for me to Bollingen and Küsnacht, not to Zurich.) The world is changing and one is getting palpably older. Both our children are now studying in Jerusalem. Everything is different. Perhaps I am getting a hint of how you are more and more forced to rise above everything so that only nature is left. It is good for me to know that at least Aniela J. is in your orbit. It was painful to me as seldom before to be so far away, for my gratitude toward your wife is great. I am happy that your wife died without much suffering, also happy for you yourself. I know this worry. My mother had a malignant stomach tumor, without knowing it, and died above all from heart failure. How much I would like to see you and speak with you! Eranos is still a long way off, but mostly it is sooner than one thinks. I think of you much; thank God I hear now and again from Aniela J. what you are doing and how you are.

My wife sends her best greetings. What you might not know is she was very attached to yours without having ever spoken very much.

As ever,
Yours,
E. Neumann

PROF. DR. C. G. JUNG   Küsnacht, Zurich,
                                  Seestrasse 228

                                  15 Dec. 1955

Dear Neumann,

Please accept my deeply felt thanks for your warm letter! Allow me to express to you for my part my sympathy on the loss of your mother. Unfortunately I can only lay barren words before you, as the shock I have experienced is so great that I am unable either to concentrate or to rediscover my ability to express myself. I would like to have told your friendly open heart that two days before the death of my wife I had—what one could call—a great epiphany that, like lightning, illuminated a secret to me, extending down through the centuries, that was embodied in my wife and that had influenced my life in unsearchable depths and to the highest degree.[553] I can only think that the epiphany originated in my wife who was then mostly unconscious and that the tremendous illumination and redemption of my insight in turn rebounded to her and was also a reason why she was able to die so painlessly and regally.

The speedy and painless end—only five days from the final diagnosis to her death—and this experience have signified a great comfort to

---

[553] In *Memories, Dreams, Reflections* Jung reports a vision, which he had after Emma's death: "I experienced this objectivity once again later on. That was after the death of my wife. I saw her in a dream that was like a vision. She stood at some distance from me, looking at me squarely. She was in her prime, perhaps about thirty, and wearing the dress that had been made for her many years before by my cousin the medium. It was perhaps the most beautiful thing she had ever worn. Her expression was neither joyful nor sad, but, rather, objectively wise and understanding, without the slightest emotional reaction, as though she were beyond the mist of affects. I knew that it was not she, but a portrait she had made or commissioned for me. It contained the beginning of our relationship, the events of fifty-three years of marriage, and the end of her life also. Face to face with such wholeness one remains speechless, for it can scarcely be comprehended." (Jung, 1961, p. 276.)

me. But the tranquility and the audible silence around me, the emptiness of the air and an interminable remoteness are hard to bear.

With best wishes to your wife also and my warmest thanks,
I remain,
Your ever loyal,

C. G. Jung

8th Feb. 1956

Dear Dr. Neumann,

I am about to forge myself a path through the forest of the contents of the cupboard and with Jung's agreement have begun to return manuscripts back to their author. On the one hand, in order to create more air and space (which is very necessary) and also so that these valuable texts will not get bogged down in the cupboards and possibly be forgotten. I am sending you what I find by *registered* post as business papers. In my experience the transit of such packages is very slow so I imagine you will not receive anything before the middle or end of March.—À propos: has the *Mysterium Coniunctionis* arrived with you now? If not, I would be grateful if you could let me know because I would then make a complaint to the post office.

Here, things are going quite well so far. Jung is indeed tired and is going on holiday at the end of the week, but he has reclaimed a part of his activity; thus he has written a foreword for the new edition of the *Words of the Buddha* (Artemis Press),[554] has had a discussion with Burghölzli psychiatrists (for 3 hours!), and has finished his stone.[555]— Now he is complaining that he is not doing enough.

But this is probably a quite good sign. The only thing to which he has an insurmountable resistance are letters, or the duty to reply to them.—I'm afraid it is now and again my task to hold him to it! But I have got used to the fact that there is a "higher" justice that has nothing to do with a Prussian regime.—And so things are actually going (unbidden) quite well. Regarding the institute here, I am—

---

[554] Jung did not write a foreword for the edition, but a statement in the publisher's brochure announcing the publication of Karl Eugen Neumann's *Die Reden Gotamo Buddho's* (Jung, 1956c).

[555] Jung carved a stone in memory of Emma. The inscription reads "She was the foundation of my house." It was placed in Bollingen between the tower and the shore of the lake, left from the covered loggia (see Hannah, pp. 327–30).

purely as far as the quantitative goes—in holiday mode. And the other does also come into it—or much more: falls away. With all necessary touching of wood I can say: I am enjoying it. Hopefully it will remain so!

I hope you and your wife are well and I also hope that the Siberian cold has not got as far as you. I thank you very much that you have let me have the recommendation of the art gallery. A carpet of Jung's (from his possession) is also on display there.[556]

Most warm greetings to you and your wife,
Yours,
Aniela Jaffé

---

[556] The exhibition on Modern Swiss Tapestries (Moderne Schweizer Bildteppiche) took place in the Helmhaus Zurich from 14 January to 12 February 1956 (Zürcher Kunstgesellschaft, 1956). The tapestry in question was Rosa Gerber-Hinnen's depiction of the Sermon on the Mount (1935–39). The Psychological Club bought it as a birthday present for Jung in 1945. Presented with the gift Jung gave a short interpretation on its motif ("Bemerkungen zu einem Wandteppich" [JA]), which was published in a newspaper article by Elsie Attenhofer (Attenhofer, 1975) as well as in a children's edition of the Sermon on the Mount with illustrations from Berger's tapestry (Ruetschi, 1988). During Jung's lifetime the tapestry hung in the smaller living room of the Küsnacht mansion, but it was returned to the Psychological Club after his death (information from the Jung family). The tapestry was first shown at the Helmhaus exhibition "Die Frau als Schöpferin und Bewahrerin von Kulturgut" ("The Woman as Creator and Custodian of Cultural Artifacts") (8 September–2 October 1946) organized on the occasion of the Dritter Kongress für Fraueninteresse (3rd Congress for Women's Interests) (Guyer, 1946); see also Jung's unpublished correspondence with the art historian Doris Gäumann-Wild [JA]). Today the tapestry can be seen in the lecture hall of the Psychological Club Zurich (information from the president, Andreas Schweizer).

Dear Dr. Neumann,

Many thanks for your card. The weather does not seem to be treating you too badly and I warmly wish you a good recovery. Enclosed the letter from you. You belong apparently to the monsters who do not write a date (or date without a year). This is why the search was protracted, but successful in the end. I am not sending the "entire correspondence." If you are exhausted anyway why do you want to invoke all *tempi passati* again? One has enough to deal with in the present! It was only my suggestion too.

I hope that the gentleman from St. Gallen has reached you. In the Seidenhof they told me that they had been sending letters on to Bern up until yesterday (10th).

I am also becoming very ready for a holiday and am looking forward to "far away."

To you and your wife, warmest greetings,
Yours,
A. J.

Your dream interpretation very much had—and is continuing to have—an effect. It came at just the right moment.

110 N

Dr. Erich Neumann,
Analytical Psychologist

Tel Aviv, 12th Nov. 56

Dearest C. G. Jung,

I would like to send you just a quick greeting, as at the moment peace reigns and we are all well. My son who participated in the Sinai campaign[557] is studying medicine in Jerusalem again, and the work here is continuing. Your telegram moved and comforted me, a thousand thanks for it, it arrived quickly and reached us at a time when such a sign of solidarity was more necessary and affected us more deeply than at any other time. A letter about the problems that we discussed when I was last with you is slowly taking shape, it needs time.

I hope you are well, even in Switzerland the fear of Russia seems to have increased very much, it hangs above us like a cloud, but this seems to belong to our fate. In an emergency, the *I Ching* has always orientated me, it is curious that one is so immersed in a situation of

---

[557] The Sinai campaign, also known as the Suez crisis, took place after Egypt under Gamal Abdel Nasser nationalized the Suez Canal and closed the Straits of Tiran to Israeli shipping on 26 July 1956. This, together with Nasser's support of regular raids into Israel by the Palestinian Fedayeen and Egypt's recent arms deal with the Soviet Union, triggered Israel's wish to conduct a military campaign in order to occupy the Sinai Peninsula. The attack started on 29 October. Isreal's war effort was secretly coordinated with France and Britain, who waited until the Israeli troops had reached a certain distance to the canal in order to send ultimatums for withdrawal from the area to both parties (30 October). Thus Britain and France were provided with an official reason to enter the conflict and attack the Egyptian forces. Under pressure of the United States and the Soviet Union a cease fire was announced on 6 November and the Anglo-French and, in March 1957, the Israeli troops had to withdraw, being replaced by UN peace-keeping units. Although the campaign was seen as a major success for Israel, it damaged the relationship between France and the United States and led to the resignation of the British prime minister Anthony Eden for his attempt to mislead the parliament (Gilbert, 2008, pp. 320–28).

being in an outpost, inside and out. It is indeed demanding, but one does not have the feeling that it is without meaning.

With warmest greetings,
Yours,
E. Neumann

Dr. Erich Neumann,
Analytical Psychologist

Tel Aviv, 25. V. [57]

Dearest C. G. Jung,

It has now been some time since I received and, of course, also read your fine text *Present and Future*.[558] In my opinion you have succeeded in an enviable way in saying the most vital thing in a popular, comprehensible form. Precisely because I know so well how difficult that is, it is important for me to place at the beginning this "technical" thing that is, however, so essential in reality. Despite this, I have the impression that you are a little too pessimistic or better, that you could be understood to be pessimistic. In my opinion, individuation is, after all, a collective process within humanity that takes precedence. That this is a process that takes a century should not discourage one, if one knows how young the consciousness of man actually is and that these processes of the collective psyche always call for long development times. For me personally it was a pleasure, besides, that your text extends a hand to my *New Ethic*, which fared so badly, even if in secret, of course. For if a reader of your work now asks himself, so what can actually be done, then he comes up against the problems that compelled me to this work back then in the second world war, with Rommel[559] at the door. But, in fact, this genesis is not quite

---

[558] First published in *Schweizer Monatshefte* 36, no. 12 in March 1957 (Jung, 1957).

[559] Erwin Rommel (1891–1944): German field marshal of World War II, commander of the *Deutsche Afrikakorps*. His 1941 campaign in North Africa was highly successful and was only brought to a hold by Field Marshal Montgomery's troops at El Alamein, sixty-six miles west of Alexandria, at the end of 1942. Rommel was involved in the failed putsch against Hitler of 20 July 1944. Because of his huge popularity Hitler feared a public trial and execution and forced Rommel to commit suicide. The truth was concealed to the public and Rommel's burial was used for Nazi propaganda purposes.

correct, for the deeper causes were internal images where it was all about evil and the "ape men" as destroyers, internally and externally.

The delay in my reply was caused by the fact that I wanted to complete a book that I have been working on for several years, the exemplification of the origins history, of child psychology, and of the ontogenetical construction of the personality.[560] (Please do not be afraid of the typo "ontological,"[561] I just had to read some Heidegger.[562]) I have now pretty much got far enough with this after a small break due to exhaustion that, freed from this work, the Eranos lecture can take me in its, I hope, friendly embrace. Strange hobbies one has.

I heard via Mrs. J. that you are quite well, thank God; that you continue to work constantly arouses my admiration, and your recurring communications that you can now no longer write are to all our delight only the—so understandable—exclamations that accompany the work. I am looking forward to hearing about what you are now up to when I am in Switzerland again. My notes with questions to you in connection with my lecture on the problem of reality have

[560] Neumann (1963). See also introduction, pp. lv–lvi.

[561] Neumann wrote ontological instead of onto-genetical, which he crossed through.

[562] Martin Heidegger (1889–1976): German philosopher, who, in *Being and Time* (1927), developed the concept of a fundamental ontology. According to Heidegger it is the task of philosophy to trace back the origins of *Sein* (being, essence) to the *Dasein* (existence). In later years he changed his understanding of the primacy of the Dasein, which is known as Heidegger's *Kehre* (turn). During the first year of the National Socialist rule in Germany, Heidegger was rector of the University of Freiburg. His notorious inauguration speech of 27 May 1933, titled "The Self-Assertion of the German University" ("Die Selbstbehauptung der deutschen Universität"), in which he endorsed the concept of the leader, has been widely read as proof of his affiliation with the Nazis. Heidegger's involvement with National Socialism in 1933–34 and the avoidance of any public admission of guilt after the war has been fiercely discussed (Wolin, 1998), also in regard to his relationship with the Jewish philosopher Hannah Arendt (1906–1975). In 1925 Heidegger, then lecturer in Marburg, had an affair with his student Arendt (Arendt and Heidegger, 1999). Probably to avoid a scandal the married Heidegger urged Arendt to continue her studies with Karl Jaspers in Heidelberg, where she formed a friendship with Karl Frankenstein, Erwin Loewenson, and Erich Neumann (Young-Bruehl, p. 66). A photograph of Neumann and Arendt can be found in Loewenthal-Neumann (2006, p. 158). When Neumann died in 1960 Arendt wrote a poem in her diaries: "*den 30. Nov. 1960 / Erich Neumanns Tod. Was von Dir blieb? Nicht mehr als eine Hand, / nicht mehr als Deiner Finger bebende Gespanntheit, / wenn sie ergriffen und zum Gruss sich schlossen. / Denn dieser Griff verblieb als Spur / in meiner Hand, die nicht vergass, die / wie Du warst noch spürte, als Dir längst / Dein Mund und Deine Augen sich versagten*" (30 November 1960 / *Erich Neumann's death*. What remains of you? Nothing more than a hand, / nothing more than the expectancy quivering in your fingers, / when they grasped and closed in greeting. / For this grasp remained as a trace / in my hand, which did not forget, which / still sensed how you used to be when / your mouth and your eyes long since failed you" (Arendt, 2002, p. 613).

sadly come to nothing,[563] the other work pushed itself forward, but I fear I will still have to bother with them once again despite this.

Please do not be angry about either my delayed thanks or the brevity of my letter, but I will not steal any more time from you than is necessary, especially as I will hopefully see you soon and in good health and speak with you.

As ever, most warmly,
Yours,
E. Neumann

---

[563] Presumably Neumann refers to his 1955 Eranos lecture titled "Die Erfahrung der Einheitswirklichkeit und die Sympathie aller Dinge" ("The Experience of the Unitary Reality") (Neumann, 1956a). A revised version was published in his collection of articles *Der schöpferische Mensch* (Neumann, 1959).

PROF. DR. C. G. JUNG   KÜSNACHT, ZURICH
SEESTRASSE 228

3rd June 1957

Dr. E. Neumann,
1 Gordon St.,
Tel Aviv,
ISRAEL

Dear Neumann,

I was very pleased to hear from you once again and to hear that you have read my small brochure. It seems to have been a hit here as there is already a second print run underway.

In relation to the so-called *New Ethic* we are basically quite in agreement, but I prefer to express this delicate problem in a rather different language. It is not really a question of a "new" ethic. Evil is and always remains the thing one knows one should not do. Man overestimates himself unfortunately in this respect: he thinks it is within his discretion to intend good or evil. He can persuade himself of this, but in reality he is, in view of the greatness of these opposites, simply too small and too unconscious to be able to choose the one or the other in free will and under all circumstances. It is much more the case that he does or does not do the good that he would like to for overwhelming reasons, and that in the same way, evil just happens to him like misfortune.

Ethics is that which makes it impossible for him to do evil intentionally and encourages him to do good—and indeed often with little success. I.e., he can do good and cannot avoid evil, although his ethic causes him to test the powers of his will in this regard. In reality he is the victim of these powers. He must admit to himself that under no circumstances can he absolutely avoid sin, as he also on the other hand may hope to be able to do good. Now, as evil is unavoidable, so one never completely evades sin and it is a fact that one must accept. It gives cause not for a new ethic, but for differentiated ethical considerations, namely, to the question: how do I behave toward the fact that I cannot escape sin? The instruction that is given in Christ's words: "If thou knowest what thou doest . . ."[564] shows a way to the ethical surmounting of the problem: I know that I do not wish to do evil and do it all the same, not from my own choice but because it overpowers me. As a human being I am a weakling and vulnerable so that evil can overwhelm me. I know that I do it and what I have done and know that I will stand in the torment of this contradiction for my lifetime. I will, where I can, avoid evil and will always fall into this hole. But I will endeavor to live as if this were not the case; I will therefore grin and bear it and will by this means be pleasing to the Lord, like the unfaithful householder who knowingly produced a false account. I do not do this because I wish to deceive myself or even the Lord, but so that I do not cause any public offense for the sake of my brothers' weakness, and I preserve my moral standing and human dignity to some degree. I am therefore in the situation of a human being who experiences a terror in the middle of a dangerous situation and would prefer to flee if he does not pull himself together for the sake of the others and feigns courage to himself and the others by which the situation can perhaps be saved. In this case, while I have not made my panic imaginary, I have hidden my good success behind the mask of courage. It is an act of supreme hypocrisy,

---

[564] According to an apocryphal text of the New Testament, Jesus while defending his disciples who have been picking corn on the Sabbath (Luke 6:1–5; Matthew 12:1–9; Samuel 21:1–6) is reported to have said to a man working on the Sabbath: "Man, if indeed thou knowest what thou doest, thou art blessed: but if thou knowest not, thou art cursed, and a transgressor of the law" (James, 1924, p. 32) This agraphon—a saying of Jesus that has not been included in the canonical Gospels—is found in addition to Luke 6:4 in the Codex Bezae from the fifth century. Jung discusses the text in *Answer to Job* (Jung, 1952b, § 696), stating that this logion—by replacing the moral criteria of law and convention through consciousness—already exceeds the traditional ethical teaching of Christianity. Jung cites this passage also in a letter to Walter Robert Corti (30 April 1929; Jung, 1973, p. 65) and disccuses its meaning in his seminar on Nietzsche's *Thus Spoke Zarathustra* (Jung, 1934–39, pp. 993–96). It is also quoted in the chapter "Späte Gedanken" ("Late Thoughts") of *Memories, Dreams, Reflections*. When Neumann read the draft of this chapter, he saw in it a confirmation of his *New Ethic* (see 118 N). See also Bishop (2002), pp. 134–35.

therefore another sin, but without which we would all be lost. This is not a new ethic, but simply a more differentiated one with fewer illusions, but the same as it always was.

You can relate these subtle considerations to Zeus, but not to the ox.[565] They are in fact subtle because they presuppose very special conditions. They achieve their validity only for the man who is really conscious of his shadow, but for one who treats his shadow either as a casual inconvenience or who trivially dismisses it out of a lack of scruples and moral responsibility, it signifies a dangerous possibility of the aberration of moral judgment as is characteristic for the man who, as a result of his moral defect, possesses a corresponding intellectual inflation. One can relieve oneself of some conflict by closing the moral eye for "all guilt avenges itself on earth."

I am just occupied with a work that has a completely different theme, but the discussion has meant that I had to also mention the ethical problem. I could not do otherwise than embark on a repudiation of the expression "new ethic," without naming names.[566] This is once again one of those sins, a faithlessness as it were, which imposes itself like a disaster at the moment when I had to protect the disproportionately higher aspect of our psychology from the coarseness of vulgar appreciation and, this, to general advantage. The entire difficulty lies in this case in the slipperiness of the language. Therefore one is forced to strew sand, which occasionally also lands in the eyes of the audience.

I am looking forward to your application of the origins history to the psychology of children. There would indeed be illustrative material there.

I feel myself very uncertain in relation to the question of pessimism and optimism and must leave the solution to fate. The only

[565] Jung refers to the Latin proverb "Quod licet Iovi, non licet bovi," translated as "What is permitted to Jove (Jupiter) is not permitted to an ox." It is probably a medieval rhyme adaptation of Terence's account of Jupiter's rape of Europa: "Aliis si licet, tibi non licet" ("If others are allowed to, that does not mean you are").

[566] Jung might be referring here to his lecture on "Das Gewissen in psychologischer Sicht" ("A Psychological View of Conscience") (Jung, 1958a), which was part of the lecture series on "Das Gewissen" ("Conscience") held at the C. G. Jung Institute Zurich in the winter term 1957/58. Jung's lecture was read by Franz Riklin and later published in the institute's volume titled *Conscience*. The reference to Neumann's ethical concept was left aside after Jung had read Neumann's response to his letter (see letter 114 J).

one who could decide this dilemma, that is dear God himself, has withheld his answer from me so far.

Hopefully you are well *dans ce meilleur des mondes possibles. Tout cela est bien dit, mais il faut cultiver notre jardin.*[567]

With best wishes,
Your ever devoted,
C. G. Jung

---

[567] "Cela est bien dit," répondit Candide, "mais il faut cultiver notre jardin." ("All that is very well," answered Candide, "but let us cultivate our garden.") The finishing sentence of Voltaire's *Candide*, which is Candide's final response to the optimistic summary of his friend Pangloss, a caricature of the German philosopher Gottfried Wilhelm Leibniz: "There is a concatenation of events in this best of all possible worlds: for if you had not been kicked out of a magnificent castle for love of Miss Cunegonde: if you had not been put into the Inquisition: if you had not walked over America: if you had not stabbed the Baron: if you had not lost all your sheep from the fine country of El Dorado: you would not be here eating preserved citrons and pistachio-nuts."

Dr. Erich Neumann,
Analytical Psychologist

Tel Aviv, 14. VI. 57

Dear C. G. Jung,

I am very moved by your quick reply to my letter, and since the problem broached concerns me very much I would like to try to clarify my position somewhat in the debate with you. While I concur in much, I have the feeling that, for me, it is still about something else than it is for you, or that something threatens to obliterate for me what I have to hold on to when compared with your formulation. Let's start with the main event. *The New Ethic* was the attempt to process a series of phantasies that roughly corresponded timewise with the exterminations of the Jews, and in which the problem of evil and justice was being tossed around in me. I am still gnawing away at these images at the end of which, in brief, stands the following. I seemed to be commissioned to kill the apeman in the profound primal hole. As I approached him, he was hanging, by night, sleeping on the cross above the abyss, but his—crooked—single eye was staring into the depths of this abyss. While it at first seemed that I was supposed to blind him, I all of a sudden grasped his "innocence," his dependence on the single eye of the Godhead, which was experiencing the depths through him, which was a human eye. Then, very abridged, I sank down in opposite this single eye, jumped into the abyss, but was caught by the Godhead, which carried me on the "wings of his heart." After that, this single eye opposite the apeman closed and it opened on my forehead. (Bit difficult to write this, but what should one do.) Working outward from the attempt to process this happening, I arrived at *The New Ethic*. For me, since then, the world looks different. Your formulations in the letter are also valid for me, but they do not go far enough. "As a man, I am a weakling and susceptible to being overcome by evil" is superficially all too true, but does not go far enough. I have subsequently had to do "evil," for these images are to be fulfilled personally, but I did not experience it as a sin but as a necessary action. That has changed nothing in the suffering I have caused and into which I have fallen, but my feeling experience was different. You write: "I will avoid evil, when I can, and will still fall into this hole all the same"—as I see it, I do not fall, but jump, and I know that the danger exists that I will die, but my prayer goes that "wings of the heart" may hold me. This means that I am, in my action, within and not outside of the Godhead,[568] because it is not about an action of the ego, but about a happening that I must hand myself over to. If the issue of "Job" is relevant, according to which the Godhead wishes to come to consciousness, an aspect of its subjectivity is evident, then I have to live with the single eye of the Godhead and also to experience the darkness of the abyss. But then evil is not a sin, but part of the world to be experienced. That is not "putting a brave face on it," but reverence before the numinosum of the Godhead, in which I am also implicated with the knowledge that there is no justice and no judge because the measure of God's eye surpasses all this. A moral attitude and human dignity no longer consist in "not exciting any bother," hiding something etc., but in enduring the responsibility for action in the certainty that behind it all there is one hidden who is superior to me who guides me, and what is required from man is to follow the instructions in vigilance and in willingness even to be destroyed. To tear down old gods is not a sin, but it is exactly the reverse that is a sin,—not to place oneself at the disposal of the new aspects of the divine. It could appear that my other temperament defends itself against "strewing sand," I also do not believe in the possibility and necessity "of protecting the disproportionately higher aspect of our psychology from the coarseness of vulgar understanding." "Our" psychology is that of modern man, whom should one protect against whom in this? If one cannot believe in man in spite of everything—do you not emphasize that he is the seat of the divine?—what then is the point of psychology anyway?

---

[568] [handwritten note:] "one is never outside"

The theologians are a more evil enemy than the *profanum vulgus*,[569] whose suffering is great and that therefore opens them up. Do not be so bitter, I have heard precisely from you that ordinary people have understood your alchemy and the educated have not. I have learned from you that one does not need to hide secrets, as they will do it for themselves. I believe that the old concept of sin has become untrue, it is no longer effective, and that is not due to the decline of man but to his new understanding of himself and of God. Are these not also "new"? The settlement of the debt that I also believe in is simply not a punishment but the expression of a moral in man that compels him to integration in which even evil is included. If you thus express yourself against *The New Ethic*, then please name names and I will reply if it is necessary, in good faith, for I believe that faithlessness exacts revenge, and would not even know why it would be necessary between us.

In old faithfulness and friendship,
Yours,
E. Neumann

---

[569]"odi profanum vulgus et arceo" ("I loathe and shun the uninitiate crowd"), Latin, from Horace, *Odes* III, 1.

PROF. DR. C. G. JUNG

KÜSNACHT, ZURICH
SEESTRASSE 228

29th June 1957

Dear Neumann,

Many thanks for your detailed letter. I have studied the same thoroughly and have decided in response to drastically modify or delete my small side excursion from my work.[570] I see that this problem is so substantial and even urgent, that it is impossible for one to illuminate it in a few words. There would be so much to say about it that one should either explore it fully in all its complexities or be silent about it. I myself would hardly know where to begin as so infinitely many factors come into play. Quite for this reason it seems to me also so exceedingly difficult to express anything really of general validity about it. I also feel something like resistance in me about making the shortcomings of my intellect liable for this supreme problem; it is a question of a numinous issue par excellence, a type of temenos[571] where one can only whisper *in conspectu genii*.[572]

Given enough time and work strength, the problem of the *Ethic* could form the content of an extended conversation and indeed not only between two, but among several. Albeit not among a great number at the same time, but as a particular debate between pairs;

---

[570] See n. 566.

[571] *Temenos*, Greek from temnō (τέμνω), "to cut," means a piece of land that is cut off and dedicated to the worship of a god, a sacred precinct such as a sanctuary or temple. Jung uses the word in a psychological sense to describe the space created between the analyst and the patient in the therapeutic process. It provides a designated container for the encounter with the unconscious (Jung (1943, § 63), which puts both into the presence of unknown and unpredictable forces. Furthermore, the term *temenos* is used in connection with the realm associated with the numinosity of the Self. The mandala is understood as a symbol for the temenos, for the protection of the center of the personality against outer forces (Jung, 1935b § 410).

[572] *in conspectu genii*, Latin, in the presence of the guiding spirit.

this in order to allow as many aspects of the question as possible to emerge. The individual differences that would reveal themselves in such a discussion are indeed very considerable, which is also to be expected with such complexity. In the face of this difficulty I cannot think, in writing, i.e., in letter form, of discussing the questions thrown up by you in an appropriate manner. Every letter would achieve the scope of a small treatise. That sadly exceeds my capability even though the matter would interest me very much. So it is not a lack of engagement on my part but much more an excess of it that hinders me from elaborating on your letter.

In the hope that you understand my point of view, I am,
With warm wishes,
Your devoted,
C. G. Jung

I assume that I will be able to welcome you here again on the occasion of the Eranos conference.

Dr. Erich Neumann,
Analytical Psychologist

Tel Aviv, 20. XII. [1957]

Dearest C. G. Jung,

I am writing to you by hand this time because this is just a greeting and an inquiry.

Despite sputniks[573] and flying saucers, I wish you and us a peaceful and healthy year. Since your admirable capacity for work has always remained loyal to you, despite your grumbles to the contrary, may it continue so to your and our pleasure and gratitude.

Now the question. Since my congress lecture[574] also concerns the genetic-phylogenetic aspect of analytical psychology, I would like to inquire of you what Fordham's[575] for me, suspect, sentence is on about: "This clear identity of the view Jung held till recently when, under pressure from biologists, he abandoned the heredity of archetypal images" (*Journal*, II 2 p. 197 below).[576] You abandoned the he-

---

[573] The USSR launched the first artificial Earth satellite, Sputnik 1 (Russian for "companion"), on 4 October 1957. In these days of the cold war the successful launch caused widespread fear of the technologically advanced powers of the Soviet Union in Western Europe and the United States ("Sputnik crisis").

[574] The First International Congress for Analytical Psychology was held in Zurich from 7 to 12 August 1958. Neumann was invited to give one of the ten extended lectures. The title of his presentation was "Die Deutung des genetischen Aspekts für die Analytische Psychologie" ("The Significance of the Genetic Aspect for Analytical Psychology") (Neumann, 1961a). On details of the congress see Adler (1959; 1961a). Due to Neumann's efforts Israel became a charter group member of the IAAP in 1958 (Thomas Kirsch, 2000, p. 181).

[575] On Fordham see n. 366 and introduction, pp. lvi–lviii.

[576] Fordham reviewed the collection of essays titled *New Directions in Psycho-Analysis*, edited by Melanie Klein, Paul Heimann, and Roger Money-Kyrle (Klein, Heimann, and Money-Kyrle, 1956) (Fordham, 1957a). He argued that the Kleinian school of psychoanalysis was getting closer to analytical psychology than to classical psychoanalysis (p. 200). In regard to a contribution by Heimann he stated that this "clear identity of the view Jung held till recently when, under pressure from biologists, he abandoned the heredity of archetypal images, together with

redity of "perceptions" long since, not recently. What is F. referring to[?] What, if anything, has changed in your views. The "sun phallus" example cannot be refuted by "biologists."[577] You will understand that the problem is important to me. F. seems to me rather hasty. In this way he also dismissed *Origins* with one wave of his hand because ontogenesis does not correspond to phylogenesis without his having noticed that it is about that of humanity here, not about the connection with animal evolution.[578] I have never had the impression until now that my writings deviate from this in relation to the genetic connections, therefore await your answer with anticipation. With F.'s comment one can easily go further and let the entire "collective unconscious" go by the board, which can get highly dangerous, both subjectively and objectively.

Once again all the best, we are pretty well, my wife and I hope the same is true for you,

Ever yours,
E. Neumann

---

the new view of counter-transference already described, led me to consider how much further the Kleinian school has approached analytical psychology and what differences remained" (pp. 197–98).

[577] Neumann refers to the case of Emile Schwyzer (1862–1931), a patient at the Burghölzli diagnosed with paranoid dementia. Jung reported on this case in *Wandlungen und Symbole der Libido* (*Transformations and Symbols of the Libido*) (1912) to support his theory that the mythological material of the phylogenetic level repeats itself in images of dreams and psychotic delusions on an ontogenetic level: "The patient sees in the sun a so-called 'upright tail' (i.e., much like an erect penis). When the patient moves his head back and forth, the sun's penis also moves back and forth and from this the wind arises" (Jung, 1912, § 173). Jung showed the similarities between Schwyzer's delusion and a mithraic vision first rendered by Albrecht Dieterich in *A Mithras Liturgy* (1903), a text that Jung claimed could not have been known to the patient due to a lack of education. But it has been argued by Shamdasani (2003, p. 216) that Schwyzer was far from unknowledgeable in things mythological, as Johann Honegger's (1885–1911) presentation of the case at the Second International Psychoanalytic Congress in Nuremberg demonstrated ("Analysis of a Case of Paranoid Dementia"). Jung's further argument of the unavailability of the mythological material to the patient—Jung, at first, mistook the second edition of Dieterich's book from 1910 as the original—has also been questioned, as similar material had already been presented by Creuzer in his influential *Symbolism and mythology of the ancient peoples, particularly the Greeks* (*Symbolik und Mythologie der alten Völker, besonders der Griechen*) (1810–12). There is also a discrepancy between *Transformations and Symbols of the Libido*, where Jung refers to Honegger as his source, and later accounts—e.g., in *Symbols of Transformations* (1952a) and *The Concept of the Collective Unconscious* (1936/37, §§ 104–10), where he stated that he himself was told the story by Schwyzer in 1906. See also Shamdasani (1990).

[578] On Fordham's critique of Neumann see introduction, pp. lvi–lviii.

PROF. DR. C. G. JUNG   **KÜSNACHT, ZURICH**
SEESTRASSE 228

3rd January 1958

Dear Neumann,

While thanking you for your kind New Year's wishes, I would like to hasten to correct Fordham's statement. The exciting novelty is that Fordham has evidently discovered that archetypal perceptions are not inherited; however, it is the archetypes themselves, namely, the underlying archetypal forms that are. I am always and everywhere coming up against the fact that epistemology is deficient. People cannot see the difference between image and reality. A problem that is completely obvious—as an artist once said to me—by never ignoring the difference between the portrait and the original. Absolutely nothing has happened "recently": I have changed nothing in my understanding. It is merely Fordham himself who has been taken in by his own concretism. I have read the sentence in the original. Who the "biologists" could be is an absolute mystery to me. I have at least not sensed any "pressure." I will write to Fordham on this point.[579]

[579] Jung's letter to Fordham is missing, but in his letter of 30 May 1958 Fordham deemed it necessary to defend his position: "I want to bother you further on your views about heredity, for I believe these could be clarified by annotations in the forthcoming volumes 8 and 9 of your Collected Works. May I start by classifying the theories of heredity that have gained general acceptance: (a) the genetic theory, now widely accepted; (b) the theory of the inheritance of acquired characteristics, now generally rejected; (c) the theory of transmission by verbal and other means. You state in more than one place that inheritance comes about through repeated experience but the inherited entity, being the primordial image or archetype, is evidently not the experience itself since it is the possibility of experience. This view does not appear to fit in with any of the ones I have enumerated above, since theory (a) does not allow for the inheritance of experience, but the genes create the experience. Theory (b) handles only the characteristic, that is, the experience. I note that the biological references you give are scanty. [. . .] I suspect that your sources were more philosophical than biological when you say, as you did in your last letter, that 'I always knew that images should not be inherited'" (Fordham to Jung, 20 May 1958 [MFP]). This prompted a harsh reaction by Jung in his letter of 14 June 1958: "I don't flatter myself to have a theory of heredity. I share the ordinary views about it. I am convinced that individual acquisitions under experimental conditions are not inherited. I don't believe that this statement could be generalized, since changes in individual cases must have been inherited, otherwise no

I, too, most warmly wish you and your family a good and fruitful New Year.

Ever yours,

C. G. Jung

P.S. By the way, à propos: Fred Hoyle, the English astronomer, appears to have written a novel in which a cloud endowed with intelligence approaches the earth. Evidently, flying saucers have also got to him. My text is now in print and unfortunately I can no longer mention this particular joke.[580]

Greetings and good wishes once again.

Yours,

C.G.J.

---

change would have come about in phylogenesis; or we would be forced to assume that a new variety, or a new species was shaped by the creator on the spot without inheritance. Concerning archetypes migration and verbal transmission are self-evident, except in those cases, where individuals reproduce archetypal forms outside of all possible influences (good example in childhood dreams!). Since archetypes are instinctual forms, they follow a universal pattern, as the functions of the body. [...] It is true that I have set aside hitherto general biology. This for good reasons! We know yet far too little about human psychology as to be able to establish a biological basis for our [views]. [...] The real connections with biology are only in the sphere of the unconscious, i.e., in the realm of the instinctive activities. [...] For our purposes it is highly indifferent, whether archetypes are handed down by tradition and migration, or by inheritance. It is an entirely secondary question, since comparable biological facts, i.e., instinctual patterns with animals are obviously inherited. I see no reason to assume, that man should be an exception. The assumption therefore, that the (psychoid) archetypes are inherited, is for many reasons far more probable than that they are handed down by tradition. Instincts are not taught, as a rule. The childish prejudice against inherited archetypes is mostly due to the fact, that one thinks, archetypes to be representations; but in reality they are preferences or 'penchants', likes and dislikes" (Jung to Fordham, 14 June 1958 [MFP]). Finally, Fordham conceded to Jung "that the subject of heredity is of no empirical importance at the present time" and that "heredity is a necessary part of the definition of archetypes" (Fordham to Jung, 24 June 1958 [MFP]). On the question of the heredity of archetypes and the relationship between analytical psychology and biology, see Stevens (2002).

    [580] The book in question is Fred Hoyle's *The Black Cloud* (1957). Sir Fred Hoyle (1915–2001) was an English astronomer, cosmologist, writer, and broadcaster. He was the Plumian Professor of Astronomy and Experimental Philosophy at St. John's College, Cambridge (1958–73) and director of the Cambridge Institute of Theoretical Astronomy (1967–73). Hoyle famously opposed the Big Bang theory of the origin of the cosmos, championing his own "Steady State" theory. Other fictional works incluce *Ossian's Ride* (1961), *October the First Is Too Late* (1974), and *Comet Halley* (1985). In his afterword to the 2010 edition of *The Black Cloud* Richard Dawkins expressed his opinion that this book is "one of the greatest works of science fiction ever written, up there with the best of Isaac Asimov and Arthur C. Clark" (Dawkins, 2010, p. 212). Regardless of his remark to Neumann, Jung extended the epilogue to "A Modern Myth" substantially and dedicated the final pages to a psychological reading of Hoyle's novel (Jung, 1958, §§ 810–20). Jung's library contains Hoyle's *Frontiers of Astronomy* (1955) and the German edition of the *The Nature of the Universe* (1950).

11th October 58

Dearest C. G. Jung,

I almost have a bad conscience that I have not emerged out of con-
templation before now. I wanted to write even from Tel Aviv and at
least thank you for the off-prints. As I had to write the lectures for the
3 congresses, Zurich, Eranos, and Barcelona,[581] naturally, alongside
my practice, I was quite unable to read and was not inclined just to
"pretend" to thank you. But in Zurich I was able to read the piece
of autobiography *written by you*.[582] But congress, people—I did not

[581] Neumann refers to the following three conferences: The First International Congress for
Analytical Psychology, Zurich, 7–12 August 1958 (see n. 574; Neumann, 1961a); "Mensch und
Frieden" ("Human Being and Peace"), Eranos conference, Ascona, 14–22 August 1958: Neu-
mann's lecture was titled "Frieden als Symbol des Lebens" ("Peace as the Symbol of life")
(Neumann, 1959a); and the Fourth International Congress of Psychotherapy, Barcelona, 1–7
September 1958: the congress in Barcelona was dedicated to the topic of "Psychotherapy and
Existential Analysis" and led to the foundation of the International Federation for Medical
Psychotherapy under Medard Boss. Neumann's lecture was titled "Das Schöpferische als Zen-
tralproblem der Psychotherapie" ("The Creative as a Central Problem of Psychotherapy") (Neu-
mann, 1960). In his review Erwin Straus describes the aim of the conference as follows: "Obvi-
ously, then, Daseins-Analyse raises almost as many questions as it answers: Must we accept
Heidegger's ontology as the final word? Or what modifications are possible and necessary? Is
Binswanger's Daseins-Analyse the legitimate application of Heidegger's Analytik des Daseins?
If not, is Daseins-Analyse the only form of Existential Analysis? These were some of the major
problems which—more or less clearly formulated—confronted the Barcelona Congress and
for which Sarro, Boss, Minkowski, Ey, Ibor, Neumann, and other speakers offered their solutions" (Straus, 1959, p. 161), and he remarks that "Neumann (Tel Aviv) impressed the audience
with a lecture in which he presented creative man as the central problem of psychotherapy"
(Straus, 1959, p. 163).

[582] Most chapters of *Memories, Dreams, Reflections* resulted from interviews Aniela Jaffé con-
ducted with Jung. However, according to her introduction, Jung wrote parts of it by himself. In
April 1958 Jung completed the three chapters on his childhood, school years, and the time of
his medical studies. These must have been the parts to which Neumann alludes in this letter.
The chapter titled "Late Thoughts" was written by Jung at the beginning of 1959. Jung sent it to
Neumann in February 1959, who discussed the content in his letter from 18 February (118 N).
In addition, Jung also wrote the chapter on "Kenya and Uganda" in the summer of 1959. Those
chapters were heavily edited by Jaffé, before they were incorporated in the manuscript. On the
problematic status of *Memories, Dreams, Reflections* see Shamdasani (1995).

Figure 9. Neumann lecturing at the Eranos conference 1958 (Eranos Archive; courtesy of Paul Kugler).

permit myself to speak with you in your exhaustion. Then came a month of congress in Barcelona and a wonderful trip through Spain whose abundance is still giving me much to think about as not only were landscape, art, and history very striking, but on top of that, so was the Jewish problem, with the synagogues transformed into churches and the many modern Hebrew inscriptions on the walls where "one" scribbles the names. To say nothing of the bullfight and its completely unexpected impact in contrast with the humane bias against it.[583]

Now we are recovering in the mountains in a small place in the Valais alps. On c. 20th October we will be in Zurich, I have a "Fear"

---

[583] On their journey through Spain Erich and Julie Neumann were accompanied by their daughter Rali and one of her friends. Among other places they visited Toledo, Sevilla, and Granada with their rich Sephardic history from the Muslim reign. The visit of the *corrida* (bullfight) in Barcelona was part of the entertainment program of the International Congress of Psychotherapy. (Information from Rali Loewenthal-Neumann.)

lecture at the Institute on 4th Nov. that I must still write.[584] But I would like to be able to speak with you twice, if it is at all possible for you, I am also writing to Aniela J., and am looking forward to it very much. My link with you is, as you know, not dependent on writing and speaking, or no longer dependent, I should say, but meeting with you always brings me a substantial affirmation that cannot be found anywhere else in the world. I hope you understand what I mean. Even the Jungian Congress,[585] which was so positive, only confirmed this for me. For me, there is only you yourself as a "connecting point" in the center, as far as the task of the work is concerned.

I hope to see you again soon and in good health.

As ever,
Yours,
E. Neumann

---

[584] Neumann gave a paper at the C. G. Jung Institute Zurich as part of the 1958–59 lecture series on "Die Angst" ("The Fear"). His lecture was titled "Die Angst vor dem Weiblichen" ("The Fear of the Feminine") (Neumann, 1959c).

[585] The First International Congress for Analytical Psychology, Zurich, 7–12 August 1958 (see n. 574).

18. II. 59

Dearest C. G. Jung,

What a month! After quite a long time, I have just landed in an "episode" of active imagination, and added to that comes your manuscript with the chapters on the afterlife.[586] Firstly, I would like to thank you very much for it. I have no "opinion" about this, nor about this entire book, but am deeply moved once again. For me, it is the finest thing you have written. I must however admit that this is for personal reasons because I do not know anything else in writing that is closer to me and to the nature of my life experience. You will not perceive this as immodesty for it is not here a question of differences in dimension, but of the nature of life experience, and you know well how closely the "myth" I wrote when I was 16 led to all of this, and if I survey my development as I get older and trace its stages, I have a very similar experience of life as the one that speaks out of this book.

If I now bring some comments, "objections," etc., you will understand these as questions that cannot be avoided. They must be asked, for the depth of these things that affect me cannot not remain without reaction, and it seems to me that I must direct this question back to you. But none of my questions should place a burden of a reply on you; you know, that in all these things I have nothing to expect from you but everything from myself. Some of it seems to me to be explained by my Jewish and thus more Eastern background that does not quite overlap with your Christian and more Occidental one. But despite this, I am still posing these questions because it seems to me that in some places as if deeper answers are conflicted in you yourself with—perhaps?—less deep ones, if I understand you correctly. I definitely do not mean the necessary paradox of statements here.

---

[586] Neumann refers to chapter 11 of *Memories, Dreams, Reflections*, titled "Über das Leben nach dem Tod" ("On Life after Death") (Jung, 1962).

If I am formulating it simplistically in the form of opposing theses, then you will please not misunderstand me. But I can, I hope, formulate it more succinctly in this way. It does indeed look as if I wish to correct you, perhaps another person sees something from his distance that is more difficult to assess for oneself. At the risk of making myself very unpopular with you, I would like then to raise some issues with the thesis so beloved of you of the "becoming conscious of God," and moreover, some issues that arise out of your own material. Could it not be the case that precisely the thesis of your consciousness should be compensated for? A thesis whose aspect of development is perhaps still tied to a particular time? If the Self contemplates you as the ego, then the Self is not unconscious. If you are told, which amounts to the same thing, C. G. Jung is a projection of the Great Unknown, then he is clearly communicating that he is not unconscious, it seems to me. In reality it could then only be a question of a variation of the myth of man as conceived by you. If we humans are complexes of the divine unconscious, which he or it becomes conscious of while we make conscious our individuality with our human consciousness, the accent on the individual would be still greater without our having to formulate the Self or God as unconscious. If we were the unconscious complexes of God that are endowed with consciousness and the possibility of consciousness, our task of consciousness and integration would also be sacred. The function of the cells of an organism, of our organism, does not imply that we are unconscious, although we cannot "replace" this function. The small unique experience of the individual is impossible to the great as the great, through metastasis into the small and smallest the great experience differentiates itself unendingly just as the image of the whole is reflected in a different way in a fragment. These infinite variations of infinitely more different unique experiences add something to absolute knowledge without our being able to say that absolute knowledge is unconscious. Am I making sense, have I misunderstood you very much?

This is roughly where my objection to "incarnation" comes from. "Late Thoughts" p. 9.[587] This incarnation is identical with the creation

---

[587] Not in the chapter "Late Thoughts," but in "On Life after Death" (Jung, 1962, pp. 293–96 [German, p. 319]).

of man in the image of God as an ego-Self. It is not incarnation but its becoming conscious and its realization, which leads to the new phenomenon of the birth of God in which the divine as a divine individual and a unique singularity manifests itself in man. The incarnation is already preexistent in the ego-Self unity in which the numinous ego-nucleus of the ego has the capacity for consciousness. If the task is that man becomes conscious of his Self and his creator, then it comes closer to the other mythically formulated phenomenon that the creator and the Self thereby create a new experience that did not exist beforehand, as the complex: this individual, this uniquely configured nucleus of consciousness and of the ego were not yet in existence. For me in any case, it is a fact that the Jewish historical "development" in this mortal world is becoming ever more problematic for me, the "actualization of messianism" in individuation is becoming ever more crucial. The same is true for the historical revelation as for the historical incarnation. What is relevant are the stages of development of consciousness in the development of the individual, otherwise everything "historical" belongs to the constellation of the ego as time, like family and constitution. The realization of the ego-Self unity is vertical. From there on, I have issues about your sentence: "On Life after Death," p. 31: Natural history tells us [...][588] Of course, taken as a whole it is indisputable, "haphazard and casual transformation" seems to me, however, to be a Darwinist remnant that I do not believe in without having a counterthesis to hand. This aspect of the 19th century will perhaps be superseded by a completely different theory in which your conception of the archetype as well as absolute and extreme knowledge will play a crucial role. The development theory takes as its starting point the inadequate and only the rational experience of the historical ego and was not capable of explaining

---

[588] The passage belongs to the chapter "Late Thoughts": "Natural history tells us of a haphazard and casual transformation of species over hundred of millions of years and devouring and being devoured. The biological and political history of man is an elaborate repetition of the same thing. But the history of the mind offers a different picture. Here the miracle of reflecting consciousness intervenes—the second cosmogony. The importance of consciousness is so great that one cannot help suspecting the element of *meaning* to be concealed somewhere within all the monstrous, apparently senseless biological turmoil, and that the road to its manifestation was ultimately found on the level of warm-blooded vertebrates possessed of a differentiated brain—found as if by chance, unintended and unforeseen, and yet somehow sensed, felt and groped for out of some dark urge" (Jung, 1962, p. 312).

the development, not through chance, selection, and mutation. This is why to speak of an "apparently senseless biological turmoil"[589] seems to me to be a metaphysical statement from you that you otherwise avoid. If the purpose of individual life presupposes such an advanced development in the direction of the Self, then it seems to me we may not any longer go beyond this question after the individual purpose. We are not responsible for it as an isolated, unique historical ego, and the mythical statement of the unconscious sounds completely different. Besides this we have, moreover, no satisfactory explanation, but the composition of the natural kingdoms in which the experience of the world is becoming ever more extensive seems to me to speak against the fact that the way toward the manifestation of meaning, thanks to warm-bloodedness and brain development, has been found by accident. Precisely because the psyche and the archetypes have developed with their meaning content in the development of nature, this meaning is not something foreign to nature but rather belongs to it from the outset—it seems to me. Your word: "Who has created, who has imagined" is also relevant here.

I hope you are not angry with me for raising "issues," but it all concerns me too much to be able to keep my mouth shut. Precisely the radical emphasis of the individual as a "unit of salvation," as it were, seems to me the upper waterline to the lower collective line. For this reason I am glad to rediscover also in your work the—unavoidable— "new" ethic in "Late Thoughts" p. 2.[590] This problem of evil will not let me off the hook and is forever making a reappearance in my imagination. Most difficult to swallow. "The murderer can have an epiphany by murdering and the murdered by being murdered," and if I am told "It makes no difference to the light of God if it burns on a black or a white candle," then I have almost dropped out of the Western world, almost out of Judaism, and I do not know from where else but not out of myself—or so I hope. The light wishes to illuminate, it creates dark bodies with the possibility that they will radiate light, is that a primordial mess? I believe the horizontal historical view confuses everything here, life itself is, after all, devouring and being devoured. The only thing that remains open to question is why cre-

[589] Ibid.
[590] Jung (1962), pp. 303–6.

ation, the answer, radiating in infinite variety what only radiates in itself in an unreflected way, is ancient, but satisfies me.

Most dear C. G. Jung, so please forgive the ambush, but this is how the constellation of my February has been. You know that my gratitude for your book is only greater because it compels me to respond.

In old solidarity,
[E. Neumann]

PROF. DR. C. G. JUNG   **KÜSNACHT, ZURICH**
                                            SEESTRASSE 228

10th March 1959

Dear Friend,

Many thanks for your comprehensive and thorough letter of 18/II! What Mrs. Jaffé sent you was a first draft, which I had not yet revised at all, an attempt at nailing down my volatile thoughts. Sadly the exhaustion of my great age forbids me from an equally comprehensive excursus as your letter.

[I]

The question: *an creator sibi conscious est?*[591] is not a "favorite idea" but a most painful experience of almost immeasurable impact that cannot easily be debated. If someone projects the Self, for example, then it is an unconscious act, for projection arises empirically only out of unconsciousness.

Incarnatio describes in the first instance the birth of God, which took place in XPo,[592] psychologically, therefore, also the realization of the Self as something new, not present before that. The previously created human is a "creature" even if "in the image of God," in whom the thought of *filiatio* and of the *sacrificium divinum* is not explicitly present. It is, as you say, a "new experience."

---

[591] "But is the creator conscious of himself?" In Jung's letter edition Aniela Jaffé transcribes this sentence with "an creator sibi *consciens* est?" (Jung, 1973, vol. 3, p. 238 [German]); vol. 2 p. 493 [English]). She published the letter again in the German version of her book *Der Mythus vom Sinn im Werk von C. G. Jung* (Jaffé, 1967, pp. 179–81)—also rendering "conscience." When Roderick Main republished the letter in the appendix of his study *Jung on Sychronicity and the Paranormal*, he followed Jaffé's letter edition (Main, 1997). The original handwritten letter states "conscious."

[592] The Greek capital letter X and P are the first two letters of ΧΡΙΣΤΟΣ. Together they formed a cross like monogram representing the Christ character of Jesus: ☧.

"It once happened by accident and at random that . . ."[593] this sentence should characterize the entire process of creation. The archetype is no exception to this. The starting point was that indistinct masses organized themselves into a circular shape. Thus the original type appeared as the first form of formless gas, for everything formless can only appear in a specific form or order.

The concept of "order" is not identical with that of "meaning." Even an organic being is, despite its inherent meaningful structure, not necessarily meaningful overall. If the world had come to an end in the Oligocene period,[594] then it would have had no meaning for man. Without the reflective consciousness of man, the world is of gigantic meaninglessness because man, in our experience, is the only being who can detect meaning.

We cannot claim to know of what the constituent factors of biological development consist. But we know well that warm-bloodedness and brain differentiation were necessary for the emergence of consciousness and, with that, also for the revelation of meaning. It cannot be imagined what kind of coincidences and risks creation went through, over millions of years, to evolve from a lemur tree dweller into a man. In this chaos of coincidence, synchronistic phenomena were probably at work, which in contrast to and with the help of the known laws of nature were able to achieve syntheses in archetypal moments that appear amazing to us. Causality and teleology collapse here, for synchronistic phenomena behave like coincidences. But their being consists in the fact that an objective process coincides in a corresponding way with a psychic event, i.e., for example, a physical process has a meaning in common with an endopsychic one. This sentence implies not only a (ubiquitous?) *latent* meaning that can be recognized by consciousness but also, for that preconscious time, a psychoid process that coincides in a corresponding way with a physical process. But here, meaning cannot yet be recognized by any consciousness. It is through the archetype that we come closest to this

[593] Jung refers to this passage of *Memories, Dreams, Reflections*: "Natural history tells us of a haphazard and casual transformation of species over hundreds of millions of years and devouring and being devoured" (Jung, 1961, p. 312).

[594] *Oligocene*, geologic epoch of the Paleogene period, from about 34 million to 23 million years before the present. The beginnings of the species *Homo* is usually dated with 2 millions year to the present.

early, irrepresentable, psychoid stage of conscious development; indeed, the archetype itself gives us direct intimations of it. Unconscious synchronicities are also, from experience, absolutely possible, in that one is in many cases unconscious of their occurrence or one must be made aware of them by an outsider.

II

Since the nomological probability gives no grounds for surmising that higher syntheses such as the psyche, for example, could emerge by chance arrangement[595] alone, we thus need the hypothesis of a latent meaning to explain not only the synchronistic phenomena but also the higher syntheses. Meaning is always unconscious and can only be discovered post hoc;[596] this is why the danger also always exists that meaning will be insinuated where nothing of the sort is present. We do need the synchronistic experiences to be able to justify the hypothesis of a latent meaning that is independent of consciousness.

Since a creation without the reflective consciousness of man has no recognizable meaning, with the hypothesis of latent sentience a cosmogonic significance is extended to man, a true *raison d'être*. If, on the other hand, the latent meaning is attributed to the creator as a conscious plan of creation, then the question arises: why should the creator contrive this whole world phenomenon as he already knows what he could be reflected in and why should he reflect himself since he is already conscious of himself? To what end should he create a second, inferior consciousness alongside his omniscience? In a sense, billions of dull little mirrors of which he knows in advance what the picture will be like that they will reflect back?

After all these considerations I have come to the conclusion that being made in the same image does not only apply to man, but also to the creator; he is similar to or the same as man, i.e., among other things, as unconscious as he is or even more unconscious since according to the myth of the *incarnatio* he even feels compelled to become a man and to offer himself as a sacrifice to man.

---

[595] The typescript version (B) differs from the handwritten letter (A). (B) gives "Zufälligkeit" ("randomness") instead of (A) "Zufallsanordnung" ("chance arrangement").

[596] The typescript version (B) renders "meaning seems always to be unconscious at first and therefore can only be discovered post hoc."

I must end here in the awareness that I have only touched on the main points (as it seems to me) of your letter, which is in part difficult for me to understand. It is not carelessness but rather my *molesta senectus*[597] that impose economy on me.

With best wishes,
Your devoted,
C. G. Jung

---

[597] *molesta senectus*, Latin for "arduous age."

Dr. Erich Neumann,
Analytical Psychologist

11th Sept 59

Dear C. G. Jung,

I wanted to write a big response to your letter, I wanted to thank you for the invitation to our daughter Rahli[598] which pleased me very much, to congratulate you on your birthday—I have done nothing of this. But this was not due to neglect but was the consequence of an emergency, which you will appreciate. You see, I became ill for more than 9 weeks and after that I wasn't even able to take care of anything other than my practice for a while. However, a big lecture for the Protestant Academy in Tübingen (first time in Germany!) and the Eranos lecture were unwritten.[599] So then a manuscript of 120 pages came out rather precipitously out of which I pulled both lectures. We are now in Wallis in the mountains and I certainly hope to see you *at some point between the end of September until mid-October*, wherever and however. We will then be in Zurich, the Institute, Club, etc. I will however write straightaway to Aniela J. so that she can "fit me in."

---

[598] Rali Loewenthal-Neumann came to Zurich for the first time in 1950 to recover from a tuberculosis infection. From 1956 to 1960 she studied psychology in Zurich. She visited the seminars and lectures at the Jung Institute and took part in the social activities of the Jung circles. When Jung heard about his friend's daughter studying in Zurich, he invited her to pay him a visit in Küsnacht. They sat together in the garden and spoke for half an hour. Jung was interested in the political situation in Israel and the well-being of Rali's father. The meeting took place in summer 1959. (Information provided by Rali Loewenthal-Neumann.)

[599] The conference of the Evangelische Akademie did not take place in Tübingen, but in Tutzing at the Starnberger Lake from 28 July 1959 to 4 August 1959 (see Neumann's letter to Rascher, 20 July 1959 [RA]). Neumann's contribution to the Eranos conference 1959 was titled "Das Bild des Menschen in Krise und Erneuerung" ("The Image of Man in Crisis and Renewal") (Neumann, 1960a). Both texts together formed the basis of Neumann's posthumously published book *Krise und Erneuerung* (*Crisis and Renewal*) (1961b).

Perhaps we will then have chance to continue something of what both letters have raised.

I hope my script will be decipherable, I have done my best anyway.

In old cordiality,
Yours,
E. Neumann

PROF. DR. C. G. JUNG   KÜSNACHT, ZURICH
                                            SEESTRASSE 228

23. Jan. 1961

Dear Mrs. Neumann,[600]

Finally I am getting around to thank you for your kind letter and now to express my condolences to you also in writing for the great loss that has befallen you. A dark year lies behind us: you have lost your husband and I a friend and, besides this, my youngest son-in-law.[601]

I regretted very much that I did not see Dr. Neumann once again last autumn. But at the time I was unwell myself and am still not over all after effects. To this is added the exhaustion of great age, which one would like to deny. Following on from the death of my son-in-law I was particularly shattered by the unexpected and, for me, sudden death of my friend and companion on the way in whose fate I participated in tranquility and from a distance. I still remember well our last conversation at which you were also present. May the New Year grant you consolatory fortunes!

Most warmly,
Your devoted,
C. G. Jung

---

[600] Letter to Julie Neumann addressed by Jung as "Liebe Frau Doktor."
[601] Konrad Hoerni-Jung (1910–1960), married to Jung's youngest daughter Helene Hoerni-Jung.

Appendix I

[LETTER TO THE *JÜDISCHE RUNDSCHAU* REGARDING "DIE JUDENFRAGE IN
DER PSYCHOTHERAPIE," *JÜDISCHE RUNDSCHAU*, 48, 15 JUNE 1934, P. 5:]

WE TAKE THE FOLLOWING (ABRIDGED) EXCERPTS FROM A
FURTHER LETTER ON THE SAME THEME.

Jung maintains that the Jew has a particular tendency to recognize the negative, the shadow, and he even believes that while the Aryan man requires more illusions, the Jew is more capable of living with a negative perception. Kirsch appeals against this observation behind which no negative evaluation of any sort is concealed. However, Jewish psychology does in fact demonstrate a characteristic—nothing more than this was asserted by Jung—a strong tendency to see the negative and to raise it to consciousness. On a small scale, this is symptomatic of the all too familiar "Jewish" manner of grumbling, but at the highest level this trait permeates Jewish awareness of history. Even in the Bible, the Jewish people knows its history as a history of ever repeated falling into sin, and in the prophets, who really were connected to the original source, this motif reaches its creative incarnation. Over and over again they raised the people's consciousness of the negative, the shadow side, and if one misconstrues this fundamental fact as a trait of Galut psychology, one is not doing Judaism any favors, as one robs it of the fundamental fact of its moral instinct that extends even as far as the one-sidedness of Freudian psychology.

The objection levied against Jung that he has "not reached the gen-otype of the actual Jew from the phenotype of the Jew living in exile from the shekinah" is also misguided. Jung, as a psychologist, is ad-hering to the experiences arising from his work with Jewish people, and we all belong to "the phenotype of the Jew living in exile from the shekinah," i.e., of the Jew as he is, but we also do not need to take flight into the image of a nonexistent "real" "actual" Jew. It is a false path to emphasize "a special link between the Jew and the eternal source," even if it may once have existed. Jung is not disputing that the Jews of the Bible saw and lived the "greater aspect of the human soul," but his work with the contemporary Jewish person has allowed him to see a clear and fateful tendency to repress this greater aspect, and this is what the issue is today.

Jung wrote in 1918 when Judaism had barely become aware of Zionism: "The Jew is domesticated to a high degree, but is sorely perplexed about that something in man that touches the earth, which receives new strength from below. . . . The Jew does not have enough of this—where does he make contact with his earth? The se-cret of the earth is no joke and no paradox." This is exactly the recog-nition and formulation of Zionism, and also, in his tendency to make the Jew aware of this, Jung is "more Zionist" than the Jews and Zionists who want to gloss over it.

We believe that Jungian Psychology will be crucial in the striving of the Jews to reach their foundation; it is precisely the so-called "Zi-onist" character of his perceptions that, just like Zionism does, incor-porate the irrational of the creative human source, which will be groundbreaking here. But just as it is only the making conscious of the shadow side, of the personal unconscious, which is a prerequisite for the individual to reconnect with the foundation, in precisely the same way, Zionism will have to go along a hard path of making con-scious the negative. Only then will an ultimate and deeply grounded development of Erez-Israel and a rebirth of the Jew that emerges from his creative foundation be possible.

Dr. Erich Neumann, Tel Aviv.

["Zur jüdischen Religionsgeschichte," *Jüdische Rundschau*, 60, 27 July 1934, p. 10:]

On The Jewish History of Religion

An essay by Hugo Rosenthal bestowed with the title *Opposing Types in the Jewish History of Religion* is included in the recently published collection *The Reality of the Soul* by C. G. Jung (Rascher Press, Zurich), alongside essays by Jung, the highly significant works of the famous psychologist. Rosenthal will be well known to readers of the *Jüdische Rundschau* for his numerous contributions.

Rosenthal takes as his starting point the two main types of Jungian psychology, namely, the extravert and the introvert. Both are fundamentally different in their distinct ways of relating to the world. While the extravert is orientated "outward," toward his objects, his interests are located there and he also experiences his fate there; for the introvert the emphasis is with the subject, he is orientated toward the "inner world." However, this does not mean, as is often misconstrued, that he only makes "subjective" judgments, or only behaves in a "subjective" way. The inner world is something equally as universal and objective as the external world. The extravert is directed toward the one part of the "world," to the general structure of the external world, the introvert to the other part, to the general structure of the human being. Both parts together are required before a complete image of the world is achieved, but every partial stance that suppresses and excludes one side of the world leads to a danger. But it is precisely this one-sidedness that characterizes the psychological type.

In the first part of his essay Rosenthal explores the Jew–non-Jew opposition. The most striking characteristic of the Jewish people is its awareness of being a "chosen people," i.e., being in opposition to the world and all other peoples, not being like the other peoples of the earth. However, psychologically speaking, this stance is a hallmark of introversion, for "the introvert locates himself in opposition to the world." However, Rosenthal does not pursue this fundamental insight to its very important conclusions; rather, the emphasis of his work lies in the exploration of the contrasting types as an "inner-Jewish" problem.

Tracing the contrast of types in Jewish spiritual history is exceptionally illuminating. The ever-repeating duality in Jewish development with its constant inner battle acquires quite a different face when one recognizes it as an unavoidable contest between the two warring basic types. The opposition between extravert-introvert can be traced throughout all basic Jewish opposites, from the polarity of "priest-prophet," "Halacha-Aggada" as far as the battle of Rabbinism against kabbalah and Hasidism and right into the present day. All this is only hinted at in Rosenthal's essay, but from now on, no emollient confrontation with Judaism will be able to disregard this way of thinking that is capable of clarifying some misunderstandings and illuminating some duality.

Starting from the problem of types, Rosenthal applies almost the entire framework of analytical psychology to analyze two very different biblical texts. On the one hand, he examines the figure of Saul in its contrast to that of David by which he achieves a comprehensive understanding of the personality and the destiny of this king; however, of greater importance than this part—against which some basic methodological objections can be raised—is the other section of the work which explores the Jacob-Esau opposition.

Qualms about the adequacy of a psychological exploration of texts such as the Bible are no longer appropriate today, for through Jung's discovery of the "collective unconscious" as the general foundation upon which human culture is constructed, an adequate conception of mythical material and religious phenomena became possible. The narrative of Jacob's battle with the angel, which according to received wisdom is Jacob's guardian angel, portrays, in the sense of myth, "a dream of the people." Rosenthal makes him an object of analysis which reveals the deepest layers of the national character by demonstrating that, in this battle, the battle of Judaism with itself, with its inferior side, it is "Esau" who is portrayed. The interweaving of the forefathers' narrative with the universal-mythical event which affects the entire people is traceable right into the details of the text, and it can be deduced precisely from the symbolic-mythical reality of the events just how the battle between the opposing types develops via the battle with its own inferiority toward the holy militancy of Israel.

This elaboration of the content is naturally meager and unsatisfactory, but it is also not intended to be a substitute for the reading of Rosenthal's work, which contains a plethora of important findings, even if some objections can be raised against it.

The application of analytical psychology to the study of religion—of which the Rosenthal work is a first beginning—imparts not only new answers and questions, but it can also provide a decisive contribution to the regrounding of the Jew in Judaism by facilitating for the modern man a personal access to the religious and general basics of Jewish scripture.

Dr. Erich Neumann, Tel Aviv.

(NEUMANN : Ethik.)

VORBEMERKUNG.

    Bitte verstehen Sie die hier folgenden Anregungen nur
als ergänzende Vorschläge. Sie wollen Ihren Text nicht er-
setzen, sondern nur ergänzend abrunden. Dies namentlich dort,
wo Sie sich etwas activistisch ausdrücken. Ich will nicht die
Activität decouragieren, sondern bloss betonen, dass der
Schatten bezw. das Unbewusste überhaupt nicht aus der Welt ge-
schafft und dem Bewusstsein unterworfen werden können. Wir
können nur lernen, wie sich ein Getreidekorn zwischen Hammer
und Amboss benehmen muss.

Titel: Der ethische Aspekt der Tiefenpsychologie, oder Das Problem
    der Ethik in der modernen Psychologie, oder Ethos und Erkenntnis,
    oder Consciousness and Conscience.

p.5 unten: ....und verdunkelt uns den Himmel mit Atombombern und dikta-
    torischer Massenentseelung.

p.6:   Tel-Aviv, Israel.

p.8 oben 6.Zeile: ... hat sich neuerdings als unfähig erwiesen.
    letzte Zeile: (Ich habe mich an Ort und Stelle überzeugt, dass
    die Missionäre die "Gleichberechtigung" der farbigen Primitiven
    versuchen, mit katastrophalen Resultaten. Man kann Kindern
    unmöglich dieselben Rechte geben wie den Erwachsenen. Das
    braucht Zeit.)

p.9 13.Zeile von oben: Statt "Ungültigkeit" Unwirksamkeit. p.11 sprechen
    Sie selber davon, dass die "alte Ethik" die Gegenkräfte abge-
    fangen hat.

p.10. 10.Zeile von oben: Die "alte Ethik" ist unwirksam, aber nicht not-
    wendigerweise ungültig.

p.13, 14.Zeile von oben: 100 und mehr Jahre.
    19. "   "   " : Vor Nietzsche war der Faust, der schon die
    Integration des Bösen behandelt.

p.17, 17.Zeile von oben: Neutr. καλὸν κἀγαθόν , kalon k'agathon.
    18. "   "   " : Statt "Frommheit" Frömmigkeit.

p.19, 6.Zeile von oben: (z.B. die Ausübung der Sex.) würde ich streichen.

p.25, 2.Alinea: (Der Schatten repräsentiert Minderwertigkeit in jeder
    Hinsicht, nicht nur Körper, sondern auch "Geist".)

p.35, 8.Zeile v.unten: (Der abgespaltene Inhalt verbindet sich nicht nur
    mit Negativem, sondern auch mit Positivem im Unbewussten. Reculer
    pour mieux sauter!)

p.36, 5.Zeile von oben. Das Unbewusste an sich ist nicht "anti-ethisch",
    sondern bloss amoralisch, weil reine Natur. "Anti" überhaupt
    ist nur das persönliche Unbewusste, auch gegen bewusste Unmoral.

p.46 oben: Die "alte Ethik" ist zum Teil schuld an der Negierung des
    Schattens, zum Teil besteht aber ein natürliches penchant nach
    der Seite des Lichtes. (Heliotropismus des Menschen.)

Appendix. Jung's correction of Neumann's *New Ethic* (JA).

Appendix II

[C. G. Jung: Corrections and amendments to Erich Neumann's *New Ethic* (attachment to letter 75 J, 29 March 1949):]

(NEUMANN: Ethic.)

Preliminary Remarks

Please understand the propositions that follow only as supplementary suggestions. They do not seek to *replace* your text but only to supplement it. This, particularly where you express yourself in a rather activist way. I do not wish to discourage the activism, but simply to emphasize that the shadow or the unconscious absolutely cannot be eliminated and subject to consciousness. We can only learn how a grain of corn must behave between a hammer and anvil.

Title:	The Ethical Aspect of Depth Psychology, or The Problem of Ethics in Modern Psychology, or Ethos and Perception, or Consciousness and Conscience.
p. 5 bottom:	... and darkens the sky with atomic bombs and dictatorial mass de-soulment.
p. 6:	Tel Aviv, Israel
p. 8 top	6th line: ... has shown itself to be incapable.
	Last line: (I have convinced myself in situ that the missionaries are attempting the "emancipation" of the colored primitives, with catastrophic results. It is

impossible to afford the *children* the same rights as the adults. That takes time.)

p. 9   13th line from top: Instead of "invalidity" *ineffectiveness*. P. 11 you speak yourself of the fact that the "old ethic" has absorbed the opposing forces.

p. 10   10th line from top: The "old ethic" is ineffective, but not necessarily *invalid*.

p. 13, 14th line from top: *100* years or more

19th line from top: Before Nietzsche there was *Faust* who already explored the integration of evil.

p. 17, 17th line from top: Neuter: καλόν κ'αγαθόν, kalo*n* k'agatho*n*.[602]

18th line from top: Instead of "piety," devoutness

p. 19   6th line from top: I would delete: (E.g., the practice of sex.)

p. 25   2nd para: (The shadow represents *inferiority in every respect*, not only body but also "spirit."

p. 35   8th line from bottom: (The split off content joins with not only the negative but also with the positive in the unconscious. *Reculer pour mieux sauter*! Draw back in order to jump farther!)

p. 36   5th line from top. The unconscious *per se* is not "anti-ethical," but simply *amoral*, because pure nature. Only the personal unconscious is altogether "Anti," even toward the consciously immoral.

p. 46   Top: The "old ethic" is *in part* guilty of the negation of the shadow, but in part there is a natural penchant for the side of light. (Heliotropism of man.)

p. 52 bottom: (The splitting into opposites is also an inescapable precondition of the development of consciousness, as is the disengagement from the unconscious.)

p. 54, 2nd para: (Imprecise representation: It is the *unconsciousness* of the individual and the *uncontrollability* of the drives which is immoral, not these themselves. *Concupiscentia*[603] and *superbia*[604] with Augustine, not

---

[602] *kalon k'agathon*, Greek for "the beauty and the good."

[603] *Concupiscentia*, Latin for longing or desire.

[604] *Superbia*, Latin for pride.

sexuality and power. Obsession is evil, not the natural forces per se. See line 3 from below: "being pre-ethically driven"—sin.)

p. 59   5th line from bottom: (The Oxford Group Movement[605] and "group analysis" as practiced in England and America belong here.)

p. 60   2nd para: (Hist. stratification of society from the cave dweller of 7000 B.C. until future man of 3000 A.D. Different levels of ethics needed to comprehend all.)

p. 68   8th line from bottom: (The other leitmotif of depth psychology is: "That is not you," e.g., the anima or the Self, etc.)

p. 83   10th line from bottom: (The word "absolute" displeases me. The "new" ethic is "more absolute" without being absolute because we are still unconscious to an inestimable degree.) Perhaps the adjective "new" will suffice.

p. 84,   Last para: (No one can "come to terms with" the shadow problem. That would imply a superhuman. One can firstly only be conscious of the shadow and suffer and bear it. "Come to terms with" would mean as much as being "liberated." Choice, decision, follow only after painful recognition of the inferiority. Only out of this arises the possibility of "processing" the shadow, without its ever being got rid of.)

P. 92   8th line from bottom: *a structure is to be created*: (If some such thing exists, then *we* certainly do not "make" it. It grows or evolves—concedente Deo. Through the collision of the opposites, an irrational third *is generated* from experience, which *we could never make!* It reveals itself in dreams, e.g., see *Psychology and Alchemy*.)

p. 93   7th line from top: (Here you simply propose the *democratization and parliamentary structure* of the personality. Quite right, if it's possible. The ego as "master" only

---

[605] *Oxford Group*, Christian organization, founded in 1921 by Frank Buchmann as "A First Century Christian Fellowship," which later became known as the "Oxford Group."

conditionally correct. In fact it is the Self, although
the ego is the location of the decisive showdown.)

10th line from bottom: "Processing and application of the
negative energies." (This formulation arouses the
curiosity of the reader far too much and he will then
sadly miss your more precise instructions. What *is
supposed to* happen is mostly quite clear, but, as a rule,
the ethicist does not reveal the *how* to us. It is precisely this that the reader wishes to know. At least the
old ethic said: "that isn't done." The new ethic should
say what one should do with the negative energies.
Process them? Application? But how? To this process
the individual can only contribute intelligence,
attention, good will, submissiveness, humility, willingness to suffer etc. That should probably be clearly
said somewhere.)

p. 95 top: "to live the evil" (As a freely chosen activity either highly
immoral or impossible. In reality it is really a matter
of a "meaningful suffering," a courageously borne
defeat, a humiliating disgrace, a none too good
conscience which one does not like to compare with
someone else and which is better than an innocence
which burdens others, etc.)

"incorporate the evil"—(Impossible. It incorporates itself
right in, if not directly, then indirectly. The question
is: "*How* can one bear it?")

p. 96   8th line from top: Instead of "necessity," *unavoidability*.

14th line from top: Necessities (just like unavoidabilities)
of the individual which are *often* (or occasionally) in
conflict, etc.

19th line: (The voice demands that *something* be done, but
not "evil." *We* name it thus. The voice finds its suggestion quite acceptable. See Paul: "the evil which I
would not do, that I do."[606])

---

[606] Romans 7:19. "For the good that I would I do not: but the evil which I would not, that I
do" (KJB).

P. 97   2nd para: (In the face of the "evil" we are considering, one has absolutely no free choice. To our horror, it simply *happens* to us. One can only suffer it because we cannot even delude ourselves that it would be possible to avoid it. Only after this recognition can a choice concerning one's own behavior be made.)

4th line from bottom: "at the risk that a fantastical or indirect substitute occurs" (instead of "the affected man").

p. 99 top *"The plethora etc., makes any theoretical definition of an ethical way of behaving impossible."* (This sentence is ominous and carries serious consequences and should be highlighted in spaced letters. In verification of this sentence you would have to avoid any expressions like "must, should, require, process, apply, incorporate, create, choose, give up etc."; for it is then impossible to define, for example, the recognition of the shadow as an ethical way of behaving) (C./f., p. 105). I fear you are contradicting yourself here. In any case, it would seem to me that a comprehensive *clarification* is necessary that, despite the above statement, it is not only possible but is even indicated that out of the experiences of psychology certain ways of behaving as ethical points of view at least to be approximately determined. This is the minimum that one may expect, not in fact from *ethos*, but rather from an *ethic*.

12th line from bottom: The "ambiguity of the inner experience" is in my opinion not "chosen," but is the thing that remains from the catastrophe of the old ethic! One does not have anything else.

p. 101 12th line from bottom: "The courage of individual judgment ... one of the most difficult demands of the new ethic." (Actually as yet nothing is demanded, especially nothing ethical, but there is nothing else left to one than to find some sort of subjective way out of the blasted hole one has landed in.)

p. 102   3rd line from top: instead of "processed" *suffered*. (It
sounds as if we could pluck the stems from every
cherry, or should be able to. If something turns out
well, then per gratiam, or through an appropriate
attitude.)

p. 104   14th line from bottom: Claims about the penal system in
Russia are unprovable and therefore only have the
merit of rumors. Better deleted!

p. 105   3rd para. (Here the expressions "good" and "evil" actually
lose their meaning. The formulation is becoming
confusing and sounds exaggerated. Good and evil are
the fundamental concepts of the old ethic and are
only applicable in its domain. In a new ethic, it
would be better to replace them with terms like
appropriate-inappropriate, right-wrong, expedient-
inexpedient, conducive–non-conducive, etc. The old
ethic is something like classical physics, the so-called
macrophysics; the new ethic is no longer absolute, but
rather, it is relative because of the inclusion of the
unconscious, and therefore can be compared with
microphysics, which knows no absolute laws but
only statistical probabilities. Also one could not say
quite what one could designate as "good" or "evil."
The principles of the old ethic can also all get turned
upside down in the subjective arena of the new ethic,
like, by the way, your new-ethical formulas. The
repression of evil, for example, does not always need
to be "evil," but can be "good" when in a certain case a
difficulty can only be removed in this way. The
"good" of the new ethic is not to be used without
quotation marks.) (C./f., also p. 119, line 2 ff. from
top.)

p. 107   "Holiness." (We know nothing that could not become a
"duty." Even celibacy or sexual continence can be
unavoidable in certain cases and a "task." In this case,
no indirect consequences would be expected. I have
seen so much that is remarkable that, in this respect, I

carefully reserve my judgment. I would also recommend some qualifications here.)

p. 108   Last para. (Evil is in fact never assented to, rather one is struck by it; it is suffered. Equally, the totality accrues to us fatefully. One cannot assent to it, for one is never acquainted with it. It is transcendent. But all this does not release us from the effort of finding that attitude which makes it possible for the unconscious to unite with consciousness.)

p. 109   2nd line from top: *Self* spacing!

p. 111   2nd line from bottom: instead of "foreign ethic" perhaps *"an externally applied yardstick."*

p. 112   9th line from top: (The "primary moral experience of primitive man" is *fabled*, i.e., one knows nothing about it. Inferences from our psychology about the primitive psyche are *very* reckless and seldom correct.)

p. 113   Line 7 ff. from the top: (Doubtful, because only patriarchal.)

p. 114   17th line from top: (The "voice" only has a partial "son" character. Very often, even as a rule, it is in fact "another" father.—Jesus to his mother: "I am in that which is of my father."[607] Or: *Psychol. and Alchemy* in the sense of a voice. For sure, the one who hears the voice is always the son.)

p. 115   12th line from top: (The Self cannot be "deployed." It deploys itself, for it is the totality of autonomous nature, superordinate to us; as one also cannot deploy God. One cannot "orientate" oneself to the Self, for one does not know it. We are orientated by it. C/f p. 115, 3rd line from bottom: autonomous compensation, also p.116, 1st para: "The totality asserts itself.")

p. 119   1st para: "The inclusion of the negative" (is a patiently or courageously borne defeat rather than an ethical

---

[607] Luke 2:49. "And he said unto them, How is it that ye sought me? wist ye not that I must be about my Father's business?" (KJB).

achievement. One should not be too proud of this;
otherwise, one turns black into white and becomes a
Pharisee.)

p. 125   1st para: "Beyond good and evil!" (For sure, this would be
an inflation, it seems to me. One will always suffer
this conflict, unless one can completely do away with
ethos and utterly destroy the foundation of life
energy, namely, the pairs of opposites. *Nirdvandva*
[freedom from duality] is Samadhi, *the goal of yoga.*)

p. 128   Last line: Delete "human."

It seems to me to be indicated that you should clarify even more
clearly what you understand by "voice." There are after all different
voices, even that of the evil spirit—probate spiritus![608] One also
speaks of the voice of conscience. Here the reader can easily get
confused.

The new ethical problem can probably not be dealt with by itself
since it is always connected with the transformation of the drive by
the *symbol.* Thus, the shadow can *never* be integrated by means of an
ethical decision, for it requires in addition the auxiliary energies of
the archetype. For this reason, you should really take this aspect of
the problem into consideration, because otherwise you unavoidably
fall back once again into the old ethic, namely, into the voluntaristic
decision, which has just been recognized as ineffectual. The shadow
can be integrated by means of two mutually complementary methods: by means of moral decision *plus* ritual action, based on the symbol. One cannot command the drive without repressing it; for this
reason, it must be transformed through the symbol (archetype) that
is presented by the unconscious. The confrontation with the shadow
puts you in an irresolvable difficulty, which you may wish to resolve,
but cannot. Now, the unconscious produces the archetype that per-
tains to this situation in whose numinosity the auxiliary energies are
situated. Out of this arises the "ritual" action, i.e., a way of behaving

---

[608] John 4:1. "Beloved, believe not every spirit, but *try the spirits* whether they are of God: because many false prophets are gone out into the world" (KJB) ("Carissimi nolite omni spiritui
credere sed *probate spiritus* si ex Deo sint quoniam multi pseudoprophetae exierunt in
mundum.")

that is sanctified by the archetype and elevated in the spiritual collective. One then acts as *Altjirangamitjiwia*,[609] i.e., as anthropos, and no longer as a civilian. One acts *in mysterium*. This is the ancient cathartic cultic action that is initiated through purification (consecration) and compensated through sacrifice, but exercised not in the collective but in the individual domain.

Your notion of the Judeo-Christian ethic requires critique. You locate yourself predominantly from the standpoint of the old testament ethic and less on that of the Hasidic one (in this text). What is Christian about it is entirely limited to a certain modern aspect of Protestantism, namely, that which is only ethic and which has, as it were, completely forfeited the symbol, to say nothing at all of ritual. You altogether ignore Catholic psychology. But it is precisely there that the sources of my conception of the symbol are situated.

The *shadow* needs to be qualified better and in more detail. It is not only the repressed negative, but in some cases even the repressed positive, not only the personal unconscious, but it extends into the conflicting nature of God. Therefore, it cannot be mastered simply by means of my decision from afar, otherwise I could coerce God. (I can do this however, but only with His will [symbolism]!)

You should really explain thoroughly at the beginning that your discussion *confines itself to the ethical aspect of the shadow problem without considering in the slightest the question of integration*. Your portrayal really does not explore how the shadow can be integrated by means of an ethical decision without its being repressed.

---

[609] *Altjiringa mitjina*, "the eternal dream-time" or "the Dreaming," refers in the mythology of some Australian Aborigines to a concept of sacred time or belonging to the Gods.

Bibliography

Abbreviations

AJP   Aniela Jaffé Papers, ETH Zurich University Archives, Swiss
      Federal Institute of Technology
CFB   Cary F. Baynes Papers, Contemporary Medical Archives,
      Wellcome Trust Library for the History and Understanding
      of Medicine, London.
CW   *The Collected Works of C. G. Jung*, edited by Sir Herbert Read,
      Michael Fordham, and Gerhard Adler; William McGuire,
      executive editor; trans. R.F.C. Hull (New York and Prince-
      ton, Bollingen Series 20, and London, 1953–83), 21 vols.
DLA   Deutsches Literaturarchiv Marbach.
EA   Eranos Archive, Ascona.
GEA   German Exile Archive, 1933–45, German National Library,
      Frankfurt am Main.
GW   C. G. Jung, *Gesammelte Werke*, edited by Lena Hurwitz-
      Eisner, Lilly Jung-Merker, Marianne Niehus-Jung, Franz
      Riklin, Elisabeth Rüf, and Leonie Zander (Zurich and
      Stuttgart: Rascher and Olten, Walter, 1958–94).
JA   C.G. Jung Papers Collection, ETH Zurich University
      Archives, Swiss Federal Institute of Technology
JFA   Jung Family Archive, Küsnacht.
KJB   King James Bible.
LC   Library of Congress, Washington, DC.
MFP   Michael Fordham Papers, Contemporary Medical Archives,
      Wellcome Library, London.

NP   Neumann Papers: Private collection, Rali Loewenthal-Neumann, Jerusalem.

RA   Rascher & Cie (publisher's archive), 1910–70: Zentralbibliothek, Zurich.

RKP   Records of Routledge and Kegan Paul, Special Collections, University of Reading.

LITERATURE

Abramovitch, Henry (2006): "'Erich Neumann as My Supervisor: An Interview with Dvora Kutzinski," *Harvest: International Journal for Jungian Studies* 52, no. 2, pp. 162–81.

———, and Marion Badrian (2006): "Ne've Ze'elim Children's Home: A Unique Long-Term Treatment Centre Inspired by the Teachings of Erich Neumann," *Harvest: International Journal for Jungian Studies* 52, no. 2, pp. 182–99.

Abrams, Samuel (1983): "Max H. Stern," *International Review of Psycho-Analysis* 10, p. 367.

Adler, Gerhard (1934): "Ist Jung Antisemit?" *Jüdische Rundschau* 62, 3 August, p. 2.

———(1948): *Studies in Analytical Psychology* (London: Routledge and Kegan Paul).

———(1959). "The First International Congress for Analytical Psychology," *Journal of Analytical Psychology* 4, pp. 187–89.

———(1961): *The Living Symbol* (New York: Pantheon Books).

———(1961a) (ed.): *Current Trends in Analytical Psychology: Proceedings of the First International Congress for Analytical Psychology* (London: Tavistock Publications).

———(1980): "Erich Neumann: 1905–1960," in *Kreativität des Unbewussten. Zum 75. Geburtstag von Erich Neumann (1905–1960)*, ed. H. Dieckmann, C. A. Meier, and H. J. Wilke (Basel: S. Karger), pp. 9–14. (= Special edition of *Analytical Psychology* 2, nos. 3–4, pp. 181–86).

Agassi, Judith Buber (1999): *Martin Buber on Psychology and Psychotherapy* (Syracuse, NY: Syracuse University Press).

Analytische Psychologie: Zeitschrift für Psychotherapie und Psychoanalyse (2008): *Erich Neumann*, 151, no. 1.

Arendt, Hannah (2002): *Denktagebuch*, ed. Ursula Ludz and Inge-borg Nordmann, 2 vols. (Munich: Piper).

———, and Martin Heidegger (1999): *Briefe 1925 bis 1975 und andere Zeugnisse*, ed. Ursula Ludz, 2nd ed., durchgesehene Auflage (Frankfurt: Vittorio Klostermann).

Astor, James (1995): *Michael Fordham: Innovations in Analytical Psychology* (London: Routledge).

Attenhofer, Elsie (1975): *Ein Zürcher Wandteppich: Erinnerungen von Elsie Attenhofer*, copy of an undated newspaper article in the archive of the Psychological Club, Zurich.

Avalon, Arthur [Sir John Woodroffe] (1919): *The Serpent Power, Being the Sat-Cakra-Nirupana and Paduka-Pancaka: Two Works on Laya-Yoga*, translated from the Sanskrit, with introduction and commentary by Arthur Avalon (London: Luzac).

Baechi, Walter (1936): "Der Mordfall Näf: Das Revisionsgesuch vom 28. Februar 1936" (Zurich: Aschmann and Scheller).

———(1940): "Der Mordfall Näf-Zürich. Verurteilung im Schwurgerichtsverfahren. Freispruch und 25000 Franken Entschädigung im Wiederaufnahmeverfahren. Von Rechtsanwalt Dr. W. Baechi," *Archiv für Kriminologie* 107, nos. 1/2.

Bailey, Ruth (1969–70): *Unpublished Oral Interviews with Miss Ruth Bailey* (Gene F. Nameche, interviewer). Archived in the "C. G. Jung Biographical Archive" at the Countway Library of Medicine at Harvard University.

Bally, Gustav (1934): "Deutschstämmige Therapie" ("Therapy of German Descent"), *Neue Zürcher Zeitung*, no. 343, 27 February.

———(1945): *Vom Ursprung und den Grenzen der Freiheit: Eine Deutung des Spiels bei Tier und Mensch* (*On the Scope of Freedom*) (Basel: Schwabe).

———(1961): *Einführung in die Psychoanalyse Sigmund Freuds* (*Introduction to the Psychoanalysis of Sigmund Freud*) (Reinbek: Rowohlt).

Baynes, Helton Godwin "Peter" (1940): *Mythology of the Soul: A Research into the Unconscious from Schizophrenic Dreams and Drawings* (London: Baillière, Tindall and Cox).

———(1941): *Germany Possessed: With an Introduction by Hermann Rauschning* (London: Jonathan Cape).

Baynes-Jansen, Diana (2003): *Jung's Apprentice: A Biography of Helton Godwin Baynes* (Einsiedeln: Daimon).

Bin-Gorion, Micha Josef (1913): *Die Sagen der Juden: Von der Urzeit*, collected and edited by Micha Josef Bin-Gorion, 2nd revised and extended edition (Frankfurt am Main: Rütten and Loening).

———(1919): *Die Sagen der Juden: Die Erzväter*, collected and edited by Micha Josef Bin-Gorion, 2nd revised and extended edition (Frankfurt am Main: Rütten and Loening).

Bernardini, Riccardo, Gian Piero Quaglino, and Augusto Romano (2011): "A Visit Paid to Jung by Alwine von Keller," *Journal of Analytical Psychology* 56, pp. 232–54.

Bishop, Paul (1996): "'Jung-Joseph': Thomas Mann's Reception of Jungian Thought in the 'Joseph' Tetralogy," *Modern Language Review* 91, no. 1, pp. 138–58.

———(1999): "Thomas Mann und C. G Jung," in *Jung in Context*, ed. P. Bishop (New York: Routledge), pp. 154–91.

———(2002): *Jung's Answer to Job: A Commentary* (Hove, East Sussex; New York: Routledge).

———(2009): *Analytical Psychology and German Classical Aesthetics: Goethe, Schiller, and Jung*, vol. 2: *The Constellation of the Self* (Hove, East Sussex; New York: Routledge).

Blau-Weiss Liederbuch (1914): edited by Führerschaft des Jüdischen Wanderbundes Blau-Weiss Berlin (Berlin: *Jüdischer Verlag)*.

Braband-Isaac, Margarete (1949): "Psychotherapie und Gymnastik" ("Psychotherapy and Gymnastic"), *Schweizer Zeitschrift für Psychologie und ihre Anwendungen* 8, no. 4.

———(1952): "Musik in der Psychotherapie" ("Music in Psychotherapy"), *Schweizer Musikpaedagogische Blätter* 13 (October).

Brauen, Martin (1998): *The Mandala: Sacred Circle in Tibetan Buddhism* (Boston and London: Shambhala).

Broek, Roelof van den, and Maarten J. Vermaseren (1981) (eds.): *Studies in Gnosticism and Hellenistic Religions: Presented to Gilles Quispel on the Occasion of His 65th Birthday* (Leiden: Etudes Preliminaires aux Religions Orientales dans l'Empire Romain).

Buber, Martin (1906): *Die Geschichten des Rabbi Nachman (The Tales of Rabbi Nachman)*, (Frankfurt am Main: Rütten and Loening).

———(1907): *Die Legende des Baal Schem* (*The Legend of Baal-Shem*) (Frankfurt am Main: Rütten and Loening).

———(1928): *Die chassidischen Bücher* (Berlin: Schockenverlag; Hellerau: Jakob Hegner).

———(1923): *Ich und Du* (Leipzig: Insel); English translation as *I and Thou* (New York: Charles Scribner's Sons, 1937).

———(1934): "Sinnbildliche und sakramentale Existenz des Judentums," in *Ostwestliche Symbolik und Seelenführung*, Eranos Yearbook 2 (Zurich: Rhein), pp. 339–67; English translation by Maurice Friedman, in Buber: *The Origin and Meaning of Hasidism* (New York: Horizon Press, 1960), pp. 151–81.

———(1935): *Hundert chassidische Geschichten* (Berlin: Schocken Verlag).

———(1949): *Die Erzählungen der Chassidim* (Zurich: Manesse); English translation as *Tales of the Hasidim*, by Olga Marx: vol. 1: *The Early Masters* (New York: Schocken, 1947); vol. 2: The Late Masters (New York: Schocken, 1948).

———(1952): "Religion und modernes Denken," *Merkur* 6, no. 2; reprinted in M. Buber, Werke, 3 vols., Munich: Kösel-Verlag, 1962–64, vol. 1, pp. 550–74; reprinted in English as "Religion and Modern Thinking," in *Eclipse of God: Studies in the Relation between Religion and Philosophy*, trans. Maurice Friedman (Atlantic Highlands, NJ: International Humanities Press, 1988), pp. 65–92.

———(1967): "On the Psychologizing of the World," in *A Believing Humanism: My Testament, 1902–1965*, translation and introduction by Maurice Friedman (New York: Simon and Schuster), pp. 144–52.

———, and Erich Neumann (1935): unpublished letter from Martin Buber to Erich Neumann, 13 November. Sold at Sotheby's in 2006. See "Music and Continental Manuscripts" (London: 30 November 2006), p. 128.

———, and Franz Rosenzweig (1991): *Die Schrift*. Aus dem Hebräischen verdeutscht von Martin Buber gemeinsam mit Franz Rosenzweig, 4 vols. (Stuttgart: Deutsche Bibelgesellschaft).

Bucher, Zeno (1946): *Die Innenwelt der Atome: Die Ergebnisse der Atomphysik naturphilosophisch bearbeitet* (Graz: Stocker).

Chamberlin, J. Maxwell (1956): "Jung and Christianity," *Pastoral Psychology* 7, no. 4, p. 54.

Clark, Walter Houston (1958): "Review of Carl Gustav Jung *The Undiscovered Self*," *Pastoral Psychology* 9, no. 5, pp. 61–62.

Cocks, Geoffrey Campbell (1975): "Psyche and Swastika: 'Neue Deutsche Seelenheilkunde,' 1933–1945" (PhD diss., University of California, Los Angeles).

———(1991): "The Nazis and C. G. Jung," in *Lingering Shadows*, ed. A. Maidenbaum and S. Martin (Boston: Shambhala), pp. 157–65.

———(1997): *Psychotherapy in the Third Reich: The Göring Institute*, 2nd ed. (New York: Oxford University Press).

Coward, Harold (1985): *Jung and Eastern Thought* (Albany: State University of New York Press).

———(1996): "Taoism and Jung: Synchronicity and the Self," *Philosophy East and West* 46, no. 4, pp. 477–95.

Creuzer, Georg Friedrich (1810–12): *Symbolik und Mythologie der alten Völker, besonders der Griechen*, 4 vols (Leipzig; Darmstadt: Leske [vols. 1 and 2]; Heyer and Leske [vols. 3 and 4]); second revised edition, continued from volume 5 by Franz Joseph Mone, 1819–23.

Cunningham, Adrian (2007): "Victor White: A Memoir," in *The Jung-White Letters*, ed. Ann Conrad Lammers and Adrian Cunningham, consulting ed. Murray Stein, Philemon Series (London and New York: Routledge), pp. 307–36.

Dan, Joseph (1999): *Jewish Mysticism*, vol. 3: *The Modern Period* (Northvale, NJ: Jason Aronson).

———(2007): *Kabbalah: A Very Short Introduction* (Oxford: Oxford University Press).

Dawkins, Richard (2010): Afterword to Fred Hoyle, *The Black Cloud* (London: Penguin), pp. 211–15.

Diels, Hermann, and Walther Kranz (1951–53): *Die Fragmente der Vorsokratiker: Griechisch und Deutsch*, ed. Walther Kranz, 6th rev. ed., 3 vols. (Berlin: Weidmann).

Dieterich, Albrecht (1903): *Eine Mithrasliturgie* (Leipzig: B. G. Teubner).

Dixon, Patricia (1999): *Nietzsche and Jung: Sailing a Deeper Night*, Contemporary Existentialism, vol. 3 (New York: Peter Lang).

Dohe, Carrie B. (2011): "Wotan and the 'Archetypal Ergriffenheit': Mystical Union, National Spiritual Rebirth, and Culture-Creating Capacity in C. G. Jung's 'Wotan' Essay," *History of European Ideas* 37, pp. 344–56.

Dreifuss, Gustav (1980): "Erich Neumanns jüdisches Bewusstsein," in *Kreativität des Unbewussten. Zum 75. Geburtstag von Erich Neumann (1905–1960)*, ed. H. Dieckmann, C. A. Meier, and H. J. Wilke (Basel: S. Karger, 1980), pp. 67–77 (= special edition of *Analytical Psychology* 2, nos. 3–4, pp. 239–47).

———(1988): "Obituary Rivkah Schärf Kluger," *Journal of Analytical Psychology* 33, pp. 301–2.

Droysen, Johann Gustav (1833): *Geschichte Alexander des Großen* (Hamburg: Friedrich Perthes).

Edinger, Edward (1996): *The Aion Lectures* (Toronto: Inner City Books).

Eliade, Mircea (1989): *Journal II (1957–1969)*, translated from French by Fred H. Johnson Jr. (Chicago: University of Chicago Press).

Engels, Friedrich (1877–78): *Anti-Dühring: Herr Eugen Dühring's Revolution in Science* (Chicago: Charles H. Kerr, 1935).

Eusebius (1890): *Church History*, trans. Arthur Cushman McGiffert. Nicene and Post-Nicene Fathers, Second Series, Vol. 1, ed. Philip Schaff and Henry Wace (Buffalo, NY: Christian Literature Publishing).

———(1913): *Des Eusebius Pamphili, Bischofs von Cäsarea, ausgewählte Schriften. Einleitung von Andreas Bigelmair* (Kempten; Munich: Kösel).

———(1998): *Eusebius—The Church History: A New Translation with Commentary*, by Paul L. Maier (Grand Rapids, MI: Kregel Publications).

Feuerstein, Georg (1997): *The Shambhala Encyclopedia of Yoga* (Boston and London: Shambhala).

Fordham, Michael (1944): *The Life of Childhood: A Contribution to Analytical Psychology* (London: Kegan Paul, Trench, Trubner).

———(1957): *New Developments in Analytical Psychology* (London: Routledge and Kegan Paul).

———(1957a): Review of "M. Klein, P. Heimann, and R. Money-Kyrle (eds.): *New Directions in Psycho-Analysis*," *Journal of Analytical Psychology* 2, pp. 195–200.

Fordham, Michael (1958): *The Objective Psyche* (London: Routledge and Kegan Paul).

———(1976): *The Self and Autism* (London: William Heinemann Medical Books).

———(1981): "Neumann and Childhood," *Journal of Analytical Psychology* 26, pp. 99–122.

———(1993): *The Making of an Analyst: A Memoir* (London: Free Association Books).

Franz, Marie-Louise von (1957): *Aurora Consurgens: Ein dem Thomas von Aquin zugeschriebenes Dokument der alchemistischen Gegensatzproblematik.* (= *Mysterium Coniunctionis* III), Psychologische Abhandlungen, vol. 7 (Zurich: Rascher).

———(1970): *A Psychological Interpretation of the Golden Ass of Apuleius* (New York: Spring Publications, 1970); German as *Die Erlösung des Weiblichen im Manne: Der Goldene Esel des Apuleius in tiefenpsychologischer Sicht* (Zurich: Walter, 1980).

Fröbe-Kapteyn, Olga (1957) (ed.): *25 Jahre Eranos, 1933–1957* (Zurich: Rhein Verlag).

Gauger, Kurt (1934): *Politische Medizin: Grundriß einer deutschen Psychotherapie* (Hamburg: Hanseatische Verlags-Anstalt).

———(1941): *Christoph: Roman einer Seefahrt* (Stuttgart: Hohenstaufen Verlag).

———(1943): *Herz und Anker: Seemannsgeschichten* (Stuttgart: Hohenstaufen Verlag).

Giegerich, Wolfgang (1975): "Ontogeny = Phylogeny? A Fundamental Critique of Erich Neumann's Analytical Psychology," *Spring: An Annual of Archetypal Psychology and Jungian Thought*, pp. 110–29.

Gilbert, Martin (2006): *Kristallnacht: Prelude to Destruction* (New York: Harper Collins).

———(2008): *Israel: A History*, revised and updated edition (New York: Harper Perennial).

Glover, Edward (1939): *Psycho-Analysis* (London: John Bale Medical Publication).

———(1950): *Freud or Jung*, with a foreword by James William Anderson (London: George Allen and Unwin).

————(1955): *The Technique of Psycho-Analysis* (London: Baillière, Tindall and Cox).

Goethe, Johann Wolfgang (1806): *Stella: Ein Schauspiel für Liebende*, in *Werke* (= Hamburger Ausgabe), vol. 4 (Munich: C. H. Beck, 1981[10]), pp. 306–51.

————(1819): *West-Östlicher Divan* (Stuttgart: Cotta'sche Verlagsbuchhandlung); again in *Werke* (= Hamburger Ausgabe), vol. 2 (Munich: C. H. Beck, 1981[12]), pp. 7–270; English translation by Edward Dowden: *West-Eastern Divan* (London: Dent and Sons, 1914).

————(1833): *Faust. Der Tragödie zweyter Theil in fünf Acten* (Stuttgart; Tübingen: Cotta'sche Verlagsbuchhandlung); again in *Werke* (= Hamburger Ausgabe), vol. 3 (Munich: C. H. Beck, 1981[12]), pp. 146–364; English translation by Philip Wayne: *Faust: Part Two* (Harmondsworth: Penguin Books, 1959).

————, and Friedrich Schiller (1794–1805): *Briefwechsel zwischen Schiller und Goethe in den Jahren 1794 bis 1805*, ed. Manfred Beetz, *Sämtliche Werke nach Epochen seines Schaffens* (= Münchener Ausgabe), vol. 8, 1–2 (Munich: C. H. Hanser, 1990); *Correspondence between Goethe and Schiller, 1794–1805,* trans. Liselotte Dieckmann (New York: Peter Lang, 1994).

Goldberg, Oskar (1925): *Die Wirklichkeit der Hebräer: Einführung in das System des Pentateuch* (Berlin: Verlag David).

Guyer, Lux et al. (1946): *Die Frau als Schöpferin und Bewahrerin von Kulturgut* (*The Woman as Creator and Custodian of Cultural Artifacts*), catalog of the exhibition in the Helmhaus Zurich, 8 September 1946–2 October 1946 (Zurich: Bühler).

Harding, Esther (1935): *Woman's Mysteries, Ancient and Modern: A Psychological Interpretation of the Feminine Principle as Portrayed in Myth, Story, and Dreams* (New York: Longmans Green).

Hannah, Barbara (1934–41) (ed.): *Modern Psychology: Notes on Lectures Given at the Eidgenössischen Technischen Hochschule, Zürich, by Prof. Dr. C. G. Jung*, October 1933–July 1941, compiled and translated by Elizabeth Welsh and Barbara Hannah, 3 vols (Zurich: privately published).

————(1976): *Jung: His Life and Work* (New York: G. Putnam's Sons).

Harms, Ernest (Ernst) (1931): "Die Struktur des religiösen Menschen," *Zeitschrift für Religionspsychologie* 4 (Dresden).

————(1931a): "Zur Pädagogik der Psychologie," *Psychologische Rundschau* 3, no. 3 (Basel).

————(1933): *Hegel und das zwanzigste Jahrhundert*, Beiträge zur Philosophie 24 (Heidelberg: Carl Winter).

————(1939): *Psychologie und Psychiatrie der Conversion*, with a foreword by J. van der Spek (Leiden: Sijthoff).

————(1946): "Jung: Defender of Freud and Jews; a Chapter of European Psychiatric History under the Nazi Yoke," *Psychiatric Quarterly* 20 (April), pp. 199–230; again in A. Maidenbaum and S. Martin, *Lingering Shadows* (Boston: Shambhala, 1991), pp. 17–49.

————(1967): *Origins of Modern Psychiatry* (Springfield: Charles Thomas).

Harnack, Adolf von (1886–90): *Lehrbuch der Dogmengeschichte* (Tübingen: Mohr); English translation by Neil Buchanan: *History of Dogma* (London: William and Norgate, 1894–99).

————(1921) *Marcion: Das Evangelium vom fremden Gott. Eine Monographie zur Geschichte der Grundlegung der katholischen Kirche* (Leipzig: J. C. Hinrichs); English translation by John E. Steely and Lyle D. Bierma: *Marcion: The Gospel of the Alien God* (Jamestown, NY: Labyrinth Press, 1990).

————(1923) *Neue Studien zu Marcion* (Leipzig: J. C. Hinrichs).

Harvest (2006): *Special Thematic Issue: On Erich Neumann*, guest editor: Henry Abramovich, *Harvest: International Journal for Jungian Studies*, ed. Renos Papadopoulos, vol. 52, no. 2.

Heidegger, Martin (1927): *Sein und Zeit, Jahrbuch für Philosophie und phänomenologische Forschung*, vol. 8, ed. Edmund Husserl (Halle an der Saale: Niemeyer); English translation by John Macquarrie and Edward Robinson as *Being and Time* (London: SCM Press, 1962); retranslated by Joan Stambaugh (Albany: State University of New York Press, 1996).

————(1933): "Die Selbstbehauptung der deutschen Universität" (Breisgau: Wilhelm Gottlieb Korn); English translation by K. Harries as "The Self-Assertion of the German University," *Review of Metaphysics* 38 (1985), pp. 470–80.

Heine, Heinrich (1840): *Ludwig Börne: Eine Denkschrift*, in *Heinrich Heine: Säkularausgabe. Werke, Briefwechsel, Lebenszeugnisse*, ed. Nationalen Forschungs- und Gedenkstätten der klassischen deutschen Literatur in Weimar and Centre National de la Recherche Scientifique in Paris, vol. 9 (Berlin: Akademie-Verlag, 1970–); English translation by Jeffrey L. Sammons as *Ludwig Börne: A Memorial* (Rochester, NY: Camden House, 2006).

Herzl, Theodor (1896): *Der Judenstaat: Versuch einer modernen Lösung der Judenfrage* (Leipzig; Vienna: M. Breitenstein's Verlagsbuchhandlung); English translation by Sylvie d'Avigdor as *The Jewish State* (London: Nutt, 1896).

Hiltner, Seward (1956): "Editorial: Carl Gustav Jung," *Pastoral Psychology* 6, no. 10, pp. 78–79.

———(1956a): "*Answer to Job* by Carl Gustav Jung," *Pastoral Psychology* 6, no 10, pp. 82–83.

———(1956b): "Jung and Symbols," *Pastoral Psychology* 7, no. 4, pp. 55–56.

Hinshaw, Robert, and Paul Kugler (2004): "Walking in the Footsteps of Eranos," *Proceedings of the IAAP Conference in Barcelona 2004*: http://iaap.org/congresses/barcelona-2004/walking-in-the-footsteps-of-eranos.html.

Hoyle, Fred (1950): *The Nature of the Universe: A Series of Broadcast Lectures* (Oxford: Basil Blackwell); German translation as *Die Natur des Universums* (Cologne: Kiepenheuer, 1951).

———(1955): *Frontiers of Astronomy* (London: William Heinemann).

———(1957): *The Black Cloud* (London: William Heinemann).

———(1961): *Ossian's Ride* (London: Four Square Books).

———(1974): *October the First Is Too Late* (Harmondsworth: Penguin).

———(1985): *Comet Halley: A Novel in Two Parts* (London: Joseph).

Hummel, Gerhard (2006): "Ein Sommernachmittag in Grinzing: Thomas Mann bei Sigmund Freud," *Luzifer-Amor* 38, pp. 76–101.

Hurwitz, Siegmund (1952): "Archetypische Motive in der chassidischen Mystik," in Studien aus dem C. G. Jung Institut, vol. 3 (Zurich: Rascher), pp. 121–212; English translation by H. Nagel as "Psychological Aspects in Early Hasidic Literature, in *Timeless Documents of the Soul* (Evanston, IL: Northwestern University Press, 1968), pp. 149–240.

———(1958): *Die Gestalt des sterbenden Messias: Religionspsychologische Aspekte der jüdischen Apokalyptik*, Studien aus dem C. G. Jung Institut, vol. 8 (Zurich: Rascher).

———(1980): *Lilith: Die Erste Eva. Eine Studie über dunkle Aspekte des Weiblichen* (Zurich: Daimon); English translation by Gela Jacobson: *Lilith: The First Eve; Historical and Psychological Aspects of the Dark Feminine* (Zurich: Daimon, 1992).

———(1994): "The Dark Face of God in Judaism," in *Jung and the Monotheisms: Judaism, Christianity, and Islam*, ed. Joel Ryce-Menuhin (London; New York: Routledge, 1994), pp. 45–55.

Huskinson, Lucy (2004): *Nietzsche and Jung: The Whole Self in the Union of Opposites* (Hove; New York: Brunner-Routledge).

"In Memoriam Gustav Bally, 1893–1966" (1967): *American Journal for Psychoanalysis* 27, pp. 95–96.

Jacobi, Jolan[de] (1938): "Das Altern: Versuch einer psychologischen Studie" (PhD diss., University of Vienna).

———(1940): *Die Psychologie von C. G. Jung: Eine Einführung in das Gesamtwerk* (Zurich: Rascher); English translation by K. W. Bash as *The Psychology of C. G. Jung: An Introduction* (New Haven, CT: Yale University Press, 1942).

———(1946): "Der Schattengeliebte und das Rautendelein," *DU: Schweizer Monatsschrift* 11 (November), pp. 19–20, 76.

———(1957): *Komplex, Archetypus, Symbol in der Psychologie C. G. Jung* (Zurich: Rascher); English translation by Ralph Mannheim as *Complex, Archetype, and Symbol in the Psychology of C. G. Jung* (London: Routledge and Paul, 1959).

———(1964): "Symbols in an Individual Analysis," in *Man and His Symbols*, ed. with an introduction by C. G. Jung (London: Aldus), pp. 323–74.

Jacoby, Mario (2005): "Erich Neumanns Konzept der Urbeziehung im Lichte der neueren Kleinkindforschung," in *Zur Utopie einer neuen Ethik: 100 Jahre Erich Neumann. 130 Jahre C.G. Jung*, ed. Österreichische Gesellschaft für Analytische Psychologie (Vienna: Mandelbaum Verlag), pp. 38–48.

Jaffé, Aniela (1950): *Bilder und Symbole aus E.T.A. Hoffmanns Märchen "Der goldne Topf"* (*Images and Symbols in E.T.A. Hoffmann's Fairy Tail "The Golden Pot"*), in *Gestaltungen des Unbewussten*, Psychologische Abhandlungen, vol. 7 (Zurich: Rascher), pp. 239–616; republished: Einsiedeln: Daimon, 1980.

———(1958): *Geisterscheinungen und Vorzeichen: Eine psychologische Deutung. Mit einem Vorwort von C. G. Jung* (Zurich; Stuttgart: Rascher); English translation as *Apparitions and Precognition: A Study from the Point of View of C. G. Jung's Analytical Psychology* (Hyde Park, NY: University Books, 1963).

———(1964): "Symbolism in the Visual Arts," in *Man and His Symbols*, ed. with an introduction by C. G. Jung (London: Aldus), pp. 255–323.

———(1967): *Der Mythus vom Sinn im Werk von C. G. Jung* (Zurich: Rascher); English translation by R.F.C. Hull: *The Myth of Meaning in the Work of C. G. Jung* (London: Hodder and Stoughton, 1970).

———(1968): *Aus Leben und Werkstatt von C. G. Jung. Parapsychologie: Alchemie, Nationalsozialismus, Erinnerungen aus den letzten Jahren* (Zurich: Rascher, 1968); English translation by R.F.C. Hull: *From the Life and Work of C. G. Jung* (London: Hodder and Stoughton, 1971).

———(1977): *C. G. Jung: Bild und Wort* (Olten: Walter); English translation by Krishna Winston as *C. G. Jung: Word and Image* (Princeton, NJ: Princeton University Press, 1979).

James, M. R. (1924) (ed.): *The Apocryphal New Testament: Being the Apocryphal Gospels, Acts, Epistles, and Apocalypses, with Other Narratives and Fragments* (Oxford: Clarendon Press).

Juliusburger, Otto (1934): Letter to the *Jüdische Rundschau* regarding "Die Judenfrage in der Psychotherapie," *Jüdische Rundschau* 48, 15 June, p. 5.

Jung, Carl Gustav (1912): *Wandlungen und Symbole der Libido: Beiträge zur Entwicklungsgeschichte des Denkens*, Jahrbuch für psychoanalytische und psychopathologische Forschungen 3–4 (Leipzig and Vienna: F. Deuticke, 1911–12); English translation by Beatrice M. Hinkle: *Psychology of the Unconscious: A Study of the Transformations and Symbolisms of the Libido; A Contribution to the*

History of the Evolution of Thought (New York: Moffatt Yard, 1916; and London: Kegan Paul, 1917); also in *CW*, supplementary volume B.

Jung, Carl Gustav (1916): *Septem Sermones ad Mortuos* (private print); English translation by H. G. Baynes: *The Seven Sermons to the Dead Written by Basilides in Alexandria, the City Where the East Toucheth the West* (London: private printing, 1925; reprinted, London: Stewart and Watkins, 1967).

————(1916b): *Two Essays on Analytical Psychology* (*Zwei Schriften über Analytische Psychologie*), *CW* VII; first translated by Cary and Peter Baynes (New York: Dodd, Mead, 1928).

————(1921): *Psychological Types* (*Psychologische Typen*), *CW* VI; first translated by Peter Baynes (New York: Harcourt, Brace, 1926).

————(1925): *Introduction to Jungian Psychology: Notes of the Seminar Given by Jung on Analytical Psychology in 1925*, original edition by William McGuire; revised edition by Sonu Shamdasani (Princeton, NJ: Princeton University Press, 2012).

————(1928): "The Relations between the Ego and the Unconscious" ("Die Beziehungen zwischen dem Ich und dem Unbewussten"), in *CW* VII, pp. 227–41.

————(1928a): "Die Struktur der Seele," *Europäische Revue* 4, nos. 1 and 2; extended and revised in *GW* VIII, pp. 161–82; English translation as "The Structure of the Psyche," in *CW* VIII, pp. 139–58.

————(1929): "Kommentar zu *Das Geheimnis der Goldenen Blüte*," in Wilhelm and Jung (1929), pp. 1–66; again in *GW* XIII, pp. 11–63; English translation as "Commentary on *The Secret of the Golden Flower*," by Cary F. Baynes in Wilhelm and Jung (1931); again in *CW* XIII, pp. 1–56.

————(1928–30): *Dream Analysis: Notes of the Seminar Given in 1928–1930*, ed. William McGuire (Princeton, NJ: Princeton University Press, 1984).

————(1930): "Einführung zu W. M. Kranefeldt 'Die Psychoanalyse'" (Berlin: Walter de Gruyter), pp. 5–16; again in *GW* IV, pp. 371–82; English translation by Ralph M. Eaton as "Introduction to Kranefeldt's 'Secret Ways of the Mind'" (New York: H. Holt, 1932), pp. xxv–xl; again in *CW* IV, pp. 324–32.

————(1930–34): *Visions: Notes of the Seminar Given in 1930–1934*, ed. Claire Douglas (Princeton, NJ: Princeton University Press, 1997).

————(1932): *The Psychology of Kundalini Yoga: Notes of the Seminar Given in 1932 by C. G. Jung*, ed. Sonu Shamdasani (Princeton, NJ: Princeton University Press, 1996).

————(1933): "Editorial," *Zentralblatt für Psychotherapie und ihre Grenzgebiete* 4, no. 3 (Leipzig), pp. 139–40; again in *CW* X, pp. 533–34.

————(1933a): *Modern Man in Search of a Soul*, trans. W. S. Dell and Cary F. Baynes (London: Kegan Paul, Trench, Trubner).

————(1933b): *Bericht über das Berliner Seminar von Dr. C. G. Jung, 26. Juni–1. Juli 1933* (Berlin).

————(1934): "Rejoinder to Dr. Bally" ("Zeitgenössisches"), *Neue Zürcher Zeitung* 437/443 (13/14 March); again in *CW* X, pp. 535–44.

————(1934a): "Zur gegenwärtigen Lage der Psychotherapie," *Zentralblatt für Psychotherapie und ihre Grenzgebiete* 7, no. 1 (Leipzig), pp. 1–16; again in *GW* X, pp. 181–99; English translation as "The State of Psychotherapy Today," in *CW* X, pp. 157–73.

————(1934b): "A Review of the Complex Theory" ("Allgemeines zur Komplextheorie"), *Kultur- und staatswissenschaftliche Schriften der ETH* 12 (Aarau: Sauerländer); again in *CW* VIII, pp. 92–104.

————(1934c): *Wirklichkeit der Seele: Anwendungen und Fortschritte der neueren Psychologie* (Zurich: Rascher).

————(1934d): "Zur Empirie des Individuationsprozesses," in *Yoga und Meditation im Osten und Westen*, Eranos Yearbook 1933 (Zurich: Rhein), pp. 201–14; substantially revised version in *Gestaltungen des Unbewussten* (Zurich: Rascher, 1954); again in *GW* IX/1, pp. 309–72; English translation as "A Study in the Process of Individuation," in *CW* IX/1, pp. 292–348.

————(1934e): "Vom Werden der Persönlichkeit," in *Wirklichkeit der Seele: Anwendungen und Fortschritte der neueren Psychologie* (Zurich: Rascher), pp. 180–212; again in *GW* XVII, pp. 189–211; English translation as "The Development of Personality," in *CW* XVII, pp. 165–86.

————(1934–39): *Nietzsche's Zarathustra: Notes of the Seminar Given in 1934–39*, ed. James L. Jarrett, 2 vols. (Princeton, NJ: Princeton University Press, 1989).

Jung, Carl Gustav (1935): "Über die Archetypen des kollektiven Unbewussten," in *Ostwestliche Symbolik und Seelenführung*, Eranos Yearbook 1934 (Zurich: Rhein-Verlag), pp. 179–229; again in *GW* IX/1, pp. 11–49; English translation as "Archetypes of the Collective Unconscious," in *CW* IX/1, pp. 3–41.

———(1935a): "Grundsätzliches zur praktischen Psychotherapie," *Zentralblatt für Psychotherapie und ihre Grenzgebiete* 8, no. 2 (Leipzig 1935), pp. 66–82; again in *GW* XVI, pp. 15–32; English translation as "Principles of Practical Psychotherapy," in *CW* XVI, pp. 3–20.

———(1935b): "The Tavistock Lectures: On the Theory and Practice of Analytical Psychology," *CW* XVIII, pp. 5–182; German translation by Hildegard Binswanger as "Über die Grundlagen der Analytischen Psychologie," *GW* 18/1, pp. 13–198.

———(1936): "Wotan," *Neue Schweizer Rundschau* 3, no. 11 (Zurich); again in *CW* X, pp. 203–18.

———(1936a): "Traumsymbole des Individuationsprozesses: Ein Beitrag zur Kenntnis der in den Träumen sich kundgebenden Vorgängen des Unbewussten," Eranos Yearbook 1935 (Zurich: Rhein Verlag), pp. 13–133; English translation as "Dream Symbols of the Process of Individuation," in *The Integration of the Personality* (New York: Farrar and Rinehart, 1939; London: Kegan Paul, Trench, Trubner, 1940), pp. 96–204; extended version as "Individual Dream Symbolism in Relation to Alchemy," in *Psychology and Alchemy*, *CW* XII, pp. 39–224.

———(1936b): "Yoga and the West," in *Prabuddha Bharata*, vol. 41, no. 2 (Advaita Ashrama, Mayavati Almora, Himalayas), pp. 170–77; again in *CW* XI, pp. 529–37; German in *GW* XI, pp. 531–39.

———(1936c): "Psychology and National Problems," in *CW* XVIII, pp. 566–81; German translation as "Psychology und nationale Probleme," in *GW* XVIII/2, pp. 604–21.

———(1936/37): "The Concept of the Collective Unconscious," *St. Bartholomew's Hospital Journal* XLIV: 3, pp. 46–49, and XLIV: 4, pp. 64–66; again in *CW* IX/1, pp. 42–53.

———(1936/37a): *Dream Symbols of the Individuation Process: Notes of the Seminars Given by Jung in Bailey Island and New York*, ed. Suzanne Gieser, Philemon Series (forthcoming).

————(1936–40): *Children's Dreams: Notes from the Seminar Given in 1936–1940*, ed. Lorenz Jung and Maria Meyer-Grass, translated by Ernst Falzeder with the collaboration of Tony Woolfson (Princeton, NJ: Princeton University Press, 2008).

————(1937):"Die Erlösungsvorstellungen in der Alchemie," Eranos Yearbook 1936 (Zurich: Rhein Verlag), pp. 13–111; English translation of the extended version: "Religious Ideas in Alchemy: An Historical Survey of Religious Ideas," *CW* XII, pp. 225–471.

————(1937a): "Psychological Factor Determining Human Behaviour," in *Lectures Given at the Harvard Tercentenary Conference 1936* (Cambridge, MA: Harvard University Press).

————(1937b): "Zur psychologischen Tatbestandsdiagnostik: Das Tatbestandsexperiment im Schwurgerichtsprozeß Näf," *Archiv für Kriminologie*, C, pp. 123–30; again in *GW* II, pp. 629–38; English translation as "On the Psychological Diagnosis of Evidence: The Evidence-Experiment in the Naf Trial," in *CW* II, pp. 605–14.

————(1938): "Einige Bemerkungen zu den Visionen des Zosimos," in *Gestaltung der Erlösungsidee in West und Ost (2)*, Eranos Yearbook 1937 (Zurich: Rhein Verlag), pp. 15–54; revised and considerably expanded as "Die Visionen des Zosimos," in *Von den Wurzeln des Bewusstsein: Studien über den Archetypus*, Psychologische Abhandlungen, vol. 9 (Zurich: Rascher, 1954); English translation as "The Visions of Zosimos," in *CW* XIII, pp. 57–108.

————(1938a): *Psychology and Religion: The Terry Lectures of 1937* (New Haven, CT: Yale University Press; and London: Oxford University Press); again in *CW* XI, pp. 3–106; German translation by Felicia Froboese: *Psychologie und Religion* (Zurich: Rascher, 1940).

————(1939): "Die psychologischen Aspekte des Mutterarchetypus," in *Gestalt und Kult der "Großen Mutter*," Eranos Yearbook 1938 (Zurich: Rhein Verlag), pp. 403–43; revised in *Von den Wurzeln des Bewusstsein: Studien über den Archetypus*, Psychologische Abhandlungen, vol. 9 (Zurich: Rascher, 1954); English translation as "Psychological Aspects of the Mother Archetype," in *CW* IX/1, pp. 75–112.

————(1939a): "The Dreamlike World of India," *Asia* 39, no. 1, pp. 5–8; again in *CW* X, pp. 515–24.

Jung, Carl Gustav (1939b): "What India Can Teach Us," *Asia* 39, no. 2, pp. 97–98; again in *CW* X, pp. 525–30.

———(1939c): "Geleitwort zu Daisetz Teitaro Suzuki: Die grosse Befreiung" (Leipzig: Gurt Weller), pp. 7–37; English translation as "Foreword to Suzuki's *Introduction to Zen Buddhism*," in *CW* XI, pp. 538–57.

———(1939d): "Bewusstes, Unbewusstes und Individuation," *Zentralblatt für Psychotherapie und ihre Grenzgebiete* 11, no. 5, pp. 257–70; English translation as "Conscious, Unconscious, and Individuation," in *CW* IX/1, pp. 275–89.

———(1939–40): *The Integration of the Personality* (New York: Farrar and Rinehart, 1939; London: Kegan Paul, 1940).

———(1940):"'Geleitwort zu Jacobi 'Die Psychologie C. G. Jungs,'" *GW* XVIII/2, pp. 500–501; English as "Foreword to Jacobi: 'The psychology of C. G. Jung,'" pp. 467–68.

———(1941): "Zur Psychologie des Kindarchetypus" ("The Psychology of the Child Archetype"), in *CW* IX/1, 151–81.

———(1942): "Das Wandlungssymbol in der Messe," in *Trinität, christliche Symbolik und Gnosis*, Eranos Yearbook 1940–41 (Zurich: Rhein Verlag), pp. 67–155; English translation as "Transformation Symbolism in the Mass," *CW* XI, pp. 201–52.

———(1942a): "Zur Psychologie der Trinitätsidee," in *Trinität, christliche Symbolik und Gnosis*, Eranos Yearbook 1940–41 (Zurich: Rhein Verlag), pp. 31–64; extended and revised as "Versuch einer psychologischen Deutung des Trinitätsdogmas," in *Symbolik des Geistes*, Psychologische Abhandlungen, vol. 6 (Zurich: Rascher, 1948), pp. 323–446; English translation as "A Psychological Approach to the Dogma of the Trinity," *CW* XI, pp. 107–200.

———(1942b): *Paracelsica: Zwei Vorlesungen über den Arzt und Philosophen Theophrastus* (Zurich; Leipzig: Rascher); again as *Paracelsus als geistige Erscheinung*, in *GW* XIII, pp. 123–209; English translation as *Paracelsus as a Spiritual Phenomenon*, *CW* XIII, pp. 109–89.

———(1944): *Psychologie und Alchemie* (*Psychology and Alchemy*), Psychologische Abhandlungen, vol. 5 (Zurich: Rascher); again in *CW* XII.

————(1946): *Aufsätze zur Zeitgeschichte* (Zurich: Rascher); English translation by Elisabeth Welsh as *Essays on Contemporary Events* (London: Kegan Paul, 1947).

————(1946a): *Psychologie der Übertragung* (Zurich: Rascher); English translation as "The Psychology of the Transference," *CW* XVI, pp. 163–320.

————(1946b): *Psychologie und Erziehung* (Zurich: Rascher); English as *Psychology and Education*, from vol. 17 of *The Collected Works* of C. G. Jung, Bollingen Series XX, trans. R.F.C. Hull (Princeton, NJ: Princeton University Press, 1969).

————(1947): "Der Geist der Psychologie" ("The Spirit of Psychology"), in *Geist und Natur*, Eranos Yearbook 1946 (Zurich: Rhein Verlag), pp. 385–448. Extended version published as "Theoretische Überlegungen zum Wesen des Psychischen," in *Von den Wurzeln des Bewusstseins* (Zurich: Rascher 1954), pp. 497–595; English translation as "On the Nature of the Psyche," in *CW* VIII, pp. 159–234.

————(1948): "Rede anlässlich der Gründungssitzung des C. G. Jung Institutes Zürich am 28. April 1948" ("The Structure and Dynamics of the Psyche: Address on the Occasion of the Founding of the C. G. Jung Institute, Zurich, 24 April 1948"), *CW* XVIII, pp. 471–76.

————(1948a): *Symbolik des Geistes*, Psychologische Abhandlungen, vol. 6 (Zurich: Rascher).

————(1948/1950): "Vorwort zum I Ging," in *CW* XI, pp. 587–606; the English translation from 1950 by Cary F. Baynes differs substantially from the German original from 1948; the English translation was published first in *The I Ching; or, Book of Changes: The Richard Wilhelm Translation, Rendered into English by Cary F. Baynes; Foreword by C. G. Jung* (New York: Pantheon Books, 1950), pp. i–xx; again as "Foreword to the *I-Ching*," in *CW* XI, pp. 589–608.

————(1949): "Vorwort zu Neumann *Ursprungsgeschichte des Bewusstseins*," in *GW* XVIII/2, pp. 556–57; translated by R.F.C. Hull: "Foreword to Neumann *The Origins and History of Consciousness*," in Neumann, *The Origins and History of Consciousness* (Princeton,

NJ: Princeton University Press, 1954), pp. xiii–xiv; again in *CW* XVIII, pp. 521–22.

Jung, Carl Gustav (1949a): "Vorwort zu Quispel 'Tragic Christianity'" in *GW* XVIII/2, pp. 697–699; English as: 'Foreword to Quispel: 'Tragic Christianity,'" in *CW* XVIII, pp. 651–53.

———(1950): *Zur Empirie des Individuationsprozesses*, Psychologische Abhandlungen, vol. 7 (Zurich: Rascher); again in *GW* IX/1, pp. 309–72; English translation as "A Study in the Process of Individuation," in *CW* IX/1, pp. 290–354.

———(1950a): "Über Mandalasymbolik," Psychologische Abhandlungen, vol. 7 (Zurich: Rascher); again in *GW* IX/1, pp. 373–407; English translation as "Concerning Mandala Symbolism," in *CW* IX/1, pp. 355–84.

———(1951): *Aion: Untersuchungen zur Symbolgeschichte. Mit einem Beitrag von Marie-Louise von Franz*, Psychologische Abhandlungen, vol. 8 (Zurich: Rascher); again as *Aion: Beiträge zur Symbolik des Selbst*, *GW* IX/2; English as *Aion: Researches into the Phenomenology of the Self*, *CW* IX/2.

———(1952): "*Religion and Psychology*: A Reply to Martin Buber" ("*Religion und Psychologie*: Eine Antwort auf Martin Buber"), in *Merkur* 6, no. 5 (Stuttgart, May 1952); again in *CW* XVIII, pp. 663–70.

———(1952a): *Symbols of Transformation* (*Symbole der Wandlung*), *CW* V.

———(1952b): *Antwort auf Hiob* (Zurich: Rascher); again in *GW* XI, pp. 363–471; English translation as *Answer to Job*, in *CW* XI, pp. 355–470.

———(1952c): *Synchronizität als ein Prinzip akausaler Zusammenhänge*, in *Naturerklärung und Psyche*, Studien aus dem C. G. Jung Institut, vol. 4 (Zurich: Rascher), pp. 1–107; again in *GW* VIII, pp. 457–553; English translation as *Synchronicity: An Acausal Connecting Principle*, in *CW* VIII, pp. 417–519.

———(1953): *Ansprache bei der Überreichung des Jung Codex*, in *GW* XVIII/2, addenda, pp. 890–93; English version as "Address at the Presentation of the Jung Codex," in *CW* XVIII: addenda, pp. 826–29.

———(1954): *Von den Wurzeln des Bewusstseins: Studien über den Archetypus*, Psychologische Abhandlungen, vol. 9 (Zurich: Rascher).

———(1954a): "Der philosophische Baum," in *Von den Wurzeln des Bewusstseins: Studien über den Archetypus*, Psychologische Abhandlungen, vol. 9 (Zurich: Rascher), pp. 351–469; again in *GW* XIII, pp. 271–376; English as "The Philosophical Tree," in *CW* XIII, pp. 251–349.

———(1955–56): *Mysterium Coniunctionis*, *CW* XIV.

———(1955): "Vorrede zur hebräischen Ausgabe von *Psychologie und Erziehung*," in *Psykhologiah analytit we-khinukh* (Tel Aviv: Dvir, 1958); again in *GW* XVIII/2, p. 885; English as "Foreword to the Hebrew Edition of Jung: *Psychology and education*," *CW* XVIII, p. 822.

———(1955a): "Mandalas," *Du: Schweizerische Monatsschrift* 15, no. 4, pp. 16, 21; again in *GW* IX/1, pp. 409–14; English translation in *CW* IX/1, pp. 385–90.

———(1956): "Why and How I Wrote *Answer to Job*," *Pastoral Psychology* 6, no. 10, p. 78–79.

———(1956a): "Psychotherapists or the Clergy," *Pastoral Psychology* 7, no. 3, pp. 27–41.

———(1956b): "Vorwort zu Jacobi 'Komplex, Archetypus, Symbol in der Psychologie C.G.Jungs,'" *GW* XVIII/2, pp. 569–70; English as "Foreword to Jacobi: 'Complex/archetype/symbol,'" *CW* XVIII, pp. 532–33.

———(1956c): "Zu Karl Eugen Neumann *Die Reden Gotamo Buddhos*," statement in the publisher's brochure announcing the publication of *Karl Eugen Neumanns Übertragungen aus dem Pāli-Kanon: Die Reden Gotamo Buddhos* (Zurich; Vienna: Artemis, Zsolnay 1956–57); again in *GW* XVIII/2, pp. 748–51; English as "On the Discourses of the Buddha," in *CW* XVIII, pp. 697–99.

———(1957): "Gegenwart und Zukunft," in *Schweizer Monatshefte* 36, no. 12, special supplement; again in *GW* X, pp. 275–336; English as "The Undiscovered Self (Present and Future)," in *CW* X, pp. 247–305.

———(1958): *Ein moderner Mythos von Dingen die am Himmel gesehen werden* (Zurich: Rascher); again in *GW* X, pp. 337–474; English translation as *Flying Saucers: A Modern Myth of Things Seen in the Skies*, in *CW* X, pp. 307–433.

———(1958a): "Das Gewissen in psychologischer Sicht," in *Das Gewissen*, Studien aus dem C. G. Jung Institut, vol. 7 (Zurich: Rascher,

1958), pp. 185–207; again in *GW* X, pp. 475–95; English translation as "A Psychological View of Conscience," in *CW* X, pp. 437–55.

Jung, Carl Gustav (1959): "Letter to the Editor," *Pastoral Psychology*
10, no. 3, pp. 4–5.

———(1962): *Memories, Dreams, Reflections*, recorded and edited by
Aniela Jaffé, trans. Richard and Clara Winston (New York: Pantheon Books).

———(1973): *Letters*, selected and edited by Gerhard Adler, in collaboration with Aniela Jaffé; trans. R.F.C. Hull; vol. 1: 1906–50,
vol. 2: 1951–61 (Princeton, NJ: Princeton University Press).

———(2009): *The Red Book: Liber Novus* (New York: W. W. Norton).

———, and Sigmund Freud (1974): *The Freud/Jung Letters*, ed. William McGuire, trans. Ralph Manheim and R.F.C. Hull (Princeton, NJ: Princeton University Press).

———, and Jakob Wilhelm Hauer (forthcoming): *Jung and the Indol-
ogists: Jung's Correspondences with Wihelm Hauer, Heinrich Zimmer,
and Mircea Eliade*, ed. Giovanni Sorge, Philemon Series.

———, and R.F.C. Hull: *Unpublished Correspondence* (LC).

———, and Karl Kerényi (1941): *Das Göttliche Kind: In mytholo-
gischer und psychologischer Beleuchtung*, Albae Vigiliae VI/VII
(Amsterdam; Leipzig: Pantheon Akademische Verlagsanstalt);
extended version as *Einführung in das Wesen der Mythologie.
Gottkindmythos; Eleusinische Mysterien* (Amsterdam; Leipzig: Pantheon Akademische Verlagsanstalt, 1941; Zurich: Rascher, 1951);
English translation as *Essays on a Science of Mythology: The Myth of
the Divine Child and the Mysteries of Eleusis* (Princeton, NJ: Princeton University Press, 1969).

———, and James Kirsch (2011): *The Jung-Kirsch Letters*, ed. Ann
Conrad Lammers (London; New York: Routledge).

———, and Hans Schmid-Guisan (2012): *The Question of Psychological Types. The Correspondence of C. G. Jung and Hans Schmid-
Guisan, 1915–1916*, ed. John Beebe and Ernst Falzeder, trans.
Ernst Falzeder with the collaboration of Tony Woolfson (Princeton, NJ: Princeton University Press).

———, and Victor White (2007): *The Jung-White Letters*, ed. Ann
Conrad Lammers and Adrian Cunningham, consulting ed. Murray Stein, Philemon Series (London; New York: Routledge).

Kerényi, Karl (1945): *Romandichtung und Mythologie: Ein Briefwechsel mit Thomas Mann. Herausgegeben zum siebzigsten Geburtstag des Dichters 6 Juni 1945* (Zurich: Rhein).

Khong, Belinda S., and Norman L. Thompson (1997): "Jung and Taoism: A Comparative Analysis of Jung's Psychology and Taoist Philosophy," *Harvest* 43, no. 2, pp. 82–105.

King, Pearl, and Riccardo Steiner (1991) (eds.): *The Freud-Klein Controversies, 1941–45* (London: Routledge).

Kinzig, Wolfram (2004): *Harnack, Marcion und das Judentum: Nebst einer kommentierten Edition des Briefwechsels Adolf von Harnacks mit Houston Stewart Chamberlain* (Leipzig: Evangelische Verlagsanstalt).

Kirsch, James (1934): "Die Judenfrage in der Psychotherapie: Einige Bemerkungen zu einem Aufsatz von C. G. Jung" *Jüdische Rundschau* 43 (29 May), p. 11.

———(1966): *Shakespeare's Royal Self* (Zurich: Daimon; New York: C. G. Jung Foundation of New York).

———(1973): *The Reluctant Prophet: An Exploration of Prophecy and Dreams* (Los Angeles: Sherbourne Press).

Kirsch, James, and Suzanne Wagner (1977): "Remembering Jung; A Conversation about C. G. Jung and His Work with Gilles Quispel" (Los Angeles: C. G Jung Institute).

Kirsch, Thomas B. (2000): *The Jungians: A Comparative and Historical Perspective* (London: Routledge).

———(2003): "Toni Wolff–James Kirsch Correspondence," *Journal of Analytical Psychology* 48, no. 4, pp. 499–506.

———(2011): Preface to *The Jung-Kirsch Letters*, ed. Ann Conrad Lammers (London; New York: Routledge), pp. ix–xvii.

Klein, Melanie, Paul Heimann, and Roger Money-Kyrle (1956) (eds.): *New Directions in Psycho-Analysis* (London: Tavistock Publications; New York: Basic Books).

Koigen, David (1934): *Das Haus Israel: Aus den Schriften von David Koigen* (Berlin: Schocken).

Kranefeldt, Wolfgang Müller (1930): *Psychoanalyse: Psychoanalytische Psychologie* (Berlin: Walter de Gruyter); English translation by Ralph M. Eaton as *Secret Ways of the Mind: A Survey of the Psychological Principles of Freud, Adler, and Jung* (New York: H. Holt, 1932).

Kranefeldt, Wolfgang Müller (1934): "Der Gegensatz von Sinn und Rhythmus im seelischen Geschehen," "Ewige Analyse," in Jung, *Wirklichkeit der Seele: Anwendungen und Fortschritte der neueren Psychologie* (Zurich: Rascher), pp. 231–71, 272–95.

Kreis, Georg (1995): "Philipp Etter—'voll auf eidgenössischem Boden,'" in *Intellektuelle von rechts: Ideologie und Politik in der Schweiz, 1918–1939*, ed. Aram Mattioli (Zurich: Orell Füssli, 1995), pp. 201–18.

Lammers, Ann Conrad (2011): Introduction to *The Jung-Kirsch Letters* (London; New York: Routledge), pp. xvii–xxvii.

Langwieler, Günter (2010): "*Wotan*—A Political Myth of the German Collective Unconscious: Three Debates of Shadow Aspects of the Collective Identities of Germans and Jews in the Germany of National Socialism," in *Cultures and Identities in Transition: Jungian Perspectives*, ed. Murray Stein and Raya A. Jones (London: Routledge), pp. 30–41.

Lao-t'zu (1842): [Lao-Tseu:] *Le Tao Te King: Le Livre de la Voie et de la vertu*, trans. Stanislas Julien (Paris: Imprimerie Royale).

———(1898): *Lao-Tze's Tao-Teh-King: Chinese-English, with Introduction, Transliteration, and Notes by Dr. Paul Carus* (Chicago: Open Court; London: Kegan Paul, Trench, Truebner).

———(1922): [Lao-Tzu:] *Tao Teh King*, trans. Isabella Maers (New York: Theosophical Publication House).

———(1937): *Tao Te Ching* (by Kao Tzu). A new translation by Ch'u Ta-Kao (New York: Routledge, Chapman and Hall; London: Buddhist Lodge).

Layard, John (1942): *Stone Men of Malekula* (London: Chatto and Windus).

———(1944): *The Lady of the Hare: Being a Study in the Healing Power of Dreams* (London: Faber and Faber).

Lenin, Vladimir Ilyich (1905): "Socialism and Religion," in *Collected Works*, vol. 10: Nov. 1905–June 1906 (Moscow: Progress Publisher, 1962), pp. 83–87.

Lévy-Bruhl, Lucien (1910): *Les fonctions mentales dans les sociétiés inférieures* (Paris: Les Presses universitaires de France).

Liebscher, Martin (2001): "'Wotan' und 'Puer Aeternus': Die zeithistorische Verstrickung von C. G. Jungs Zarathustrainterpretation," in *Nietzsche-Studien*, vol. 30 (2001), pp. 329–50; English translation as "'Wotan' and 'Puer Aeternus': The Historical Context of C. G. Jung's Interpretation of Zarathustra," in *New Nietzsche Studies*, vol. 6, 3/4, and vol. 7, 1/2 (2006), pp. 99–115.

Lockot, Regine (1985): *Erinnern und Durcharbeiten: Zur Geschichte der Psychoanalyse und Psychotherapie im Nationalsozialismus* (Frankfurt am Main: S. Fischer).

Lori, Aviva (2005): "Jung at Heart," *Haaretz* 28, no. 1.

Loewenthal-Neumann, Rali (2006): "My Father, Dr Erich Neumann," *Harvest: International Journal for Jungian Studies* 52, no. 2, pp. 148–60.

Löwe, Angelica (2008): "'Wir waren eine zufriedene und glückliche Familie.' Ruth Goldstone erinnert sich; Auszüge aus Briefen und Gesprächen," *Analytische Psychologie: Zeitschrift für Psychotherapie und Psychoanalyse: Erich Neumann*, 151, no. 1, pp. 41–49.

Lubbock, John (1865): *Pre-Historic Times, as Illustrated by Ancient Remains, and the Manners and Customs of Modern Savages* (London: Williams and Norgate).

Mādhavānanda(1965) (ed., trans.): *The Bṛhadāraṇyaka Upaniṣad*, with the commentary of Śaṅkarācārya and an introduction by S. Kuppuswāmi Śāstrī, 4th ed. (Calcutta: Advaita Ashrama).

Maidenbaum, Aryeh (1989): "Lingering Shadows: A Personal Perspective," in *Lingering Shadows: Jungians, Freudians, and Anti-Semitism*, ed. Aryeh Maidenbaum and Stephen A. Martin (Boston; London: Shambhala), pp. 291–300.

Main, Roderick (1997): *Jung on Synchronicity and the Paranormal* (London: Routledge).

Mann, Thomas (1929): "Die Stellung Freuds in der modernen Geistesgeschichte," *Die psychoanalytische Bewegung* 1, no. 1, pp. 3–32.

———(1933–43): *Joseph und seine Brüder*, vol 1: *Die Geschichten Jaakobs* (Berlin: Fischer, 1933); vol. 2: *Der junge Joseph* (Berlin: Fischer, 1934); vol. 3: *Joseph in Ägypten* (Vienna: Bermann-Fischer, 1936); vol. 4: *Joseph der Ernährer* (Stockholm: Bermann-Fischer, 1943); English translation by H. T. Lowe-Porter: *Joseph and His Brothers*, 4. vols. (London: Secker and Warburg, 1934–45).

———(1936): "Freud und die Zukunft. Vortrag [,] gehalten in Wien am 8. Mai 1936 zur Feier von Sigmund Freuds 80. Geburtstag" (Vienna: Bermann-Fischer); English translation by H. T.

Lowe-Porter: "Freud and the future," in *Essays of Three Decades* (New York: A. A. Knopf, 1947), pp. 411–28.

Mann, Thomas (1939): *The Living Thoughts of Schopenhauer*, translation of the introductory essay by H. T. Lowe-Porter, translation of the selection by R. B. Haldane and J. Kemp (New York; Toronto: Longmans).

———(1983): *Diaries, 1918–1939*, selection and foreword by Hermann Kesten, translated from German by Richard and Clara Winston (London: André Deutsch).

———, and Karl Kerényi (1960): *Gespräch in Briefen* (Zurich: Rhein).

Marx, Karl (1844): "Zur Kritik der Hegelschen Rechtsphilosophie: Einleitung," in *Deutsch-Französische Jahrbücher* (Paris, February), pp. 71–85; English translation by Annette Jolin and Joseph O'Malley: *A Contribution to the Critique of Hegel's Philosophy of Right: Introduction*, in *Critique of Hegel's Philosophy of Right*, ed. with an introduction and notes by Joseph O'Malley (Cambridge: Cambridge University Press, 1970), pp. 129–42.

———(1961): *Zur Kritik der Politischen Ökonomie*, in Karl Marx, and Friedrich Engels, *Werke*, vol. 13 (Berlin: Karl Dietz Verlag); English translation by S. W. Ryanzanskaya: *A Contribution to the Critique of Political Economy*, ed. M. Dobb (London: Lawrence and Whishart, 1971).

Meier, C(arl) A(lfred) (1948): "Presse Informierung anlässlich der Eröffnung des C. G. Jung Institutes Zürich, am 11. Oktober 1948 durch C. A. Meier" (n.p.).

———(1949): *Antike Inkubation und moderne Psychotherapie*, Studien aus dem C. G. Jung Institut, vol. 1 (Zurich: Rascher); English translation as *Ancient Incubation and Modern Psychotherapy* (Evanston, IL: Northwestern University Press, 1967).

———(1964): *Ansprachen gehalten anlässlich der Eröffnung der Klinik am Zürichberg* (Zurich: Klinik und Forschungsstätte für Jung'sche Psychologie).

———(1968–77): *Lehrbuch der Komplexen Psychologie C. G. Jungs*, 4 vols. (Zurich; Stuttgart: Rascher; Olten and Freiburg i. Br.: Walter); English as *The Psychology of C. G. Jung*, vols. 1–3, trans. Eugene Wolfe (Boston: Sigo Press, 1984–89), vol. 4 trans. David N. Roscoe (Einsiedeln: Daimon, 1995).

Meier, Joan, et al. (1985): *A Testament to the Wilderness: Ten Essays on an Address by C. A. Meier in Honor of His 80th Birthday* (Zurich: Daimon; Santa Monica: Lapis Press).

Mellon, Paul (1992): *Reflections in a Silver Spoon: A Memoir* (New York: William Morrow).

McGuire, William (1981): "John D. Barrett, Jr., December 8, 1903–June 28, 1981," *San Francisco Jung Institute Library Journal* 2, no. 4, pp. 45–47.

Middrash Rabbah (1939): Translation with notes, glossary, and indexes under the editorship of Rabbi Dr. H. Freedman and Maurice Simon, with a foreword by Rabbi Dr. I. Epstein, 10 vols (London: Soncino Press).

Molton, Mary Dian, and Lucy Anne Sikes (2011): *Four Eternal Women: Toni Wolff Revisited—A Study in Opposites* (Carmel, CA: Fisher King Press).

Nag Hammadi Scriptures (2007): *The Nag Hammadi Scriptures: The International Edition: The Revised and Updated Translation of Sacred Gnostic Texts*, ed. Marvin Meyer, with an introduction by Elaine H. Pagels (New York: Harper One).

Neumann, Erich (1928): *Johann Arnold Kanne: Ein vergessener Romantiker: Ein Beitrag zur Geschichte der mystischen Sprachphilosophie* (Berlin: Verlag Reuter and Reichard).

———(1932): Chapter of the unpublished novel *Der Anfang*, in *Zwischen den Zelten: Junge jüdische Autoren*, ed. Julius Wassermann (Berlin: Die Nachricht), pp. 135–55.

———(1934): Letter to the *Jüdische Rundschau* regarding "Die Judenfrage in der Psychotherapie," *Jüdische Rundschau* 48 (15 June), p. 5.

———(1934a): "Zur jüdischen Religionsgeschichte," *Jüdische Rundschau* 60 (27 July), p. 10.

———(1934b): "Zur Psychologischen Lage des Judentums," unpublished typescript (October 1934), sold at Sotheby's in 2006. See Music and Continental Manuscripts (London, 30 November 2006), p. 155.

———(1934–40): *Ursprungsgeschichte des jüdischen Bewusstseins* (*On the Origins and History of Jewish Consciousness*), vol. 1: *Beiträge zur Tiefenpsychologie des jüdischen Menschen und der Offenbarung* (*Contributions to the Depth-Psychology of the Jewish Man and to the*

Problem of Revelation), vol. 2: *Der Chassidismus und seine psycholo-gische Bedeutung für das Judentum* (*Hasidism and Its Psychological Relevance for the Jewry*), unpublished typescript, sold at Sotheby's in 2006. See Music and Continental Manuscripts (London, 30 November 2006), p. 153; also in NP.

Neumann, Erich (1937–38): *Seelenproblem des modernen Juden: Eine Reihenanalyse von Träumen, Bildern und Phantasien* (*Soul Problems of the Modern Jew: An Analysis of a Series of Dreams, Images, and Phantasies*) (unpublished seminar), Tel Aviv 1937–38 [missing].

———(1938): *Märchen und Unbewusstes* (unpublished seminar), Tel Aviv, 5 April 1938–7 May 1938 (NP).

———(1938–39): *Seelenproblem des modernen Juden: Eine Reihena-nalyse von Träumen, Bildern und Phantasien* (*Soul problems of the Modern Jew: An Analysis of a Series of Dreams, Images, and Phanta-sies*) (unpublished seminar), Tel Aviv, 10 November 1938–29 Feb-ruary 1939 (GEA).

———(1939): "Bemerkungen zur Psychologie des Kindes und der Paedagogik" ("Observations on the Psychology of the Child and Pedagogy"), unpublished typescript (NP).

———(1939–40): *Analytische Psychologie und Judentum: Der Chassi-dismus* (*Analytical Psychology and Jewry: The Hasidism*) (unpub-lished seminar), Tel Aviv, 9 November 1939–30 May 1940 (GEA).

———(1940–59): *Buch der Einweihung*, 2 vols. (unpublished); see Sotheby's, Music and Continental Manuscripts (London, 30 No-vember 2006), pp. 148–49.

———(1941–42): *Das Symbol und die Symbolgruppe zur Alchemie* (unpublished seminar), Tel Aviv, 12 November 1941–24 June 1942 (GEA).

———(1942): "Zur religiösen Bedeutung des tiefenpsychologischen Weges" ("On the Religious Significance of the Way of Depth Psy-chology"), unpublished typescript (NP).

———(1943):"Die Bedeutung des Bewusstseins für die tiefenpsy-chologische Erfahrung" ("The Significance of Consciousness for Depth-Psychological Experience"), unpublished typescript (NP).

———(1948): Fragments of a Seminar on the Female Aspect in Fairy Tales, 18 February 1948, 25 February 1948, 4 March 1948, unpublished typescript (NP).

———(1949): "Der mystische Mensch," in *Der Mensch (2)*, Eranos Yearbook 1948 (Zurich: Rhein-Verlag), pp. 317–74; again in *Kulturentwicklung und Religion*, Eranos Vorträge, vol. 1, ed. Regula Bühlmann (Rütte: Johanna Norländer Verlag, 2007), pp. 100–140; English translation as "Mystical Man," in *The Mystic Vision*, ed. Joseph Campbell (Princeton, NJ: Princeton University Press, 1968), pp. 375–415.

———(1949a): *Ursprungsgeschichte des Bewusstseins* (Zurich: Rascher); English translation as *The Origins and History of Consciousness*, trans. R.F.C. Hull (Princeton, NJ: Princeton University Press, 1954).

———(1949b): *Tiefenpsychologie und Neue Ethik* (Zurich: Rascher); English translation by Eugene Rolfe: *Depth Psychology and a New Ethic* (London: Hodder and Stoughton, 1969; reprint Boston: Shambhala, 1990).

———(1950): "Die mythische Welt und der Einzelne," in *Der Mensch und die mythische Welt*, Eranos Yearbook 1949 (Zurich: Rhein-Verlag), pp. 189–254; again in *Kulturentwicklung und Religion*, Eranos Vorträge, vol. 1, ed. Regula Bühlmann (Rütte: Johanna Norländer Verlag, 2007), pp. 52–98.

———(1950a): "Zu Mozarts Zauberflöte"; first published as "Über den Mond und das matriarchalische Bewusstsein," in *Aus der Welt der Urbilder*, Eranos vol. 18: Sonderband für C. G. Jung zum 75. Geburtstag am 26. Juli 1950 (Zurich: Rhein), pp. 323–76; revised version as "Zu Mozarts Zauberflöte," in *Zur Psychologie des Weiblichen: Umkreisung der Mitte II* (Zurich: Rascher, 1953), pp. 123–73; again in Eranos Vorträge, vol. 4 (Rütte: Johanna Norländer Verlag, 2008), pp. 92–126; English translation as "On Mozart's Magic Flute," by Esther Doughty, *Quadrant* 11, no. 2 (1978), pp. 5–32; revised translation by Boris Matthew, in Erich Neumann, *The Fear of the Feminine and Other Essays on Feminine Psychology*, ed. William McGuire, Bollingen series LXI/4 (Princeton, NJ: Princeton University Press, 1994), pp. 119–64.

———(1950b): "Über den Mond und das matriarchalische Bewusstsein," in *Aus der Welt der Urbilder*, Eranos volume XVIII: Sonderband für C. G. Jung zum 75. Geburtstag am 26. Juli 1950 (Zurich: Rhein), pp. 323–76; again in *Zur Psychologie des Weiblichen:*

Umkreisung der Mitte II (Zurich: Rascher, 1953); English translation by Boris Matthew as "The Moon and Matriarchal Consciousness," in Erich Neumann, *The Fear of the Feminine and Other Essays on Feminine Psychology*, ed. William McGuire, Bollingen series LXI/4 (Princeton, NJ: Princeton University Press, 1994), pp. 64–118.

Neumann, Erich (1951): "Die Urbeziehung zur Mutter," *Der Psychologe* 7/8, vol. 3 (Schwarzenburg: GBS-Verlag), pp. 254–61.

———(1952): "Eros und Psyche: Ein Beitrag zur seelischen Entwicklung des Weiblichen," in Apuleius, *Amor und Psyche* (Zurich: Rascher), pp. 75–217; English translation as "The Psychic Development of the Feminine: A Commentary on the Tale by Apuleius," trans. Ralph Manheim, in Apuleius, *Amor and Psyche* (New York: Pantheon Books, 1956), pp. 57–161.

———(1953): "Die psychologischen Stadien der weiblichen Entwicklung," in *Zur Psychologie des Weiblichen: Umkreisung der Mitte II* (Zurich: Rascher), pp. 1–65; again in Eranos Vorträge, vol. 4 (Rütte: Johanna Norländer Verlag, 2008), pp. 12–53; English translation as "The Psychological Stages of Woman's Development," in Erich Neumann, *The Fear of the Feminine and Other Essays on Feminine Psychology*, ed. William McGuire, Bollingen series LXI/4 (Princeton, NJ: Princeton University Press, 1994), pp. 3–63.

———(1953a): *Kulturentwicklung und Religion: Umkreisung der Mitte I* (Zurich: Rascher).

———(1953b): *Zur Psychologie des Weiblichen: Umkreisung der Mitte II* (Zurich: Rascher).

———(1953c): "Die Psyche und die Wandlung der Wirklichkeitsebenen," in *Mensch und Energie* (*Human Being and Energy*), Eranos Yearbook 1952 (Zurich: Rhein Verlag) pp. 169–216; again in *Die Psyche als Ort der Gestaltung*, Eranos Vorträge, vol. 2 (Rütte: Johanna Norländer Verlag, 2007), pp. 52–92; English translation as "The Psyche and the Transformation of the Reality Planes: A Metapsychological Essay," trans. Hildegard Nagel, completed and revised by Inge Roberts and William Goodheart, in *The Place of Creation, Essays of Erich Neumann*, vol. 3, ed. Renée Brand, William McGuire, and Julie Neumann (Princeton, NJ: Princeton University Press), pp. 3–62.

———(1954): Fragments of a Seminar for Child Psychologist Entitled *Die matriarchale Welt als seelische Ursprungswelt*, 17 June 1954–7 July 1954, unpublished typescript (NP).

———(1954a): "Die Bedeutung des Erdarchetyps für die Neuzeit," in *Mensch und Erde I (Human Being and Earth I)*, Eranos Yerabook 1953 (Zurich: Rhein Verlag), pp. xx; again in *Die Psyche als Ort der Gestaltung*, Eranos Vorträge, vol. 2 (Rütte: Johanna Norländer Verlag, 2007), pp. 11–51; English translation as "The Meaning of the Earth Archetype for Modern Times," trans. Eugene Rolf and Michael Cullingworth, *Harvest: International Journal for Jungian Studies* 27 (1980) and vol. 29 (1982); again in *The Fear of the Feminine and Other Essays on Feminine Psychology*, ed. William McGuire, Bollingen series LXI/4 (Princeton, NJ: Princeton University Press), pp. 165–226.

———(1955): Fragments of a Seminar for Child Psychologists, meeting of 13 March 1955, unpublished typescript (NP).

———(1956): *Die große Mutter: Der Archetyp des großen Weiblichen* (Zurich: Rhein-Verlag); again as *Die große Mutter: Die weiblichen Gestaltungen des Unbewussten* (Düsseldorf: Patmos, 2003); English translation as *The Great Mother: An Analysis of the Archetype*, by Ralph Manheim (London: Routledge and Kegan Paul, 1955).

———(1956a): "Die Erfahrung der Einheitswirklichkeit und die Sympathie aller Dinge," in *Der Mensch und die Sympathie aller Dinge (The Human Being and the Sympathy of All Things)*, Eranos Yearbook 1955 (Zurich: Rhein Verlag), pp. 11–54; again in *Der schöpferische Mensch* (Zurich: Rhein Verlag, 1959), p. xx; reprinted in vol. 3 of Neumann's Eranos Vorträge (Rütte: Johanna Norländer Verlag, 2008), pp. 49–83; English translation as "The Experience of the Unitary Reality," trans. Eugene Rolfe, in *The Place of Creation, Essays of Erich Neumann*, vol. 3, ed. Renée Brand, William McGuire, and Julie Neumann (Princeton, NJ: Princeton University Press), pp. 63–130.

———(1958): "Aus dem ersten Teil des Kafka-Kommentars: 'Das Gericht,'" in *Geist und Werk: Aus der Werkstatt unserer Autoren. Zum 75. Geburtstag von Dr. Daniel Brody* (Zurich: Rhein Verlag), pp. 175–96; English translation by Eugene Rolfe as "Kafka's 'The Trial': An Interpretation through Depth Psychology," in *Creative*

Man, Bollingen series LXI/2 (Princeton, NJ: Princeton University Press, 1979), pp. 3–75.

Neumann, Erich (1958a): "Die jüdische Mystik: Bemerkungen zu G. Scholems 'Die Jüdische Mystik in ihrem Hauptströmungen,'" *Mitteilungsblatt. Wochenzeitung des Irgun Olej Merkas Europa* 37/38 (Tel Aviv, 12 September), p. 10.

———(1959): *Der schöpferische Mensch* (Zurich: Rhein Verlag).

———(1959a): "Frieden als Symbol des Lebens," in *Mensch und Frieden I* (*Human Being and Peace*), Eranos Yearbook 1958 (Zurich: Rhein Verlag), pp. 1–50; extended version in *Der schöpferische Mensch* (Zurich: Rhein Verlag, 1959); reprinted in vol. 3 of Neumann's Eranos Vorträge (Rütte: Johanna Norländer Verlag, 2008), pp. 158–90; English translation as "Peace as the Symbol of Life," trans. Jan van Heurck, in *The Place of Creation, Essays of Erich Neumann,* vol. 3, ed. Renée Brand, William McGuire, and Julie Neumann (Princeton, NJ: Princeton University Press), pp. 264–319.

———(1959b): "Die Angst vor dem Weiblichen," in *Die Angst,* Studien aus dem C. G. Jung Institut, vol. 10 (Zurich: Rascher), pp. 67–112; English translation as "The Fear of the Feminine," by Irene Gad and Ruth Horine, in Jeanne Walker (ed.), *Quadrant* 19, no. 1 (1986), pp. 7–30; new translation by Boris Matthews, in Erich Neumann, *The Fear of the Feminine and Other Essays on Feminine Psychology,* ed. William McGuire, Bollingen series LXI/4 (Princeton, NJ: Princeton University Press, 1994), pp. 227–82.

———(1960): "Das Schöpferische als Zentralproblem der Psychotherapie" ("The Creative as a Central Problem of Psychotherapy"), *Acta Psychotherapeutica et Psychosomatica* (Basel; New York: Karger).

———(1960a): "Das Bild des Menschen in Krise und Erneuerung" ("The Image of Man in Crisis and Renewal"), in *Die Erneuerung des Menschen* (*Renewal of the Human*), Eranos Yearbook 1959 (Zurich: Rhein Verlag), pp. 7–46.

———(1961): *Die archetypische Welt Henry Moores* (Zurich: Rascher); English translation by R.F.C. Hull as *The Archetypal World of Henry Moore* (Princeton, NJ: Princeton University Press, 1985).

———(1961a): "Die Deutung des genetischen Aspekts für die Analytische Psychologie," in *Current Trends in Analytical Psychology:*

Proceedings of the First International Congress for Analytical Psychology, ed. Gerhard Adler (London: Tavistock Publications); first published in English as "The Significance of the Genetic Aspect for Analytical Psychology," *Journal of Analytical Psychology* 4, no. 2 (1959), pp. 125–37.

———(1961b): *Krise und Erneuerung* (*Crisis and Renewal*) (Zurich: Rhein Verlag); reprinted in vol. 5 of Neumann's Eranos Vorträge (Rütte: Johanna Norländer Verlag, 2009), pp. 96–187.

———(1961c): "Gewissen, Ritual und Tiefenpsychologie," in Schmaus Michael and Karl Forster (eds.), *Der Kult und der heutige Mensch* (Munich: Max Hueber), pp. 317–23.

———(1963): *Das Kind: Struktur und Dynamik der werdenden Persönlichkeit* (Zurich: Rhein Verlag); English translation by Ralph Manheim as *The Child: Structure and Dynamics of the Nascent Personality* (New York: Published by Putnam for C. G. Jung Foundation for Analytical Psychology, 1973).

———(1979): *Creative Man: Five Essays*, trans. Eugene Rolfe, Bollingen series LXI/2 (Princeton, NJ: Princeton University Press, 1979).

———, and Bollingen Foundation: unpublished letter from 5 April 1948, unpublished correspondence between Erich Neumann and Olga Fröbe-Kapteyn (EA).

———, and Michael Fordham: unpublished correspondence (NP).

———, and Olga Fröbe-Kapteyn: unpublished correspondence, letters from Erich Neumann to Olga Fröbe-Kapteyn (EA); letters from Olga Fröbe-Kapteyn to Erich Neumann (NP).

———, and C. A. Meier: unpublished letter (NP).

———, and Merkur (journal): unpublished correspondence (DLA).

———, and Marie-Jeanne Schmid: unpublished correspondence (NP).

Neumann, Erich W. A. (1924): "Die Schmerzlüsternheit: Fragmente einer Psychologie des Pessimismus," in *Proteus: Blätter einer Welt* 4 (Kettwig: Rödde).

Neumann, Micha (2005): "Die Beziehung zwischen C. G. Jung und Erich Neumann auf Grund ihrer Korrespondenz," in *Zur Utopie einer neuen Ethik: 100 Jahre Erich Neumann—130 Jahre C. G. Jung* (Vienna: Mandelbaum), pp. 17–37.

Nietzsche, Friedrich (1980): *Also sprach Zarathustra*, Kritische Studienausgabe, 15 vols., ed. Mazzino Montinari and Giorgio Colli, vol. 4 (Berlin; New York: de Gruyter); English translation by Adrian Del Caro as *Thus Spoke Zarathustra*, ed. Adrian Del Caro and Robert Pippin (Cambridge: Cambridge University Press, 2006).

Nieuwe Rotterdamse Courant (1961): "Dr. E. Neumann overleden" (obituary), 26 January 1961.

Origen of Alexandria (1910/11): *The Writings of Origen*, 2 vols., trans. Frederick Crombie (Edinburgh: T. & T. Clark).

Österreichische Gesellschaft für Analytische Psychologie (2005) (ed.): *Zur Utopie einer neuen Ethik: 100 Jahre Erich Neumann. 130 Jahre C. G. Jung* (Vienna: Mandelbaum Verlag), pp. 38–48.

Owens, Lance S. (2011): "Jung and Aion: Time, Vision, and a Wayfaring Man," *Psychological Perspectives* 54, pp. 253–89.

Pehle, Walter H. (1991) (ed.): *November 1938: From "Reichskristallnacht" to Genocide* (New York: Berg).

Pirke de-Rabbi Eliezer (1918), according to the text of the manuscript belonging to Abraham Epstein of Vienna, translated and annotated with introduction and indexes by Gerald Friedlander (London: Kegan Paul, Trench, Trubner; New York: Bloch).

Plaut, A. (1995): "Obituary Notice for Lotte Paulsen," *Journal for Analytical Psychology* 40, p. 110.

Poewe, Karla (2006): *New Religions and the Nazis* (Abingdon: Routledge).

Portmann, Adolf (1948): *Die Tiergestalt: Studien über die Bedeutung der tierischen Erscheinung* (Basel: Verlag Friedrich Reinhardt); English translation by Hella Czech as *Animal Forms and Patterns: A Study of the Appearance of Animals* (London: Faber and Faber, 1952).

———(1953): *Das Tier als soziales Wesen* (Zurich: Rhein Verlag); English translation as *Animals as Social Beings* (London: Hutchinson, 1961).

Psychologischer Club Zürich (1935) (ed.): *Die kulturelle Bedeutung der komplexen Psychologie: Festschrift zum 60. Geburtstag von C. G. Jung* (Berlin: Springer).

Quispel, Gilles (1943): *De Bronnen van Tertullianus' Adversus Marcionem* (Leiden: Burgersdijk and Niermans).

———(1951): *Gnosis als Weltreligion: Vier Vorträge. Allgemeine Ein-führung in die Thematik der Gnosis* (Zurich: Origo).

———(1974): *Gnostic Studies*, 2 vols., *Publication de l'institut histo-rique et archéologique néerlandais de Stamboul*, 34, 1–2.

———(1975): *Tatian and the Gospel of Thomas: Studies in the History of the Western Diatessaron* (Leiden: Brill).

———(2008): *Gnostica, Judaica, Catholica: Collected Essays of Gilles Quispel*, ed. Johannes van Oort; with additional prefaces by April DeConick and Jean-Pierre Mahé (Leiden; Boston: Brill).

Quispel, Gilles, G. Van Unik, and W. C. Puech (1955): *The Jung Codex: A Newly Recovered Gnostic Papyrus* (London: Mowbray; New York: Morehouse-Gorham).

Read, Anthony (1989): *Kristallnacht: The Nazi Night of Terror* (New York: Times Books).

Ritsema, Rudolf (1983) (ed.): "Adolf Portmann" (obituary), in *Das Spiel der Götter und der Menschen*, Eranos Yearbook 51 (Frankfurt am Main: Insel).

Remembering Jung: Rivkah and Yehezkel Kluger (2003): directed by Suzanne and George Wagner: *Remembering Jung*, no. 13 (Los Angeles: C. G. Jung Institute of Los Angeles).

Reis, Patricia, and James Harrod (1987): "The Work of Heinz West-man," *San Francisco Jung Institute Library Journal* 7, no. 2, pp. 23–50.

Roazen, Paul (2000): *Oedipus in Britain: Edward Glover and the Strug-gle over Klein* (New York: Other Press).

Rosarium philosophorum (1593): In *Artis auriferia, quam chemiam vo-cant . . .* , vol. 2. (Basel), pp. 204–384.

Rosenthal, Hugo (1934): "Der Typengegensatz in der jüdischen Religionsgeschichte," in C. G. Jung: *Wirklichkeit der Seele: Anwen-dungen und Fortschritte der neueren Psychologie* (Zurich: Rascher), pp. 355–409.

———(2000): *Lebenserinnerungen*, ed. Micheline Prüter-Müller and Peter Wilhelm A. Schmidt (Bielefeld: Verlag für Regional-geschichte).

Rüetschi, Magdalena (1988): *Die Bergpredigt: Kindern in Bildern er-zählt. Nach einem Wandteppich von Rosa Gerber. Mit einer*

Einführung von C. G. Jung (Freiburg im Breisgau; Basel; Wien: Herder).

Rüf, Elisabeth (1975) (ed.): *Experiment und Symbol: Arbeiten zur komplexen Psychologie C. G. Jungs. Festschrift zum 70. Geburtstag von Prof. Dr. C. A. Meier* (Olten; Freiburg im Breisgau: Walter).

Schär, Hans (1946): *Religion und Seele in der Psychologie C. G. Jungs* (Zurich: Rascher); translated by R.F.C. Hull as *Religion and the Cure of Souls in Jung's Psychology* (London: Routledge and Kegan Paul, 1951).

———(1950): *Erlösungsvorstellungen und ihre psychologischen Aspekte.* Studien aus dem C. G. Jung Institut Zürich, vol. 2 (Zurich: Rascher).

Schärf Kluger, Rivkah (1948): *Die Gestalt des Satans im Alten Testament*, in C. G. Jung, *Symbolik des Geistes*. Psychologische Abhandlungen, vol. 6 (Zurich: Rascher), pp. 153–322; English: *Satan in the Old Testament* (Evanston, IL: Northwestern University Press, 1967).

———(1974): *Psyche and Bible: Three Old Testament Themes* (Zurich: Spring Publication).

———(1991): *The Archetypal Significance of Gilgamesh: A Modern Ancient Hero*, ed. Yehezkel Kluger (Einsiedeln: Daimon).

Schneer, Jonathan (2010): *The Balfour Declaration: The Origins of the Arab-Israeli Conflict* (New York: Random House).

Schoenl, William J. (1998): *C. G. Jung: His Friendships with Mary Mellon and J. B. Priestley* (Wilmette, IL: Chiron).

Scholem, Gershom (1923): *Das Buch Bahir: Ein Schriftdenkmal aus der Frühzeit der Kabbala: Auf Grund der kritischen Neuausgabe* (Leipzig: Drugulin).

———(1941): *Major Trends in Jewish Mysticism* (Jerusalem: Schocken); German as *Die jüdische Mystik in ihren Hauptströmungen* (Zurich: Rhein Verlag, 1957).

———(1960): "Erich Neumann (Nachruf)," *Mitteilungsblatt: Wochenzeitung des Irgun Olej Merkas Europa* 28, no. 47, p. 4; again in *Das neue Israel* 13 (1960/61), p. 313.

———(1973): *Sabbatai Sevi: The Mystical Messiah, 1626–1676* (London: Routledge and Kegan Paul).

Sengupta, Sulagna (2013): *Jung in India* (New Orleans: Spring Publishing).

Shamdasani, Sonu (1990): "A Woman called Frank," *Spring: Journal of Archetype and Culture* 50, pp. 26–56.

———(1995): "Memories, Dreams, Omissions," *Spring: Journal of Archetype and Culture* 57, pp. 115–37.

———(1996): Introduction to C. G. Jung: *The Psychology of Kundalini Yoga: Notes of the Seminar Given in 1932 by C. G. Jung*, ed. Sonu Shamdasani (Princeton, NJ: Princeton University Press, 1996), pp. xvii–xlvii.

———(2003): *Jung and the Making of Modern Psychology: The Dream of a Science* (Cambridge: Cambridge University Press).

———(2009): Introduction to C. G. Jung, *The Red Book: Liber Novus* (New York: W. W. Norton), pp. 193–226.

Sherry, Jay (2012): *Carl Gustav Jung: Avant-Garde Conservative* (New York: Palgrave Macmillan).

Sidler, Eduard (1933–41): Unpublished notes on Jung's lectures at the Eidgenössischen Technischen Hochschule (JA).

Silberer, Herbert (1914): *Probleme der Mystik und ihre Symbolik* (Vienna: Heller); English translation: *Problems of Mysticism and Its Symbolism* (New York: Moffat, Yard, 1917).

Sotheby's (2006): Music and Continental Manuscripts (London, 30 November).

Sri Aurobindo (1943): Gedanken und Einblicke. Studie über das Yoga des Shri Aurobindo von N. K. Gupta. Vorrede von J. Herbert und Übersetzung aus der Originalausgabe in Arya Pondichery von Alwina von Keller (Zurich: Rascher).

———(1945): *Die Mutter: Zweiter Band. Indische Weisheit*, Sämtliche Werke, German translation by Alwine von Keller (Zurich: Rascher).

Steinfeld, J. (1934): Letter to the *Jüdische Rundschau* regarding "Die Judenfrage in der Psychotherapie," *Jüdische Rundschau*, 50, 22 June, p. 5.

Stephens, Barbara D. (2001): "The Martin Buber–Carl Jung Disputations: Protecting the Sacred in the Battle for the Boundaries of Analytical Psychology," *Journal of Analytical Psychology* 46, pp. 455–91.

Stern, Max M. (1988): *Repetition and Trauma: Toward a Teleonomic Theory of Psychoanalysis*, ed. Liselotte Bendis Stern, with an introduction by Fred M. Levin (Hillsdale, NJ: Analytic Press).

Stevens, Anthony (2002): *Archetype Revisited: An Updated Natural History of the Self* (London: Brunner-Routledge).

Straus, Erwin (1959): "The Fourth International Congress of Psychotherapy Barcelona, Spain, September 1 through 7, 1958" (Review), *Psychosomatic Medicine* 21, no. 2, pp. 158–64.

Thatcher, David (1977): "Eagle and Serpent in *Zarathustra*," *Nietzsche-Studien* 6, pp. 240–60.

Vivekananda (1944): *Gespräche auf den tausend Inseln*, German translation by Alwine von Keller (Zurich: Rascher).

Wälder, Robert (1941): *The Living Thoughts of Freud*, The Living Thoughts Library, vol. 19, ed. Alfred O. Mendel (New York and Toronto: Longmans, Green).

Westman(n), Heinz (1936): "Die Erlösungsidee im Judentum," in *Gestaltung der Erlösungsidee im Judentum und im Protestantismus*, complementary volume to Eranos Yearbook 1936, ed. Rudolf Ritsema (Ascona: Eranos Fundation), pp. 33–110.

———(1961): *The Springs of Creativity* (London: Routledge, Kegan and Paul).

———(1984): *The Structure of Biblical Myths: The Ontogenesis of the Psyche* (Dallas, TX: Spring Publications).

Wilhelm, Richard (1911) (trans.): *Laotse: Tao Te King. Das Buch des Alten vom Sinn und Leben* (Jena: Eugen Diederichs Verlag).

———(1924) (trans.): *I Ging: Das Buch der Wandlungen* (Jena: Eugen Diederichs); again as *I Ging: Text und Materialien*, with an introduction by Wolfgang Bauer (Kreuzlingen; Munich: Heinrich Hugendubel, 2003); English translation by Cary F. Baynes as *The I Ching; or, Book of Changes* (New York: Pantheon Books, 1950).

———(1925): *Lao-Tse und der Taoismus* (Stuttgart: Frommann).

———, and C. G. Jung (1929): *Das Geheimnis der goldenen Blüte: Ein chinesisches Lebensbuch. Übersetzt und erläutert von Richard Wilhelm, mit einem europäischen Kommentar von C. G. Jung* (Munich: Dornverlag); English translation by Cary F. Baynes as *The Secret of the Golden Flower: A Chinese Book of Life*, translated (into German) and explained by Richard Wilhelm with a European commentary by C. G. Jung (London: Kegan Paul).

Williams, Daniel H. (1994): "Harnack, Marcion, and the Argument of Antiquity," in Wendy E. Helleman (ed.): *Hellenization Revisited:*

Shaping a Christian Response within the Greco-Roman World (Lanham, MD: University Press of America), pp. 223–40.

Winchell, Wallace (1956): "Jung and Symbols," *Pastoral Psychology* 7, no. 4, pp. 53–54.

Wolff, Toni (1951): *Strukturformen der weiblichen Psyche: Eine Skizze*, in *Der Psychologe*, 7/8, vol. 3, Bern, July/August; English translation by Paul Watzlawick: *Structural Forms of the Feminine Psyche* (Zurich: Students Association C. G. Jung Institute, 1956).

———(1959): *Studien zur Psychologie C. G. Jungs* (Rhein: Zurich).

———, and Erich Neumann (1934–52): unpublished letters from Toni Wolff to Erich Neumann. Sold at Sotheby's in 2006. See Music and Continental Manuscripts (London, 30 November), p. 161; also in NP.

Wolin, Richard (1998): *The Heidegger Controversy: A Critical Reader* (Cambridge, MA: MIT Press).

Yogananda, Paramahansa (1946): *Autobiography of a Yogi* (New York: Philosophical Library); quoted from the third Indian paperback edition (Kolkata: Yoga Satsanga Society of India, 2006).

Young-Bruehl, Elisabeth (1982): *Hannah Arendt: For the Love of the World* (New Haven, CT: Yale University Press).

Zürcher Kunstgesellschaft (1956) (ed.): *Moderne Schweizer Bildteppiche* (Zurich: Berichthaus).

Index

The Collected Works of C. G. Jung

Editors: Sir Herbert Read, Michael Fordham, and Gerhard Adler; executive editor, William McGuire. Translated by R.F.C. Hull, except where noted.

The Collected Works of C. G. Jung is now available in a complete digital edition that is full-text searchable. The Complete Digital Edition includes volumes 1–18 and volume 19, the Complete Bibliography of C. G. Jung's Writings. Volumes 1–18 of The Complete Digital Edition are also available for individual purchase. For ordering information, please go to http://press.princeton.edu/titles/10294.html.

(continued)

(continued)

(continued)

(continued)

19. COMPLETE BIBLIOGRAPHY OF C. G. JUNG'S WRITINGS
(1976; 2d ed., 1992)

20. GENERAL INDEX OF THE COLLECTED WORKS (1979)

THE ZOFINGIA LECTURES (1983)
Supplementary Volume A to the Collected Works.
Edited by William McGuire, translated by
Jan van Heurck, introduction by
Marie-Louise von Franz

PSYCHOLOGY OF THE UNCONSCIOUS ([1912] 1992)
A STUDY OF THE TRANSFORMATIONS AND SYMBOLISMS OF THE LIBIDO.
A CONTRIBUTION TO THE HISTORY OF THE EVOLUTION OF THOUGHT
Supplementary Volume B to the Collected Works.
Translated by Beatrice M. Hinkle,
introduction by William McGuire

Notes to C. G. Jung's Seminars

DREAM ANALYSIS ([1928–30] 1984)
Edited by William McGuire

NIETZSCHE'S *ZARATHUSTRA* ([1934–39] 1988)
Edited by James L. Jarrett (2 vols.)

ANALYTICAL PSYCHOLOGY ([1925] 1989)
Edited by William McGuire

THE PSYCHOLOGY OF KUNDALINI YOGA ([1932] 1996)
Edited by Sonu Shamdasani

INTERPRETATION OF VISIONS ([1930–34] 1997)
Edited by Claire Douglas

CHILDREN'S DREAMS ([1936–40] 2008)
Edited by Lorenz Jung and Maria Meyer-Grass, translated by Ernst
Falzeder with the collaboration of Tony Woolfson

DREAM INTERPRETATION ANCIENT AND MODERN ([1936–41]
2014).
Edited by John Peck, Lorenz Jung, and Maria Meyer-Grass, translated by
Ernst Falzeder with the collaboration of Tony Woolfson

ANALYTICAL PSYCHOLOGY IN EXILE: THE CORRESPONDENCE
OF C. G. JUNG AND ERICH NEUMANN
Edited and introduced by Martin Liebscher, translated by
Heather McCartney